Reading Ovid

Reading Ovid presents a selection of stories from Ovid's *Metamorphoses*, the most famous and influential collection of Greek and Roman myths in the world. It includes well-known stories like those of Daedalus and Icarus, Pygmalion, Narcissus and King Midas. The book is designed for those who have completed an introductory course in Latin and aims to help such users to enjoy the story-telling, character-drawing and language of one of the world's most delightful and influential poets. The text is accompanied by full vocabulary, grammar and notes, with assistance based on two widely used beginners' courses, *Reading Latin* and *Wheelock's Latin*. Essays at the end of each passage are designed to point up important detail and to show how the logic of each story unfolds, while study sections offer ways of thinking further about the passage. No other intermediate text is so carefully designed to make reading Ovid a pleasure.

PETER JONES is well known as an author, journalist, lecturer and publiciser of classics. He is co-founder of the charity *Friends of Classics* and regularly contributes columns, reviews and features on classical topics in the national media in the UK. His books include *Learn Latin* (1998), *An Intelligent Person's Guide to Classics* (2002) and (with Keith Sidwell) *Reading Latin* (1986).

Reading Ovid

Stories from the *Metamorphōsēs*

PETER JONES

CAMBRIDGE
UNIVERSITY PRESS

CAMBRIDGE UNIVERSITY PRESS
Cambridge, New York, Melbourne, Madrid, Cape Town, Singapore, São Paulo

Cambridge University Press
The Edinburgh Building, Cambridge CB2 2RU, UK

Published in the United States of America by Cambridge University Press, New York

www.cambridge.org
Information on this title: www.cambridge.org/9780521613323

First published 2007

Printed in United Kingdom at the University Press, Cambridge

A catalogue record for this book is available from the British Library

ISBN-13 978-0-521-84901-2 hardback

ISBN-13 978-0-521-61332-3 paperback

Contents

Illustrations

Maps

Preface

This selection of stories from Ovid's *Metamorphōsēs* is designed for those who have completed a beginners' course in Latin. Its purpose is restricted and unsophisticated: to help such users, who will have read little or no Ovid, to enjoy the story-telling, character-drawing and language of one of the world's most delightful and influential poets. Assistance given with vocabulary and grammar is based on two widely used beginners' courses, *Reading Latin* and *Wheelock's Latin* (for details, see *Vocabulary, grammar and notes* below).

My general principle is to supply help on a need-to-know basis for the story in hand. The **Vocabulary, grammar and notes** and **Learning vocabularies** accompanying the text speak for themselves. The **Comment** at the end of each passage is an occasionally embellished paraphrase whose main purpose is to point up important detail and show how the logic of each story unfolds. I make no apology for this. With the minimal amount of time today's students have for learning the language, the demands of translation alone can be so heavy that it is all too easy to miss the wood for the trees and hamper the whole purpose of the exercise – pleasure, one of the most useful things in the world. The **Study sections** offer ways of thinking further about the passage.

My debt to W. S. Anderson's excellent *Ovid's Metamorphoses Books 1–5* (Norman and London: University of Oklahoma Press, 1997) and *Ovid's Metamorphoses Books 6–10* (Norman and London: University of Oklahoma Press, 1972) will be obvious. The translations by David Raeburn, *Ovid: Metamorphoses: A New Verse Translation* (Penguin Classics, 2004, brilliantly readable) and A. D. Melville, *Ovid Metamorphoses* (Oxford World's Classics, 1986, with a first-rate Introduction by E. J. Kenney) made stimulating companions. Arthur Golding's *Ovid's Metamorphoses* (1565, used by Shakespeare, the spelling modernised for Penguin Classics, 2002) remains peerless.

My best thanks go to Andrew Morley for the maps.

Peter Jones
Newcastle upon Tyne, July 2005

Abbreviations

1f., 2m., etc. refer to the declension and gender of a noun
1/2/3/4 and 3/4 (which some grammars call 5) refer to the conjugation of a verb

abl.	ablative	part.	participle
abs.	absolute	pass.	passive
acc.	accusative	perf./pf.	perfect
act.	active	pl.	plural
adj.	adjective	plupf./plup.	pluperfect
adv.	adverb	p.p.	principal part
cf.	*cōnfer*, 'compare'	prep.	preposition
comp.	comparative	pres.	present
conj.	conjugation,	prim.	primary
	conjugated	pron.	pronoun
dat.	dative	q.	question
decl.	declension	rel.	relative
dep.	deponent	*s.*	singular
dir.	direct	*sc.*	*scīlicet*, 'presumably'
f.	feminine	sec.	secondary
fut.	future	seq.	sequence
gen.	genitive	sp.	speech
imper.	imperative	subj.	subjunctive
impf./imperf.	imperfect	sup.	superlative
indecl.	indeclinable	trans.	transitive
ind.	indicative	tr.	translate
indir.	indirect	vb.	verb
inf.	infinitive	voc.	vocative
intrans.	intransitive		
irr.	irregular		
l(l)	line(s)		
lit.	literally		
m.	masculine		
m./f.	masculine/feminine		
neg.	negative		
n.	neuter		
nom.	nominative		

Introduction

Metamorphōsēs *and this selection*

Ovid's roughly twelve-thousand-line, fifteen-book *Metamorphōsēs* ('Changes of shape') is classed as an epic (like all epics it was composed in hexameters). It offers a supposedly temporal sequence of myths that starts with the formation of the world and ends with Ovid's contemporary, the emperor Augustus. Its title derives from the fact that almost all the stories involve transformations of one sort or another, about two hundred and fifty in all, mostly of humans. Ovid treats each one with inimitable brilliance, turning *Metamorphōsēs* into (if nothing else) a treasure-house of wonderful stories. But since these stories of transformation are all self-contained narratives, often without any obvious connection with each other, Ovid has to employ a range of ingenious devices in order to weave them together into a continuous narrative. As a result, *Metamorphōsēs* is quite unlike any other epic, and rather difficult to summarise. One (among many) ways of doing so is to divide it into three sections. In books 1–6 it recounts stories mainly of gods (e.g. Apollo and Daphne, Jupiter and Io, Jupiter's rape of Europa, Dionysus and Pentheus, Mars and Venus); books 7–10 concentrate on the heroes of myth (e.g. Jason and the Argonauts, Medea, the Minotaur, the Calydonian boar, Hercules, Orpheus and Eurydice); and in books 11–15 Ovid turns to 'history' (the siege of Troy, the stories of Aeneas, Romulus and early Roman kings like Numa), before unfolding some lengthy 'philosophical' speculations on vegetarianism and the nature of change by the sixth-century BC Greek philosopher Pythagoras. With a positively phosphorescent temporal leap at the finish, the poem ends with the assassination of Julius Caesar and his transformation into a star, so that his adopted son and heir Augustus can be proclaimed offspring of a god. But this way of summarising the poem, like every other way, merely indicates the problems there are in trying to define what the poem is 'about', especially as no story, or sequence of stories, seems to be given special status over any other. In other words, as soon as one attempts to pin the poem down by means of e.g. an over-arching structure or dominant theme, it promptly wriggles free. Ovid clearly did not see this as a problem. Neither should we.

The stories in this selection represent about one-sixth of the whole. They have been selected primarily because each is (broadly) self-contained and has high entertainment value. As can be inferred from the summary above, they do not represent every side of Ovid's vast poem (which is much longer than the *Aeneid*); in other words, there is more to *Metamorphōsēs* than this selection can suggest.

Herewith four caveats, all essential for understanding what this book, which is aimed at post-beginners, is trying and not trying to do:

- This brief introduction is designed to apply only to the contents of this reader. It does not engage with all the problems or issues implicit in a bewilderingly kaleidoscopic work like *Metamorphōsēs*.
- Ovid drew on many different sources for his tales. These are sometimes quoted in the **Study sections**, so that readers can reflect on how and why Ovid's version differed. In general, where I attribute originality to Ovid, please preface my remarks with 'If Ovid is not drawing this detail from his sources . . .'
- Detailed analysis of the various genres of writing of which Ovid was master is inappropriate in a reader designed for those whose experience of Latin is limited. I have restricted comment here to a few aspects of epic as exemplified by Homer and Virgil and some references to Ovid's earlier elegiac love-poetry. I recommend the following epic prose translations in the Penguin Classics series for their accessibility: *Homer: The Iliad*, tr. E. V. Rieu, rev. Peter Jones (Penguin Classics, 2003); *Homer: The Odyssey*, tr. E. V. Rieu, rev. D. C. H. Rieu (Penguin Classics, 2003); *Virgil: The Aeneid*, tr. David West (rev. edn., Penguin Classics, 2003). For Ovid's love-poetry, see, e.g., *Ovid: The Erotic Poems*, tr. Peter Green (Penguin Classics, 1982) and *Ovid: The Love Poems*, tr. A. D. Melville (Oxford World's Classics, 1990).
- Where I attribute beliefs or attitudes to Ovid on the strength of what he writes, please preface my remarks with 'Ovid writes as if he believes that . . .'

Ovid's life

Publius Ovidius Naso ('Nose') was born on 20 March 43 BC in Sulmo (modern Sulmona in the Abruzzi, ninety miles east of Rome over the Apennines). It was the year after Julius Caesar had been assassinated. After another period of civil war, Caesar's heir, Octavian, fought his way to sole power by defeating Mark Antony and his Egyptian lover Cleopatra at Actium in 31 BC (they committed suicide a year later) and in 27 BC became Rome's first emperor, universally known as Augustus. During this period, Ovid's wealthy parents were putting Ovid (he tell us, *Tristia* 4.10), through a standard rhetorical education in Rome, designed to equip young Romans with the verbal skills needed to make a public career in prestigious and lucrative areas like politics or law (i.e. where one climbed the ladder by one's ability to communicate persuasively). The elder Seneca tells us that Ovid excelled in the element of rhetorical training called *suāsōria*, an exercise in which the student had to advise a figure from legend or history on the course of action he should take, e.g. what would one say to Agamemnon when he was told that, if the Greek fleet were to sail for Troy, he had first to sacrifice his daughter Iphigeneia? Such training would stand Ovid in very good stead for all his work (his *Hērōides* (*Heroines*), for example, in which famous mythical women – like Penelope, Medea, Dido, Phaedra – write impassioned letters to their men, and sometimes exchange letters with them). After this, Ovid travelled round Sicily and Greece (still regarded as the cultural hot-bed of the ancient world). Ovid's parents presumably had in mind a career for him in some official capacity in public service, but a brief experience of minor judicial posts turned out not to be to Ovid's taste, and he gave it all up to become a full-time poet. His father, apparently, disapproved.

There was strong competition in Rome at this time – Virgil (b. 70 BC: Ovid had seen him), Horace (b. 65 BC: Ovid had heard him give a reading), Tibullus (b. 55 BC: Ovid knew him), Propertius (b. 50 BC: a close friend of Ovid's). But perhaps as early as the mid-twenties BC Ovid had made his mark with his *Amōrēs*, a selection of elegiac love-poetry in three (originally five) books. It was a stunning debut for one so young. Further slender elegiac volumes poured out, most controversially his light-hearted instruction manual *Ars Amātōria* in three books (how to get your girl/boy), soon to be followed by his *Remedia Amōris* (how to lose your girl/boy). All these books treat the subject-matter lightly, wittily and ironically – Ovid's escapades in love have at times an almost soap-opera element to them – and parody and self-mockery are well to the fore. They also use myth extensively to illustrate the dilemmas of young lovers.

When it came to love, Ovid did not feel he had to stir his soul to its depths with a pole, as Tibullus and Propertius rather tended to. To give an example: in *Amōrēs* 3.2, Ovid imagines himself at the chariot-races with a woman he wants to sleep with. After admitting he couldn't care less about the races but it's a great place to be with the woman he's after (various *doubles entendres* on 'riding'), he presses up close to her ('one advantage of the narrow seating'), picks up her dress ('it's trailing on the ground') to admire her legs (just like Atalanta's or Diana's, he comments) and admits he's feeling 'hot' ('let me fan you – unless it's just *me*'). Look! Some dust on your dress! Let me brush it off. Then the race starts. Ovid urges on his girl's favourite, the crowd goes wild ('hide your head in my cloak in case your hair gets spoiled'), the right chariot wins and

Her prayers are fulfilled, but mine aren't.
That charioteer won the prize: I still have mine to win.
She laughed. Her eyes sparkled, and she promised – something.
That'll do for me here. Do the rest for me . . . somewhere else.

Ovid's sexy, witty and indiscreet elegiacs, which made *pleasure* the purpose of love and poetry, were quite unique. No Roman had ever written love-poetry like this, nor ever would again: the genre died out with Ovid. But around about AD 1, Ovid struck out in a new direction and started on *Fastī* ('Calendar'), a twelve-book account of the origins of and reasons for Rome's festivals and cults (only six have come down to us), and *Metamorphōsēs*, a vast 'epic' in hexameters, the metre used by Homer and Virgil. These were quite different in concept, but still used myth and legend extensively. Ovid had just about finished but not revised *Metamorphōsēs* (as he tells us in *Tristia* 1.7) and was half-way through *Fastī* when, in AD 8, Augustus suddenly exiled him to Tomis on the Black Sea (modern Romania). Augustus' decision was connected, Ovid tells us, with the *Ars Amātōria* and some *error* about which Ovid never comes clean but was clearly not prosecutable. Since Augustus had a moralistic streak to him, it may be that he regarded Rome's leading poet as a bad influence, and took the opportunity presented by Ovid's *error* (perhaps a sexual scandal of some sort) to justify banishing him. Ovid died in Tomis in AD 17, still writing poems asking for a recall (*Tristia* and *Epistulae ex Pontō*) to which Augustus remained as hostile as his successor, Tiberius (AD 14–37). The whole episode makes one wonder what Rome would have been like had Mark Antony, and not Octavian-Augustus, won the battle of Actium in 31 BC and become first Roman emperor. Life, one feels, would have been rather more fun, and Ovid, surely, would never have been exiled.

In all this it is apparent that, in strong contrast with today, the Roman ruling classes took poetry seriously as a *potential* political force. In such a milieu, a widely acclaimed poet like Ovid, making his living out of witty elegiac poetry, fascinated by sex, indifferent to, even defiant of, political projects, but composing at a time of imperial legislation regulating morals and family life, was not likely to come to heel merely to suit his masters. Least of all was he about to produce an epic like Virgil's *Aeneid*, with its dignified Jupiter, strong sense of destiny and vision of Roman history reaching its climax with the Great Leader himself. Ovid talks about his own priorities at *Ars Amātōria* 3.121–8, where he says other people can get their pleasures from the past, but he is thrilled to be have been born now, not so much because of Rome's material and politicial domination, *sed quia cultus adest* 'but because this is a sophisticated/refined/elegant/cultured age'.

Some features of this selection

Ovid is an entertainer, the performing flea of Roman poetry, but that should not be taken to mean that he is lightweight. Far from it. One of the many things he does in his *Metamorphōsēs* is to take the fantasies of myth and, using them as a way of talking about human experience, ask 'What if these stories involved real people? How might they work in real life? What would the characters be like and what would they do and say?' He then applies all his ingenuity to humanise them and bring them vividly to life in a way his readership would enjoy. Having a more powerful and inventive imagination than perhaps any other ancient poet, he is able to find the contemporary human angle in even the most fantastic of ancient myths. This selection concentrates on stories of this sort.

Since Ovid is particularly fascinated by relationships between men and women, he revels in myths in which he can explore such relationships, especially ones where powerful emotions and great passions – often amounting to abnormal psychological mind-sets (e.g. passage 8, Narcissus, and passage 15, Byblis) – are involved. He does this not only through what he makes the characters do and say (their actions regularly signal their emotional state of mind), but in the way in which he interprets their interior thought-processes. There is an issue here: it is often difficult to determine whether an Ovidian comment on a situation is supposed to be taken *as* an authorial comment, or rather as an insight into the thought-processes of the character concerned.

Ovid is a master of pathos: he sees into the human heart, understands it all too well and can write sympathetically about the sufferings to which it is all too prone (although sometimes his exploitation of those sufferings can seem rather cold). He is able to see the funny side of human frailties, but is equally unflinching in his depiction of the catastrophic ruin that obsessive feelings (e.g. passage 15, Byblis) can bring. Being Ovid, he is also able to depict what we would call loving married relationships (passage 1, between Deucalion and Pyrrha, and passage 14, between Baucis and Philemon). Ovid was himself married three times, his last marriage apparently a devoted one.

The transformations in Ovid serve a purpose. They can provide an escape-route for a character (e.g. Daphne being turned into a tree to escape Apollo), or a reward (Baucis and Philemon being joined in death as they were in life), or a punishment (e.g. Arachne being turned into a spider); sometimes they are central to the story (e.g. passage 17, Pygmalion, where the metamorphosis is the whole point); and sometimes they are simply a means of bringing it to an end (e.g. Adonis being turned into an anemone). Sometimes one can see a psychological point, the characters turning into a form appropriate to them (though obviously not in Adonis' case; and e.g. Io may be transformed into a cow, but she seems quite relieved to reassume her original human shape. In a story not in this selection, the mighty Ajax, craggy defensive rock of the Greek army at Troy, is turned into a hyacinth. If one has no sense of humour, *Metamorphōsēs* is perhaps best avoided). Most interesting of all, Ovid loves trying to make poetic *sense* of the absurdities apparent in e.g. a stone turning into a human, or a woman into a spider. What would it really be like? How might it actually work? To these situations (as to everything else) he brings all his glorious imagination, ingenuity and sense of humour, the supreme poet of 'What if?' and 'Why not?'

But Ovid is not just a brilliant story-teller who grapples with trying to understand how humans in extreme situations might react and to persuade us this is how it *must* have been. He is a connoisseur of the literary world too. He knows how to compose in any style, from comedy (e.g. passage 14, Baucis and Philemon) to tragedy (e.g. passage 12, Cephalus and Procris), from the pastoral songs of rustic shepherds tootling away on their pipes (e.g. passage 3, Io and Syrinx) to romantics bemoaning their love (e.g. passage 9, Pyramus and Thisbe) and obsessives in the grip of uncontrollable passions (e.g. passage 15, Byblis); and he happily switches from one style to another within the same story. He makes constant references to earlier Greek and Roman literature (this reader will concentrate on Ovid's references to Homeric epic in particular). He constantly revisits and reworks his own poetry (e.g. passage 13, Daedalus and Icarus, differs in many interesting ways from his version in *Ars Amātōria*). He makes little jokes about the act of writing (see notes on, e.g., 11.549, 551). Above all, he is a master of rhetoric, witty (juxtaposing unlikely ideas to amusing effect, e.g. when Deucalion says to Pyrrha that the two of them are the earth's sole remaining *turba* ['mob, crowd'], 1.355); brilliant at snappy, balanced expressions (should the deer-Actaeon return home, or hide? *pudor hoc, timor impedit illud* 'shame inhibits the one course, fear the other', 3.205); adept at intense word-games (e.g. passage 8, Echo and Narcissus); and able to soar into passionate registers with powerful emotional speeches in the high style which he promptly proceeds to undercut with a moment of low bathos (e.g. passage 9, 4.121–4). This facility did not meet with the approval of Roman literary critics, who wanted epic to be didactic, setting a good, wholesome example. They felt that Ovid was treating the epic genre flippantly, without an appropriate sense of seriousness or decorum: 'too much in love with his own inventiveness', pouts Quintilian (*Institutes* 10.1.88); 'doesn't know how to leave well alone' moans the elder Seneca (*Contrōuersiae* 9.5.17), and 'he was well aware of his faults – and adored them' (2.2.12). Given Ovid's reputation, those 'faults' never troubled his readers – let alone him. Ovid knew exactly what he was doing in taking a tradition and seeing what *he* could make of it, whatever anyone else thought.

Ovid's gods

The West has inherited a Judaeo-Christian tradition which holds that there is one God, and He is good. But pre-Christian pagans acknowledged a multiplicity of gods, for whom 'goodness' was usually irrelevant, and epic took full advantage of them. In the *Iliad* of Homer (epic's founding father in the Western tradition c. 700 BC), the gods loom large, constantly squabbling among themselves to support their human favourites and establishing the tradition that, morally and ethically, there need be little to distinguish the human from the divine, if the poet so wished. So in epic, men and gods interact in whatever way the poet requires. For Virgil in his *Aeneid*, Jupiter, the king of the gods, is a figure of some gravity: he has a serious plan in mind – the founding of the Roman race – and he ensures it happens. Ovid will have none of this. He provides no consistently intelligible account of divine activity, let alone any theory of divine morality, justice or vision. The gods act precisely as he wants them to, which, in this selection, often means (for males) pursuing beautiful women through woods and (for females) taking revenge for perceived slights to their honour. Yet while the gods can be selfish, petty and cruel, they can occasionally act with dignity as upholders of the moral order. In other words, Ovid manipulates these gods as earlier epic poets had done – for his own literary purposes.

Women and woods

There is a reason for the predominantly wooded locations of Ovid's stories. Myths do not take place in cities: they take place (for the most part) in the Great Outdoors, especially in places where men hunted. Hunting was the sport of kings and their aristocratic followers, which is what characters in myth tended to be. It was physically hard, requiring fitness, muscle, speed, endurance and courage. It was not, in other words, a sport for aristocratic women, whose priorities were expected to lie elsewhere. But the deity of hunting was, interestingly, a goddess, Artemis/Diana; and there was something else odd about her too – she was a virgin, rejecting all male advances. The ancients put two and two together: a woman keen on this most manly of sports could not be a woman with 'normal' female appetites.

For Ovid, therefore, a woman without interest in men is signalled by her enthusiasm for the sport of hunting. Further, if a woman goes off men, she immediately takes up hunting to prove it (see, e.g., Procris in passage 12, 7.744–6). The 'rule' is proved by the exception: when Aphrodite, the goddess of sex, is fired with *amor* for the youthful hunter Adonis, she immediately takes up hunting to be with him all the time. Naturally, it absolutely exhausts her, and she is only too keen to lie down at every opportunity and have a rest with her young lover in her arms (passage 18, 10.544–9).

By the same token, however keenly a woman races about in the forest chasing things, she is still a woman, and therefore, in the woods and fields, far from the protection of home and family (where she 'should' be), vulnerable. Add in the sort of clothing any hunter or huntress will wear – as little as possible – and the dangers are immediately apparent. The huntress in her innocence will not recognise any of this; but any god strolling about the forest will not fail to see an opportunity. The irony of the situation is that the place where a woman goes to show that she is not interested in men turns into exactly the place where she will be most accessible to them.

In such woods it is common to come across a *locus amoenus*, 'idyllic spot', one of literature's favourite locations. It is characterised by its trees, shade, running water, breezes, grassy banks/meadows, caves, flowers etc. (wall-paintings from Pompeii offer a number of luscious examples). In the innocent 'golden age', when men lived at ease and free from labour, and in the fields of the blessed in Elysium, one cannot move for *locī amoenī*; nor in Ovid, where its appearance is usually marked by an opening like *est locus . . .* or *fōns erat . . .* Hunters and huntresses, sweating from the day's work, are drawn to it like a magnet. But there is an ironic Ovidian sting in the tail. In *Metamorphōsēs*, its attractiveness is nearly always deceitful. Gods are everywhere, and the more peaceful and secret the location, the greater the hidden danger of stumbling across a deity unawares, and paying the price.

Amor *and rape in Ovid*

Amor, wholesome or obsessive, is at the centre of eight of the stories in this selection (Semele, Echo and Narcissus, Pyramus and Thisbe, Cephalus and Procris, Byblis, Orpheus, Pygmalion, and Venus and Adonis). Rape or attempted rape, defined in *our* terms, which occurs about fifty times in the fifteen books of *Metamorphōsēs*, occurs in three of the stories (Apollo and Daphne, Io, Arethusa). While the topic of relationships between the sexes (or should that be genders?) is as much a modern preoccupation as it was an ancient one, rape in particular makes for uncomfortable reading in today's world, and raises a number of serious issues. It may, for example, be worth considering whether Ovid is offering any significant critique of rape or whether he simply endorses it as a fact of mythical life. Before engaging with that particular question, however, it is worth taking the following points into account:

- First, Ovid is not *inventing* the rapes contained in the myths he relates: they are built into the stories, which go back hundreds of years.
- Second, since many Romans regarded gods as slaves to their passions, amoral if not immoral, and happy to take their pleasure where they found it, they would not have been surprised by divine proclivities.
- Third, Ovid lived in a world where absence of female consent was not a *necessary* defining feature of rape (it is *the* defining feature in our world).
- Fourth, the audience for myth may have considered insemination by a god, whether by force or not, a great honour for a mere mortal, since it brought with it the prospect of semi-divine offspring.

It is also worth checking carefully on the context in which *rapiō*, usually translated 'rape', occurs, since its basic meaning is 'carry off, abduct, take'. The latter meaning is clearly more appropriate in e.g. passage 12, where the hunter Cephalus is *raptus* by Aurora, goddess of the Dawn (7.704, 725, 732). Then again, when Cephalus says that his beloved wife Procris was sister of the *rapta* Oreithyia, he comments that Procris was more *digna rapī* (7.697) – surely not that she would have made a better *rape* victim? In passage 13, Theseus escapes with his lover, who is called the *rapta* Ariadne – scarcely 'raped' if they were lovers (8.174). To complicate matters further, in passage 10 (5.576), Arethusa, who is about to describe how Alpheus tried to rape her, says she will tell the story of Alpheus' *amōrēs*. Likewise, in the story of Apollo and Daphne, Apollo feels *amor* for Daphne (passage 2, 1.452, 474) and immediately attempts to – 'rape' her?

Amor only rarely appears in relationships which might seem to us driven by 'love' in our broadest sense, possibly because in Ovid it usually has such strong sexual overtones (I emphasise here that I am concentrating on Ovid's usage in this selection and not taking into account other writers' views of *amor*). For example, it never occurs in passage 1, between Deucalion and Pyrrha (who seem old), and passage 14, between Baucis and Philemon (who are old). Cephalus uses *amor* of his relationship with his beloved wife Procris, but qualifies it as *amor sociālis* (passage 12, 7.800) and glosses it with *mūtua cūra*, and in the next line uses *amor*, unqualified, in its sexual sense (7.801). Orpheus talks of the divinity *Amor* existing among the gods, but again in the sexual sense, if that is how *rapīnae* (passage 16, 10.28) should be understood. If it is fair to say that *amor* in passage 2 (Apollo and Daphne), passage 3 (Io), passage 8 (Narcissus) and passage 15 (Byblis) is predominantly sexual, its use to describe the 'first love' of Pyramus and Thisbe (passage 9) and Pygmalion (passage 17) may be more innocent, but may not – after all, the innocent Atalanta feels *amor* for the first time at 10.637 (passage 18), but *sociāre cubīlia* and *cupīdō* (635–6) indicate what she actually has in mind; and Hippomenes falls for Atalanta when he sees her naked (10.578–82). For Ovid in these passages, then, sexual desire is at the root of *amor*, however *sociālis* it might subsequently become. It is a psychology which is not entirely unfamiliar in the third millennium.

On issues like slavery, killing, poverty, war, child-labour, the treatment of animals (and rape), the difference between our world and the ancient world is very great indeed. This raises a historical issue (is it possible to understand the ancients if we do not do so on their terms?) and a literary one (is literature best judged by its capacity to appeal to the reader's conscience, so that moral edification is the main index of aesthetic and cultural merit? Is literature 'the handmaid of ethics'?). To put it bluntly, can we understand and enjoy the ancient world only if we personally *approve* of the way they did things? Finally, if Ovid's account of rape challenges us, did it challenge the Romans? Was it Ovid's purpose so to do? Is it relevant that only one of the rapes in *Metamorphōsēs* is carried out by a human?

Ovid and epic

Gravity and high seriousness are not Ovid's priorities. So his *Metamorphōsēs*, though technically an epic, often lacks what we might think of as epic grandeur. Certainly the poem does not lack for emotion, pathos and human feeling, but the vast range of disparate myths Ovid includes and the tension between the setting of the stories in far-off times and places and the contemporary angle Ovid gives to his characters seem designed to generate amusing incongruity, as does the picture of gods behaving exactly like mortals, especially in affairs of the heart; and jokes keep breaking in anyway. The explanation might lie in the prevalence of Ovid's favourite subject, *amor*, and his 'neoteric' way of handling poetry.

Greeks and Romans were highly suspicious of 'love/lust/sex' because it tended to make one look such a fool. But most people are subject to it, some throughout much of their lives, and (as we have seen) Ovid had put it and its usually disastrous consequences at the centre of his early work. By also putting it at the centre of his *Metamorphōsēs*, he signals that this is going to be an epic with a difference – an epic where the 'moving toyshop of the heart' (Pope), in all its folly and feeling, is one of the main ingredients.

'Neoteric' is the term applied to Roman poetry influenced by Hellenistic Greek poets ('Hellenistic' means 'Greek-like', 'Greek-style', and refers to the Greek world from 323 to 331 BC when Alexander had spread Greek culture far and wide). It derives from the Greek *hoi neōteroi* 'the younger/modern/fashionable [poets]', a term used by Cicero of trendy poets in Rome in the first century BC. Broadly, neoteric poetry is characterised by its sophistication, elegance, cleverness, minia-turism, contrived literary self-consciousness and allusiveness to other poetry. At the beginning of the Apollo and Daphne story, for example, Ovid consciously refers back to his *Amōrēs* (see **Comment** on 1.452–62); in his Narcissus story, Narcissus takes on all the characteristics of the 'haughty lover' of Ovid's early poetry (see **Comment** on 10.351–61). In other words, grand, sonorous, noble Roman epic has, in Ovid's hands, become transformed in terms of style, form and content.

All this raises questions about the sense in which *Metamorphōsēs* can be said to be an epic at all. It *looks* epic in size, metre (hexameter is the traditional epic form) and some of its reflexes (e.g. the interventions of the gods, similes, speeches, catalogues, and so on). But if 'epic' is 'great heroes fighting it out on the battlefield while the greatest of them all battles with his inner demons' (like the *Iliad*), or 'a great hero overcoming obstacles to return home' (like the *Odyssey*), or 'a great hero on a mission to found a nation with the help of the gods' (like the *Aeneid*), *Metamorphōsēs* is automatically defined out of the equation (a constant problem with definitions of any sort). For example, *Metamorphōsēs* does not have a central hero on a mission of any sort (and the serious fighting tends to take place at weddings). The great hero Theseus simply sits down and listens to stories. Highly articulate and sexually charged women ruthlessly pursue their own desires (e.g. Byblis). The poem is highly episodic, one myth loosely strung together with the next, rather like an anthology (indeed, *Metamorphōsēs* has its basic origins in collections of myths made by earlier Greek poets). There is no sense of narrative direction. More than one-third of the poem is told through the mouth of someone other than the narra-tor Ovid. The often trivial or downright demeaning loves/lust of men and gods are a major feature: the sort of fun Ovid had with people-in-love in his earlier elegiac work keeps on breaking through. But nor is it exactly mock-epic: Ovid is not obviously *laughing* at the genre, but doing something quite different, and very Ovidian, with it. It is as if he wants to show that he can do 'epic' too, but that there is no point in doing a 'Homer' or 'Virgil'. They had already been done. So he does an 'Ovid' instead, producing something quite unique in the process, characterised by an unmatched multiplicity and diversity of genres, subject-matter and styles.

Irony and paradox

One especial feature of life and language appeals to Ovid: its paradoxes. His char-acters constantly embark on courses of action designed to bring them happiness but doomed only to bring them misery. Sometimes it is their fault; sometimes they are led into it by the gods. *amor* is one obvious example, bringing with it both intense pleasure and intense pain. The irony of these situations is that both gods and humans *think* they are acting in their own interests when Ovid makes it transparent to the reader that they are not: by acting in certain ways, they lay themselves open to being acted upon (often reflexively, i.e. by themselves) in ways they did not, or could not, expect. Passage 8, Narcissus, offers the most obvious example. Ovid's language constantly points up the paradoxes and ironies inherent in such situations.

Style

Ovid is a highly rhetorical poet. This simply means: (i) that he takes extraordinary care over every single word – words are there to be *enjoyed*; (ii) that he composes in a language rich in figures of speech that particularly favours repetition, balance, contrast and climax (see the **Glossary of technical literary terms** for some of the most common); and (iii) that he is looking to invent plausible ways of arousing his readers' emotions, especially by making his characters act and speak in ways that will persuasively reproduce (in his readers' eyes, he hopes) their states of mind. In other words, Ovid sees a connection between painting persuasive characters and touching his readers' hearts. The technical rhetorical term for 'thinking up ways of making the action and characters sound as plausible as possible' is *inuentio*. The word is most obviously applicable to pleading cases at law, but Ovid is its literary master.

Whereas Virgil dwells on his subject, repeating ideas in different forms in the same line, Ovid gets on with it. The story is what counts; what people say or do next is his main interest. The result is that, to generalise, there is a *consistent* emotional profundity to Virgil that one does not find in Ovid.

By the same token, there is a speed in Ovid one does not regularly find in Virgil (see e.g. **Study section** to passage 16). Comparisons between the two show that Ovid's grammar is simpler; metrically he uses more dactyls and fewer elisions; and sense-breaks tend to recur at the main caesuras (see on **Metre** (12) below). In this sense, Ovid's surface style is more 'Homeric' than Virgil's.

There is another very Homeric feature of Ovid's work: the simile. Homer started this trend; there are about three hundred similes in the *Iliad*, about eighty in the *Odyssey*. In *Metamorphōsēs*, about the same length as the *Odyssey* and one-fifth shorter than the *Iliad*, there are over two hundred and fifty. For an example of how Ovid uses similes, see **Comment** on 1.490–503.

Some assessments

Because it is almost impossible to pin Ovid down, it may be helpful to offer some general assessments made of *Metamorphōsēs* and various features of it by scholars of the past fifty years.

L. P. Wilkinson (1955, 155) suggests we:

approach the *Metamorphoses* with no preconception about what we are to get out of it, taking each episode as we find it, letting the 'most capricious poet', as Touchstone called him, lead us through romance, burlesque, splendour, horror, pathos, macabre, rhetoric, genre-painting, debate, landscape-painting, antiquarian interest, patriotic pride – wherever his own fancy leads him.

Brooks Otis (1966, 323) summarises as follows:

Virgil is an author who enters into his readers' and characters' feelings in order to enhance the majesty of his epic and Roman theme, to suggest the symbolic relevance of even the most incredible scenes. Ovid, instead, exhibits all the incongruities and absurdities, all the unpalatable truth behind the epic décor, all the scandal of myth, in order to shock, amuse or, sometimes, even enrage. Ovid's approach to epic was thus subject to very severe limitations: wherever he could treat epic or heroic material in a light, satiric or humorous way, he was almost uniformly successful in realizing his essentially comic or critical aims . . . But when he tried to treat heroic themes in a serious or a Virgilian way, he met an absolute check, and fell into the worst sort of bathos. His misfortune was that his epic plan and purpose could not be made to fit his peculiar abilities and deficiencies. His poem is thus a combination of true comedy, real pathos and false heroics, of intentional and unintentional humour, of conscious and unconscious grotesquerie, of brilliant design and disastrous mistake. No wonder it has been so often, so usually misunderstood!

O. S. Due (1974, 164–5) argues:

Metamorphoses are not really an epic poem. They are a descriptive poem. And what is described is the innumerable aspects of man, and not least of woman, and of their behaviour as individuals in this fantastic world. Ovid's gods reveal nothing about religion, and his Kings nothing about the state. Ovid's animals are not zoological but psychological phenomena. This vast gallery of virgins, mothers, wives, young men, fathers, and husbands, heroes, nymphs, gods, monsters, and plain people, with their different human characters, good and bad or both, and their strange experiences, happy or more often unhappy, in their imaginary world broaden the reader's human knowledge as they pass before his eyes. Ovid does not point a moral. Any moral would narrow the import of the description: life may be just, but is far from always just, it is often comic or pathetic or stark or cruel or grotesque and macabre. It is always fascinating and interesting – as interesting and fascinating as our own lives and that of our neighbour when looked upon with fresh eyes . . . *Man* is what all revolves around, his shortcomings, his passions, his aggressions, his pretensions, and his love, a mixture of heroism, tragedy, comedy, romance and elegy, true as only life itself.

Philip Hardie (2002a, 4–8, *passim*) summarises modern approaches, which seem to concentrate on finding in Ovid support for various literary and linguistic theories:

What formerly was seen as superficial wit and an irredeemable lack of seriousness has been reassessed in the light of a postmodernist flight from realism and presence towards textuality and anti-foundationalism. 'Parody', a term often used in dismissive acknowledgement of Ovid's entertainment value, has moved to the theoretical centre of studies of allusion and inter-textuality. Ovid exults in the fictiveness of his poetry, that written in the first person singular quite as much as self-evidently tall tales like that of the beautiful girl Scylla changed into a hideous sea-monster (*Met.* 13.732–4). At the heart of the *Metamorphoses* we come across a debate on the truth or fiction of stories of metamorphosis, conducted by fictional characters at the dinner-table of a river-god, himself a shape-shifter (*Met.* 8.611–19).

The later twentieth-century novel saw a significant shift from the prevailing nineteenth-century realist tradition that concealed its own devices, back towards the seventeenth- and eighteenth-century self-conscious novel, defined by Robert Alter as 'a novel that systematically flaunts its own condition of artifice and that by so doing probes into the problematic relationship between real-seeming artifice and reality'. The line of Cervantes, Sterne, and Diderot may be traced back directly to the ancient prose novel, but also to Ovid . . .

Ovid has often been accused of mocking and trivializing love, and in effect bringing about the death of love elegy. This might seem strange for a poet described by Chaucer as 'Venus' clerk' (*House of Fame* 1487). Recent theorizations of desire offer opportunities to move beyond the stereotype of Ovid the cynical realist. The teasing revelation that the elegist's object of desire, Corinna (Ovid's girl-friend in *Amōrēs*), may be no more than an effect of the text confronts us with an awareness of our own investment of desire in the process of reading. 'Reading about desire provokes the desire to read.' Ovid complains that he has prostituted his girl-friend to the reader in his poems *(Am.* 3.12.5–8). In the *Metamorphoses* Ovid offers virtuoso experiences of a Barthesian 'plaisir du texte'. An episode like the story of Mercury's enchantment of Argus *(Met.* 1.668–723) thematizes the model of reading as seduction.

Peter Brooks puts Freudian theories of desire to work in analyses of the workings of texts, both in the dynamic of desire and repetition that structures narrative plots, and in the inscription of meaning on desired bodies within such narratives, the 'semioticization of desire'. Ovidian narrative repetition lends itself readily to the former kind of analysis; with regard to the latter a body like that of Daphne, in the archetypal erotic narrative of the *Metamorphoses* (1.452–567), is transformed into a multiply determined site of signification, the deposit of a desire whose satisfaction is for ever deferred . . .

After-life

Ovid's influence on writers, artists and composers from the twelfth century onwards was very great indeed. For some in the Middle Ages, he was the rakish man of the world, the secular antidote to the puritan teachings of the Church. The Church responded by moralising him (*Ovide moralisé* was the title of a fourteenth-century 70,000-line poem), finding in him a thinker, philosopher and theologian whose fictional myths conveyed deep and familiar truths. For example, Daedalus and Icarus were taken to represent Christ's ascension to heaven, with a warning to man not to aspire too high. Arthur Golding's *Epistle* (1567), which introduces his translation of *Metamorphōsēs*, gives an idea of the general approach. In all the myths, he says, are:

> pithy, apt and plain
> Instructions which import the praise of virtues and the shame
> Of vices, with the due rewards of either of the same.
> As, for example, in the tale of Daphne turned to bay
> A mirror of virginity appear unto us may;
> Which, yielding neither unto fear, nor force, nor flattery,
> Doth purchase everlasting fame and immortality.
> In Phaeton's fable unto sight the poet doth express
> The natures of ambition blind and youthful wilfullness,
> The end whereof is misery, and bringeth at the last
> Repentance when it is too late, that all redress is past . . .
> Tiresias wills inferior folk in any wise to shun
> To judge between their betters, lest in peril they do run.
> Narcissus is of scornfulness and pride a mirror clear
> Where beauty's fading vanity most plainly may appear.
> And Echo in the selfsame tale doth kindly represent
> The lewd behaviour of a bawd and his due punishment.
> The piteous tale of Pyramus and Thisbe doth contain
> The heady force of frantic love, whose end is woe and pain . . .

Chaucer saw in Ovid a fellow-spirit, the great story-teller embracing all genres and styles, but did not take him as in any way authoritative. Nor did the Elizabethans who, fascinated by sex, generation and death, found in Ovid the perfect combination of sensuousness and wit: Ovid was there to be used, not revered. His influence is strong, for example, in Shakespeare (via Golding's translation). As Francis Meres famously put it in his *Palladis Tamia, Wits Treasury* (1598):

As the soule of *Euphorbus* was thought to live in *Pythagoras*: so the sweet wittie soule of *Ovid* lives in mellifluous & honytongued *Shakespeare*, witnes his *Venus* and *Adonis*, his *Lucrece*, his sugred Sonnets among his private frinds, &c.

Until the eighteenth century, virtually all art was based on the Bible, Virgil, Homer and Ovid, but artists, like writers, did not necessarily set out to reproduce Ovid's words in pictures (see **Study section** on passage 18, Venus and Adonis). They had patrons, who actually commissioned the art, to satisfy. These patrons might want anything from high-class decoration, full of Cupids and naked women, to didactic interpretation of famous mythic moments. The two were not necessarily exclusive, and a prestigious poet like Ovid could be mined to supply both. Operatic composers too like Handel (e.g. *Semele*, 1744), Gluck (e.g. *Orphée et Euridice*, 1774) and Offenbach (e.g. *Orpheus in the Underworld*, 1858) have found *Metamorphōsēs* a rich source. Richard Strauss's *Daphne* (1938), partly inspired by the famous Bernini statue of Daphne turning into a tree in the Villa Borghese, ends with Daphne's on-stage transformation to the accompaniment of suitably metamorphic music. The simple story-lines of Ovid's tales, full of sharply focussed human characters in emotionally dramatic situations, all worked out in highly rhetorical fashion, fitted the medium to perfection, and (if required) a moral lesson could always be tacked on at the end. As Norman Vance says:

the brilliant artifice of opera, offering spectacle and dramatic feeling, found Ovid indispensable . . . the operatic qualities of Ovid were as well suited to comedy as tragedy, for his narratives offered a sometimes evasive, even equivocal tone or quality of feeling which could be rendered sympathetically, or comically subverted according to taste. (quoted from Martindale 1988, 229–30)

This is an enormous subject that cannot be usefully taken further here. To get some idea of its range, however, and to witness the richness of the tradition, look up e.g. 'Daphne' in J. D. Reid, *The Oxford Guide to Classical Mythology in the Arts 1300–1990s* (Oxford: Oxford University Press, 1993). It names 272 artists, writers and composers who have dealt with the story, many more than once (e.g. Froissart [d. 1410] evoked the subject in four poems, Poussin [d. 1665] produced five paintings and sketches, Handel [d. 1759] two compositions, Ossip Zadkine [d. 1967] three sculptures, and so on). Narcissus attracts about the same number of entries; Orpheus nearer 800 . . . Wilkinson (1955, 366–438), Martindale (1988) and Christopher Allen in *The Cambridge Companion to Ovid* (Hardie, 2002a, 336–67) offer fine introductions to this endlessly rich topic.

Glossary of technical literary terms

Technical literary terms are used throughout the book (cf. the Grammar to *Reading Latin*, 314–20 – see p. 20 below). These include:

Aetiology: an explanation of something's origin (humans were made from stones, 'as a result of which we are a hard race', *inde genus dūrum sumus*, 1.414).

Anaphora: a figure of speech in which a sequence of phrases or clauses begins with the same word(s) (*ō soror, ō coniunx, ō fēmina sōla superstes*, 'O sister, O wife, O sole remaining female', 1.351).

Antithesis: the choice or arrangement of words to produce a strong contrast (e.g. 'such *hard* pride in so *tender* a form', *in tenerā tam dūra superbia fōrmā*, 3.354).

Apostrophe: a figure of speech in which a third person narrative reverts to the second person ('A did this, and B did this, and C did this, and *you, B, said*', cf. [Mercury killed Argus] 'and you, Argus, lie there', *Arge, iacēs*, 1.720).

Asyndeton: a figure of speech in which conjunctions (especially 'and') are omitted (e.g. 'Friends, Romans, countrymen', cf. *ō soror, ō coniunx, ō fēmina sōla superstes*, 'O sister, O wife, O sole remaining female' 1.351).

Chiasmus: two corresponding pairs of words or phrases placed 'criss-cross', i.e. in the order ABBA ('You (A) I love (B), I hate (B) him (A)', cf. *nōs* (A) *turba* (B) *sumus* (C), *possēdit* (C) *cētera* (B) *pontus* (A), 1.355).

Clause: a speech unit with a subject and finite verb (a main clause or subordinate clause, e.g. 'Charlotte said this', 'When Charlotte said this').

Golden line: a line of poetry in which two nouns, each with an adjective in agreement, and a verb are placed in the order A B (verb) A B or A B (verb) B A ('The winds in her face ruffled her clothes against her', *obuiaque* (A) *aduersās* (B) *uibrābant* (V) *flāmina* (A) *uestēs* (B), 1.528).

Hyperbaton: the upsetting of the natural word-order (e.g. 'Pleasures the sex as children birds pursue' [Pope], i.e. 'The sex [=women] pursue pleasures as children [pursue] birds', cf. 'the naked nymphs, the man seen, beat their breasts', *nūdae uisō sua pectora nymphae / percussēre uirō*, 3.178).

Oxymoron: an apparently contradictory use of words, producing a paradoxical fusion (e.g. '*Wisest fool* in Christendom'; 'save me from this *seductive curse*', *speciōsōque ēripe damnō*, 11.133).

Phrase: a speech unit without a main verb (e.g. '*Saying this*, Charlotte . . .', 'In Charlotte's house').

Polyptoton: a sequence in which the same word is used in different forms ('*torus iūnxit, nunc ipsa perīcula iungunt*, 'the marriage-bed *linked*, now dangers themselves *link*', 1.353).

Syllepsis: a figure of speech in which a word is used correctly both in syntax and meaning in relation to two other words, but in such a way as to produce an amusing effect (e.g. 'he took tea and a taxi'; 'he ejected him from his life and chariot', *animāque rotīsque / expulit*, 2.312–13).

Tetracolon: a four-fold repetition of the sort described under 'Tricolon' (*quam commūne mihī genus et patruēlis orīgō, / deīnde torus iūnxit, nunc ipsa perīcula iungunt*, 'whom shared race (1) and brotherhood of fathers (2), then the marriage-bed (3) linked, *now dangers themselves (4)* link', 1.353).

Tricolon: a unit of words, phrases or clauses repeated three times; often 'rising' (each element getting longer), sometimes 'decreasing', and regularly used with asyndeton (e.g. 'Friends, Romans, countrymen') and anaphora ('O sister, O wife, O sole remaining female', *ō soror, ō coniunx, ō fēmina sōla superstes*, 1.351).

Notes for the reader

Text-markings

1. In general, the text has been over-punctuated in an attempt to clarify word-groups.
2. Macra (s. macron; i.e. syllables pronounced long) are marked throughout, e.g. *ā*, *ē*, etc. *hūīc* and *cūī* are taken as one syllable, *hūīus* and *cūīus* as two syllables.
3. (a) Words to be taken together for translation purposes (almost always because they agree) are linked A^ . . . ^B. Thus:

   redditus orbis erat; quem^ postquam uīdit ^inānem
   et dēsōlātās^ agere alta silentia ^terrās

   i.e. *quem* agrees with *inānem*, *dēsōlātās* agrees with *terrās*.

   (b) When more than two words are so linked, the sequence continues A^ . . . ^B . . . ^C . . . ^D, etc. Thus:

   haec^ quoque adhūc uītae nōn est ^fidūcia nostrae
   ^certa satis

   i.e. *haec* agrees with *fidūcia* and *certa*.

   The sequence A^ . . . ^B . . . C^ . . . ^D would mean that A agrees with B, and C agrees with D.

   (c) When other words agree inside the ^ . . . ^ pattern, A* . . . *B is used. Thus:

   haec^ quoque adhūc uītae nōn est ^fidūcia *nostrae*
   ^certa satis

   i.e. *uītae* agrees with *nostrae*.

Note that these linking-marks are gradually phased out.

4. An underlined vowel is to be disregarded for the purpose of scansion (see below on 'Metre'). Thus:

   haec^ quoqu<u>e</u> adhūc uītae nōn est ^fidūcia *nostrae*

The *e* of *quoque* is to be disregarded. This convention is discontinued after passage 3.

Vocabulary, Grammar and Notes (VGN)

1. A running *VGN* accompanies each passage. It cross-refers users to the Grammars of two commonly used beginners' Latin courses:

   RL = Peter Jones and Keith Sidwell, *Reading Latin: Grammar, Vocabulary and Exercises* (Cambridge: Cambridge University Press, 1986). A plain number, e.g. **RL88**, refers to sections of the Running Grammar; letter + number, e.g. **RLA4**, refers to the Reference Grammar at the back.
   W = F. M. Wheelock, *Wheelock's Latin* (sixth edn., rev. R. A. LaFleur, New York: HarperCollins, 2000). The number, e.g. **W38**, refers to the grammatical chapters; *Suppl.Syntax* = Supplementary syntax.

2. It is assumed that students will know the meaning of those words which **RL** and **W** *between them* share as set to be learned (so if any word appears for learning in **RL** but not in **W**, and vice-versa, it will not be assumed that it has been learned). All those shared words are in the **Total Learning Vocabulary** at the back of this book (pp. 255–69), and are not glossed in the running *VGN* that accompanies each passage. All other words are glossed in the running *VGN*.

3. In passages 1–8, words marked with an * in the running *VGN* must be learned because they will not appear in the *VGN* again. These words are listed from time to time in alphabetical order within the *VGN*, under the heading *Learning Vocabulary* (e.g. p. 34). At the end of each passage's *VGN*, all the words listed under *Learning Vocabulary* are repeated as *Learning Vocabulary for Passage X* (e.g. p. 42). All these words have also been added to the **Total Learning Vocabulary**, in case you forget them.

4. From passage 9 onwards, there will still be words marked * in the *VGN*. These will be gathered in the *Learning Vocabulary for Passage X* at the end of the passage's *VGN*. These will be words which, while (obviously) not appearing in the **Total Learning Vocabulary**, appear *more than once* in that passage. However, we assume no learning carry-over of these words into any other passage in passages 9–16. As a result, if they appear again in any other passage, they will be glossed. The consequence of this decision is: read passages 1–8 first. From then on, all words not in the **Total Learning Vocabulary** will be glossed.

5. In passages 12–16, there is a modest further refinement. Words whose meaning is guessable because they are compounds of words you (should)

already know, or because they are very close to English, appear in their dictionary form in the *VGN* but are *not* glossed. Instead, they are marked with an *. For example, you should by then be thoroughly familiar with *amplector* 'I embrace'. When therefore you meet *amplexū*, it appears as *amplex-us ūs* 4m.*, and you will have to work out what it means.

6. Since Ovid is dealing with Greek myths, he frequently uses Greek names for people and places. But Greek nouns do not decline like Latin. Therefore the Greek form and its case will be glossed in full.

For information, many Greek nouns take a nom. s. in *-ōn* or *-ēs*, acc. s. in *-ēn* or *-a*, nom. pl. in *-es* and acc. pl. in *-as* (note the short vowels). Also common are forms ending in *-adēs* and *-idēs* meaning 'son/descendant of' (patronymic, 'father-name', is the technical term).

Translating Ovid

1. Latin generally subordinates phrases and clauses ('Prayers having been said, they went home'), while English tends to pile them up ('They said prayers and went home').
2. Ovid often uses 'poetic' plurals where we would use the singular, e.g. Thisbe embraces the dead Pyramus, *gelidīs in uultibus ōscula figēns* 'planting kisses on his cold face(s)' (4.141).
3. Ovid favours syncopated perfect forms, e.g. *agitāsse* for *agitāvisse*, *tetigēre* for *tetigērunt*.
4. The relative often precedes the word to which it is referring. Consider (2.309–10):

sed neque quās^ posset terrīs indūcere ^nūbēs
tunc habuit, nec quos^ caelō dēmitteret ^imbrēs

'But [Jupiter] neither what^ he was able to draw over the lands ^clouds / then he had, nor what^ from the sky he might let fall ^showers', i.e. Jupiter then had neither clouds which he was able to draw over the lands, nor showers which he might let fall from the sky.

Metre

Heavy and light syllables

1. In Latin verse, *every* syllable counts for the sake of the metre as either heavy or light.
2. Heavy syllables consist of: •

   (a) vowels that are *pronounced* long, e.g. *dēsōlātās* – four vowels pronounced long and therefore four heavy syllables.
   (b) vowels that are followed by two consonants or a double consonant (x, z) e.g. *ingentēs* – the first two syllables are heavy as the vowel of each is followed by two consonants, the last vowel is pronounced long and the syllable is therefore heavy. Observe that the rule holds even if words are divided. For example, *et* is light, but would become heavy in *et fugit*, because *e* is then followed by two consonants, *t* and *f*.

   NB Observe the rule for the formation of syllables: a syllable starts with a consonant *if it can*. So the three syllables of *ingentes* are *in-gen-tēs* (not e.g. *ing-ent-ēs*). This means that, *technically speaking*, a syllable ending in a consonant is heavy, because (by the rule) if a syllable *ends* in a consonant, the next syllable must *begin* with a consonant.
   (c) a short vowel followed by a mute consonant (p, b, ph, f; t, d, th; k, c, g, ch) + l or r may remain light or become heavy. See e.g. *lacrimīs, patruēlis* (350 and 352 below), where the initial *a* in both cases is short and the syllable is light.
   (d) diphthongs, e.g. *Dēūcaliōn* – first syllable heavy as it is a diphthong, last syllable heavy by pronunciation.

3. All other syllables are light, e.g. *nūbila mentem* – *nū* heavy by pronunciation, *bi* light, *la* light, *men* heavy as *e* is followed by two consonants, *tem* light. Cf. *Dēūcaliōn*, where *ca* and *li* are light.
4. *h* does not count as a consonant for metrical purposes. So *et* in *et habuit* scans light.
5. *i* and *u* sometimes count as vowels, sometimes as consonants like the English j and v. Thus for metrical purposes *coniunx* = *conjunx*, *uideō* = *video*, *Iuppiter* = *Juppiter*, *Iūnō* = *Jūnō*, etc. *x* (ks) and *z* (ds) count as *two* consonants.

6. Some vowels admit of alternative lengths. For example, both vowels in *mihi*, *tibi* and *sibi* are usually pronounced short, but can be pronounced short-long, where they will be so marked (*mihĭ*, *tibĭ* and *sibĭ*).

Elision

7. If a word *ends* in a vowel or *-m*, and is followed by a word *beginning* with a vowel or *h*, the final vowel is *elided* (lit. 'crushed') and does not count for the purpose of the metre. Observe:
    ego et tū for metrical purposes = *eg et tū*
    quam et for metrical purposes = *qu et*
    cum habēs for metrical purposes = *c abēs*
8. 'Hiatus' ('yawning gap') is the term applied when elision is not observed. An example is passage 1, l.363 *ō utinam*, where *ō* is not elided, and is thus 'in hiatus'.

Pronunciation

9. The pronunciation of a syllable is affected *only* by whether the vowel is long or short, *not* by whether it is heavy or light. Thus *et* is short. It is therefore pronounced short. If it becomes heavy because it is followed by a consonant, e.g. *et fugit*, it is still pronounced short. There are no circumstances in which you would ever pronounce it long, *ēt*. Thus, in this text of Ovid's, all single vowels *pronounced* long are *marked* long (and automatically count heavy for scansion purposes). All *other* vowels are pronounced *short*, though (like *et* in *et fugit*) they may be heavy for the purposes of scansion.

Exercise
Read the first twenty lines of passage 1, pronouncing all syllables short except where they are marked as long.

The hexameter

10. Ovid's *Metamorphōsēs* is composed in hexameters ('six metra/feet'). This consists of a metron/foot called a 'dactyl' (heavy-light-light, $-\smile\smile$, tum-ti-ti) and a metron/foot called a 'spondee' (heavy-heavy, $--$, tum-tum), on the following pattern:

1	2	3	4	5	6
tūm-tĭ-tĭ	tūm-tĭ-tĭ	tūm-tĭ-tĭ	tūm-tĭ-tĭ		
or	*or*	*or*	*or*	tūm-tĭ-tĭ	tūm-tūm/
tūm-tūm	tūm-tūm	tūm-tūm	tūm-tūm	(tūm-tūm)	tūm-tĭ

In other words, the first four 'feet' can be a dactyl or a spondee. Foot 5 is virtually always a dactyl, and foot 6 a spondee, though the last syllable is allowed to be short.

Caesura

11. There is nearly always a division between words in the third or fourth foot of the hexameter. This is called 'caesura' (from *caedō*, 'I cut'), e.g.

1	2	3	4	5	6
rēddĭtŭs	ōrbĭs	ĕrāt;// quēm	pōstquām	uīdĭt	ĭnānĕm

Exercises

A. Examine carefully the opening lines of passage 1 ('long' pronunciation marks removed), here scanned for you. Underlined vowels are elided and do not count for the purpose of scansion; caesuras are marked //

rēddĭtŭs ōrbĭs ĕrāt;// quēm pōstquām uīdĭt ĭnānĕm
ēt dēsōlātās // ăgĕr<u>e</u> āltă sīlēntĭă tērrās,
Dēucălĭōn lăcrĭmĭs // ĭtă Pȳrrh<u>am</u> ādfātŭr ŏbōrtis: 350
'ō sŏrŏr, ō cōniunx, // ō fēmĭnă sōlă sŭpērstĕs,
quăm cōmmūnĕ mĭhĭ // gĕnŭs ĕt pătrŭēlĭs ŏrĭgō,
deīndĕ tŏrūs iūnxĭt, // nūnc ipsă pĕrĭcŭlă iūngūnt.
tērrārūm, quāscūmquĕ // uĭdēnt ōccāsŭs ĕt ōrtŭs,
nōs dŭŏ tūrbă sŭmŭs; // pōssēdĭt cētĕră pōntŭs.   355

B. Now scan the following lines. Hints:
   (i)   Every new foot must begin -.
   (ii) If a foot begins – ˘, the next syllable must be ˘ and the next -.
   (iii) The last five syllables of a line will virtually always scan – ˘ ˘ – – or – ˘ ˘ – ˘.
   (iv) Check for elisions.
   (v)   Mark caesuras in the third or fourth foot.

haec quoque adhuc uitae non est fiducia nostrae
certa satis; terrent etiam nunc nubila mentem.

quīs tǐbǐ, sī sǐnĕ mē fātīs ērēptǎ fuīssēs,
nūnc ǎnǐmūs, mǐsěrāndǎ, fǒrēt? quǒ sǒlā tǐmǒrēm
fērrě mǒdō pōssěs? quǒ cōnsōlāntě dǒlěrēs?

Effect of the metre

12. Galinsky (1975, 21) neatly summarises the effect of Ovid's use of metre. See also Anderson (1972, 24–30) for more detail:

> Ovid's favourite arrangement of dactyls and spondees in the first four feet of the hexameter is exactly the reverse of Virgil's. The eight most frequent patterns in the *Metamorphōsēs* exhibit an average ratio of twenty dactyls to twelve spondees; in the *Aeneid*, it is exactly the other way around. These eight patterns account for 81.62 per cent of Ovid's verses. All eight have an initial dactyl. Only one of the eight uses more than two spondees, as compared to three of eight in the *Aeneid*. Ovid makes far less use of elision, again quite in contrast to Virgil, who 'made elision one of the important features of his hexameter, using it frequently and with great art to interlock phrases and reinforce the complexity of his design'. (1972, 26)

> Furthermore, Ovid is intent on combining sense-units with metrical units. Phrases or clauses that form a meaningful unit do not overrun the major caesuras of the hexameter nearly as often as they do in Virgil. The result is that the narrative is perspicuous and flows along smoothly and quickly. It is worth quoting Brooks Otis' succinct, if slightly exaggerated, summary:

> In a word, Ovid puts in everything (dactyls, regular pauses, coincidence of ictus and accent, rhyme, alliteration, grammatical simplicity and concision) that will speed up and lighten; leaves out everything (elision, spondees, grammatical complexity, clash of accent and ictus, overrunning of metrical by sense unit) that will slow down and encumber his verse.

Suggestions for further reading

The *Main text* section contains almost nothing written after 1990 because I consider much modern literary scholarship on *Metamorphōsēs* to be rather too advanced for the intended readers of this book, although I have included examples of what it has to offer. The **Study sections**, however, refer to modern works from time to time and the books quoted there appear in the *Study section* below.

Main text

Anderson, W. S. 1972.*Ovid's Metamorphoses Books 6–10* (Norman and London: University of Oklahoma Press)

   1997. *Ovid's Metamorphoses Books 1–5* (Norman and London: University of Oklahoma Press)

Anderson, W. S. and Frederick, M. P. 1998. *Selections from Ovid's Metamorphoses* (White Plains, N.Y.: Prentice Hall)

Barkan, L. 1986. *The Gods Made Flesh* (New Haven and London: Yale University Press)

Binns, J. W. (ed.) 1973. *Ovid* (London: Routledge)

Brown, S. A. 1999. *The Metamorphosis of Ovid: From Chaucer to Ted Hughes* (London: Duckworth)

Due, O. S. 1974. *Changing Forms: Studies in the Metamorphoses of Ovid* (Copenhagen: Gyldendal)

Galinsky, G. K. 1975. *Ovid's Metamorphoses* (Oxford: Blackwell)

Henderson, A. A. R. 1979. *Ovid Metamorphoses III* (Bristol: Bristol Classical Press)

Hill, D. E. 1985. *Ovid: Metamorphoses I–IV* (Warminster: Aris and Phillips)

   1992. *Ovid: Metamorphoses V–VIII* (Warminster: Aris and Phillips)

   1999. *Ovid: Metamorphoses IX–XII* (Warminster: Aris and Phillips)

Hollis, A. S. 1970. *Ovid: Metamorphoses Book VIII* (Oxford: Clarendon Press)

Jestin, C. A. and Katz, P. B. 2000. *Ovid: Amores, Metamorphoses: Selections* (2nd edn., Wauconda, Ill.: Bolchazy-Carducci)

Kenney, E. J., in Kenney, E. J. and Clausen, W. V. (eds.) 1982. *The Cambridge History of Classical Literature*, II.420–57 (Cambridge: Cambridge University Press)

Lee, A. G. 1953, 1984. *Ovid: Metamorphoses I* (Cambridge: Cambridge University Press, 1953; repr. Bristol: Bristol Classical Press, 1984)

Mack, S. 1988. *Ovid* (New Haven and London: Yale University Press)

Martindale, C. (ed.) 1988. *Ovid Renewed* (Cambridge: Cambridge University Press)

Murphy, G. M. H. 1972. *Ovid: Metamorphoses Book XI* (Oxford: Oxford University Press)

Otis, B. 1966. *Ovid as an Epic Poet* (Cambridge: Cambridge University Press)

Solodow, J. B. 1988. *The World of Ovid's Metamorphoses* (Chapel Hill and London: University of North Carolina Press)

Syme, R. 1978. *History in Ovid* (Oxford: Clarendon Press)

Wilkinson, L. P. 1955. *Ovid Recalled* (Cambridge: Cambridge University Press)

Study section

Brown, S. A. 2005. *Ovid: Myth and Metamorphosis* (Bristol: Bristol Classical Press).

Fantham, E. 2004. *Ovid's Metamorphoses* (Oxford: Oxford University Press)

Fowler, D. 2000. *Roman Constructions* (Oxford: Clarendon Press)

Hardie, P. 2002. *Ovid's Poetics of Illusion* (Cambridge: Cambridge University Press)

Hardie, P. (ed.) 2002a. *The Cambridge Companion to Ovid* (Cambridge: Cambridge University Press)

Hardie, P., Barchiesi, A. and Hinds, S. (eds.) 1999. *Ovidian Transformations* (Cambridge Philological Society, Supplementary Volume 23)

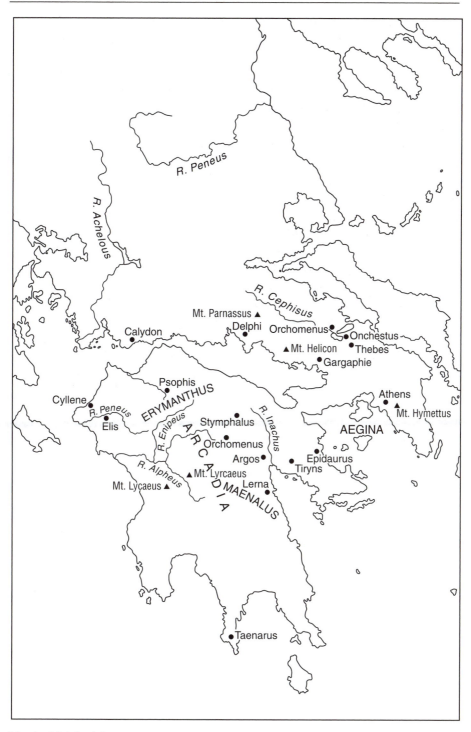

Map 1   Mainland Greece

Map 2   The Western Aegean and Asia Minor

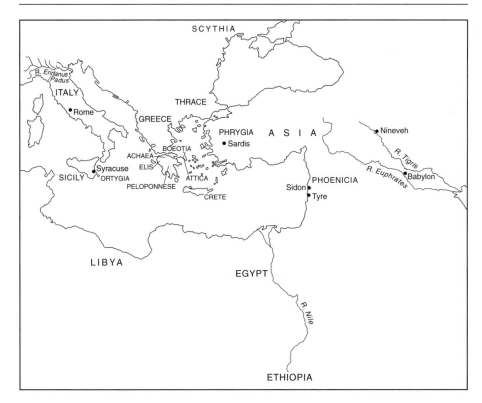

Map 3   The Central and Eastern Mediterranean

1 Deucalion and Pyrrha, *Metamorphōsēs* 1.348–415

Background

The universe has been created, but man has become greedy and aggressive. The Giants launch an attack on Jupiter, and his lightning strikes them down, but from the Giants' blood springs a yet more savage race. Jupiter summons the gods and tells them that he has decided to destroy mankind; when the gods object, he promises to replace men with a better race. He sends a flood, which overwhelms the earth and kills everyone – except Deucalion and Pyrrha. Sailing in their little boat, they come ashore near Delphi on Mount Parnassus, the only place not yet submerged. Jupiter sees them and, realising what a god-fearing, right-minded and devout couple they are, he stays the flood, which slowly retreats. As the waves die down, the earth rises up – empty and bare.

Deucalion was son of Prometheus ('Forethought'), who was credited with making mankind out of the clay of the earth. Prometheus' brother was Epimetheus ('Afterthought'), and Pyrrha was his daughter. Prometheus and Epimetheus were sons of Iapetus, one of the gods known as the Titans.

1.348–57: *Deucalion realises that he and Pyrrha are alone and in danger*

redditus orbis erat; quem^ postquam uīdit ^inānem
et dēsōlātās^ agere alta silentia ^terrās,
Deucaliōn lacrimīs^ ita Pyrrham adfātur ^obortīs:　　　　　　　　350

---

348 *reddō* 3 *reddidī redditus* restore to view, return
*orb-is is 3m. physical world. See p. 20 n.3
quem . . . uīdit: *quem* refers to the world, i.e. 'after he [i.e. Deucalion] saw *it*', a connecting relative, **RL**107; for relatives generally, see **RL**106, **W**17; *uīdit* also controls *agere . . . terrās*, an acc. and inf. i.e. 'and [after he saw] that the *dēsōlātās terrās agere alta silentia . . .*' etc., **RL**98–9, **W**25
inān-is e empty

349 *dēsōlāt-us a um* deserted. An impressively doom-laden word, with its four heavy syllables, to be followed by an *alta silentia*
silentia agō be silent (lit. 'pass-time-in silences').
　　Note *silentia*, 'poetic' pl., where we would expect s
350 *Deucaliōn* 3m. Greek nom. s., Deucalion
*lacrim-a ae 2f. tear. For the scansion, see **Metre** 2(c)
adfor adfārī 1 dep. address
obortus: 4th p.p. *oborior* 4 dep. spring up, well up (abl. abs. with *lacrimīs*, **RL**150–1, **W**24)

348–57: The scene is initially focussed through the eyes of Deucalion (*uīdit*, 348) as he reacts to the world's emptiness and silence (348–9); and tearful emotions run high throughout (350, cf. *flēbant* 367). Note that he does not begin by lamenting the

'ō soror, ō coniunx, ō fēmina sōla superstes,
quam commūne^ mihī ^genus et patruēlis orīgō,
deīnde torus iūnxit, nunc ipsa perīcula iungunt.
terrārum, quāscumque uident occāsus et ortus,
nōs duo turba sumus; possēdit cētera pontus.
haec^ quoque adhūc uītae* nōn est ^fidūcia *nostrae
^certa satis; terrent etiam nunc nūbila mentem.'

355

351 *soror -is* 3f. sister (first cousins, actually: see below). Note the three word-groups ('tricolon'), beginning with the same word *ō* ('anaphora'), increasing in length ('rising') and without a word for 'and' ('asyndeton'). These are common rhetorical features in Ovid

coniunx coniug-is 3m/f. wife, husband. The *o* scans heavy because it is followed by two consonants, *n* + consonantal *i* (=*j*, cf. 'conjugal'; see **Metre** 5). The derivation is *con* (=*cum*) + *iungō*, cf. *iūnxit*, *iungunt* below

superstes superstit-is surviving

352 *quam*: object of *iūnxit*, *iungunt*

patruēl-is e from a paternal uncle. Pyrrha was the daughter of Epimetheus, brother of Deucalion's father Prometheus. For the scansion, see **Metre** 2(c)

genus . . . orīgō . . . torus: the subjects of *iūnxit* (353); they develop *soror* and *coniunx* (351) in slightly different terms. As often in Latin, even though there are plural subjects, the verb is in the singular. This forms another tricolon, but is capped by a fourth item, *nunc . . . iungunt* (making a tetracolon), strongly contrasting past and present

origō origin-is 3f. birth, origin

353 *deīnde*: *eī* is not a diphthong; the two vowels are slurred into one ('synizesis')

tor-us ī 2m. marriage-bed. *-us* scans heavy because the next word, *iūnxit*, begins with consonantal *i*

iungō 3 iūnx-ī iūnct-um join. Note the rhetorical contrast of *deīnde . . . nunc* and *torus . . . perīcula*. The different forms of *iungō* exemplify the figure

of speech known as polyptoton (see the **Glossary of Technical Literary Terms**)

354 *terrārum*: '[and] of the lands, whichever (object) *occāsus et ortus* (subjects) *uident* . . .'

quī/quae/quod- cumque who/which/what-ever

occās-us ūs 4m. setting

ort-us ūs 4m. rising (of the sun)

355 *turba*: i.e. the sum total, the whole lot – a fine example of Ovid's wit in combining such contrary ideas

possideō 2 possēd-ī possess-um hold, possess

pont-us ī 2m. sea. More fine balance – *nōs* (A) *turba* (B) *sumus* (C) – *possēdit* (C) *cētera* (B) *pontus* (A). This 'reversed' order is known as 'chiasmus'. It is common in Ovid. Note *cētera* – n. pl.: everything, not just humans, has been submerged

356 *adhūc . . . nōn*: not yet

fidūci-a ae 1f. trust, faith (in [the chances of] *nostrae uītae*)

357 *nūbil-um ī* 2n. cloud, mist

Learning vocabulary

coniunx coniug-is 3m/f. wife, husband, spouse
iungō 3 iūnx-ī iūnct-um join
lacrim-a ae 2f. tear
nūbil-um ī 2n. cloud, mist
orb-is is 3m. physical world
origō origin-is 3f. birth, origin
pont-us ī 2m. sea
possideō 2 possēd-ī possess-um hold, possess
quī/quae/quod- cumque who/which/what-ever
soror -is 3f. sister

destruction of the human race; he knows that the gods have been at work (366, cf. their assumed anger, 378) and they can do no wrong (392 – there is a charming innocence to Deucalion's piety); but lovingly, his first thoughts and fears turn to his wife, not himself. The *ō* tricolon (351) makes for an emotional start to the speech: Pyrrha is kin, wife and womankind – three categories, she the sole representative of them all. He begins by pointing out that they are now linked not only by their relationship but also by the dangers they jointly face (353): note the increasing intimacy of *genus*, *origō* and *torus* – family (in general), birth (more particular), bed. Their adversity binds them yet closer, and it needs to – not only are they all that is left (354–5), but even now they still cannot be certain that they will survive (356–7).

1.358–62: *Deucalion expresses his fears, should they be parted*

'quis^ tibi, sī sine mē fātīs ērepta fuissēs,
nunc ^animus, miseranda, foret? quō^ sōla timōrem
ferre ^modō possēs? quō cōnsōlante dolērēs?   360
namque ego (crēde mihī), sī tē quoque pontus habēret,
tē sequerer, coniunx, et mē quoque pontus habēret.'

1.363–6: *They are the sole remnants of the human race*

'ō utinam possim populōs reparāre paternīs
artibus, atque animās formātae īnfundere terrae!
nunc genus^ in nōbīs* restat ^mortāle *duōbus –   365
sīc uīsum superīs – hominumque exempla manēmus.'

358 *quis . . . quō* (360) *. . . quō . . .* (362): note the
tricolon of three questions, each clause this time
becoming shorter. *quis*, usually 'who?', can be
used as an adjective, as here (*quis . . . animus*
'what . . . state of mind?', **RL**I4, **W**19)
*fāt-um ī 2n. fate, destiny. Here dat. pl., 'from
destiny' (i.e. death)
fuissēs: plupf. subj., 'you had (been) . . .'. This starts
a long sequence of conditional thoughts, 'if X had
happened, what would the situation be *now*?',
ending at 362; **RL**139, 173, **W**33
359 *miserand-us a um* pitiable, piteous. Gerundive of
miseror 1 dep. 'pity', **RL**161, **W**39
foret: impf. subj., 'would [now] be', **RL**E1
quō . . . modō how
360 *possēs*: impf. subj., on the pattern of *foret* above
quō cōnsōlante: abl. abs., lit. 'with whom consoling
 . . . ?' i.e. 'who would there be to console you as'
dolērēs: see on *possēs* above, and cf. the subjunctives
in 361–2
361 *tē quoque . . . habēret*: this half-line is repeated at
362, with *mē* for *tē*. It is a common device in
Ovid; here it emphasises the determination of
Deucalion to align himself with his wife, even in
death. The two are devoted to each other

363 *ō*: note the emotional hiatus with *utinam* (hiatus
is quite common after such interjections; perhaps
the effect is to give special emphasis to the cry)
*utinam would that, O that (+ subj., **RL**153)
reparō 1 restore
*patern-us a um father's, paternal. At *artibus*, it looks
as if Deucalion is lamenting the fact that there is
no way the two of them can repopulate the whole
world by the time-honoured methods (*paternīs
artibus*), cf. 355, 365. But 364 indicates that *pater-
nus* refers specifically to his father Prometheus,
who moulded humans from clay and breathed life
into them – a rather less demanding and certainly
speedier solution to the problem, if only they had
the know-how
364 **anim-a ae* 1f. soul, spirit, breath
*fōrmō 1 shape, form, mould
īnfundō 3 pour; inf. after *possim* (364)
365 *restō* 1 survive, hang on
*mortāl-is e mortal, human
366 *uīsum*: supply *est*; *uideor* here means 'seem
good'
*super-ī ōrum 2m. powers above, gods
exempl-um ī 2n. (sole) model, example, pattern,
copy

359–62: Deucalion now contemplates how his wife could possibly handle his death (358)
with a tricolon of unanswerable questions *quis* (358) . . . *quō* (359) . . . *quō* . . . (360),
each beginning with a form of *quis* ('polyptoton'), with asyndeton, the subjunctives
emphasising how unreal the situation would be. He hints from the example he proposes
for himself that suicide would be her best option (361–2).

363–6: But immediately he pulls himself together: it may be impossible to imagine how
they can solve the world's problems (363–4), but they are the world's last hope, and this
is the will of the gods (365–6).

1.367–74: *In tears, they decide to seek an oracle at the deserted temple*

dīxerat, et flēbant; placuit caeleste∧ precārī *dep'*
∧nūmen, et auxilium per sacrās∧ quaerere ∧sortēs.
nūlla mora est; adeunt pariter Cēphīsidas undās∧,
ut nōndum ∧liquidās, sīc iam uada nōta ∧secantēs.   370
inde ubi libātōs∧ irrōrāuēre ∧liquōrēs
uestibus et capitī, flectunt uestīgia sānctae∧
ad dēlūbra ∧deae, quōrum fastīgia turpī∧
pallēbant ∧muscō, stābantque sine ignibus ārae.

Learning vocabulary

anim-a ae 1f. soul, spirit, breath
fāt-um ī 2n. fate, destiny
fōrmō 1 shape, form, mould
mortāl-is e mortal, human
patern-us a um father's, paternal
super-ī ōrum 2m. powers above, gods
utinam + subj. would that, o that

367 **fleō 2 flēuī flētum* weep
placuit: impersonal verb, **RL**154, **RLF**2, **W**37
*precor 1 dep. pray to, entreat
368 **nūmen nūmin-is* 3n. power, divinity (here = Themis, 379)
*sors sort-is 3f. oracle, lot
369 *pariter* equally, together, side by side
Cēphīsidas: Greek acc. pl. 'of the river Cephisus' (Ovid means the sacred Castalian spring at Delphi, into whose waters there was presumably a tradition that the Cephisus flowed)
*und-a ae 1f. wave, water
370 *ut . . . sīc* as . . . so, though . . . but
liquid-us a um clear, limpid. It is still muddy because of the effects of the flood
uad-um ī 2n. course, channel
*nōt-us a um familiar, well-known, usual
secō 1 cut through
371 **inde* (if taken with *libātōs . . . liquōrēs*) from there; or as a result, hence. Begin translating with *ubi*
libō 1 draw (of water). One had to be physically pure to approach a god; a ritual sprinkling of water was enough. Since *libō* also means 'pour' and is used of making libations (liquid offerings poured out to the gods, usually wine), Ovid might be suggesting that the couple also make a libation with some of the water before using the rest to purify themselves. They are a very pious pair

irrōrō 1 sprinkle X (acc.) over Y (dat.). *irrōrāuēre = irrōrāuērunt*, **RL**A4; so also *tetigēre* 375, *trāxēre* 412
liquor -is 3m. water
372 **uest-is is* 3f. clothes, dress, cloth
*flectō 3 flexī flexum bend, curve, avert, steer
*uestīgi-um ī 2n. footstep, footprint, track, walk, trace
*sānct-us a um sacrosanct, sacred, holy, blessed, upright, pure
373 *dēlūbr-um ī* 2n. shrine, temple. Presumably readers were supposed to think of the great temple of Apollo at Delphi, though he did not have an oracle there at this time, and the deity to whom they are appealing is in fact Themis (see below)
*de-a ae 1f. goddess
fastīgi-um ī 2n. roof, summit, tip (here, 'pediment'?). Subject of *pallēbant*
374 *palleō* 2 be yellow, sallow
musc-us ī 2m. moss. There is no one looking after this holy place

Learning vocabulary

de-a ae 1f. goddess
flectō 3 flexī flexum bend, curve, avert, steer
fleō 2 flēuī flētum weep
inde from there
nōt-us a um familiar, well-known, usual
nūmen nūmin-is 3n. power, divinity
precor 1 dep. pray to, entreat
sānct-us a um sacrosanct, sacred, holy, blessed, upright, pure
sors sort-is 3f. oracle, lot
uestīgi-um ī 2n. footstep, footprint, track, walk, trace
uest-is is 3f. clothes, dress, cloth
und-a ae 1f. wave, water

367–74: They must therefore try to discover what the divine will now is (367–8). What else, after all, can they do? This is indeed a devout couple, an impression reinforced by the measures they take to carry out the correct rituals (371–2). There is no sign of human activity at the temple: it has not been cleaned, nor do altar-fires burn (373–4). Nor do they have any sacrifice to offer.

1.375–80: *They prostrate themselves and ask for help*

ut templī tetigēre gradūs, prōcumbit uterque   375
prōnus humī, gelidōque∧ pauēns dedit ōscula ∧saxō,
atque ita 'sī precibus∧' dīxērunt 'nūmina* ∧iūstīs
*uicta remollēscunt, sī flectitur īra deōrum,
dīc, Themi, quā∧ generis* damnum reparābile *nostrī
∧arte sit, et mersīs∧ fer opem, mītissima, ∧rēbus!'   380

1.381–9: *The goddess Themis gives them baffling instructions*

mōta dea̧ est, sortemque dedit: 'discēdite templō,
et uēlāte caput, cīnctāsque∧ resoluite ∧uestēs,

375 *grad-us ūs* 4m. step. One worshipped the god outside at the altar, not inside the temple
prōcumbō 3 prostrate oneself, fall down
*uterque utriusque both, each (cf. *uter utr-a um*)
376 *prōn-us a um* flat, prone. The *-us* is short because the following *h* does not count for metrical purposes
*humī on the ground
*gelid-us a um cold
*paueō 2 be frightened, fear
*ōscul-um ī 2n. kiss
*sax-um ī 2n. stone
377 *sī . . . sī*: ancient prayers are full of 'ifs'. In fact, the 'ifs' represent the reasons why a human thinks a god ought to act; but since humans cannot know for *certain* what persuades a god to act in any situation, 'if' is used rather than e.g. 'since'
*prec-ēs –um 3f. pl. prayers. *precibus* is abl. of means after *uicta*, **RL**100A(b), **W**14
*iūst-us a um just, righteous, lawful, fair
378 *remollēscō* 3 be softened
*īr-a ae 1f. anger, rage, wrath
379 *Themi*: Greek voc. of Themis, Greek god of the earth and prophecy, embodying order and justice. Prior to the establishment of Apollo's oracle there was an ancient sanctuary to Earth-Themis at

Delphi, a circle of rocks surrounding a cleft in the ground
damn-um ī 2n. loss
reparābil-is e retrievable, recoverable
380 *sit*: subj. in indir. q. beginning *dīc . . . quā*
mergō 3 *mersī mersum* submerge, deluge, drown.
rēbus = 'the world'
*ops op-is 3f. help, aid
mīt-is e gentle, kind. Prayers are always intended to flatter the god

Learning vocabulary
gelid-us a um cold
humī on the ground
īr-a ae 1f. anger, rage, wrath
iūst-us a um just, righteous, lawful, fair
ops op-is 3f. help, aid
ōscul-um ī 2n. kiss
paueō 2 be frightened, fear
prec-ēs -um 3f. pl. prayers
sax-um ī 2n. stone
uterque utriusque both, each (cf. *uter utr-a um*)

381 *templō*: a 'true' ablative, indicating the point *from which* an action moves; **RL**100A,Survey(a)
382 **uēlō* 1 veil, cover, conceal. The head being considered sacred, and therefore to be respected,

375–80: All they can do is prostrate themselves at the temple steps – a most dramatic gesture, emphasising their sense of helplessness – kiss the cold stone (375–6 – cold because the powerful Greek sun has not been shining on it) and offer prayers (377). Observe too their prayer – not for themselves, but for a just cause, as they see it (377), the restoration of the human race ('submerged' indeed, 379–80). Further, observe who the prayer is directed at: the couple can hardly appeal to Jupiter, whose anger at human wickedness caused the destruction in the first place.

381–9: We know of about 300 oracular shrines from the ancient world. To judge by the records (left on inscriptions) of visits to them, an oracle was perfectly capable of giving

ossaque post tergum magnae∧ iactāte ∧parentis!'
obstipuēre diū; rumpitque silentia uōce
Pyrrha prior, iussīsque deae pārēre recūsat,   385
detque sibī ueniam pauidō∧ rogat ∧ōre, pauetque
laedere iactātīs∧ māternās* ∧ossibus *umbrās.
intereā repetunt caecīs∧ obscūra* ∧latebrīs
*uerba datae sortis, sēc<u>um</u> inter sēque uolūtant.

Romans veiled their heads on some ritual occasions, e.g. sacrifice. But Deucalion and Pyrrha were Greeks, who did not. Ovid was not alone among Roman writers in foisting Roman customs on others

cingō 3 *cīnxī cīnctum* surround, encircle, gird up

resoluō 3 undo, untie. Knots in anything (rope, hair, clothes) were thought to impede divine powers, perhaps because they were bindings and could therefore bind, i.e. prevent or hinder, divine interventions

383 **os oss-is* 3n. bone
**terg-um* ī 2n. back, rear, far side
magnae: -*ae* counts metrically because the next letter is consonantal *i*; cf. the scansion of *laedere* 387, *dīcī* 394, *fēmina* 413
iact-ō 1 throw
parentis: the last word of the god's command – making the orders utterly baffling. But note *magnae*, feminine. This is the clue, which Pyrrha fails to understand by interpreting too literally (*māternās*, 387)
384 *obstipescō* 3 *obstipuī* be dumbfounded, struck dumb
rumpō 3 break

silenti-um ī 2n. silence (note 'poetic' pl. again)
385 **prior -is* earlier (of two), former, having prior place, elder
**iuss-um* ī 2n. injunction, order, command
recūsō 1 refuse
386 *detque*: subj., 'Themis' understood as subject – indirect command after *rogat*, with *ut* suppressed: '[Pyrrha] asks *that* [Themis] . . .', **RL**134, **W**36
ueni-a ae 1f. pardon, forgiveness
**pauid-us a um* terror-struck, fearful
387 *laedō* 3 harm, hurt, offend
**mātern-us a um* mother's, maternal
388 **repetō* 3 *repetīuī repetītum* return/go back to, recall, repeat, attack again
caec-us a um blind, dark
obscūr-us a um puzzling
latebr-a ae 1f. obscure expression, hidden recess. This is abl. of cause after *obscūra*, i.e. puzzling *because of* . . ., **RL**108.2, **RLL**(f)4(iii), **W**Suppl.syntax. Even though this is the temple of Themis, the latter meaning hints at the recess in Apollo's temple at Delphi where the prophetess gave her oracles
389 *sēcum inter sēque*: i.e. each with him/her self, and then between them
uolutō 1 turn over

clear answers to questions, especially those dealing with religious ritual (like 'Which gods should we worship if we want to achieve X?'). In myth, however, the oracle's utterances were traditionally baffling and needed interpretation to understand; the will of the gods was not expected by ancients to be crystal clear to mere mortals (any more than the will of God is today). So the couple's baffled reaction to Themis' command (384) was only to be expected, and sets the tone for this scene. It was a fearful thing (386) to reject a divine command, especially for people as pious as Pyrrha and Deucalion, but Pyrrha's refusal to carry out her orders (385) is not surprising, given that the gods were traditionally severe on those who mistreated the dead, especially their own parents – which the oracle here seems to be inviting them to do. Deucalion clearly agrees with her initial reaction – the oracle surely cannot refer to their literal mothers – so, knowing as they do that oracles are bewildering (388–9), they debate the matter between themselves (389).

1.390–7: *Deucalion guesses at the oracle's meaning*

inde Promēthīdēs placidīs Epimēthida dictīs   390
mulcet, et 'aut fallāx' ait 'est sollertia nōbīs,
aut (pia sunt nūllumque nefās ōrācula suādent!)
magna parēns terra est; lapidēs in corpore terrae
ossa reor dīcī; iacere hōs post terga iubēmur.'
coniugis auguriō quamquam Tītānia mōta est,   395
spēs tamen in dubiō est: adeō caelestibus ambō
diffīdunt monitīs; sed quid temptāre nocēbit?

390 *Promēthīdēs*: Greek nom., son of Prometheus (= Deucalion). Such 'patronymics' (calling a son by the father's name) are regularly found in epic. Pro-metheus means 'before-thinker'; Deucalion has inherited his father's intelligence
placid-us a um gentle, soothing. With *dictīs*, this is abl. of means, **RL**84, **RLL**(f)4(ii), **W**22
Epimēthida: Greek acc., daughter of Epimetheus (= Pyrrha). Epi-metheus means 'after-thinker', i.e. slow to catch on. Pyrrha is daughter of her father
*dict-um ī 2n. word, saying
391 *mulceō* 2 calm
fallāx fallāc-is misleading, deceptive
sollerti-a ae 1f. cleverness, skill
nōbīs: dat. indicating possession, **RL**48.2, 88.1(b), **W**Suppl.syntax. Is this the royal 'we', or is the kindly Deucalion also crediting Pyrrha?
392 **pi-us a um* holy, dutiful, faithful, just
*nefās n. wrong, crime, sacrilege, horror
*ōrācul-um ī 2n. oracle
*suādeō 2 *suāsī suāsum* recommend, urge, advocate
393 *terra*: 'mother' earth (Greek *Gaia*). Greek myth told how in the beginning the empty world was filled when Sky (Ouranos) mated with Gaia, who gave birth to everything in it – mountains, rivers, night, day, gods, etc.
lapis lapid-is 3m. stone
394 *reor* dep. believe, suppose. Note the following acc. and inf., '*reor* the *ossa dīcī* [to be] the *lapidēs*', i.e. '*reor* by *ossa* she means . . .'
*iaciō 3 *iēcī iactum* throw (away), hurl; pile up

395 *auguri-um ī* 2n. prediction, interpretation
Tītāni-a ae 1f. daughter of the Titan (Epimetheus), i.e. Pyrrha
396 **in dubiō* = in doubt; *dubi-us a um* uncertain, doubtful, ambiguous
*adeō to such an extent, so
ambō (nom.) both
397 *diffīdō* 3 mistrust, distrust (+ dat.)
*monit-a ōrum 2n. pl. advice, warning, precepts
*temptō 1 try out, test, investigate, examine, try

Learning vocabulary
adeō to such an extent, so
cingō 3 *cīnxī cīnctum* surround, encircle, gird up; pass. be situated, lie round
dict-um ī 2n. word, saying
iaciō 3 *iēcī iactum* throw (away), hurl; pile up
in dubiō = in doubt; *dubi-us a um* uncertain, doubtful, ambiguous
iuss-um ī 2n. injunction, order, command
mātern-us a um mother's, maternal
monit-a ōrum 2n. pl. advice, warning, precepts
nefās n. wrong, crime, sacrilege, horror
ōrācul-um ī 2n. oracle
os oss-is 3n. bone
pauid-us a um terror-struck, fearful
pi-us a um holy, dutiful, faithful, just
prior -is earlier (of two), former, having prior place, elder
repetō 3 *repetīuī repetītum* return/go back to, recall, repeat, attack again
suādeō 2 *suāsī suāsum* recommend, urge, advocate
temptō 1 try out, test, investigate, examine, try
terg-um ī 2n. back, rear, far side
uēlō 1 veil, cover, conceal

390–7: Now Deucalion gently proposes the solution (393–4). Observe how piously cautious he is: they might be wrong (391), but the gods can never do wrong (392), so . . . Pyrrha is not immediately persuaded (395–6), and Deucalion too shares her doubts (396–7) – these two work as a pair – but they see that no harm can come from at least giving it a try (397).

1.398–402: *They take a chance and start throwing stones behind them*

dēscendunt, uēlantque caput, tunicāsque recingunt,
et iussōs lapidēs sua post uestīgia mittunt.
saxa∧ (quis hoc crēdat, nisi sit prō teste uetustās?)   400
pōnere dūritiam coepēre, suumque rigōrem
mollīrīque morā, ∧mollītaque dūcere fōrmam.

1.403–15: *A new race is formed*

mox ubi crēuērunt, nātūraque mītior illīs
contigit, ut quaedam∧ – sīc nōn ∧manifesta – uidērī
∧fōrma potest hominis, sed utī dē marmore ∧coepta,   405

---

398 **dēscendō* 3 *dēscendī dēscēnsum* descend, go down
tunic-a ae 2f. robe, tunic. They now carry out the divine orders (382)
recingō 3 ungirdle, loosen
399 *lapis lapid-is* 3m. stone
400 *crēdat*: note the conditional pres. subj., and the following *sit*; see **RL**139, 173, **W**33
prō teste 'for/as witness, testimony [to it]'
uetustās uetustāt-is 3f. ancient tradition, antiquity
401 *dūriti-a ae* 1f. hardness
coepēre = *coepērunt*, the subject being *saxa* (l. 400). *coepēre* explains the inf. *pōnere*, *mollīrī* and *dūcere*
rigor -is 3m. rigidity. Here it is acc. of respect after *mollīrique*, **RL**6.3

402 **molliō* 4 soften, calm, weaken, appease, allay, tame. *mollīta* refers to *saxa*. Note the 'soft' *m*s and *l*s in the first half of this line
morā: lit. 'with delay', i.e. gradually
dūcō 3 take on, assume
403 **crēscō* 3 *crēuī crētum* grow, be born, increase, swell, advance
mīt-is e gentle
illīs: dat. (referring to *saxa*)
404 *contingō* 3 *contigī* come about, happen to
ut quaedam: 'as a certain *fōrma potest uidērī*'. *sīc* = though
manifest-us a um clear, well-defined, distinct
405 *utī* = *ut* as, just as
marmor -is 3m. marble

398–402: They carry out the ritual preparation ordered by the god (398) and lo, Deucalion's suggestion works (400 ff.). Observe the rhetorical question *quis crēdat*: Ovid loves to tease by dropping into mock historical mode, like a serious historian supplying the 'evidence' of 'witnesses'. Observe that they throw the stones *post uestīgia* (399) – i.e. as they walk away from the temple, they pick up whatever stones they see and lob them behind them.

So far, Ovid has provided us with a delightful picture of a loyal, loving and devout couple doing all they can between themselves to retrieve a desperate situation in the interests of all mankind, by seeking divine help and trying to make sense of it. Now Ovid faces a 'what if?' problem of the sort he revelled in. What would it actually be *like* if stones turned into humans? How would it actually *work*? What would be the *logic* behind it? Here one can sense the endlessly ingenious, inventive and imaginative Ovidian brain going into overdrive to come up with a suitably convincing poetic solution. First, he reasons, rocks are hard: they must therefore become soft (401–2). Only thus can they begin, gradually, to take on a different shape (402).

403–15: But rocks are also small, at least those which the couple can pick up. They must therefore increase in size, and in so doing their essential nature as stones begins unalterably to yield (403–4). Their shape can now *come to seem* like that of a man: not yet obvious (404), not yet the finished article, but very like a carved statue emerging

nōn ^exācta satis, rudibusque* ^simillima *signīs.
quae^ tamen ex illīs aliquō* ^pars ūmida *sūcō
et ^terrēna fuit, ^uersa est in corporis ūsum;
quod solid<u>um</u> est flectīque nequit, mūtātur in ossa;
quae^ modo ^uēna fuit, sub eōdem nōmine mānsit;   410
inque breuī spatiō, superōrum nūmine, saxa
missa uirī manibus faciem trāxēre uirōrum,
et dē fēmineō^ reparāta est fēmina ^iactū.
inde genus dūrum sumus experiēnsque labōrum,
et documenta damus quā^ sīmus ^orīgine nātī.   415

406 *exāct-us a um* finished, exact
rud-is e rough (-hewn)
sign-um ī 2n. statue
407 *quae . . . pars* 'what part', better 'the part which'.
    Continue translating with *ex illīs fuit ūmida aliquō sūcō*
ex illīs: i.e. the rocks
ūmid-us a um moist
sūc-us ī 2m. juice, sap, vigour
408 *terrēn-us a um* earthy, of the earth/soil
*ūs-us ūs 4m. use, employment, function, utility, need. *in corporis ūsum* means 'to serve as flesh' (see the **Comment** on this issue)
409 *solid-us a um* solid
nequeō irr. be unable
410 *uēn-a ae* 1f. vein
411 *spati-um ī* 2n. space
412 **faci-ēs –ēī* 5f. looks, appearance, sight, beauty, face
*trahō 3 *trāxī tractum* attract, bring in one's wake; drag, draw after, carry off, acquire, extend
413 **fēmine-us a um* woman's, feminine, female
reparō 1 reconstruct
iact-us ūs 4m. throw

414 **dūr-us a um* hard, tough, robust, harsh, severe, strict
experiēns experient-is enterprising, active in (+ gen.)
415 *document-um ī* 2n. proof, example (often of something implying some sort of warning or instruction)
*nāscor 3 dep. *nātus* be born, arise, come into being, be suited. *sīmus nātī* is subj. of indirect question, **RLR3, W**30. *nāt-us a um* son/daughter of (lit. 'born from' + 'true' abl. of source/origin, **RL**108.1); also = (x years) old

Learning vocabulary
crēscō 3 *crēuī crētum* grow, be born, increase, swell, advance
dēscendō 3 *dēscendī dēscēnsum* descend, go down
dūr-us a um hard, tough, robust, harsh, severe, strict
faci-ēs –ēī 5f. looks, appearance, sight, beauty, face
fēmine-us a um woman's, feminine, female
molliō 4 soften, calm, weaken, appease, allay, tame
nāscor 3 dep. *nātus* be born, arise, come into being, be suited; *nāt-us a um* son/daughter of; = (x years) old
trahō 3 *trāxī tractum* attract, bring in one's wake; drag, draw after, carry off, acquire, extend
ūs-us ūs 4m. use, employment, function, utility, need

from (hard) stone (405–6). Ovid now homes in on the details. Stones have earthy and wet parts, Ovid claims: these become the flesh (407–8). Is he talking of rocks covered in wet earth after the flood? No: the Latin does not say that. Ovid is repeating an ancient theory articulated by the Greek philosopher Xenophanes that mud could turn into stone. This is in fact true of e.g. sedimentary rock formed out of mud, clay and sand which had been deposited and subjected to immense pressures for millions of years. Xenophanes, of course, did not know that, but he had observed fossils imprinted in stone and drawn the right conclusion (the matter was of some interest: there is a lost work by the Greek Theophrastus *On Things Turned to Stone*). So while the muddy parts turn to flesh, the solid parts of the rock become bones (409); and Ovid knows that rocks can be veined, or marbled, so these parts become veins (410 – Ovid has been inspecting the backs of his hands). Finally, Ovid reverts to tradition to

Learning vocabulary for Passage 1, Deucalion and Pyrrha

adeō to such an extent, so

anim-a ae 1f. soul, spirit, breath

cingō 3 *cīnxī cīnctum* surround, encircle, gird up; pass. be situated, lie round

coniunx coniug-is 3m/f. wife, spouse

crēscō 3 *crēuī crētum* grow, be born, increase, swell, advance

de-a ae 1f. goddess

dēscendō 3 *dēscendī dēscēnsum* descend, go down

dict-um ī 2n. word, saying

dūr-us a um hard, tough, robust, harsh, severe, strict

faci-ēs –ēī 5f. looks, appearance, sight, beauty, face

fāt-um ī 2n. fate, destiny, death

fēmine-us a um woman's, feminine, female

flectō 3 *flexī flexum* bend, curve, avert, steer

fleō 2 *flēuī flētum* weep

fōrmō 1 shape, form, mould

gelid-us a um cold

humī on the ground

iaciō 3 *iēcī iactum* throw (away), hurl; pile up

in dubiō = in doubt; *dubi-us a um* uncertain, doubtful, ambiguous

inde from there, as a result, hence

īr-a ae 1f. anger, rage, wrath

iungō 3 *iūnx-ī iūnct-um* join

iuss-um ī 2n. injunction, order, command

iūst-us a um just, righteous, lawful, fair

lacrim-a ae 2f. tear

mātern-us a um mother's, maternal

molliō 4 soften, calm, weaken, appease, allay, tame

monit-a ōrum 2n. pl. advice, warning, precepts

mortāl-is e mortal, human

nāscor 3 dep. *nātus* be born, arise, come into being, be suited; *nāt-us a um* can = (x years) old; son/daughter of + abl.

nefās n. wrong, crime, sacrilege, horror

nōt-us a um usual, well-known, familiar

nūbil-um ī 2n. cloud, mist; cf. *nūb-ēs is* 3f. cloud

nūmen nūmin-is 3n. power, divinity

ops op-is 3f. help, aid

ōrācul-um ī 2n. oracle

orb-is is 3m physical world

orīgō orīgin-is 3f. birth, origin

os oss-is 3n. bone

ōscul-um ī 2n. kiss

patern-us a um father's, paternal

paueō 2 be frightened, fear

pauid-us a um terror-struck, fearful

pi-us a um holy, dutiful, faithful, just

pont-us ī 2m. sea

account for male and female by the sex of the thrower (412–13; see Apollodorus below). Naturally, the metamorphoses happen very quickly, thanks to the gods (411) – obviously, no human eye could *quite* describe it – and the problem of repopulating the world is solved, with gods and men now working in harmony again (cf. the divine anger, 378).

Ovid ends with an aetiology ('explanation of causes': Greek *aitia* 'cause' + *logos* 'account, explanation') – men's origin in rocks (415) is the cause of us being a 'hard race' (414). This idea is a poetic commonplace, occurring widely in Greek and Latin literature, e.g. Virgil's *Georgics* 1.61–3: *quō tempore prīmum / Deucaliōn uacuum lapidēs iactāuit in orbem / unde hominēs nātī, dūrum genus* 'from the time when Deucalion first threw stones over the empty world, from which men were born – a hard race', and cf. Lucretius *dē rērum nātūrā* 5.925 and the **Study section**. The central point, however, is that Ovid is the only poet who attempts to explain how the transformation might actually have *worked*. Observe that aetiology of this sort can sometimes suggest that a metamorphosis has a 'logic' to it – physical, or emotional, or psychological (as if the metamorphosis somehow 'fits' or has appropriate consequences for the person or thing transformed). Finally, note that for Ovid, the origins of our race lie not with great heroes, but with a simple, pious and loving couple.

Learning vocabulary for Passage 1, Deucalion and Pyrrha (continued)

possideō 2 *possēd-ī possess-um* hold,
    possess
prec-ēs -um 3f. pl. prayers
precor 1 dep. pray to, entreat
prior -is former, earlier (of two), having prior
    place, elder
quī- quae- quod- cumque who/which/what-ever
repetō 3 *repetīuī repetītum* return/go back to,
    recall, repeat, attack again
sānct-us a um sacrosanct, sacred, holy, blessed,
    upright, pure
sax-um ī 2n. stone
soror-is 3f. sister
sors sort-is 3f. oracle, lot
suādeō 2 *suāsī suāsum* recommend, urge,
    advocate

super-ī ōrum 2m. powers above, gods
temptō 1 try out, test, investigate, examine, try
terg-um ī 2n. back, rear, far side
trahō 3 *trāxī tractum* attract, bring in my wake;
    drag, draw after, carry off, acquire, extend
uēlō 1 veil, cover, conceal
uestīgi-um ī 2n. footstep, footprint, track,
    walk, trace
uest-is is 3f. clothes, dress, cloth
und-a ae 1f. wave, water
ūs-us ūs 4m. use, employment, function,
    utility, need
uterque utriusque both, each (cf. *uter utr-a um*)
utinam would that, O that (+ subj.)

Study section

1. Write out and scan ll.363–6, 408–15.
2. At 398, many texts prefer to print *discēdunt*. Why? See 381. How might one defend *dēscendunt*?
3. What picture does Ovid present of the relationship between Deucalion and Pyrrha, and how does he do it?
4. Take any five lines, consecutive or not, and explain why they give you pleasure.
5. Here are two versions of the story by the Greek myth-collector, Apollodorus (third century BC) and the Latin myth-collector, Hyginus (probably second century AD). How is Ovid's version different, and with what result?

Apollodorus

'Prometheus' son was Deucalion . . . he married Pyrrha, the daughter of Epimetheus and Pandora (the first woman made by the gods). And when Zeus had it in mind to destroy the race of bronze, Deucalion, on Prometheus' advice, constructed a chest, filled it with provisions and got on board with Pyrrha. Zeus's storms flooded the greater part of Greece . . . but Deucalion, floating in the chest over the sea for nine days and nights, drifted to Parnassus, and there, when the rain stopped, he landed and sacrificed to Zeus God of Escape. And Zeus sent Hermes to him and allowed him the choice of whatever he wanted; and Deucalion chose to have people. On Zeus's orders, he took up stones and threw

them over his head, and the stones which Deucalion threw became men, and the stones which Pyrrha threw became women. This is how people came to be called people (Gk. *laos*), from (Gk.) *laas*, a stone.'
Apollodorus, *Library* 1.7.2

Hyginus

'After the flood . . . the whole human race perished except for Deucalion and Pyrrha, who took refuge on Etna, said to be the highest mountain in Sicily. Since they could not live on account of their loneliness, they asked Jupiter either to provide humans or drown them too. Then Jupiter ordered them to throw stones behind them. Those thrown by Deucalion became men, those by Pyrrha, women. For this reason they are called *laos*, since *laas* in Greek means "stone".'
Hyginus, *Genealogiae* 153

2 Cupid, Apollo and Daphne, *Metamorphōsēs* 1.452–567

Background

The earth is now repopulated with humans, and Ovid goes on to describe how spontaneous self-generation engendered other creatures, including monsters. This *mise-en-scène*, which is still Parnassus, leads Ovid to concentrate on one particular monster, the Python, a vast and hideous snake, swollen with poison, which sprawled over Parnassus and terrorised Delphi until Apollo killed it with his arrows. To celebrate his victory, Apollo established at Delphi the 'Pythian' Games, whose winners would at first be crowned with oak-leaves. This changes, however, when Apollo is hit by Cupid's golden arrow and falls hopelessly for Daphne ('laurel').

Ovid is extremely skilful at connecting one myth with another. Here, the connection is forged by Apollo's boasting about his skill with the bow in killing the Python and going on to demean Cupid and his bow. The angry Cupid decides to take revenge and demonstrate how much more powerful his bow is than Apollo's.

1.452–62: *Apollo mocks Cupid (who is playing with a bow) and boasts of his own killings*

prīmus amor Phoebī Daphnē Pēnēia, quem nōn
fors ignāra dedit, sed saeua^ Cupīdinis ^īra.

---

452 *prīmus*: Ovid will tell the stories of more lovers to come for Apollo, male and female, including the prophetic Sibyl and the boy Hyacinth.
 Understand *erat* as the main verb
Phoeb-us ī 2m. Phoebus ('bright, shining'), i.e. Apollo; also, the sun
Daphn-ē f. Greek nom. of Daphne, daughter of Peneus
Pēnēi-us a um descended from the river Peneus. This means the *god* of the river Peneus. All physical features of the world, being of divine origin, were thought to be also personified as gods.

'Peneus' is the name both of the river and the river-god
quem: note the gender, m. So it cannot refer to Daphne: that leaves *amor* or *Phoebus*. Which?
453 **fors fort-is* 3f. chance, luck, destiny (usually only in nom. or abl. *forte*, 'by chance')
*ignār-us a um ignorant, unaware, i.e. blindly
*saeu-us a um savage, cruel
Cupīdō Cupīdin-is 3m. Cupid, the god of carnal lust. He is depicted as a winged (466) mischievous little boy playing with a bow, who excites sexual desire (with golden arrows) or extinguishes it (with lead) (468–9)

452–62: Ovid starts the story with a teasing paradox: Apollo is fired with *amor* for Daphne not out of mere chance but because of Cupid's *anger* (452–3). Now 'anger' is a suitably epic theme (Homer's *Iliad*, the first work of Western literature c. 700 BC, begins

[45]

Dēlius^ hunc,* nūper uictō serpente ^superbus,
uīderat adductō^ *flectentem cornua ^neruō,   455
'quid' que 'tibī, lascīue puer, cum fortibus armīs?'
dīxerat; 'ista^ decent umerōs ^gestāmina nostrōs,
quī dare certa^ ferae, dare ^uulnera possumus hostī,
quī modo pestiferō^ tot iūgera ^uentre prementem*
strāuimus innumerīs *tumidum *Pȳthōna sagittīs.   460
tū face^ nescioquōs* estō contentus *amōrēs
irrītāre ^tuā, nec laudēs adsere nostrās!'

---

454 *Dēli-us a um* Apollo, lit. 'from Delos', the Greek
island where Apollo was born
hunc: m., i.e. Cupid
*nūper recently
serpēns serpent-is 3m. snake, serpent, i.e. the Python,
here abl. abs. with *uictō*, explaining why Apollo
was *superbus*
superb-us a um proud, haughty
455 *uīderat*: note the plup., and cf. *dīxerat* 457. Ovid
uses these tenses to indicate that all this is background to the real story. This almost begins at
474, before Ovid backtracks to tell Daphne's
story, and finally starts at 490
addūcō 3 draw back, pull tight
cornu-a 3n. pl.: lit. 'horns', i.e. bow, whose tips were
often made of horn; here object of *flectentem*
neru-us ī 2m. bow-string (made of sinew or horse-
hair)
456 *quid . . . tibī*: lit. 'What . . . for you?', i.e. 'What's
your interest?', 'What are you doing?'
lascīu-us a um playful, mischievous, sexually unre-
strained
457 *deceō* 2 (impersonal vb.) suit, fit, be proper (for
+ acc.), **RL**154, **W**37
umer-us ī 2m. shoulder
gestāmen gestāmin-is 3n. gear, ornament
458 *quī*: m. pl., picking up *nostrōs*, i.e. '[we] who *possumus dare certa uulnera* both *ferae* and *hostī*'
*fer-a ae 1f. wild animal
459 *pestifer -a um* deadly, noxious. *pestiferō . . . prementem* describes the Python (460), the object of
strāuimus

tot: scans heavy because the next word begins with a
consonantal *i*
iūger-um ī 2n. acre (= two-thirds of a modern acre)
uenter uentr-is 3m. belly, stomach
460 *sternō* 3 *strāuī* flatten, stretch lifeless
innumer-us a um countless
tumid-us a um swollen, gross (with poison, as Ovid
had earlier explained)
Pȳthōn -is 3m. Python
sagitt-a ae 1f. arrow
461 *fax fac-is* 3f. torch, brand, love-flame
nescioqui quid some X or other (usually contemptu-
ous in tone)
estō be! (imper.). This is an archaic imperative form,
RLE1: is Apollo further mocking Cupid ('be
thou!')?
content-us a um satisfied, content (to + inf.)
462 *irrītō* 1 stir up, excite
*laus laud-is 3f. reputation, praise, merit; cf. *laudō* 1
praise
adserō 3 lay claim to

Learning vocabulary

fer-a ae 1f. wild animal
fors fort-is 3f. chance, luck, destiny (usually only in
nom. or abl. *forte*, 'by chance')
ignār-us a um ignorant, unaware, i.e. blindly
laus laud-is 3f. reputation, praise, merit; cf. *laudō* 1
praise
nūper recently
Phoeb-us ī 2m. Phoebus ('bright, shining'), i.e.
Apollo; also, the sun
saeu-us a um savage, cruel

---

with the word 'anger' – the anger of the mighty hero Achilles), but the *saeua īra* of a trivial
god like Cupid sounds like a contradiction in terms anyway; and why would his anger fire
Apollo with *amor*? Cupid surely *wanted* his victims to experience *amor*? But we know,
like the Romans, that *amor* can be a painful business; and Cupid, being the mischievous
god he is (456), is intent on taking revenge on Apollo for an insult. The result will be that
the *amor* with which he fires Apollo will be frustrated. The path of true *amor* never does
run smooth for humans, nor does it for gods either. But as *prīmus* indicates – first word,
in strongly emphatic position – there will be a lot of it about in *Metamorphōsēs* for Apollo

1.463–73: *Cupid shoots different arrows at Apollo and Daphne*

filius^ hūic ^Veneris 'figat tuus omnia, Phoebe,
tē meus arcus' ait; 'quantōque̯ animālia^ cēdunt
^cūncta deō, tantō minor est tua glōria nostrā.'   465

463 *hūic*: 'to him', dative after *ait* (464)
Venus Vener-is 3f. Venus, goddess of sex. Cupid is
her son
*figō 3 *fixī fixum* pierce, transfix. *figat* (subj. of
command [jussive], 'let . . .', **RL**152, **W**28) is the
verb controlling *figat tuus* [*arcus*] *omnia* (463);
but for *tē meus arcus* (464), supply *figet*, future.
Cupid implies that anyone can deal with
creatures; it takes real power to deal with
gods

464 *arc-us ūs* 4m. bow
quantō . . . tantō by how much . . . by so much. This
is ablative of difference, **RL**100B.5,
WSuppl.syntax
animal -is 3n. mortal creature
*cēdō 3 *cess-ī cess-um* yield to (+ dat.), step aside; go,
withdraw, come to an end
465 *cūnct-us a um all
nostrā: note the case (abl.) – used of comparison
after *minor*, **RL**J5, **W**26/Suppl.syntax

(and many other gods too). Would Romans have seen a feeble joke, therefore, in *MetAMORphōsēs*? Possibly, though the word is Greek and splits *meta* ('change') *morphōsis* ('shape').

At which point, a word of warning: *amor* covers a range of meanings, from sexual passion, sexual intercourse and strong desire at one extreme, to affection, liking and fondness at the other (see Introduction, pp. 9–10). Where exactly on the scale does Apollo's *amor* come? Is his 'love' nothing but lust in fancy dress?

Something else is going on here. At *Amores* 1.1.5, Ovid describes how he was about to write an epic in hexameters ('arms and the violent deeds of war') when Cupid interrupted to force him to write elegiacs, on love-themes, instead. *quis tibi, saeve puer, dedit hoc in carmina iūris*, Ovid asks ('Who gave you, cruel boy, this right over poems?'). Now, at 456, Cupid has popped up again, and Apollo asks what this 'lustful' boy has got to do with mighty weapons. Here, then, in one of the first stories of what, with its hexameters, looks as if it is going to be a great epic, Cupid is interfering yet again. This will be an epic with an elegiac difference.

superbus (454) sets us on the narrative path: Apollo is feeling very pleased with himself after killing the Python with his bow and arrows. It is Apollo's character that motivates the story. When he sees Cupid playing with a bow and arrow too, he mocks him and tells him to go play with his torch (lighting flames of *amor* in his victims) and leave bows and arrows to the big boys, for serious business (455–62). Apollo sings up his own achievements (457–62) in lines of tremendous bravura: note the repeated *quī* and *dare*, the second *quī* (459) leading to two magnificently ringing, boastful lines – *strāuimus innumerīs* is especially grandiose in a semi-golden line while *pestiferō, tot* and *tumidum* all lay on thick the danger he faced. Observe too the haughty royal 'we' (459–60). Apollo's final mocking dismissal of Cupid, especially *face . . . tuā, nescioquōs* and *irrītāre* (461–2) – as if Cupid really were attempting to rival him – is an insult too far.

463–73: Cupid is all too ready to take up the challenge. A god is not mocked, and even in a mighty epic, the little god of love has a role to play (cf. *Aeneid* 1.664–722, where Venus sends Cupid to ensure Dido falls in love with Aeneas). To prove his point, Cupid selects Apollo as his first victim – for if Apollo can master all mortal creatures with his bow but

dīxit et, ēlīsō^ percussīs ^āere pennīs,
impiger umbrōsā^ Parnāsī cōnstitit ^arce,
ēque sagittiferā^ prōmpsit duo tēla* ^pharetrā
*dīuersōrum operum: fugat hoc, facit illud amōrem.
quod facit, aurātum est et cuspide fulget acūtā;
quod fugat, obtūsum est et habet sub harundine plumbum.
hoc deus in nymphā Pēnēide fīxit, at illō
laesit Apollineās^ trāiecta per ossa ^medullās.

470

466 *ēlīdō* 3 *ēlīsī ēlīsum* remove by force, sweep aside.
   ēlīsō . . . āere is abl. abs., the idea being that
   Cupid's wings face powerful resistance as he
   labours upwards
percutiō 3/4 percussī percussum beat, strike
āēr āer-is 3m. air, atmosphere, sky
penn-a ae 1f. wing, feather
467 *impiger impigr-a um* active, energetic
umbrōs-us a um shadowy
Parnās-us ī 2m. Parnassus, a mountain overlooking
   Delphi
468 *ēque = ē(x) que*
sagittifer-us a um arrow-bearing
prōmō 3 *prōmpsī prōmptum* bring out, produce
tēl-um ī 2n weapon
pharetr-a ae 1f. quiver
469 *dīuers-us a um* opposite. *dīuersōrum operum* is
   genitive of description, preparing us for the
   description of the function of the two arrows,
   RL101, **W**40
hoc . . . illud: subjects, referring to the arrows, 'the
   one', 'the other'. Note the word-play *fugat . . . facit*
470 *quod facit*: subject, 'the one that makes [one fall
   in love]', paralleled by *quod fugat* (471)
aurāt-us a um golden, gilded. This line sounds sharp
   and crisp
cuspis cuspid-is 3f. point, tip
acūt-us a um sharp
471 *obtūs-us a um* blunt. This line sounds heavy and
   solid, full of *u*'s and *b*'s
harundō harundin-is 3f. shaft. *sub* here means 'at the
   tip of'

plumb-um ī 2n. lead
hoc: i.e. the latter (lead) arrow. *illō* (472) = the
   former (golden) arrow; *hīc* and *ille* are often
   used in this sense, *hīc* meaning 'this one here',
   i.e the nearer, i.e. the latter; *ille* meaning that
   one over there, i.e. the further away, i.e. the
   former
472 *nymph-a ae* 1f. young woman, semi-divine
   female spirit
Pēnēis Pēnēid-is descended from Peneus (cf. *Pēnēi-
   us*, 452)
473 *laedō* 3 *laesī laesum* wound, hurt, injure,
   annoy
Apolline-us a um of Apollo
trāiciō 3/4 trāiēcī trāiectum pierce
medull-a ae 1f. marrow, innermost being

Learning vocabulary
āēr āer-is 3n. air, atmosphere, sky
cēdō 3 *cess-ī cess-um* yield to (+ dat.), step aside; go,
   withdraw, come to an end
cūnct-us a um all
fīgō 3 *fīxī fīxum* pierce, transfix
hīc . . . ille the one (this one here, latter) . . . the
   other (that one there, former)
laedō 3 *laesī laesum* wound, hurt, injure, annoy
nymph-a ae 1f. (also *nymph-ē*) young woman, semi-
   divine female spirit
penn-a ae 1f. wing, feather
percutiō 3/4 percussī percussum beat, strike
pharetr-a ae 1f. quiver
tēl-um ī 2n weapon

Cupid can master Apollo with *his*, who is the true master then, Cupid argues (464–5)? Note
Cupid's ironic use of the royal 'we' at the end of *his* boast (*nostrā*, 465). At once Cupid flies
up to the top of Parnassus (where he can see Daphne). This makes for an amusing picture:
the chubby little god Cupid energetically (*impiger*) thrashing his way on his tiny wings up
to the top of Parnassus, as if he were one of Parnassus' eagles that still fly above the mountain to this day (466–7). Once there, he uses his arrows to make sure that Apollo is filled
with *amor*, but that Daphne utterly rejects him (466–73). There is a pleasing contrast in
Ovid's treatment of the two victims. Daphne, a river nymph, simply needs to be hit (472);
Apollo, a god, needs to have the arrow driven through his bones right into his marrow
(473). Cupid, too, is now *deus* (472), not a silly little boy (though *puer* would fit the metre).

1.474–89: *Daphne's beauty and desire to remain a virgin for ever*

prōtinus alter amat, fugit altera^ nōmen amantis,
siluārum latebrīs captīuārumque ferārum   475
exuuiīs ^gaudēns innūptaeque ^aemula Phoebēs;
uitta coercēbat positōs sine lēge capillōs.
multī illam petiēre; illa, āuersāta petentēs,
impatiēns expersque uirī, nemora āuia lūstrat,
nec, quid Hymen, quid Amor, quid sint cōnūbia cūrat.   480
saepe pater dīxit: 'generum mihi, filia, dēbēs,'
saepe pater dīxit: 'dēbēs mihi, nāta, nepōtēs.'
illa^, uelut crīmen taedās ^exōsa iugālēs,
pulchra^ uerēcundō suffūderat ^ōra rubōre,
inque patris^ blandīs* haerēns ^ceruīce *lacertīs,   485

474 *prōtinus* at once; straight on
475 *latebr-a ae* 1f. hiding place, retreat. *latebrīs* and
    exuuiīs (476) are both controlled by *gaudēns*,
    'finding/who found pleasure/joy in'
captīu-us a um captive
476 *exuui-ae ārum* 1f. pl. spoils, prize
gaudeō 2 semi-dep. *gāuīsus* find pleasure, rejoice, be
    happy in (+ abl.)
innūpt-us a um unmarried
aemul-a ae 1f. rival. This is Daphne, whose ambition
    is to match Diana in hunting and avoiding sex
Phoebēs: Greek gen. s. of Phoebe, i.e. Diana, goddess
    of chastity and the hunt (Greek Artemis); she was
    sister of Apollo
477 *uitt-a ae* 1f. headband
coerceō 2 hold back
sine lēge: upper-class Roman women usually took
    great care to see that their hair was done properly
capill-us ī 2m. hair
478 *multī*: i.e. many suitors. For other examples of
    suitors seeking the hand of a girl, see e.g.
    10.569–74 (passage 18, Atalanta), and cf. e.g.
    Penelope in Homer's *Odyssey*
petiēre = petiuērunt **RLA4, W12**(footnotes)
āuersor 1 dep. *āuersātus* turn from, reject
479 *impatiēns impatient-is* intolerant, impatient (of)
expers expert-is inexperienced, lacking knowledge
    (of)
nemus nemor-is 3n. wood, forest, grove

āui-us a um trackless, out of the way
lūstrō 1 rove, move through
480 *quid . . . quid . . . quid*: indirect question in the
    form of a tricolon, with anaphora, after *cūrat*
Hymen Hymen-is 3m. marriage hymn, god of
    marriage
cōnūbi-um ī 2n. marriage, right to marry
cūrat: we might expect 'know' – we get
    'care'!
481 *saepe . . . dīxit*: here the repeated clause mimics
    her father's insistence. An unmarried child was a
    useless child in the ancient world
gener -ī 2m. son-in-law
482 *nepōs nepōt-is* 3m. grandchild
483 *uelut* like, as if, as
crīmen crīmin-is 3n. crime, scandal, offence
taed-a ae 1f. torch (accompanying marriage-cere-
    mony)
exōs-us a um hating, loathing
iugāl-is e to do with marriage, nuptial
484 *uerēcund-us a um* bashful, shy
suffundō 3 *suffūdī* suffuse
rubor rubōr-is 3m. blush, redness, modesty
485 *inque*: begin with *haerēns*, take *in* with *ceruīce*
bland-us a um coaxing, flattering, charming
haereō 2 *haesī haesum* cling (to), be fixed to; doubt,
    hesitate
ceruīx ceruīc-is 3f. neck (controlled by *inque*)
lacert-us ī 2m. (upper) arm, embrace

474–89: Ovid now dramatises Daphne and the beauty that will be her (unwitting) undoing. She is depicted as a rival – perhaps 'admirer' would be better – of Diana, finding pleasure in animal lairs and the spoils of the hunt (475–6); her hair is loose and free (477); she has no interest in men, marriage or sex (478–80); her father keeps dropping insistent hints about grandchildren (481–2), but she uses her innocent female charm on him alone (pleasant irony) to persuade him otherwise (483–7). He agrees (488): but, of course, he

'dā mihi perpetuā∧, genitor cārissime,' dīxit
'∧uirginitāte fruī! dedit hoc pater ante Diānae.'
ille quid<u>em</u> obsequitur, sed tē decor iste quod optās
esse uetat, uōtōque tuō tua fōrma repugnat.

1.490–503: *Apollo is overwhelmed with desire; fire simile*

Phoebus amat, uīsaeque∧ cupit cōnūbia ∧Daphnēs,   490
quodque cupit, spērat, suaqu<u>e</u> il<u>lum</u> ōrācula fallunt.
utque leuēs stipulae dēmptīs∧ adolentur ∧aristīs,

486 *dā mihi*: 'grant to me to/that I should' + inf.
  (*fruī*)
perpetu-us a um eternal, perpetual
genitor -is 3m. parent
cār-us a um dear, beloved
487 *uirginitās uirginitāt-is* 3f. virginity
fruor 3 dep. *frūctus/fruitus* enjoy (+ abl.)
pater: i.e. Jupiter
ante: adverbial, i.e. 'previously'
* *Diān-a ae* 1f. Diana, goddess of chastity and the
  hunt
488 *obsequor* 3 dep. *obsecūtus* give in, agree
tē: object of *uetat* (489). Note the 'apostrophe'
  (moving into the second person to address
  Daphne)
*decor decōr-is 3m. beauty, grace, charm
quod optās/esse 'to be what you desire'
489 *uetō 1 *uetuī uetitum* forbid
*uōt-um ī 2n. prayer, desire, vow
tuō tua: a pointed contrast
*repugn-ō 1 fight against (+ dat.)

Learning vocabulary
bland-us a um coaxing, flattering, charming
capill-us ī 2m. hair
cōnūbi-um ī 2n. marriage, right to marry
crimen crimin-is 3n. crime, scandal, offence
decor decōr-is 3m. beauty, grace, charm
Diān-a ae 1f. Diana, goddess of chastity and the
  hunt

gaudeō 2 semi-dep. *gāuīsus* find pleasure, rejoice, be
  happy in (+ abl.)
haereō 2 *haesī haesum* cling (to), be fixed to; doubt,
  hesitate
lacert-us ī 2m. (upper) arm, embrace
nemus nemor-is 3n. wood, forest, grove
prōtinus at once; straight on
*repugn-ō 1 fight against (+ dat.)
rubor rubōr-is 3m. blush, redness, modesty
uelut like, as if, as
uetō 1 *uetuī uetitum* forbid
uōt-um ī 2n. prayer, desire, vow

490 *Phoebus*: the background has been filled in; now
  the action begins with Apollo's pursuit of Daphne
Daphnēs: Greek gen. s. of Daphne
491 *quodque*: = *quod* + *que* 'and what'
ōrācula: Apollo was god of prophecy
*fallō 3 *fefellī falsum* cheat, deceive, fail
492 *utque*: 'and as', to be followed by two similes
  (the second, beginning *ut*, at 493), the similes
  finally referred back to the subject with *sic* (495):
  'as . . . as . . . so . . .'
*leu-is e light
stipul-a ae 1f. stalk, stubble
dēmō 3 *dēmpsī dēmptum* take away, i.e. harvest
adoleō 2 burn
arist-a ae 2f. ear (of corn). The grain having being
  harvested, the stubble is now burnt to increase
  soil-fertility

can do nothing about her when she is alone in the woods. As Ovid comments, her own
beauty will prove her downfall (488–9) – as it often does in Ovid. The 'lesson' is, perhaps,
marked by Ovid's sudden sympathetic, intimate, personalising 'apostrophe' – that is,
referring to a person in the second person (*tē . . . optās . . . tuō tua* 488–9) where the third
person has been the norm.

490–503: The narrative now returns to the point where Ovid left it to describe Daphne
(*amat* 474, *amat* 490) – Apollo in *amor*, and so intensely that he wants to marry Daphne
(*cōnūbia* 490: it is worth emphasising that *cōnūbium* does not mean simply 'going to bed

ut facibus saepēs ardent, quās forte uiātor
uel nimis admōuit, uel iam sub lūce relīquit,
sīc deus in flammās abiit, sīc pectore tōtō   495
ūritur, et sterilem∧ spērandō nūtrit ∧amōrem.
spectat inōrnātōs∧ collō pendēre ∧capillōs,
et 'quid, sī cōmantur?' ait. uidet igne micantēs∧
sīderibus similēs ∧oculōs; uidet ōscula, quae nōn
est uīdisse satis; laudat digitōsque manūsque   500
brācchiaque et nūdōs∧ mediā plūs parte ∧lacertōs;
sī qua latent, meliōra putat. fugit ōcior aurā∧
illa ∧leuī, nequ̲e ad haec∧ reuocantis ∧uerba resistit:

493 *fax fac-is* 3f. torch (i.e. 'because of the torches
    which [*quās*] . . .')
saep-ēs is 3f. hedge
ardeō 2 *arsi arsum* burn, blaze; be in turmoil
uiātor -is 3m. traveller
494 *nimis*: i.e. too close
*admoueō 2 *admōuī admōtum* move, bring
sub lūce: i.e. at daybreak. The torch has been used as
    a night-light (there was no street-lighting in
    Rome) and abandoned
ōscula: 'poetic' pl. for s., 'little mouth'
495 **pectus pector-is* 3n. breast, chest
496 **ūrō* 3 *ussi ustum* burn up, set on fire,
    inflame
steril-is e fruitless, sterile
nūtriō 4 suckle, foster, feed
497 **spectō* 1 look at, observe, see
inōrnāt-us a um not made up; cf. 477
pendeō 2 *pependī* hang, hang down, be uncertain.
    This is an inf. in an acc. and inf. after *spectat*
498 *cōmō* 1 do up, arrange. The understood subject
    is *capillī* (488)
micō 1 flash
500 **digit-us ī* 2m. finger
501 **brācchi-um ī* 2n. arm, fore-arm
*nūd-us a um naked

mediā plūs parte: 'more than by the middle part [of
    the arm]', i.e. almost to the shoulder. *plūs* is used
    here adverbially, with *quam* (as often) omitted,
    and *mediā parte* an abl. of difference, **RL**100B.5,
    WSuppl.syntax
502 *qua* anywhere
*lateō 2 lie hidden, be covered. Understand as
    subject 'features of her body', and take *meliōra*
    (object of *putat*) to refer to them
ōcior -is faster, swifter
*aur-a ae 1f. breeze, wind. It is abl. of comparison
503 *reuocō* 1 call back. *reuocantis* = 'of the one (i.e.
    Apollo) calling [her] back'

Learning vocabulary

admoueō 2 *admōuī admōtum* move, bring
aur-a ae 1f. breeze, wind
brācchi-um ī 2n. arm, fore-arm
digit-us ī 2m. finger
fallō 3 *fefellī falsum* cheat, deceive, fail
lateō 2 lie hidden, be covered
leu-is e light
nūd-us a um naked
pectus pector-is 3n. breast, chest
spectō 1 look at, observe, see
ūrō 3 *ussi ustum* burn up, set on fire, inflame

with'). That is the inevitable effect of Cupid's darts. Further, he is so blinded that (lovely
irony) even his own prophetic powers fail him – he hopes and desires, but cannot see that
he will never succeed (491). Two similes now follow to describe the god's passion: one of
a field of stubble being set on fire after the harvest has been collected, and one of a traveller accidentally setting roadside hedges on fire (492–4). Similes at moments of high
drama are common in epic: Homer's *Iliad* provides the model, which was widely imi-
tated. Is Ovid playing literary games with us here, introducing high epic into a jolly
romp? Note that Ovid does not begin the simile by telling us to what the simile refers: he
goes straight in 'and like light stubble . . .' For the connection we have to wait till 495
(another typical Homeric feature) – the fires are the fires burning in Apollo's breast, all
in the cause of an unfulfilled *amor* (495–6). It is always worth investigating the simile to

1.504–11: *Apollo begs her to slow her flight*

'nympha, precor, Pēnēi, manē! nōn īnsequor hostis;
nympha, manē! sīc agna lupum, sīc cerua leōnem,   505
sīc aquilam pennā^ fugiunt ^trepidante columbae,
hostēs^ quaeque ^suōs: amor est mihi causa sequendī!
mē miserum! nē prōna cadās, indignaue^ laedī
^crūra notent sentēs, et sim tibi causa dolōris!
aspera, quā properās, loca sunt; moderātius, ōrō,   510
curre fugamque inhibē; moderātius īnsequar ipse.'

504 *Pēnēi* (voc.) daughter of Peneus. Note the
slightly panting quality, in rhythm and sound, to
the whole *nympha . . . manē* clause
*īnsequor 3 dep. follow, pursue
hostis: in apposition to understood *ego* of *īnsequor*,
RL17B, **W**3; cf. 511 *ipse*, 562 *custōs*
505 *agn-a ae* 1f. lamb. *agna . . . cerua . . . columbae*
(505–6) are all subjects of *fugiunt*, a splendid
'rising' tricolon with anaphora (*sīc*), climaxing
with the strong contrast of Apollo's motive (507)
lup-us ī 2m. wolf
ceru-a ae 1f. deer
leō leōnis 3m. lion
506 *aquil-a ae* 1f. eagle
trepidō 1 be terrified, tremble

columb-a ae 1f. dove
507 *quaeque*: 'each one (i.e. of the named animals)
fugit . . .'
508 *nē* + subj. = 'don't/don't let . . .'. It applies to
cadās, *notent* and *sim*, **RLL**-V(a)3, **W**28; another
tricolon
prōn-us a um headlong, flat
indign-us a um unworthy to X (inf.); *-ue* = 'or'
509 *crūs crūr-is* 3n. leg
notō 1 mark, scratch
sent-is -is 3f. bramble. It is subject of *notent*
510 **properō* 1 hurry
moderāt-us a um restrained, moderate
511 **currō* 3 *cucurrī cursum* run
inhibeō 2 hold back

see what precise relation it bears to the subject. *spērat* of 491, for example, connects to *spērandō* of 496; *adolentur, facibus* and *ardent* (492–3) all look forward to *in flammās* and *ūritur* (495–6). But can one make any other connections? Is Apollo in any sense *leuēs stipulae*? Or *saepēs*? Does the activity of the *uiātor* connect with anything in particular? If we find connections hard to make, this is often the case in Homer. In other words, it is sometimes the overall picture that counts, not the detail – in this case, the raging fire burning in the fields/hedges and the god's heart. The hopelessness of it all is beautifully caught by the crunchy word-order and sentiment of *sterilem spērandō nūtrit amōrem* – 'useless' – 'hope' – 'feed' – '*amor*'. All too common a human experience . . .

We now picture Daphne through Apollo's eyes. Inevitably, it is her physical appearance that so excites him – the face to start with (hair, eyes, 'little lips'); then the arms (progression up the arm from fingers, hands, fore-arm, upper arm); the nakedness of her arms suggests that what he cannot see (which presumably he now scans) is even more exciting to him (501–2). This is a psychology all males will understand. But what Apollo sees means nothing to Daphne: she's off. So he must attempt to communicate his feelings, and Ovid tells us it will be pointless before he even begins, making his speech all the more deliciously amusing for the reader (502–3). But there is no pretence or hypocrisy in Apollo's words. He has been struck by Cupid's arrow: he is head over heels in *amor*.

504–11: Ovid here goes into full 'what if?' mode. What *would* a god say to a fleeing mortal to persuade her to stop? His argument moves through four stages:
(a) 504–7 – I intend you no harm – it is *amor* that drives me (no effect)
(b) 508–11 – to prove it, look how concerned I am for your safety (no effect)

1.512–24: *Apollo boasts of who he is*

'cūī placeās, inquīre tamen. nōn incola montis,
nōn ego sum pāstor, nōn hīc armenta gregēsque
horridus obseruō. nescīs, temerāria, nescīs,
quem fugiās, ideōque fugis: mihi Delphica tellūs   515
et Claros et Tenedos Patarēaque rēgia seruit;
Iuppiter est genitor; per mē, quod eritque fuitque
estque, patet; per mē concordant carmina neruīs.
certa quidem nostra^ est, nostrā tamen ^ūna ^sagitta
certior, in uacuō* ^quae uulnera *pectore fēcit!   520
inuentum medicīna me͟u͟m est, opiferque per orbem

512 *inquīrō* 3 inquire, find out. *cūī placeās* is an indi-
      rect question after *inquire*
incol-a ae 1m. inhabitant, native. This begins
      another fine 'rising' tricolon, with anaphora
      (*nōn*)
513 **pāstor -is* 3m. shepherd
arment-um ī 2n. herd
grex greg-is 3m. flock
514 *horrid-us a um* rough, uncouth, dishevelled
obseruō 1 watch over
temerāri-us a um thoughtless, hasty. Note more
      emotional repetitions in 514–15
515 *fugiās*: note subj. – why?
ideō for that reason
mihi: object of *seruit*, 516
Delphic-us a um of Delphi
*tellūs tellūr-is 3f. earth
516 *Claros, Tenedos* (both nom.) and Patara were all
      sites of Apolline oracles in Asia (modern western
      Turkey)

Patarē-us a um of Patara
rēgi-a ae 1f. palace
seruiō 4 wait on, be subject to (+ dat.)
517 *genitor -is* 3m. father
518 *pateō* 2 be made clear, revealed
concordō 1 be harmonised with (+ dat.)
carmen carmin-is 3n. song, poem, music
neru-a ae 1f. string
519 *certa . . . nostra*: refers to *sagitta*. Apollo
      contrasts his *certa* arrow with Cupid's *certior*
      arrow
sagitt-a ae 1f. arrow
520 *uacuō*: i.e. a heart empty of *amor* and waiting to
      be filled
521 *inuent-um ī* 2n invention, discovery.
      This begins the first colon of another
      tricolon
medicīn-a ae 1f. medicine
opifer -a um help-bringer, helper

512–24: Any mere mortal could have said all that, of course. Apollo needs to raise the
stakes:
(c) 512–18 – my credentials
     (i) what I am not (512–15)
     (ii) what I am (515–18):
          royal power (515–16)
          paternity (517)
          personal capacities – prophecy and the lyre (517–18) (no effect)
(d) 519–24 – but none of this counts beside my *amor* for you
          my mastery of the bow is as nothing to Cupid's (519–20)
          my mastery of medicine cannot cure me of my feelings for you (521–4) (no effect).
     Apollo plays card after card. When the straight appeals (a)–(b) fail, he plays the power
card (c); when that fails, he plays the helplessness card (d) – and he a god! But all to no
avail whatsoever. One almost feels sorry for him: the *ēi mihi* (523) is surely heartfelt, such
is the power of Cupid (as Apollo has effectively admitted). Apollo's humiliation is nearly

dīcor, et herbārum subiecta potentia nōbīs.
ēi mihi, quod nūllīs^ amor est sānābilis ^herbīs,
nec prōsunt dominō, quae prōsunt omnibus, artēs!'

1.525–39: *Daphne becomes more beautiful in flight; hunting simile*

plūra locūtūrum timidō Pēnēia cursū   525
fūgit, cumque ipsō uerba imperfecta relīquit –
tum quoque uīsa decēns. nūdābant corpora uentī,
obuiaque^ aduersās uibrābant ^flāmina uestēs,
et leuis^ impulsōs retrō dabat ^aura capillōs,

522 *herb-a ae* 1f. herb, plant, grass
subiect-us a um subject to, in control of (+ dat.)
*potenti-a ae 1f. power
523 *ēi* alas!
quod: explains the reason for Apollo's cry of *ēi*, and
    prepares the ground for a fine paradox
sānābil-is e curable
524 **prōsum prōdesse prōfui prōfutūrum* be an
    advantage to (+ dat.). *artēs* is the subject

Learning vocabulary
currō 3 *cucurri cursum* run
herb-a ae 1f. herb, plant, grass
insequor 3 dep. follow, pursue
pastōr -is 3m. shepherd
potenti-a ae 1f. power
properō 1 hurry
prōsum prōdesse prōfui prōfutūrum be an advantage
    to (+ dat.)
tellūs tellūr-is 3f. earth

525 *plūra locūtūrum*: 'him about to say more', object
    of *fūgit*, RL81, W23
*timid-us a um fearful, timid. *timidō cursū* is abl. of
    manner, **RL**100B.3, **W**14
Pēnēia: i.e. Daphne
526 *imperfect-us a um* unfinished
527 *decēns decent-is* beautiful. *uīsa* suggests
    that 527–30 describe Daphne as Apollo sees
    her
nūdō 1 strip, lay bare. Here begins a tetracolon, with
    golden lines!
528 *obui-us a um* in her face. This is a golden line
aduers-us a um back, against (her), i.e. outlining her
    body
uibrō 1 shake, make flutter
flāmen flāmin-is 3n. wind, breeze
529 *impuls-us a um* streaming (back). Nearly a
    golden line
retrō backwards

complete, from mighty Python-slayer to love-sick, baffled suitor. Even his divinity is of
no use to him in this situation.

There are delightful moments in this episode: Apollo's informed critique of Daphne's
hair-style (498); the ascending tricolon (505–6) with its powerful conclusion at 507; his
lover's anguish (*mē miserum*, 508) that she may hurt herself; his (wonderful) assurance
that he will slow down if she does (508–11) – only Ovid could have thought of that one;
the ascending tricolon describing who he is not – the fastidious *horridus* is very amusing
(512–14); and the resounding conclusion of 523–4 – the physician who heals others but
is helpless to heal himself (cf. 491). A third tricolon occurs at 521–2: it is a favourite
Ovidian device.

525–39: And there was yet more to come from Apollo, apparently (525), but Daphne still
did not want to know (525–6). Yet her flight makes no difference to Apollo. He has eyes
only for her, and her beauty (527) is increased by her flight (530), not because she is
announcing an unattainability which challenges his manhood, but because the winds are
stripping her (527), revealing yet more of the beauty that earlier Apollo could only guess

auctaque fōrma fugā est. sed enim nōn sustinet ultrā   530
perdere blanditiās iuuenis deus, utque monēbat
ipse amor, admissō^ sequitur uestīgia ^passū.
ut canis^ in uacuō leporem cum ^Gallicus aruō
uīdit, et hīc praedam pedibus petit, ille salūtem;
alter, inhaesūrō similis, iam iamque tenēre   535
spērat, et extentō^ stringit uestīgia ^rōstrō,
alter in ambiguō est, an sit comprēnsus, et ipsīs
morsibus ēripitur tangentiaque ōra relinquit;
sīc deus et uirgō est: hīc spē celer, illa timōre.

1.540–56: *Daphne cries out for help and is transformed into a laurel*

quī tamen īnsequitur, pennīs^ adiūtus ^amōris,   540
ōcior est, requiemque negat, tergōque fugācis

---

530 *augeō* 2 *auxī auctum* increase. This could mean
   that she looks bigger, and therefore more
   desirable, too. See on Venus (passage 18) 10.534
sed enim however. *enim* is used here in its original
   intensifying form 'indeed, truly'
*sustineō 2 endure, bear
ultrā any more
531 *blanditi-a ae* 1f. flattery, blandishment. Apollo was
   not going to waste any more breath on soft words
532 *admiss-us a um* released, headlong
*pass-us ūs 4m. step, stride, pace
533 *ut*: 'as' introduces a long simile (begin *ut canis
   cum uīdit* . . . , **RLT**(d), **W**31): the picture is of a
   dog chasing a hare (533–4), with the one (*alter*
   535) closing in for the kill (535–6) and the other
   (*alter* 537) just evading the death-bite (537–8);
   the simile is resolved by *sīc* (539), cf. on 492 above
lepor -is 3m. hare
Gallic-us a um Gallic, from Gaul (France) – a Roman
   hunting-dog (greyhound?). The huntress is now
   being hunted
*aru-um ī 2n. field
534 *hīc . . . ille*: cf. on 469 above

praed-a ae 1f. prey, catch
535 *inhaereō* 2 close in on. This is a fut. part., 'one
   about to . . .'
iam iamque at every moment
536 *extent-us a um* extended, at full stretch
stringō 3 graze, touch
uestīgia: here used to mean 'feet'
rōstr-um ī 2n. muzzle
537 *in ambiguō* in doubt
an whether, if
comprehendō 3 *comprehendī comprēnsus* seize, catch
538 *mors-us ūs* 4m. jaw, bite, teeth
ēripitur: here used in reflexive rather than passive
   sense, 'snatch oneself away from'
est: a dramatic example of the pl. subject taking a s. vb.
539 *hīc . . . ille*: an exception to the rule at 472 above!
   Cleverly balanced paradox – both are *celer*, but for
   quite opposite reasons
540 *quī*: 'he who'
541 *ōcior -is* quicker, too quick. A 'rising' tetracolon
   follows
requi-ēs requi-ēī 5f. rest
fugāx fugāc-is fugitive, swift, in flight

---

at (502). Note the precise tricolon: the winds reveal her limbs, the breezes flutter her dress, the light air blows back her tresses (527–9). Urged by *amor*, Apollo abandons all thought of persuasion and steps on it (530–2). Since this is another important moment, an extended simile decorates it (533–9), this one based on Virgil: Aeneas chases Turnus like a stag which 'runs and runs back a thousand ways, but the untiring Umbrian hound / stays with him, jaws gaping; now he has him; now he seems to have him; / his jaws snap shut but, thwarted, he bites the empty air' (*Aeneid* 12.753–5, adapted from West).

540–56: The race is coming to an end, and Ovid shows us how both sides are progressing. Apollo is pressing Daphne hard, driven by *amor* (540), and almost on her (541–2). The

imminet, et crīnem sparsum ceruīcibus adflat.
uīribus absūmptīs expalluit illa, citaeque^
uicta labōre ^fugae, spectāns Pēnēidas undās,
'fer, pater,' inquit 'opem! sī flūmina nūmen habētis,   545
quā nimium placuī, mūtandō perde figūram!'
[   ]
uix prece finītā, torpor grauis occupat artūs;
mollia^ cinguntur tenuī ^praecordia librō;
in frondem crīnēs, in rāmōs brācchia crēscunt;   550

---

542 *immineō* 2 threaten, press on (+ dat.)
*crīn-is is 3m. hair
spars-us a um spread out (i.e. further reference to
    that loose hair)
ceruīc-ēs um 3f. (pl.) neck
adflō 1 breathe on
543 *absūmō* 3 *absūmpsī absūmptum* exhaust, use up
expalleō 2 grow pale
cit-us a um swift, speedy
544 *Pēnēidas*: Greek acc. pl. 'of the river Peneus'
546 *quā*: refers forward to *figūram*, i.e. '(destroy the
    beauty) *as a result of which . . .*'
nimium too much
mūtandō: gerund, showing how Peneus is to destroy
    her beauty, **RL**175, **W**39
*figūr-a ae 1f. beauty, shape
(non-Ovidian lines omitted here: see the **Comment**)

548 **uix* scarcely, hardly
prece finītā: abl. abs.
torpor -ris 3m. numbness
art-us -ūs 4m. limb
549 **moll-is e* soft, tender, pleasant, weak. A golden
    line
*tenu-is e thin, slim, fine, clear
praecordi-a ōrum 2n. pl. breast
liber libr-ī 2m. bark. This is the same word as
    'book'. Is Ovid joking here about *tenuis liber*,
    the technical term for a 'slender volume'
    of short poems (of the sort Ovid used to write),
    when in fact Daphne is featuring in a
    mighty epic?
550 *frōns frond-is* 3f. leaf, foliage
*rām-us ī 2m. branch
brācchi-um ī 2n. arm

---

picture of him literally breathing down her neck is lifted from Homer, when, in the
funeral games for Achilles' close companion Patroclus, Odysseus is hard on Locrian
Ajax's heels in the foot-race and 'kept up so well that his breath fanned Ajax's head' (*Iliad*
23.765–6, Rieu–Jones). Daphne is physically spent (expressed in three different ways,
543–4; people do indeed go grey with exhaustion) but sees her father's river and calls
upon him for help. He had, after all, agreed that she remain a virgin (488), and she asks
him now to ensure that promise is kept by transforming her and her beauty (546).
Observe that she wonders whether rivers have the power so to do (545); and since some
ancient editors thought they did *not*, they replaced our lines 545–6 with the following
(whose omission is noted by [ ]), giving the transformative role to Earth: 'Overcome by
the toil of flight [=first half of 544] she says "Earth, open up, or destroy my beauty by
transforming it [=second half 545], that beauty which causes me to be harmed."' But
these lines miss the pathos of the appeal to her father; *quā nimium placuī* is a typically
ironical Ovidian turn of phrase, while 'that beauty that causes me to be harmed' is
wooden by comparison; and since Ovid anyway does not actually *say* which god transformed Daphne, nothing hangs on who actually did it.

'What if?' looms: how does a girl turn into a tree? First, she must stop; Ovid tells us she
can feel her limbs growing heavy (547). Next, bark begins to encase her body: since the
purpose of her prayer is that her desirability should be destroyed, it begins by covering
her breasts (549: note the sympathetic *mollia*). Leaves? Her hair. Branches? Her arms.

pēs modo tam uēlōx pigrīs rādīcibus haeret;
ōra cacūmen habet; remanet nitor ūnus in illā.
hanc quoque Phoebus amat, positāque^ in stīpite ^dextrā,
sentit adhūc trepidāre nouō sub cortice pectus,
complexusque suīs^ rāmōs ut membra ^lacertīs,   555
ōscula dat lignō; refugit tamen ōscula lignum.

1.557–67: *Apollo vows to make the laurel his own tree*

cūi deus 'at, quoniam coniunx mea nōn potes esse,
arbor eris certē' dīxit 'mea! semper habēbunt
tē coma, tē citharae, tē nostrae, laure, pharetrae;

---

551 *uēlōx uēlōc-is* fast, speedy. This line seems to 'slow down', like Daphne. Ovid may be playing on *pēs*, a physical and metrical foot
piger pigr-a um slow, sluggish. Cleverly placed next to *uēlōx*, creating a pleasing antithesis
rādix rādic-is 3f. root
552 *cacūmen cacūmin-is* 3n. tree-top
remaneō 2 remain
nitor -is 3m. youthful splendour, shine (bay-leaves are especially shiny)
ūnus: i.e. *sōlus*
553 *stīpes stīpit-is* 3m. trunk
554 *trepidō* 1 flutter, tremble. This is an inf. in acc. and inf. after *sentit*
cortex cortic-is 3m. bark

555 *complector* 3 dep. *complexus* embrace, surround
*membr-um ī 2n. limb
556 *lign-um ī* 2n. wood
refugiō 3 shrink from
557 *cūi*: 'to whom', after *dīxit* (558)
quoniam since, because
559 *com-a ae* hair: i.e. my hair (etc.) will always be decorated with laurel. Note the 'rising' tricolon with anaphora (*tē*). Repeated *tē* is common in hymns in which a mortal praises or appeals to a god; here it is a god praising a mortal! For explanations of the references in 558–65, see the end of the **Comment**
cithar-a ae 1f. lyre
laur-us ī 2f. bay-tree, laurel

Roots? Her feet (note the crunchy *uēlōx pigrīs*). Tree-top? Her face. The only indication of her human beauty is the shine of the leaves (549–52). Her body grows into the tree-trunk (553), in which Apollo can still feel her *heart beating* – a wonderful conceit (554). Even better is yet to come: his *amor* for her has not changed, and he embraces the branches as if they were her limbs, kisses the bark – and it recoils back from him (555–6)! Only Ovid could get away with this, but it serves to raise the question: is this a story of a potentially brutal, but frustrated, rape? What would a rapist do if the object of his lust turned into a tree? It seems to make no difference to Apollo's feelings; nor to hers either. At least we can conclude – game, set and match to Cupid.

557–67: The story ends, as often, with aetiology: in this case, the explanation of how the bay-tree/bay-laurel/laurel (Greek *daphnē*) came to play such an important part in the cult of Apollo and in Roman life (Ovid, again, using Greek myth to explain Roman customs). In depictions of Apollo, the laurel does indeed frequently decorate his hair, lyre and arrows (559); Roman generals wore wreaths of laurel, signifying victory, when they led triumphs into Rome, consisting of long (561) processions of senators, magistrates, soldiers, booty, captives and bands weaving their way from the Campus Martius to the great temple of Jupiter on the Capitoline hill, and the happy watching crowds

tū ducibus Latiīs aderis, cum laeta∧ Triumphum   560
∧uōx canet et uīsent longās∧ Capitōlia ∧pompās.
postibus Augustīs eadem fidissima custōs
ante forēs stābis, mediamque tuēbere quercum.
utque me<u>um</u> intōnsīs∧ caput est iuuenāle ∧capillīs,
tū quoque perpetuōs∧ semper gere frondis ∧honōrēs!'   565
fīnierat Paeān; factīs modo laurea rāmīs
adnuit, utque caput uīs<u>a</u> est agitāsse cacūmen.

---

560 *Lati-us a um* Latin
*laet-us a um joyful, happy
Triumph-us ī 2m. triumph(al procession)
561 *canō* 3 sing
uīsō 3 witness, see
Capitōli-a ōrum 2n. pl. the Capitol
pomp-a ae 1f. procession
562 *post-is is* 3f. column, pl. porch
August-us a um of Augustus
fīd-us a um faithful, loyal
563 *for-ēs um* 3f. pl. door, entrance
tueor 2 dep. guard, watch over. For the form, see
   RLC2
querc-us ūs 4f. oak-tree
564 *intōns-us a um* uncut
iuuenāl-is e youthful
565 *frōns frond-is* 3f. leaf, foliage
honōs honōr-is 3m. honour, glory. The point is
   that the laurel is an evergreen, and its leaves,
   like Apollo's hair, will always retain their
   glory
566 *Paeān*: i.e. Apollo. 'Paean' is a cult-title
   associated with Apollo as god of healing
factīs: i.e. newly made; abl. of means, **RL**100A(b),
   W14
laure-a ae 1f. laurel-tree

567 *adnuō* 3 agree, assent. Daphne is Apollo's tree
   for ever, and Ovid tells us that she accedes to her
   everlasting fame with a nod (567)
utque and like/as
uīsa est: 'seemed' or 'was seen'? Obviously the latter:
   Daphne has to respond to Apollo's wish and,
   since she cannot speak, Ovid is explaining how
   she was able to signal agreement. Or is this the
   way Ovid has decided to tell us that she might *not*
   have assented (see the **Study section**)?
agitō 1 move, nod. For the form, see **RLA4**
cacūmen cacūmin-is 3n. tree-top

Learning vocabulary
aru-um ī 2n. field
crīn-is is 3m. hair
figūr-a ae 2f. beauty, shape
laet-us a um joyful, happy
membr-um ī 2n. limb
moll-is e soft, tender, pleasant, weak
pass-us ūs 4m. step, stride, pace
rām-us ī 2m. branch
sustineō 2 endure, bear
tenu-is e thin, slim, fine, clear
timid-us a um fearful, timid
uēlōx uēlōc-is fast, speedy
uix scarcely, hardly

---

crying *iō triumphe!* as they did so (560); outside the entrance to the emperor Augustus'
palace on the Palatine hill, two laurel trees grew, and on the palace door was hung a
wreath of oak-leaves (562–3). This was an award for saving a soldier's life in battle,
granted by the Romans to Augustus for saving the nation. Ovid is laying on the Augustan
associations pretty thick here. Finally, Apollo makes the laurel an evergreen: as his own
youthful hair is never cut (564), the leaves of the laurel will never fall and will thus eternally signal the honour Apollo has bestowed on them (565) – an outcome to which
Daphne accedes, *adnuit* (566–7). Ovid has moved, effortlessly, from the heroic destruction of the hideous Python, via Cupid's darts and a humiliating sylvan failure for the
Python's destroyer, to Augustus and contemporary Rome. This poet is the master of all
literary genres, styles and effects.

Learning vocabulary for Passage 2, Cupid, Apollo and Daphne

admoueō 2 *admōuī admōtum* move, bring
āēr āer-is 3m. air, atmosphere, sky
aru-um ī 2n. field
aur-a ae 1f. breeze, wind
bland-us a um coaxing, flattering, charming
brācchi-um ī 2n. arm, fore-arm
capill-us ī 2m. hair
cēdō 3 *cess-ī cess-um* yield to, step aside; go, withdraw, come to an end
cōnūbi-um ī 2n. marriage, right to marry
crīmen crīmin-is 3n. crime, scandal, offence
crīn-is is 3m. hair
cūnct-us a um all
currō 3 *cucurrī cursum* run
decor decōr-is 3m. beauty, grace, charm
Diān-a ae 1f. Diana, goddess of chastity and the hunt
digit-us ī 2m. finger
fallō 3 *fefellī falsum* cheat, deceive, fail
fer-a ae 1f. wild animal
fīgō 3 *fīxī fīxum* pierce, transfix
figūr-a ae 2f. beauty, shape
fors fort-is 3f. chance, luck, destiny (usually only in nom. or abl. *forte*, 'by chance')
gaudeō 2 semi-dep. *gāuīsus* find pleasure, rejoice, be happy
haereō 2 *haesī haesum* cling (to), be fixed to; doubt, hesitate
herb-a ae 1f. herb, plant, grass
hic . . . ille the latter . . . the former
ignār-us a um ignorant, unaware
insequor 3 dep. *īnsecūtus* follow, pursue
lacert-us ī 2m. (upper) arm, embrace
laedō 3 *laesī laesum* wound, hurt, injure, annoy
laet-us a um joyful, happy
lateō 2 lie hidden, be covered
laus laud-is 3f. reputation, praise, merit; cf. *laudō* 1 praise

leu-is e light
membr-um ī 2n. limb
moll-is e soft, tender, pleasant, weak
nemus nemor-is 3n. wood, forest, grove
nūd-us a um naked
nūper recently
nymph-a ae 1f. (and *nymph-ē*) young woman, semi-divine female spirit
pass-us ūs 4m. step, stride, pace
pāstor -is 3m. shepherd
pectus pector-is 3n. breast, chest
penn-a ae 1f. feather, wing
percutiō 3/4 *percussī percussum* beat, strike
pharetr-a ae 1f. quiver
Phoeb-us ī 2m. Phoebus ('bright, shining'), i.e. Apollo; used also of the sun
potenti-a ae 1f. power
properō 1 hurry
prōsum prōdesse prōfuī prōfutūrum be an advantage
prōtinus at once; straight on
rām-us ī 2m. branch
repugn-ō 1 fight against
rubor rubōr-is 3m. blush, redness, modesty
saeu-us a um savage, cruel
spectō 1 look at, observe, see
sustineō 2 endure, bear
tellūs tellūr-is 3f. earth
tēl-um ī 2n weapon
tenu-is e thin, slim, fine, clear
timid-us a um fearful, timid
uēlōx uēlōc-is fast, speedy
uelut like, as if, as
uetō 1 *uetuī uetītum* forbid
uix scarcely, hardly
uōt-um ī 2n. prayer, desire, vow
ūrō 3 *ussī ustum* burn up, set on fire, inflame

Study section

1. Write out and scan ll.469–73, 476–9.
2. At 452, some manuscripts read *quam* for *quem*. To whom would that refer, and would it be preferable?
3. At 532, some texts print *Amor* (the god of love) instead of *amor* (and again at 540). Is that god needed at this moment?

4. Is it possible to tell whether Apollo is motivated by love or lust? Should Cupid's part in the action be taken into account?
5. Take any five lines, consecutive or not, and explain why they give you pleasure.
6. 'It is also a story about the god of knowledge's frustrated pursuit of sexual knowledge, as the male gaze proves unable to penetrate the secrets of the female body' (Hardie, 2002, 46). Is it?
7. 'It is famously unclear . . . whether Daphne in shaking her head really means to say "yes" or "no" to Apollo's proposition . . . If [Daphne] had her voice, the matter would not be in doubt. But her voice has perished, and with it perhaps her ability to make meaning at all' (Farrell in Hardie et al. 1999, 135). Cf. Hardie (2002, 130 note 46), who wonders 'whether Apollo's laurel was nodding in response to anything more than a puff of wind'. Discuss.
8. 'Although neither Ovid nor Apollo enjoys Daphne sexually, they could be said to collaborate in an artistic exploitation of her transformed body' (Brown, 2005, 50). What significance can you attach to this claim?

3 Io (and Syrinx), *Metamorphōsēs* 1.583–746

Background

When Daphne is transformed, Ovid tells us that all the other river-gods come to visit her father Peneus, not knowing whether to congratulate or console him. That is a shrewd observation. These are tactful river-gods, sensitive to a difficult social occasion; they have to find out Peneus' reaction before knowing how best to respond to him (not that Ovid tells us Peneus' feelings). Ovid at once goes on to say, however, that one river-god is absent: Inachus, because he is grieving for his lost daughter Io. With this 'negative association' – a common device in Ovid – the poet Ovid constructs the transition from Apollo and Daphne to the next metamorphosis.

1.583–7: *Inachus does not know where his daughter Io has gone*

Īnachus ūnus abest, īmōque reconditus antrō,
flētibus auget aquās, nātamque^ miserrimus ^Īō
lūget ut ^āmissam: nescit, uītāne fruātur,   585
an sit apud mānēs; sed quam nōn inuenit usquam,
esse putat nusqu<u>am</u>, atqu<u>e</u> animō pēiōra uerētur.

---

583 *īm-us a um* deep, bottom (of)
recondit-us a um hidden away
*antr-um ī 2n. cave. Abl. of place
584 *flēt-us ūs* 4m. weeping. This is an abl. of means, showing how he increased his own waters
augeō 2 increase
Īō: Greek acc. s. of Io
585 *lūgeō* 2 grieve, mourn for
ut: 'as one *āmissam*'
nescit: note that 'whether' in the following indir. q. is expressed by *-ne*

fruor 3 dep. enjoy (+ abl.). Io is the subject
486 *mān-ēs ium* 3m. pl. shades, spirits of the dead
sed quam: 'but [she] whom . . . [her] *putat esse nusquam*'
usquam anywhere
587 *nusquam* nowhere
animō: abl. of place
pēiōra: i.e. 'the worse' of the two options on offer (life and death)
uereor 2 dep. fear

583–7: Ovid simply but powerfully paints Inachus' emotional state. He is hidden away deep in his cave (583) – already we wonder what the description tells us – he is crying profusely (584), and with one word crunching against another ('child – most miserable – Io – grief – as lost') we cannot but feel sympathy for a father's despair (584–5). Psychologically, Ovid is spot on to see both that it is the not knowing that is the real torture (585–6) and that there is a logic to fearing the worst (586–7): after all, Inachus is a god, and if *he* does not know where she is, what possible conclusion can he draw?

[61]

1.588–600: *In fact Jupiter had spotted and ravished her*

uīderat ā patriō∧ redeuntem* Iuppiter *illam
∧flūmine, et 'ō uirgō∧ Ioue ∧digna, tuōque* beātum
nescioquem ∧factūra *torō, pete' dīxerat 'umbrās   590
altōrum nemorum' (et nemorum mōnstrāuerat umbrās)
'dum calet, et mediō∧ sōl est altissimus ∧orbe!
quodsī sōla timēs latebrās intrāre ferārum,
praeside∧ tūta ∧deō, nemorum sēcrēta subībis –
nec dē plēbe deō, sed quī caelestia magnā∧   595
scēptra ∧manū teneō, sed quī uaga fulmina mittō.
nē fuge mē!' fugiēbat enim. iam pāscua Lernae
cōnsitaque∧ arboribus ∧Lyrcēa relīquerat ∧arua,
cum deus inductā∧ lātās ∧cālīgine terrās
occuluit, tenuitque fugam, rapuitque pudōrem.   600

588 *uīderat*: note the plupf. Ovid goes back in time to establish the background to the tale
patri-us a um of one's father, paternal
beāt-us a um happy, blessed, fortunate
590 *nescioquī/quae/quod* someone or other
tor-us ī 2m. bed, marriage-bed
591 *mōnstrō* 1 show, point out. Ovid commonly repeats himself in this chatty, spontaneous way, as if giving a stage direction, cf. 597
592 *caleō* 2 grow warm
593 *latebr-a ae* 1f. hiding place, lair
594 *praeses praesid-is* 3m. guardian. Take this with *tūta* 'safe with *deō praeside*'. Note the hypocrisy of Jupiter, claiming to protect her from the beasts in the woods when in fact he intends to rape her there
sēcrēt-us a um set apart, remote, withdrawn, secluded. This is n. pl., used as a noun, **RL**14.7, **W**4
sub-eō īre pass into
595 *dē . . . sed quī*: 'nor [am I a god] from [one of the] *plēbs* gods . . . but [a god] who . . .' Note the dismissive air of *plēbs* (as if some gods were patricians – patricians and plebs were contrasted in Roman society – and others not!), the repeated *sed quī* and grand pomposity of tone (compare Apollo's boasting in passage 2, 1.504–24). Here

are the two sides of Jupiter: mighty ruler of the universe and cynical serial adulterer, all in one
plēbs plēb-is f. common (people), mob
596 *scēptr-um ī* 2n. sceptre
uag-us a um free-moving, wide-ranging
fulmen fulmin-is 3n. thunderbolt
597 *nē fuge*: an amusing change of tone – all Jupiter can do is utter this comically bewildered protest as Io races off before he can finish (like Daphne, 1.503, 526). *nē* with the imperative is common in poetry, **RLL-V**(a)3
pāscu-um ī 2n. pasture
Lern-a ae 1f. Lerna (a town near Argos in Southern Greece)
598 *cōnsit-us a um* sown, planted (*cōnserō*)
Lyrce-us a um of Mt. Lyrceus (near Argos)
599 *indūcō* 3 spread, bring over
lāt-us a um wide, broad
cālīg-ō -inis 3f. darkness, gloom, mist
600 *occulō* 3 *occuluī* hide

Learning vocabulary
antr-um ī 2n. cave
fulmen fulmin-is 3n. thunderbolt
lāt-us a um wide, broad
patri-us a um of one's father, paternal
tor-us ī 2m. bed, marriage-bed

588–600: Ovid now fills us in on how Io came to be missing – the 'background' to the story (note how Ovid moves from the pluperfect tense 588, to the perfect 600, and finally the vivid present 605). Jupiter saw her in the woods, and it was lust at first sight (no Cupid's revenge here, cf. Apollo and Daphne). His motivation is transparently self-interested in a way that Apollo's was not (the *torus* 590, a hypocritical hint at marriage; the

1.601–9: *Juno suspects something is up and dispels the clouds*

intereā mediōs* Iūnō^ dēspexit in *Argōs,
et noctis faciem nebulās fēcisse uolucrēs
sub nitidō* ^mīrāta *diē, nōn flūminis illās
esse nec ūmentī^ sēnsit ^tellūre remittī;
atque suus coniunx ubi sit circumspicit, ut quae   605
dēprēnsī^ totiēns iam nōsset fūrta ^marītī.
quem postquam caelō nōn repperit, 'aut ego fallor
aut ego laedor' ait, dēlāpsaque ab aethere summō,
cōnstitit in terrīs, nebulāsque recēdere iussit.

601 *Iūnō Iūnōn-is 3f. Juno (in Greek, Hera), wife of Jupiter
dēspiciō 3 *dēspexi* look down
Arg-ī ōrum 2m. pl. Argos (an important town in southern Greece, a major cult centre for the worship of Hera/Juno in the Greek world)
602 *nebul-a ae* 1f. cloud, mist
fēcisse: the verb in an acc. and inf. construction after *mīrāta* (603), with *nebulās . . . uolucrēs* as its subject
uolucer uolucr-is e sudden, swift, flying
603 *nitid-us a um* bright, shining
*mīror 1 dep. wonder, be amazed at
flūminis illās: i.e. [that] *illās* (i.e. the clouds – still acc. and inf. after *mīrāta*) [were not] *flūminis*, lit. 'of the river', i.e. arising from the river (like e.g. morning mists emerging out of it), a gen. of origin/source, **RL**6.5; 'clouds' are still the subject of *remittī* (acc. and inf. after *sēnsit*, 604)

604 *ūmeō* 2 be wet, moist
remittō 3 send up (from)
605 *suus coniunx*: subject of *ubi sit*
circumspiciō 3 look around
ut quae: *ut qui/quae/quod*, lit. '[she/Juno] as one who, being the sort of person who' takes the subj. (*nōsset*), **RL**166, **W**38
606 *dēprendō 3 *dēprēndi dēprēnsum* catch out, catch red-handed (often *dēprehendō*)
totiēns so often
nōsset=nōuisset*, **RLA5
fūrt-um ī 2n. deceit (especially in sexual escapades), theft
*marit-us a um married; husband; *marita* wife
607 *quem*: connecting relative, **RL**107. Begin with *postquam*
caelō: abl. of place
608 *dēlābor* 3 dep. *dēlāpsus* glide down
*aethēr -is 3m. upper air, heaven
609 *nebul-a ae* 1f. cloud, mist
recēdō 3 depart, recede

invitation into a shady nook out of the hot sun, 591–4, and apparent 'care' for Io who, being no huntress, may well fear the woods; the cynical *praeside tuta deo*). Jupiter shows little sign of concern for Io (contrast Apollo); and his boasting about his identity (595–6) is crude. He is most affronted when she simply runs for it (his shocked reaction, 597), and he shows not the slightest hesitation in trapping and ravishing her. Ovid's description is cold and clinical (599–600). We have Jupiter's measure. Io's reaction, however, is not revealed.

601–9: But how is Juno to find out? Ovid makes her suspicious of the clouds over Argos (her 'home' town) on such a sunny day (602–4). Further, she knows Jupiter has 'form' in this respect (605–6), and when she looks round for her husband, he is not at home (607). Adding two and two, she swoops down to investigate, scattering the clouds (607–9). She admits she may be wrong (*fallor*) – but also that she may be being wronged (*laedor*). We now have Juno's measure.

1.610–24: *An embarrassed Jupiter has turned Io into a cow and gives her to Juno as a present*

coniugis aduentum praesēnserat, inque nitentem^   610
Īnachidos uultūs mūtāuerat ille ^iuuencam
(bōs quoque fōrmōsa est). speciem Sāturnia uaccae,
quamquam inuīta, probat, nec nōn et cūius et unde
quōue sit armentō, uērī quasi nescia, quaerit.
Iuppiter ē terrā genitam mentītur, ut auctor   615
dēsinat inquīrī. petit hanc Sāturnia mūnus.
quid faciat? crūdēle suōs addīcere amōrēs,
nōn dare suspectum est; pudor est quī suādeat illinc,

---

610 *aduent-us ūs* 4m. arrival
praesentiō 4 *praesēnsī praesēnsum* sense in advance.
   Jupiter is the subject
niteō 2 dep. shine
611 *Īnachid-os*: Greek gen. s. of *Īnachis*, 'daughter of
   Inachus', i.e. Io
*iuuenc-a ae 1f. cow, heifer. Note consonantal *i*
612 *bōs bou-is* 3 m./f. bull, ox; cow
fōrmōs-us a um beautiful, shapely
speci-ēs ēī 5f. look, sight, appearance
*Sāturni-a ae 1f. daughter of Saturn, i.e. Juno.
   Sāturnius = Jupiter
*uacc-a ae 1f. cow
613 *probō* 1 approve of, prove
nec nōn and also (= 'nor . . . not')
cūius . . . unde . . . quōue: indirect questions after
   quaerit (614), all with *sit* as the main verb
614 *arment-um ī* 2n. herd
*nesci-us a um ignorant (of)
615 *genit-us a um* born. This is f., referring to the
   cow, and supply *esse*, acc. and inf. after *mentītur*.

To be 'born from the earth' meant that one's
   origin was unknown
mentior 4 dep. lie
ut: explains Jupiter's purpose in lying
auctor -is 3m. inventor (of the cow's origin, i.e.
   Jupiter)
616 *dēsinō* 3 stop, cease
inquīrō 3 examine, inquire into
mūnus: in apposition to *hanc* = the cow
617 *faciat*: 'deliberative' subj. (Jupiter is the subject),
   RL152. Ovid here signals that we are about to see
   Jupiter's thought-processes at work
addīcō 3 surrender. This is inf. after *crūdēle* (*est*).
   Since Jupiter is reflecting what to do, translate 'it
   would be cruel to . . .' Jupiter knows that if he lets
   Juno have the cow, that would be the end of his
   affair with Io
618 *nōn dare*: '[but] not to hand it over'
suspect-us a um suspicious
*illinc from there; from that/one point of
   view

610–24: Juno finds (a forewarned) Jupiter, plus cow (and a pretty one, too – 612). She knows her man (note *uērī quasi nescia*), and starts gently turning the screws with a range of 'innocent' questions about the cow's origin (613–14). Ovid does not need to depict Jupiter squirming under the cross-examination: 'Where did it come from?' 'Er, no idea, no idea at all', he whistles hopelessly (615), desperate to get Juno to stop (616). But Juno knows something is up and is taking no chances: 'Present it to me, then' (616). Jupiter is now on the back foot, and Ovid shows us his thought-processes. One wonders to whom precisely it would be *crūdēle* to have to surrender Io (617 – only to Jupiter, of course); and his shame at being caught – or losing out to his wife? – battles with desire for Io (618–19). A conflict between *pudor* and *amor* (hardly 'love' in this instance) is the sort of debate one might expect feckless humans to have; but Jupiter can be as feckless as any human (see Introduction, p. 7). But Jupiter realises he is trapped – why should he be so keen on *not* handing over an unimportant (*leue*) cow when he is trying to persuade Juno that he just happened to stumble across it (620–1)? So he gives up Io, imagining that this will prove

hinc dissuādet amor. uictus pudor esset amōre,
sed leue sī mūnus sociae generisque torīque   620
uacca negārētur, poterat nōn uacca uidērī.
paelice dōnātā, nōn prōtinus exuit omnem^
dīua ^metum, timuitque Iou<u>em</u>, et fuit ānxia fūrtī,
dōnec Arestoridae^ seruandam trādidit ^Argō.

1.625–38: *Argus guards an Io baffled by her new state*

centum lūminibus cīnctum caput Argus habēbat;   625
inde suīs uicibus capiēbant bīna quiētem,

619 *hinc*: from this/another point of view
dissuādeō 2 hold back, dissuade
esset . . . uictus: note the conditional plupf. subj.,
  'would have been . . .'
620 **leu-is e* light, trivial, capricious, inconstant.
  With *mūnus*, it is in apposition to *uacca* (621),
  RL17B, **W**3
soci-a ae 1f. partner of (+ gen.), i.e. Juno. *sociae* is
  dative after *negārētur*, 'should be denied to . . .'
generis: *genus*, not *gener*!
negārētur: note conditional subj., **RL**139, 173, **W**33
621 *poterat*: *possum* is often used in conditions in the
  ind., where we would expect the subj.: 'it would
  be possible to seem [to be] *nōn uacca*',
  RLS2(c)Notes(6)
622 **paelex paelic-is* 3f. mistress (Io)
dōnō 1 give as a gift, donate
exuō 3 *exui* cast off, lose. Note the tricolon of Juno's
  fears – *nōn exuit . . . timuit . . . anxia*
623 **diu-us a um* divine; (when used as a noun)
  god(dess)
ānxi-us a um worried, uneasy about (+ gen.)
fūrt-um ī 2n. theft (of the cow); deceitfulness
624 **dōnec* until
Arestoridae: Greek dat. s. of *Arestoridēs* = son of
  Arestor (an Argive hero of some sort), i.e. Argus;
  dative of agent with a gerundive, **RL**L(e)1(iv),
  W24

seruandam: f., referring to Io. Note the gerundive
  idiom 'hand over X *to be -ed*', **RL**161, **W**39
Arg-us ī 2m. Argus (the hundred-eyed guardian)

Learning vocabulary
aethēr -is 3m. upper air, heaven
dēprendō 3 *dēprēndī dēprēnsum* catch out, catch red-
  handed (often *dēprehendō*)
diu-us a um divine; as noun, god(dess)
dōnec until
illinc from there; from that/one point of view
Iūnō Iūnōn-is 3f. Juno (in Greek, Hera), wife of
  Jupiter
iuuenc-a ae 1f. cow, heifer
leu-is e light, trivial, capricious, inconstant
marit-us a um married; husband; *marīta* wife
miror 1 dep. wonder, be amazed at
nesci-us a um ignorant (of)
  nōsset=nōuisset
paelex paelic-is 3f. mistress
Sāturni-a ae 1f. daughter of Saturn, i.e. Juno;
  Sāturnius = Jupiter
uacc-a ae 1f. cow

625 **lūmen lūmin-is* 3n. eye, light
626 *inde*: i.e. 'of these [eyes]'
suīs uicibus: 'by turns', 'in their turn'
bīn-us a um two at a time (understand *lūmina* as
  subject; so too with *cētera*, 627)

his innocence and, when Juno has forgotten all about it, he can start again. But Juno
knows all about her husband and his tricks, and puts a guard on Io (622–4). This is the
comic battle of the sexes: exquisitely amusing, and beautifully observed – the sharp, suspicious Juno boxing into a corner a desperately evasive Jupiter who imagines he may
have got away with it. The mighty gods of Olympus have here become a very human
couple. Io's feelings still remain a mystery.

625–38: Hundred-eyed Argus is a formidable prison-guard, as Ovid makes clear:
unsleeping by day (625–30), he ties Io up at night (630–1) when his hundred eyes would

cētera seruābant atque in statiōne manēbant.
cōnstiterat quōcumque modō, spectābat ad Īō;
ante oculōs Īō, quamuīs auersus, habēbat.
lūce sinit pāscī; cum sōl tellūre sub altā est,   630
claudit et indignō circumdat uincula collō.
frondibus arboreīs et amārā pāscitur herbā;
prōque torō terrae^ nōn semper grāmen ^habentī
incubat īnfēlīx, limōsaque flūmina pōtat.
illa etiam supplex Argō cum brācchia uellet   635
tendere, nōn habuit quae brācchia tenderet Argō;
cōnātōque querī mūgītūs ēdidit ōre,
pertimuitque sonōs, propriāque exterrita uōce est.

627 *statiō statiōn-is* 3f. guard-duty
628 *quōcumque modō*: 'in whatever position [Argus
    cōnstiterat]'
Īō: Greek acc. of Io in 628 and 629
629 *āuers-us a um* turned away. This line makes for
    an amusing paradox!
630 *lūce* by daylight
sinō 3 allow, permit (understand 'Io' as object)
pāscor 3 dep. graze
631 *claudō* 3 close up, enclose
indign-us a um innocent, blameless, undeserving
circumdō 1 put X (acc.) round Y (dat.), surround
uincul-um ī 2n. halter, binding, chain
632 *frōns frond-is* 3f. leaf. Ovid now describes
    (632–4) what might in other circumstances be a
    locus amoenus for Io (see Introduction, p. 8) – but
    not in her present transformed state as a cow
arbore-us a um of/from trees
amār-us a um bitter
pāscor 3 dep. graze on (+ abl.)
633 *grāmen grāmin-is* 3n grass
634 *incubō* 1 lie down on (dat.)
īnfēlīx īnfēlic-is unhappy, unfortunate
limōs-us a um muddy

pōtō 1 drink
635 *supplex supplic-is* supplicating, entreating
636 *tendō* 3 *tetendī tēnsum* stretch out, draw,
    proceed, reach, aim (at)
quae brācchia: 'arms which she could', 'arms to'.
    Note *tenderet*, subj. in a relative clause of purpose,
    RL145(3); a repetition full of pathos
637 *cōnātō . . . ōre*: abl. abs., 'when her mouth tried
    . . .'
mūgīt-us ūs 4m. mooing (listen to the sound of the
    word!)
ēdō 3 *ēdidī* utter, give out
638 *pertimēscō* 3 *pertimuī* be afraid of
son-us ī 2m. sound
propri-us a um own
exterrit-us a um terrified

Learning vocabulary
arbore-us a um of/from trees
circumdō 1 put X (acc.) round Y (dat.), surround
īnfēlīx īnfēlic-is unhappy, unfortunate
lūmen lūmin-is 3n. eye, light
pertimēscō 3 *pertimuī* be afraid of
tendō 3 *tetendī tēnsum* stretch out, draw, proceed,
    reach, aim (at)

be less useful. And at last we turn to Io. What must it be like, Ovid thinks, to find your-
self unexpectedly turned into a cow? Ovid amusingly suggests the way Io must be thinking about it. First, there would be the strange food (note *amārae*, 632); then sleeping on
the ground (not always grassy either, 633); and only muddy water to drink (633). No
arms with which to plead with Argus (635–6), and no voice either – just moos, which
frighten even herself (637–8). Poor Io! Amusing it may be, but one's heart goes out to
her.

1.639–50: *Io finally manages to communicate with Inachus*

uēnit et ad rīpās, ubi ludere saepe solēbat,
Īnachidas rīpās, nouaque‸ ut cōnspexit in undā   640
‸cornua, pertimuit sēque exsternāta refūgit.
Nāides ignōrant, ignōrat et Īnachus ipse,
quae sit; at illa patrem sequitur, sequiturque sorōrēs
et patitur tangī sēque admīrantibus offert.
dēcerptās‸ senior porrēxerat Īnachus ‸herbās;   645
illa manūs lambit, patriīsque dat ōscula palmīs,
nec retinet lacrimās et, sī modo uerba sequantur,
ōret opem, nōmenque suum cāsūsque loquātur.
littera‸ prō uerbīs, ‸quam pēs in puluere dūxit,
corporis‸ indicium ‸mūtātī trīste perēgit.   650

639 *rīp-a ae* 1f. bank

640 *Īnachidas*: Greek acc. pl. of Ínachis, 'of (the river/god) Inachus'. Another pathos-filled repetition, as throughout 642–3

cōnspiciō 3 *cōnspexī cōnspectum* catch sight of, see, observe

641 *exsternāt-us a um* in consternation, panic

refugiō 3 *refūgī* recoil from

642 *Nāis Nāid-is* 3f. water nymph. These are Io's sisters; note the ABBA word-order (chiasmus) *Nāides ignōrant, ignōrat . . . Īnachus*, and in 643

ignōrō 1 be ignorant, not know

644 *admīror* 1 dep. be surprised, wonder at

offerō 3 put forward, offer

645 *decerpt-us a um* plucked, pulled (*dēcerpō*). A chiastic golden line

senior –is 3m./f. older, senior (= *senex*)

porrigō 3 *porrēxī porrēctum* stretch out, offer

646 *lambō* 3 lick

palm-a ae 1f. palm

647 *retineō* 2 *retinuī retentum* hold back, keep

sequantur . . . ōret . . . loquātur: 'vivid' pres. subj. in an unfulfilled condition

649 *littera*: subject of *perēgit* (650)

puluis puluer-is 3m. dust

dūcō = trace

650 *indici-um ī* 2n. evidence, sign

trīste: if the word Io wrote was her own name, it would be *trīste* indeed, since *iō* in Greek meant 'alas, woe'. Inachus picks up the refrain with *mē miserum* in 651 and 653

peragō 3 *perēgī* provide

Learning vocabulary

admīror 1 dep. be surprised, wonder at
cōnspiciō 3 *cōnspexī cōnspectum* catch sight of, see, observe
ignōrō 1 be ignorant, not know
Nāis Nāid-is 3f. water nymph
refugiō 3 *refūgī* recoil from
retineō 2 *retinuī retentum* hold back, keep
rīp-a ae 1f. bank

639–50: It gets worse. She finds herself by the banks of the Inachus, her home, and sees her reflection in the river! Horns! (*cornua*, emphatic first word of a new line.) Not a fashion statement. No wonder she runs a mile (639–41). But it is her inability to make herself known to her family that is most frustrating. They obviously do not recognise her (642–3); all she can do is follow them, nuzzle up to them; eat from Inachus' hands, lick them, kiss them, weep – all no use (643–7). Ovid looks into her thoughts and tells us what she would have said had she been able (647–8). What despair, until finally she cracks it – and writes with her hoof in the dust (649–50)!

1.651–67: *Inachus' lament for Io*

'mē miser<u>um</u>!' exclāmat pater Īnachus*, inque gementis^
cornibus et niueā *pendēns ceruīce ^iuuencae,
'mē miser<u>um</u>!' ingeminat; 'tūn<u>e</u> es quaesīta per omnēs^
nāta mihī ^terrās? tū nōn inuenta reperta
luctus erās leuior; reticēs, nec mūtua^ nostrīs   655
^dicta refers, altō^ tantum suspīria dūcis
^pectore, quodqu<u>e</u> ūnum potes, ad mea uerba remūgis!
at tib<u>ī</u> eg<u>o</u> ignārus thalamōs taedāsque parābam,
spēsque fuit generī mihi prīma, secunda nepōtum.
dē grege nunc tibi uir, nunc de grege natus habendūs.   660
nec fīnīre licet tantos^ mihi morte ^dolōrēs;
sed nocet esse deum, praeclūsaque iānua lētī
aeternum^ nostrōs lūctus extendit in ^aeuūm.'
tālia maerentem stellātus submouet Argus,

---

651 *exclāmō* 1 cry out
inque: controls *cornibus* and *niueā . . . ceruīce* (652)
gemō 3 groan, cry
652 *niue-us a um* snow-white
*pendeō 2 *pependī* hang on, be uncertain; depend on
653 *ingeminō 1 repeat, intensify
tūne . . . terrās: take in order *tūne es [ea] nāta quaesīta mihi* (dat. of agent, **RL**(e)1(iv), **W**24) *per . . . ?'*
654 *repertā*: abl. of comparison, 'than [you] having-been-found', 'than now that you have been found'
655 *luct-us ūs 4m. cause of grief, mourning, lamentation
reticeō 2 be silent
mūtu-us a um mutual, in return
nostrīs: i.e. words
656 **referō referre rettulī relātum* bring/carry/put back, tell, answer, record, pay
*tantum only

suspīri-um ī 2n. sigh
657 *quodque ūnum* 'and what only', 'and the only thing'
remūgiō 4 moo/low in reply
658 *thalam-us ī 2m. marriage (bed)
taed-a ae 1f. torch (accompanying marriage)
659 *nepōs nepōt-is 3m./f. grandchild
660 *grex greg-is* 3m. herd
tibi: dative of agent
661 *fīniō 4 end, finish
662 *nocet*: impersonal, 'it hurts', **RLF**2, **W**37
praeclūs-us a um closed, shut
lēt-um ī 2n. death
663 *aetern-us a um* eternal
extendō 3 extend, stretch
*aeu-um ī 2n. age
664 *maereō* 2 lament (referring to Inachus)
stellāt-us a um starred (because of his many eyes)
submoueō 2 move along, push away

651–67: A father finds his daughter transformed into a cow. He embraces her (651–2), but what does he say? *mē miserum*, rather than *tē miseram*, establishes the tenor of Inachus' speech: it is all about himself. Shock (653–4) and despair at his own situation – his grief at her loss is now even more acute (654–5) – come first; and communication with her is impossible, he observes, since all she can do is sigh and moo (655–7). Since the main purpose of daughters in the ancient world was to produce heirs, his thoughts now turn to the destruction of any prospects for him in that respect (658–60), and he ends by reflecting that, since he is a god, even death can never end his torment (661–3: *praeclūsaque . . . aeuum* is a finely expressed sentiment). He seems unable to offer any sympathy to her. One wonders if a Roman father would have felt about his own

ēreptamque^ patrī dīversa in pāscua ^nātam   665
abstrahit. ipse procul montis sublīme cacūmen
occupat, unde sedēns partēs speculātur in omnēs.

1.668–77: *Jupiter instructs a disguised Mercury to kill Argus*

nec superum rēctor mala tanta Phorōnidos ultrā
ferre potest, nātumque uocat, quem lūcida^ partū
^Plēias ēnixa est, lētōque det imperat Argum.   670
parua mora est alas pedibus uirgamque^ potentī*
^somniferam sūmpsisse *manū, tegumenque capillīs.
haec ubi disposuit, patriā^ Ioue nātus ab ^arce
dēsilit in terrās; illīc tegumenque remōuit,
et posuit pennās; tantummodo uirga retenta est: 675

665 *patrī*: dat. of loss or disadvantage, **RL**48.1
dīvers-us a um distant
pāscu-um ī 2n. pasture
666 *abstrahō* 3 drag away
somnifer *procul* at a distance
sublīm-is e high, lofty
cacūmen cacūmin-is 3n. peak, summit
667 *sedeō* 2 *sēdī sessum* sit
speculor 1 dep. watch, gaze
668 *superum* = *superōrum*
rēctor -is 3m. ruler, i.e. Jupiter
Phorōnidos: Greek gen. s. of *Phorōnis* 'woman con-
    nected with (i.e. sister of) Phoroneus' (Inachus'
    son, another Argive hero) – a dramatic way of
    referring to Io
ultrā beyond, further
669 *nātumque* = Mercury (Greek Hermes)
lūcid-us a um bright, shining
part-us ūs 4m. birth
670 *Plēias Plēiad-is* 3f. Pleias or Maia (one of the

stars known as the Pleiades, mother of
    Mercury)
ēnitor 3 dep. *ēnixus* produce, give birth to
lēt-um ī 2n. death
det: subj. of indir. command after *imperat*. Jupiter is
    ordering Mercury [*ut*] *lētō det* [*Argum*]
671 *parua mora est*: controls [*Mercuriō*] *sūmpsisse*
    'for Mercury to . . .', 'while Mercury . . .'
**āl-a ae* 1f. wing
**uirg-a ae* 1f. rod, wand
**potēns potent-is* powerful
672 *somnifer -a -um* sleep-inducing
sūmpsisse: perfect to show how quickly Mercury
    acted
tegumen tegumin-is 3n. covering, hat
673 *dispōnō* 3 *disposuī dispositum* arrange
patriā . . . arce: i.e. Olympus
674 *dēsiliō* 4 leap down
**illīc* there
675 *tantummodo* only (so much as)

daughter in such terms. Anyway, Argus moves him along and takes Io elsewhere: does
ēreptam patrī reflect her feelings?

668–77: Jupiter cannot bear to see Io treated like this (668–9) – pity? Or because he still
has primarily his own interests at heart? – and summons his son Mercury, his general fac-
totum on all sorts of adventures, to kill Argus. Mercury dresses – epics always have dress-
ing-scenes (cf. *Odyssey* 5.43–8) – and takes with him his famous sleep-inducing wand
(672). Arriving on earth, he immediately (and unepically) undresses, ridding himself of
everything except the wand, and appears as an innocent herdsman (676), putting his
wand to novel use, stealing some goats to play the part convincingly and tootling away on

hāc agit, ut pāstor, per dēuia rūra capellās∧
dum uenit ∧abductās, et strūctīs cantat auēnīs.

1.678–88: *Argus is not sent to sleep by Mercury's pan-pipes*

uōce nouā captus, custōs Iūnōnius 'at tū,
quisquis es, hōc∧ poterās mēcum cōnsīdere ∧saxō'
Argus ait; 'neque enim pecorī fēcundior ūllō∧   680
herba ∧locō est, aptamque∧ uidēs pāstōribus ∧umbram.'
sēdit Atlantiadēs, et euntem∧ multa loquendō
dētinuit sermōne ∧diem, iūnctīsque∧ canendō
uincere ∧harundinibus seruantia lūmina temptat.
ille tamen pugnat mollēs ēuincere somnōs   685
et, quamuīs sopor est oculōrum parte receptus,

---

676 *hāc*: abl. of means
dēui-us a um remote
rūs rūr-is 3n. country, countryside
capell-a ae 1f. goat
677 *dum uenit*: take this clause closely with *abductās*
abdūcō 3 *abdūcere abductum* steal
struō 3 *strūxī strūctum* fit together, construct
cantō 1 play on (+ abl.)
auēn-a ae 1f. oat-stalk; pipe

Learning vocabulary
aeu-um ī 2n. age
āl-a ae 1f. wing
finiō 4 end, finish
illīc there
ingeminō 1 repeat, intensify
luct-us ūs 4m. cause of grief, mourning, lamentation
nepōs nepōt-is 3m/f. grandchild
pendeō 2 *pependī* hang on, be uncertain; depend on
potēns potent-is powerful
procul at a distance
referō referre rettulī relātum bring/carry/put back, tell, answer, record, pay
sedeō 2 *sēdī sessum* sit

tantum only
thalam-us ī 2m. marriage (bed)
uirg-a ae 1f. rod, wand

678 *uōce*: = music
Iūnōni-us a um of Juno
679 *poterās*: a polite invitation, = 'why don't you?' (a sort of suppressed condition: 'if you wanted to, you could ', cf. **RLS**2(c)Notes(6)
cōnsīdō 3 *cōnsēdī cōnsessum* sit, settle down
680 *pecus pecor-is* 3n. flock, herd (which Mercury has stolen 677 and brought with him)
fecund-us a um lush
ūllō . . . locō: abl. of comparison after *fēcundior*
681 *apt-us a um* fitted for, suitable for (+ dat.)
682 *Atlantiadēs*: Greek nom., grandson of Atlas, i.e. Mercury
loquendō: gerund (**RL**175, **RLN**, **W**39) with *multa* (**RL**14.7, **W**4Footnotes 5) as object
683 *dētineō* 2 *dētinuī dētentum* occupy, engage
canō 3 play; sing
684 *harundō harundin-is* 3f. reed, pipe
685 *ēuincō* 3 overcome
686 *sopor -is* 3m. sleep

---

his pipes (677). There was a long tradition of pastoral, or bucolic, poetry in Greek and Latin literature. Ovid shows that he can play that game too.

678–712: Argus, charmed by the music, is happy to let Mercury chat and play away, but none of this lulls him to sleep (678–87). One wonders why Mercury does not use his wand, but Ovid has other ideas – a story within a story, a favourite Ovidian device. So Ovid puts the story of Syrinx in Mercury's mouth. Note the number of repeated ideas and words in 682–8 and the *loquendō . . . canendō* rhyme. Is Ovid trying to create a sense of monotony, as Mercury attempts to lull Argus to sleep? Anyway, this finally does the

parte tamen uigilat. quaerit quoque (namque reperta
fistula nūper erat), quā sit ratiōne reperta.

The story of Syrinx ('Pan-pipe')

Then the god said 'In the cool mountains of Arcadia
[690] where the Arcadian wood-nymphs lived,
there was a famously beautiful nymph called Syrinx.
Satyrs had pursued her more than once – so had every other god
that lived in those shady woods and fertile country – but she had
given them all the slip. It was Diana to whom she dedicated
[695] both her devotion and her virginity. She dressed
deceptively like Diana and could be taken for her, except that
her bow was made of horn, and Diana's of gold.
Even so, she passed for her. As she returned
from the Lyrcaean hill, Pan, his head garlanded with pine-needles, saw her,
[700] and began to say' – but Mercury never finished to describe how,
spurning his pleas, she raced off through the trackless paths
till she reached the peaceful stream of sandy
Ladon; how there, since the stream barred her escape, she
begged her watery sisters to transform her, so that
[705] when Pan clutched what he thought was Syrinx,
he found he was holding not her but marsh reeds;
how the frustrated sighs Pan uttered stirred the wind in these reeds,
producing a thin, plaintive sound;
how, entranced by the sweet sound of this new music,
[710] Pan said 'I shall always be able to talk with you like this!';
and how he fixed the reeds of different lengths together
with wax, and gave them the name of the girl.

687 *uigilō* 1 stay awake

688 *fistul-a ae* 1f. pipe

quā . . . ratiōne how, by what means

trick (688–712), though Ovid has to finish the story himself since Argus drops off half-way through it (713) – an amusing device, breaking the dramatic illusion. Note that this story-within-a-story is, again, of divine *amor* with all the usual features: beautiful girl, dedicated to Diana, roaming the woods, seen by a deity, runs for it, begs for transformation and (like Daphne) is honoured by the smitten deity even in her transformed state. It is also aetiological, explaining how pastoral (=bucolic) poetry came into existence, when Pan, god of the countryside (his name means 'guardian of flocks'), discovered the pan-pipes (Greek *surinx*). From then on herdsmen (which Mercury was pretending to be) used them to accompany their songs, passing the lonely hours as their flocks grazed remote pastures and hills. By making Mercury sing pastoral poetry to get Argus to sleep, one wonders, idly, whether Ovid was making a little joke about the tedium of the genre.

1.713–23: *Mercury kills Argus, whose eyes Juno transplants into the peacock's tail*

tālia dictūrus, uīdit Cyllēnius omnēs∧
succubuisse ∧oculōs, adopertaque lūmina somnō.
supprimit extemplō uōcem, firmatque sopōrem,   715
languida∧ permulcēns medicātā ∧lūmina uirgā.
nec mora, falcātō∧ nūtantem uulnerat ∧ēnse,
quā collō est cōnfine caput, saxōque cruentum
dēicit, et maculat praeruptam sanguine rūpem.
Arge, iacēs, quodque in tot lūmina lūmen habēbās,   720
exstinctum est, centumque oculōs nox occupat ūna.
excipit hōs uolucrīsque suae Sāturnia pennīs
collocat, et gemmīs caudam stellantibus implet.

---

713 *dictūrus*: Argus had fallen completely asleep
  before Mercury could finish
Cyllēni-us ī 2m. Mercury (who was born on
  Mt. Cyllene in Arcadia)
714 *succumbō* 3 *succubuī* fall asleep
adopert-us a um covered
715 *supprimō* 3 suppress, check
extemplō immediately, suddenly
*firmō 1 reinforce, strengthen
sopor -is 3m. sleep
716 *languid-us a um* drowsy (a nearly golden
  line)
permulceō 2 soothe
medicāt-us a um magic, charmed
717 *falcāt-us a um* hooked
nūtō 1 nod (with sleep)
uulnerō 1 wound
ēns-is is 3m. sword
718 *cōnfin-is e* joined to
saxōque: 'true' abl., **RL**100A, Survey(a)
cruent-us a um bloody (acc., referring to
  Argus)
719 *dēiciō* 3/4 *dēiēcī dēiectum* throw X (acc.) down
  from Y (abl.)

maculō 1 smear, stain
praerupt-us a um steep, sheer
*sanguis sanguin-is 3m. blood
rūp-ēs is 3f. rock, cliff
720 *iacēs*: note the shift to the second person
  ('apostrophe')
quodque . . . lūmen: 'whatever light', object of
  habēbās, subject of *exstinctum est*
in tot lūmina: 'for/in so many eyes'. Ovid plays on
  lūmen 'light/eye'
721 *exstinct-us a um* extinguished, put out
722 *excipiō* 3/4 pick out, remove (Juno (*Sāturnia*) is
  the subject)
hōs: i.e. the eyes
uolucr-is is 3f. bird (here gen. s.), i.e. the peacock
  (brought to the Mediterranean from India and
  Sri Lanka)
723 *collocō* 1 place
*gemm-a ae 1f. gem
*caud-a ae 1f. tail
stellāns stellant-is starry
*impleō 2 *implēuī implētum* fill

713–23: Now that Argus is asleep, Mercury finally brings his wand into play, ensuring he stays asleep (715–16). This seems rather unnecessary, since without delay Mercury beheads Argus (but where did he get the sword from?) and throws the head down from the rock where Argus had earlier been on guard (717–19, cf. 666–7). A sympathetic 'apostrophe' contrasts the single night (of death) with the hundred eyes that Argus was once able to use, eyes now at any rate preserved for ever in the tail of Juno's sacred bird, the peacock (720–3) – more aetiology.

1.724–33: *The enraged Juno maddens Io, who begs Jupiter for release*

prōtinus exārsit, nec tempora distulit īrae,
horriferamque^ oculīs animōque obiēcit ^Erīnyn   725
paelicis Argolicae, stimulōsque in pectore caecōs
condidit, et profugam per tōtum exercuit orbem.
ultimus immēnsō^ restābās, Nīle, ^labōrī;
quem simulac tetigit, positīsque^ in margine rīpae
prōcubuit ^genibus, resupīnōque ardua collō,   730
quōs potuit sōlōs, tollēns ad sīdera uultūs,
et gemitū et lacrimīs et luctisonō mūgītū
cum Ioue uīsa querī, finemque ōrāre malōrum.

724 *exardēscō* 3 *exarsī* flare up
differō differre distulī dīlātum put off, delay
725 *horrifer -a -um* horrific, shuddersome
obiciō 3 *obiēcī* place X (acc.) before Y (dat.)
Erīnyn: Greek acc. s. of *Erīnys*, tormenting fury,
  demon
726 *paelex*: = Io, here gen. with *oculīs animōque*
Argolic-us a um from Argos
stimul-us ī 2m. goad (lit., cattle-prod)
caec-us a um blind
727 **condō* 3 *condidī conditum* hide; build, found;
  compose
profug-a ae 1m./f. exile, fugitive. Here it is in apposition to (understood) 'her' (Io), **RL**17B, **W**3
exerceō 2 *exercuī* drive on, chase
728 **ultim-us a um* final, last. Here = 'final destination', in apposition to the 'you' of the Nile
*immēns-us a um immeasurable
restō 1 be left as X (nom.) for Y (dat.). Note the
  'apostrophe'
Nīl-us ī 2m. Nile

729 *quem*: i.e. the Nile. It is a connecting relative,
  RL107
simulac as soon as. This controls only *tetigit* (of
  which Io is the subject)
*margō margin-is 3m. edge, border
730 *prōcumbō* 3 lie down
*genū gen-ūs 4n. knee
resupīn-us a um bent back
*ardu-us a um looking upwards, steep, difficult,
  high
731 *quōs potuit sōlōs*: refers to *uultūs*, 'which alone
  she could [raise]', 'which was all she could
  [raise]'; humans raised hands to the gods in
  prayer and supplication
732 **gemit-us ūs* 4m. groan
luctison-us a um grief-sounding, heart-rending (a
  one-off word in extant Latin)
mūgīt-us ūs 4m. moo. Note the rare (and here very
  effective) spondaic fifth foot
733 *uīsa*: supply *est*
*fin-is is 3f. end

724–33: The death of Argus enrages Juno, and she takes it out not on Jupiter but on the hapless Io. She terrifies Io with visions of the Furies (725) and plants goads in her (*stimulus* is literally a cattle-prod, an apt choice of word, 726), as a result of which she careers madly all over the world (727). There can be few passages in Ovid more sweetly touching than Io's appeal for mercy on the banks of the Nile: as a prayerful suppliant (729–30), she lifts her face to the heavens (all she could lift, as Ovid says – she has no arms to use, cf. 636–7) – and seems to take issue with Jupiter and beg for release (733); 'seems', of course, because she cannot speak. All she can offer is the (wonderfully onomatopoeic and pathos-filled) tricolon of groans and tears and *luctisonō mūgītū* (732) – made all the more heart-rending by the one-off *luctisonus*.

1.734–46: *Jupiter makes his peace with Juno, and Io becomes a woman again*

coniugis^ ille ^suae complexus colla lacertīs,
fīniat ut poenās tandem rogat, 'in' que 'futūrum   735
pōne metūs' inquit; 'numquam tibi causa dolōris
haec erit,' et Stygiās^ iubet hōc audīre ^palūdēs.
ut lēnīta dea est, uultūs^ capit illa ^priōrēs,
fitque quod ante fuit; fugiunt ē corpore saetae,
cornua dēcrēscunt, fit lūminis artior orbis,   740
contrahitur rictus, redeunt umerīque manūsque,
ungulaque in quīnōs^ dīlāpsa absūmitur ^unguēs.
dē boue nīl superest, fōrmae nisi candor in illā.
officiōque pedum^ nymphē contenta ^duōrum,
ērigitur metuitque loquī, nē mōre iuuencae   745
mūgiat, et timidē uerba intermissa retemptat.

734 *ille*: i.e. Jupiter
complex-us a um embracing
735 *ut*: take with *fīniat* after *rogat*, '[Jupiter] *rogat*
   that she *tandem fīniat . . .* '
futūr-um ī 2n. the future
737 *haec*: i.e. Io
*Stygi-us a um Stygian, underworld, hellish. Jupiter
   is telling the (god of the) river Styx to hear
   because gods swore oaths in the name of the river
   (Homer *Iliad* 15.37–8). This was a reward which
   Zeus/Jupiter gave Styx for supporting him in a
   war against the Titans
hōc: object of *audīre*
palūs palūd-is 3f. marsh, swamp
738 *lēnīt-us a um* soothed, placated
dea: i.e. Juno
illa: i.e. Io
739 *fit . . . fuit*: a neat word-play and contrast
saet-a ae 1f. animal hair, coat
740 *dēcrēscō* 3 shrink
art-us a um narrow
741 *contrahō* 3 close, become smaller
rict-us ūs 4m. gaping mouth
umer-us ī 2m. shoulder
742 *ungul-a ae* 1f. hoof
quīn-us a um five
dīlābor 3 dep. *dīlāpsus* disperse, dissolve
absūmō 3 (passive) vanish, fade
ungu-is is 3m. nail
743 *bōs bou-is* 3m./f. ox, cow
*nīl nothing

**supersum superesse superfuī* remain,
   be left over, survive
candor is 3m. brightness (take with *fōrmae*; cf. 610, 612)
744 *offici-um ī* 2n. use, function
nymphē: Greek nom., nymph
content-us a um happy with (+ abl.)
745 *ērigor* stand up
*metuō 3 *metuī metūtum* fear
mōre: abl. of *mōs*, 'in the manner of, like'
746 *mūgiō* 4 moo
timidē fearfully, hesitantly
intermiss-us a um interrupted
retemptō 1 try again

Learning vocabulary
ardu-us a um looking upwards, steep, difficult, high
caud-a ae 1f. tail
condō 3 *condidī conditum* hide; build, found; compose
fīn-is is 3f. end
firmō 1 reinforce, strengthen
gemit-us ūs 4m. groan
gemm-a ae 1f. gem
genu gen-ūs 4n. knee
immēns-us a um immeasurable
impleō 2 *implēuī implētum* fill
margō margin-is 3m. edge, border
metuō 3 *metuī metūtum* fear
nīl nothing
sanguis sanguin-is 3m. blood
Stygi-us a um Stygian, underworld, hellish
supersum superesse superfuī remain, be left over, survive
ultim-us a um final, last

734–46: This time, even Jupiter agrees enough is enough. He embraces his wife (734), promises never to stray again – at least with Io – and confirms his promise with an oath (735–7). Peace between the two is (temporarily) restored, and Ovid must now turn Io

Learning vocabulary for Passage 3, Io and Syrinx

admīror 1 dep. be surprised, wonder at

aethēr -is 3m. upper air, heaven

aeu-um ī 2n. age

āl-a ae 1f. wing

antr-um ī 2n. cave

arbore-us a um of/from trees

ardu-us a um looking upwards, steep, difficult, high

caud-a ae 1f. tail

circumdō 1 surround, put X (acc.) round Y (dat.)

condō 3 *condidī conditum* hide; build, found; compose

cōnspiciō 3 *cōnspexī cōnspectum* catch sight of, see, observe

dēprendō 3 *dēprēndī dēprēnsum* catch out, catch red-handed (often *dēprehendō*)

dīu-us a um divine; as noun, god(dess)

dōnec until

fīniō 4 end, finish

fin-is is 3f. end

firmō 1 reinforce, strengthen

fulmen fulmin-is 3n. thunderbolt

gemit-us ūs 4m. groan

gemm-a ae 1f. gem

genu gen-ūs 4n. knee

ignōrō 1 be ignorant, not know

illīc there

illinc from there; from that/one point of view

immēns-us a um immeasurable

impleō 2 *implēuī implētum* fill

īnfēlīx īnfēlīc-is unhappy, unfortunate

ingeminō 1 repeat, intensify

Iūnō Iūnōn-is 3f. Juno (Greek Hera), wife of Jupiter

iuuenc-a ae 1f. cow, heifer

lāt-us a um wide, broad

leu-is e light, trivial, capricious, inconstant

luct-us ūs 4m. cause of grief, mourning, lamentation

lūmen lūmin-is 3n. eye, light

margō margin-is 3m. edge, border

marīt-us a um married; husband; *marīta* wife

metuō 3 *metuī metūtum* fear

miror 1 dep. wonder, be amazed at

Nāis Nāid-is 3f. water nymph

nepōs nepōt-is 3m./f. grandchild

nesci-us a um ignorant (of)

nīl nothing

nōsset=nōuisset

paelex paelic-is 3f. mistress

patri-us a um paternal, of one's father

pendeō 2 *pependī* hang on, be uncertain; depend on

pertimēscō 3 *pertimuī* be afraid of

potēns potent-is powerful

procul at a distance

referō referre rettulī relātum bring/carry/put back, tell, answer, record, pay

refugiō 3 *refūgī* recoil from

retineō 2 *retinuī retentum* hold back, keep

rīp-a ae 1f. bank

sanguis sanguin-is 3m. blood

Sāturni-a ae 1f. daughter of Saturn, i.e. Juno; *Sāturnius* = Jupiter

sedeō 2 *sēdī sessum* sit

Stygi-us a um Stygian, (of the) underworld, hellish

supersum superesse superfuī remain, be left over, survive

tantum only

tendō 3 *tetendī tēnsum* stretch out, draw, proceed, reach, aim (at)

thalam-us ī 2m. marriage (bed)

tor-us ī 2m. bed, marriage-bed

uacc-a ae 1f. cow

uirg-a ae 1f. rod, wand

ultim-us a um final, last

back into a woman (animal rarely changes into human in Ovid). He begins with the whole body (the coat falls off, 739), then works down from the head (horns, eyes, mouth), to shoulders and legs (739–41), focussing on the way the hooves split into fingers (742). Io is as beautiful now as she was before (743, cf. 612). Delighted to be back on two feet, she lifts herself up onto them (she has been prone, in suppliant position) – but dare she utter a noise? She can *see* she has been physically changed (744, cf. 640–1), but has no idea what noise she will make until she actually tries it (745, cf. 637–8). How awful to be restored to beauteous womanhood, yet able only to moo! Timidly, she gives it a go . . . (746). Pathos and comedy sit easily side by side in this little masterpiece.

Study section

1. Write out and scan ll.724–33.
2. Compare and contrast the stories of Daphne and Io in terms of character and the structure and complexity of the story. In what respects, for example, are Apollo and Jupiter similar and different? What sort of a woman is Juno, and how does her entry into the story affect it? Are Daphne and Io merely foils for the depiction of divine passions?
3. 'From Io's point of view Argus' boredom is a grim reminder that male violence against women is an everyday occurrence, not worth staying awake for' (Brown, 2005, 30–1). Justify, or attack, this claim.
4. Give a feminist and anti-feminist perspective on this story.
5. Take any five lines, consecutive or not, and explain why they give you pleasure.

4 Phaethon, *Metamorphōsēs* 2.150–216, 227–38, 260–71, 301–39

Please note that elisions are no longer marked, and linking devices will be more sparingly used, largely to mark agreements between words in different lines.

Background

Io bears a son Epaphus, who has a friend Phaethon ('Shining'). When Phaethon boasts that he is the son of Sol, the sun-god, Epaphus challenges the claim; but Phaethon's mother Clymene swears it is true, and sends Phaethon to Sol to confirm it. Sol does so, promising Phaethon to grant him any wish. When Phaethon asks to take charge of the chariot in which he rides across the sky every day, Sol is distraught and tries to persuade him of the appalling difficulty and danger of what he wants to do. But a promise is a promise: Phaethon is adamant. So Sol tries to advise the young man:

'If you can at least comply with your father's advice in this respect,
be sparing with the whip, but work the reins hard.
The horses need no encouragement to gallop ahead; it's restraint they need . . .
Keep to the route marked out by the wheel-tracks.
So that earth and sky do not become over-heated,
Don't drive the chariot too low or too high:
Too high, and heaven will burn,
Too low, and earth will. Your safest route is in the middle . . .'

2.150–60: *Phaethon boards the chariot, the gates open and the horses race off*

occupat ille leuem iuuenali corpore currum,   *ICTUS*   150
statque super, manibusque leues contingere habenas
gaudet, et inuito grates agit inde parenti.

150 *iuuenāl-is e* youthful   *contingō* 3 seize
*curr-us ūs 4m. chariot   **habēn-a ae* 1f. rein
151 **super* up, i.e. high, tall; *super* + acc., above

With Deucalion, the world was transformed by flood. Here it will be transformed by fire.
150–60: *leuem* and *iuuenālī*, significantly juxtaposed (150), prepare us for two major

intereā uolucrēs Pyroïs et Eōus et Aethōn,
Sōlis equī, quārtusque Phlegōn hinnītibus^ aurās
^flammiferīs implent, pedibusque repāgula pulsant.   155
quae postquam Tēthys, fātōrum ignāra nepōtis,
reppulit, et facta est immēnsī cōpia caelī,
corripuēre uiam, pedibusque per āera mōtīs,
obstantēs scindunt nebulās, pennīsque leuātī
praetereunt ortōs īsdem dē partibus Eurōs.   160

2.161–70: *The horses, sensing a light chariot, veer off-course, leaving Phaethon helpless*

sed leue pondus erat, nec quod cognōscere possent
Sōlis equī, solitāque iugum grauitāte carēbat.

153 *uolucer uolucr-is e* swift
Pyroïs, Eōus, Aethōn . . . Phlegōn: Greek noms., horses
 of the sun ('Fiery', 'Dawn', 'Blazing', 'Burning')
154 *hinnīt-us ī* 4m. whinnying
155 *flammifer -a um* flaming
repāgul-a ōrum 2n. door-bars
pulsō 1 beat on
156 *Tēthys*: Greek nom.; Tethys was grandmother of
 Phaethon and goddess of the sea, from which Sol
 arose (as if 'released'?) every day
157 *repellō* 3 *reppulī* thrust back
cōpi-a ae 1f. use of, access to
158 *corripiō* 3/4 *corripuī* seize, charge at
159 *obstō* 1 be in the way

scindō 3 cut through
nebul-a ae 1f. cloud
leuō 1 raise up, lift up
160 *Eur-us ī* 2m. east wind
161 **pondus ponder-is* 3n. weight
nec quod 'and not [a weight of the sort] that' + subj.
 The subj. here is 'generic', or 'characteristic', that
 is, the relative clause defines the sort of thing that
 would usually happen; in this case, the weight was
 not the sort of thing Sol's horses normally
 expected, **RL**140, **W**38
162 *solit-us a um* usual, customary
iug-um ī 2n. yoke
*careō 2 lack, be lacking, be free of, lose (+ abl.)

themes of the Phaethon story: Sol's chariot is light and will therefore need firm control, but Phaethon is a young man and will lack both the physical weight/strength to control it and the experience too. This combination of incapacities will prove fatal. At the moment, however, he is full of confidence, standing tall in the chariot (151), as charioteers did, and thrilling in anticipation at the touch of the reins (151–2: if he were in a modern sports-car he would be playing with the steering wheel and gears and going 'vrrm vrrm'). There is pathos in the crunch of *inuītō grātēs*: Phaethon will soon be regretting his decision (182–4), as will Sol (329–32). What horse-power this chariot carries, too – horses with fiery names matched by their fiery whinnying, their desire to be off making them kick at the door-bars (153–5: note the urgent dactyls of 153 and the *ps* alliteration of *pedibusque repāgula pulsant*). Granny Tethys pulls back the bolts, and off they go: goddess of the sea she may be, but even she does not know the disaster that awaits (156: note the heavy, fateful spondees) in the *immēnsī cōpia caelī* (157) – where the chariot is to run riot, with devastating consequences. They're off! Hooves and wings working, the horses soon cut through the low clouds clinging to the horizon into the clear sky (158–60: note the dashing dactyls of 158).

161–70: Now the trouble starts. Note *leue* (161) – so *leue* indeed that by 166 the chariot may as well be empty. This important moment is marked by a simile: like a ship without ballast

utque labant curuae^ iūstō sine pondere ^nāuēs,
perque mare ^īnstabilēs nimiā leuitāte feruntur,
sīc, onere adsuētō uacuus, dat in āera saltūs,   165
succutiturque altē, similisque est currus inānī.
quod simulac sēnsēre, ruunt trītumque^ relinquunt
quadriiugī ^spatium, nec quō prius ōrdine currunt.
ipse pauet, nec quā commissās flectat habēnās
nec scit quā sit iter, nec, sī sciat, imperet illīs.   170

2.171–7: *Cold stars heat up, slow stars flee*

tum primum radiis gelidī caluēre Triōnēs,
et uetitō frūstrā temptārunt aequore tingī.

163 *utque*: 'and as' (introducing a simile, picked up
  by . . .) *sīc* (165) 'so . . .'
labō 1 roll, lurch
*curu-us a um curved
pondere: i.e. its ballast (or cargo)
164 *instabil-is e* unsteady, unstable
leuitās leuitāt-is 3f. lightness
165 *adsuēt-us a um* usual, accustomed
uacuus: refers to Phaethon's chariot (*currus*, 166)
salt-us ūs 4m. jump, leap
166 *succutiō* 3/4 drive from below
altē on high, up in the air
inān-is e empty
167 *quod*: tr. 'this', object of *sēnsēre*, whose subject is
  quadriiugī, 168
simulac as soon as
*ruō 3 run wild
trit-us a um trodden, worn (by the horses making
  previous runs – through the air!)
168 *quadriiug-ī ōrum* horses yoked four-abreast
quō prius ōrdine 'in what order [they ran] before'
169 *committō* 3 *commīsī commissus* entrust
flectō 3 handle
170 *sciat . . . imperet*: note subj., indicating a conditional: 'even if he had known, he would not . . .'

Learning vocabulary
careō 2 lack, be lacking, be free of, lose (+ abl.)
curr-us ūs 4m. chariot
curu-us a um curved
habēn-a ae 1f. rein
pondus ponder-is 3n. weight
ruō 3 run wild
super up, i.e. high, tall; *super* + acc., above

171 *radi-us ī* 2m. ray (of the sun)
caleō 2 grow warm
Triōnēs: nom. pl., 'the Oxen', which the ancients
  imagined to be hard at work in this constellation,
  also known as the Great and Little Bear. Ancients
  turned groups of stars into 'constellations' (*cum* +
  stella) and gave them names according to the
  shapes they could make out of them by 'joining
  the dots' in the sky. The *Triōnēs* were located in
  the far northerly (and therefore freezing) regions
172 **aequor -is* 3m. sea
tingō 3 wet, bathe in. Ovid plays with astronomy
  here, imagining that the Oxen/Bears, which are
  never seen to sink below the horizon (and therefore get wet) by people living in the north, desperately wish to do so now

being tossed about in the waves (note *leuitāte* 164), so the chariot without its usual cargo (165: note the metre) leaps about, jumping up and down. The horses have already realised something is not quite right (161–2); but now, feeling the chariot bucking about, they career away (167–8). The 'camera' turns to the terrified Phaethon. Vividly, Ovid depicts the fearful (*pauet*, 169) thoughts flashing through his mind (169–70). He had paid no attention, of course, to anything Sol had told him, such was his excitement at the prospect of showing off in the driving seat of his new toy. Never say Ovid did not understand a young man's mind.

171–7: So what *would* happen if the sun strayed wildly off its usual route? We are in Ovid's favourite 'what if?' territory again, and he imagines the firmament responding like

quaeque polō posita est glaciālī proxima Serpēns –
frīgore pigra prius nec formīdābilis ūllī –
incaluit, sūmpsitque nouās feruōribus īrās.   175
tē quoque turbātum memorant fūgisse, Boōte,
quamuīs tardus erās et tē tua plaustra tenēbant.

2.178–92: *Phaethon is terrified, out of control like a rudderless ship*

ut uērō summō dēspexit ab aethere terrās∧
īnfēlīx Phaethōn penitus penitusque ∧iacentēs,
palluit, et subitō genua intremuēre timōre,   180
suntque oculīs tenebrae per tantum lūmen obortae.
et iam māllet equōs numquam tetigisse paternōs,
iam cognōsse genus piget et ualuisse rogandō;
iam Meropis dīcī cupiēns, ita fertur ut acta∧
praecipitī ∧pīnus Boreā, cūī uicta∧ remīsit   185

---

173 *quaeque . . . Serpēns*: 'and what Serpent', i.e.
'and that Serpent which . . .'; the Serpent (also
known as *Dracō*) is a northern constellation
which coils between the Oxen/Bears
pol-us ī 2m. pole
glaciāl-is e icy, freezing
174 *frīgus frigor-is* 3n. cold
piger pigr-a um lazy, sluggish
formīdābil-is e frightening
175 *incaleō* 2 grow warm
feruor -is 3m. high temperature. Snakes become
aroused when warm
176 *turbō* 1 disturb
memorō 1 say, tell
Boōte: Greek voc. of the constellation Bootes, 'Ox-
driver' (hence his slowness); he 'drove' the
Triōnēs
177 *plaustr-um ī* 2n. wagon (which the *Triōnēs*
pulled)
178 *dēspiciō* 3/4 *dēspexī* look down on
179 *penitus* far below
180 *palleō* 2 grow pale

intremō 3 *intremuī* tremble
181 *tenebr-a ae* 1f. shadow, darkness, i.e. dizziness or
a fainting fit brought on by the height
per: almost 'in spite of'
182 *māllet*: note conditional subj.
183 *genus*: 'birth', i.e. who his father was (the Sun),
which earlier in the story he had foolishly
demanded to know (1.757 ff.)
piget (impersonal) it is a matter of regret, **RLF2**,
W37
rogandō: i.e. in asking to drive the chariot
184 *Merops Merop-is* 3m. Merops, the husband of
Phaethon's mother
dīcī: sc. 'to be called/said to be [the son] of', gen. of
origin/source, **RL6.5**
ita . . . ut: *ita*, 'so', prepares us for *ut* 'like, as',
introducing a simile
185 **praeceps praecipit-is* headlong
pīn-us ūs 4f. pine (tree), i.e. ship
Boreā: abl. s. of Greek Boreas, the north wind
cūī: '[the wind] to which/to whose control'
*remittō 3 *remīsī* let go of, hand over

---

a living being: cold stars trying to cool down (171–2); the Serpent heating up (173–5);
and Bootes lumbering away (176–7). Note the lightly ironical *memorant* (176) – Ovid
teasing again, as if this were a real historical event of which an oral record survives.

178–92: Back to Phaethon. He is now at a giddy height, and faster and further the world
is receding (178–9: note how far *terrās* is away from *iacentēs* – a good verbal, and on the
page visual, joke). His terror is evinced by his physical reactions (180–1); and we see into
his mind as he repents of his foolish actions (182–4) in words that reconstruct the story

^frēna suus rēctor, quam dīs uōtīsque relīquit.
quid faciat? multum caelī post terga relictum,
ante oculōs plūs est: animō mētītur utrumque,
et modo, quōs illī fātum contingere nōn est
prōspicit occāsūs, interdum respicit ortūs;
quidque agat ignārus, stupet et nec frēna remittit
nec retinēre ualet, nec nōmina nōuit equōrum.

190

2.193–209: *Phaethon spots Scorpio, drops the reins in fear and the horses bolt*

sparsa^ quoque in uariō passim ^mīrācula caelō
uastārumque uidet trepidus simulācra ferārum.

186 **frēnum ī* 2n. rein, control. Ovid here uses a
   metaphor from charioteering to describe the loss
   of control on board ship
rēctor -is 3m. captain, helmsman
quam: i.e. the *pīnus*
187 *faciat*: note deliberative subj., **RL**152
multum caelī: take closely together
188 *plūs*: i.e. sky
mētior 4 dep. measure
189 *modo . . . interdum* 'now . . . sometimes'
quōs . . . occāsūs: take in order *prōspicit occāsūs quōs illī
contingō* 3 reach
190 *prōspiciō* 3/4 look forward towards

occās-us ūs 4m. setting (of the sun) i.e. west
respiciō 3/4 look back at
ort-us ūs 4m. rising (of the sun), i.e. east
191 *quidque agat*: indirect question after *ignārus*
stupeō 2 be bewildered, in a daze
193 **spars-us a um* scattered
passim far and wide
mīrācul-um ī 2n. wonder, marvel
194 *uast-us a um* huge
trepid-us a um trembling
simulācr-um ī 2n. image. These are the images made
   by the constellations, which Phaethon takes to be
   genuine celestial monsters

of his folly: from wanting to know who he was, to succeeding in his request to Sol and picking up the reins. It was his divine birth that led him into all this; now he wishes he had, after all, been the son of a mortal. Another naval simile ensues, this time from the viewpoint of the steersman abandoning control of his ship in a storm and leaving his fate to the gods (185–6): Ovid again using an everyday image with which his readers would be well acquainted to make real the fantasies of space travel. *quid faciat* (187) re-introduces us to Phaethon's thought-processes: he sees the vast space of the skies ahead and behind (cf. 157) and measures how far there is to go – but (Ovid comments) in vain (187–90, cf. 156). This story is going to have no happy ending; no 'gods and prayers' (186) will save him. He knows he does not know what to do; *stupet* (191) reinforces the idea of his paralysis; unlike the steersman of the simile (185), he can bring himself neither to abandon nor actively control the reins; if only he knew the horses' names it might help, he seems hopelessly to be saying to himself (191–2). Here, as often, it is not clear whether Ovid is merely recounting the facts or inviting us to look into his character's mind.

193–209: Phaethon has looked in front and behind (190); now he looks up, surveys the canopy of the heavens and *trepidus* sees monsters everywhere, which he takes to be real (193–4, cf. 171–7). The sight of a gigantic Scorpio(n), covering two signs of the zodiac and apparently threatening him with its sting (195–9), is enough to make him drop the

est locus, in geminōs ubi brācchia concauat arcūs   195
Scorpius et, caudā flexīsque utrimque lacertīs,
porrigit in spatium signōrum membra duōrum.
hunc^ puer ut nigrī ^madidum sūdōre uenēnī
uulnera curuātā* ^minitantem *cuspide uīdit,
mentis inops gelidā formīdine lōra remīsit.   200
quae^ postquam summum tetigēre ^iacentia tergum,
exspatiantur equī, nūllōque inhibente per aurās
ignōtae regiōnis eunt, quāque impetus ēgit,
hāc sine lēge ruunt, altōque sub aethere fīxīs^
incursant ^stellīs, rapiuntque per āuia currum   205
et modo summa petunt, modo per dēclīue uiāsque^
^praecipitēs spatiō terrae propiōre feruntur,
īnferiusque suīs frāternōs^ currere Lūna
admīrātur ^equōs, ambustaque nūbila fūmant.

---

195 *locus*: take *ubi* next. *est locus* (or equivalent) usually introduces an idyllic *locus amoenus* (see Introduction, p. 8). As usual, the *locus* here is far from *amoenus* for poor Phaethon
gemin-us a um twin
brācchia: here = 'Claws', a sign of the zodiac, also known as *Libra* 'the Balance'
concauō 1 curve
arc-us ūs 4m. arc
196 *Scorpi-us ī* 2m. Scorpio, a constellation and sign of the zodiac
flex-is: describes both *caudā* and *lacertis*
utrimque from/on both sides
197 *porrigō* 3 stretch out, expand
in spatium: i.e. to cover a space of
signōrum duōrum: i.e. Scorpio and Claws/Libra
198 *hunc*: i.e. Scorpio; begin *ut puer* . . . *uīdit* (199)
madid-us a um wet, dripping
sūdor -is 3m. sweat
uenēn-um ī 2n. poison, venom
199 *curuāt-us a um* curved
minitor 1 dep. threaten
cuspis cuspid-is 3f. sting
200 *inops inop-is* devoid of, out of (+ gen.)
formīdō formīdin-is 3f. fear, terror

lōr-um ī 2n. rein
201 *quae*: i.e. *lōra* (subject)
tergum: i.e. the horses' backs; the horses can feel the reins (subject of *tetigēre*) lying uselessly there
202 *exspatior* 1 dep. veer off-course
inhibeō prevent, stop
203 *ignōt-us a um* unknown
regiō -nis 3f. territory, region
quāque and wherever
impet-us ūs 4m. urge
204 *hāc* by this route, here
fīx-us a um fixed, located. The ancients believed the stars were stationary in the firmament
205 *incursō* 1 run among (+ abl.)
stell-a ae 1f. star
āui-a ōrum 2n. trackless places (n. pl., like *summa* 206)
206 *dēclīu-e* 3n. slope
207 *spati-um ī* 2n. place, area
propior -is too near (to)
208 *inferius suīs* 'lower than his own [horses]'
frātern-us a um of a brother (Moon and Sun were brothers)
209 *ambust-us a um* scorch, burn up (*ambūrō*)
fūmō 1 smoke

---

reins out of sheer terror (200). The horses, realising that even Phaethon's (minimal) control over them has lapsed, bolt (201–2). Now the whole sky is open to them; they can go where they will, without let or hindrance (202–4; note the insistent *nūllōque inhibente . . . quāque impetus ēgit . . . sine lēge*), and so they do: *incursant . . . rapiunt . . . āuia . . . modo/modo* all emphasise the horses' random swooping up and down among the *fīxīs . . . stellīs* (204–7), as does the great surprise of the duly anthropomorphised Moon (208–9; other heavenly bodies have reacted rather differently, as we have seen). Phaethon is now too close to the earth (207), and the consequence is that the clouds catch fire (209).

2.210–16: *The earth is engulfed in flames*

┌corripitur flammīs, ut quaeque altissima, tellūs   210
fissaque agit rīmās et sūcīs āret adēmptīs.
pābula cānēscunt, cum frondibus ūritur arbor,
māteriamque suō praebet seges ārida damnō.
┌parua queror: magnae pereunt cum moenibus urbēs,
cumque suīs tōtās^ populīs incendia ^gentēs   215
in cinerem uertunt; siluae cum montibus ardent; . . .

[Ovid provides a catalogue of mountains that burst into flame]

2.227–38: *Phaethon too feels the fiery heat*

tum uērō Phaethōn cūnctīs ē partibus orbem^   227
adspicit ^accēnsum, nec tantōs sustinet aestūs,

Learning vocabulary	
aequor -is 3n. sea	*āreō* 2 dry up
frēnum i 2n. rein, control	*adēmpt-us a um* removed (*adimō*)
fūmō 1 smoke	212 *pābul-um i* 2n. pasture, field
gemin-us a um twin	*cānēscō* 3 turn white
lōr-um i 2n. rein	*frōns frond-is* 3f. leaf
praeceps praecipit-is headlong	213 *māteri-a ae* 1f. fuel
remittō 3 *remīsī remiss-um* let go of, hand over	**praebeō* 2 supply, provide
spars-us a um scattered	*seges seget-is* 3f. corn-field, crop
	*ārid-us a um dry, parched
	damn-um i 2n. destruction
210 *corripiō* 3/4 grip	214 *moeni-a um* 3n. pl. walls
ut quaeque: quaeque is f., referring to *tellūs*, lit. 'inasmuch as each (*tellūs*) [*sc.* was] *altissima*', i.e. in all the land's highest parts	215 **incendi-um i* 2n. fire, conflagration
	216 **cinis ciner-is* 3m./f. ashes
	ardeō 2 burn
211 *fiss-us a um* split open (*findō*)	228 *adspiciō* 3/4 see
*rīm-a ae 1f. crack	*accēns-us a um* ablaze, on fire (*accendō*)
sūc-us i 2m. juice, i.e. rivers, etc.	**aest-us ūs* 4m. heat

210–16: Next, logically, the earth catches fire too, starting (naturally) with the mountain tops (210). The fire spreads, engulfing nature first – the very earth itself, cracked and parched, crops, trees (211–12), all providing material for their own destruction (213 – Ovid enjoys the irony inherent in reflexive events, especially self-destruction); then cities, walls, whole peoples are consumed; and woods with the mountains (214–16). Ovid has in fact already described their conflagration (210), but he wants to roll out a catalogue of flaming mountains (Ovid adores catalogues: they are a regular feature of epic), and this gives him the cue. Note *parua queror* (214): the poet inserts himself into the third-person narrative to highlight a particularly dreadful moment, the destruction of cities and people. Ovid was an urban sophisticate; for him, the destruction of nature is *parua* by comparison.

227–38: Phaethon now begins to feel the effects of the infernos he has himself begun, and 227–34 are surely seen through his eyes. One would not have thought a chariot that

feruentēsque aurās uelut ē fornāce profundā
ōre trahit, currūsque suōs candēscere sentit.   230
et neque iam cinerēs ēiectātamque fauillam
ferre potest, calidōque inuoluitur undique fūmō.
quōque eat aut ubi sit, piceā cālīgine tēctus,
nescit, et arbitriō uolucrum raptātur equōrum.
sanguine^ tum crēdunt in corpora summa ^uocātō   235
Aethiopum populōs nigrum trāxisse colōrem;
tum facta est Libyē, raptīs ūmōribus aestū,
ārida . . .

[Ovid provides a catalogue of rivers of the world that dried up]

229 *ferueō* 2 boil
fornāx fornāc-is 3f. furnace, oven
profund-us a um deep
230 *candēscō* 3 glow, light up
231 *ēiectō* 1 throw out
fauill-a ae 1f. spark
232 *calid-us a um* hot
inuoluō 3 wrap
undique on all sides
fūm-us ī 2m. smoke
233 *eat . . . sit*: subjs. after *nescit* (234). It is odd that
  the horses do not seem to be affected by the chaos
  around them
pice-us a um pitch (i.e. made of pitch, resinous)
cālīgō cālīgin-is 3f. darkness, gloom
234 *arbitri-um ī* 2n. will
uolucer uolucr-is e swift, speedy

raptō 1 carry/drag off
235 *crēdunt*: 'they (i.e. people) believe . . .'; Ovid
  does not commit himself
in corpora summa: i.e. to the surface of the bodies.
  Ovid ingeniously rationalises that the blood
  rushing to the surface of the body to cool
  it would eventually cause the skin to
  turn black (blood does congeal black,
  after all)
236 *Aethiop-es -um* 3m. Ethiopia(ns); these are
  gen. after *populōs*, subject of the acc. and inf.
  trāxisse. Phaethon originated from Ethiopia
  (778)
color -is 3m. colour
237 *Libyē*: Greek nom., Libya
ūmor -is 3m. moisture

was pulling the sun could be combustible, or that Phaethon would not have felt the
sun's heat already, but Ovid ignores any contradiction, perhaps because he could not
think of a way round it (even he could hardly have imagined a heat-shield). First
Phaethon sees, and then he feels (227–8). Ovid had presumably been in a forge and
knew what it was like to breathe in hot air (229–30) – a homely, vivid image. The
chariot begins to glow, ash and dust everywhere, all unendurable, scorching smoke,
pitch black, where am I?, horses in charge, running where they will (231–4): it all makes
a picture of terrifying confusion as Ovid switches dramatically between Phaethon's
thoughts and the surrounding heat, smoke, ash and darkness. Ovid now steps back to
draw some aetiological conclusions: this is how Ethiopians (the usual name for black
Africans) became black, and how Libya became a desert (235–8). The thought of
moisture being sucked out of the earth leads him into another epic list, of rivers that
dried up.

2.260–71: *The earth splits open, the sea contracts, fish die*

dissilit omne solum, penetratque in Tartara rīmīs   260
lūmen, et infernum terret cum coniuge rēgem;
et mare contrahitur, siccaeque est campus harēnae
quod modo pontus erat; quōsque altum tēxerat aequor,
exsistunt montēs et sparsās Cycladas augent.
ima petunt piscēs, nec sē super aequōra curvī∧   265
tollere cōnsuētās audent ∧delphīnes in aurās;
corpora phōcārum, summō resupīna profundō,
exanimāta natant; ipsum quoque Nērea fāma est
Dōridaque et nātās tepidīs latuisse sub antrīs.
ter Neptūnus aquīs cum torvō brācchia vultū   270
exserere ausus erat, ter nōn tulit āeris ignēs.

[Mother Earth, choking in the smoke and heat, complains to Jupiter]

260 *dissiliō* 4 burst apart
sol-um ī 2n. earth
penetrō 1 reach
261 *infern-us a um* belonging to the lower regions
262 *contrahō* 3 shrink
sicc-us a um dry
est: the subj. of *est* is *quod modo . . . erat* (263)
camp-us ī 2m. expanse
harēn-a ae 1f. sand (gen. of content/material,
    RLL(d)3, **WSuppl.**syntax)
263 *quōsque*: *quōs* refers to *montēs* (264); take in
    order *montēs quōs . . . exsistunt et . . .*
264 *exsistō* 3 stick out
Cycladas: Greek acc. pl. (f.), Cyclades, the Cycladic
    isles, a chain of mountainous-looking islands in
    the Aegean
augeō 2 multiply
265 *īm-a -ōrum* n. pl. the depths, **RL**14.7, **W**4
pisc-is is 3m. fish

266 *cōnsuēt-us a um* usual, accustomed
delphīn delphīn-is 3m. dolphin
267 *phōc-a ae* 1f. seal
resupīn-us a um on one's back
profund-um ī 2n. the deep
268 *exanimāt-us a um* lifeless
natō 1 swim, float
Nērea . . . Dōrida: Greek accs. of Nereus and his wife
    Doris (sea-gods), subjects of the acc. and inf.
    following *fāma est*
269 *tepid-us a um* warm
270 *Neptūn-us ī* 2m. Neptune, god of the sea, tem-
    porarily powerless to do anything about the
    destruction of his domain
aquīs: 'from the waters' ('true' abl.,
    RL100A,Survey(a))
torv-us a um stern, grim
271 *exserō* 3 stretch out, raise

260–71: The earlier cracks in the earth (211) are as nothing to what occurs when the rivers have all dried up: the light reaches down even to Hades (260–2)! This is another Homeric moment, based on the tumult which shakes the earth when the gods in the *Iliad* join battle with each other ('in the underworld, Hades, lord of the dead, took fright and leapt with a cry from his throne. He was afraid earthshaker Poseidon might split open the ground above his head and expose to mortal and immortal eyes the horrible decaying chambers that fill the gods themselves with loathing', *Iliad* 20.61–5, Rieu–Jones). Ovid also loves paradoxes, and as the sea contracts, sandy plains and mountains appear where once the seas had been (262–4). What would be the consequence of that, ruminates Ovid? Clearly, the fish would have to dive even deeper (265); dolphins would not dare to leap out of the water (265–6); seals would die and float lifeless on the surface (267–8). And what of the gods of the sea? Too hot for them, too, even for 'grim-faced' Neptune – three quick looks are quite enough for him (268–71).

2.301–18: *Jupiter smashes the chariot with a thunderbolt*

dīxerat haec Tellūs; neque enim tolerāre uapōrem   301
ulterius potuit nec dīcere plūra, suumque∧
rettulit ∧ōs in sē propiōraque mānibus antra.
at pater omnipotēns, superōs testātus et ipsum
quī dederat currūs, nisi opem ferat, omnia∧ fātō   305
∧interitūra grauī, summam petit arduus arcem,
unde solet nūbēs lātīs indūcere terrīs,
unde mouet tonitrūs uibrātaque fulmina iactat.
sed neque quās∧ posset terrīs indūcere ∧nūbēs
tunc habuit, nec quōs∧ caelō dēmitteret ∧imbrēs.   310
intonat, et dextrā lībrātum fulmen ab aure
mīsit in aurīgam, pariterque animāque rotīsque
expulit, et saeuīs compescuit ignibus ignēs.

301 *tolerō* 1 endure, put up with
uapor -is 3m. heat
302 *ulterius* (adv.) further, any more
in: controls both *sē* and *antra*. It is hard to envisage
how *Tellūs* can 'withdraw her face into herself'
until one remembers that *Tellūs* is both an individual deity (a goddess) and the Earth (in the
same way that e.g. Peneus was both the river and
the river-god; see on passage 2, 1.452). She had
begun her speech after poking her head out of the
ashes of the earth (275–7, 282–4, not included in
these extracts); now, as a goddess, she pokes it
back again and retreats
303 *propior -is* nearer to (+ dat.)
mān-ēs –ium 3m. pl. shades of the underworld (contrast *man-us ūs* 4f. hand)
304 *omnipotēns omnipotent-is* all-powerful
testor 1 dep. call on X (acc.) as witness that (+ acc.
and inf., *omnia interitūra* [*esse*] *fātō grauī*). Since
gods do not usually interfere with each other's
decisions, Jupiter alerts the Sun to the seriousness
of the situation to explain his decision to inter-
vene (cf. passage 7, 3.336–7)
306 *intereō interīre interiī interitum* die, perish
ardu-us a um on high

307 **indūcō* 3 draw X (acc.) over Y (dat.)
308 *tonitr-us ūs* 4m. thunder
uibrō 1 shake
iactō 1 throw, hurl
309 *quās*: refers to *nūbēs*. Begin *neque tunc habuit
nūbēs quās . . . nec imbrēs quōs*; *posset*, like *dēmitteret* (310), is subj., because the relative clause
expresses purpose, 'clouds to . . .', **RL**145(3)
310 *dēmittō* 3 let down/fall
imber imbr-is 3m. shower, rain
311 *intonō* 1 thunder
lībrō 1 balance
aur-is 3f. ear
312 **aurīg-a ae* 1m. charioteer, lit. 'one who works
the reins' (*aureae* + *agō*) – which Phaethon no
longer does
pariter equally, at the same time
*rot-a ae 1f. wheel, i.e. chariot (cf. 'wheels')
313 *expellō* 3 *expulī* expel X (acc., understand
'Phaethon') from Y (abl.). Note the syllepsis of
Phaethon's expulsion from 'life and chariot'
saeuīs: Jupiter's fire is much more powerful than
ordinary fire, and therefore by Ovidian logic puts
it out
compescō 3 *compescuī* restrain, check

301–18: Ovid now faces a problem. The horses of the sun are running wild, and all nature
is in turmoil. How is the situation to be resolved? He gets Mother Earth (*Tellūs*) to complain to Jupiter, though even that is nearly beyond her: her speech comes to a halt because
she can endure the heat no longer, nor even speak any more (301–2), and therefore with-
draws back deep into her underground caves (302–3). With a grandly resounding *at
pater omnipotēns*, Ovid makes Jupiter swing into action: a very different picture of Jupiter
from the cruelly deceitful, trivialised husband of the Io incident (though Jupiter will
shortly revert to type). Calling on gods and Sol to witness the threat to the world (304–6),

cōnsternantur equī et, saltū in contrāria factō,
colla iugō ēripiunt abruptaque lōra relinquunt.   315
illīc frēna iacent, illīc tēmōne reuulsus
axis, in hāc^ radiī frāctārum ^parte rotārum,
sparsaque sunt lātē lacerī^ uestīgia ^currūs.

2.319–28: *Phaethon falls to earth like a comet, and is buried by Naiads*

at Phaethōn, rutilōs flammā populante capillōs,
uoluitur in praeceps, longōque per āera tractū   320
fertur, ut interdum dē caelō stella serēnō
etsī nōn cecidit, potuit cecidisse uidērī.
quem procul ā patriā dīuersō maximus^ orbe

---

314 *cōnsternō* 1 throw into confusion
salt-us ūs 4m. leap
in contrāria: 'in opposite directions' (there are four
  horses in all)
315 *iug-um ī* 2n. yoke
abrupt-us a um torn off (*abrumpō*)
316 *tēmō -nis* 3m. pole
reuuls-us a um ripped from (+ abl.) (*reuellō*)
317 *ax-is is* 3m. axle
radi-us ī 2m. spoke
frāct-us a um broken (*frangō*)
318 *lacer -a um* mangled, torn

Learning vocabulary
aest-us ūs 4m. heat
ārid-us a um dry, parched
aurig-a ae 1m. charioteer
cinis ciner-is 3m/f. ashes
incendi-um ī 2n. fire, conflagration

indūcō 3 draw X (acc.) over Y (dat.)
  praebeō 2 supply, provide
    rim-a ae 1f. crack
    rot-a ae 1f. wheel

319 *rutil-us a um* ruddy, glowing red
populor 1 dep. ravage
320 *uoluō* 3 roll/spin along
in praeceps headlong
tract-us ūs 4m. trail
321 *ut*: 'as', introducing a simile
interdum from time to time
serēn-us a um clear
323 *quem*: i.e. Phaethon
dīuers-us a um different (part of). Here it is
  abl. of place with *orbe*

---

he climbs to the high position from which he controlled the weather to launch his bolts –
only to find a complete absence of clouds and showers with which to dowse the flaming
chariot (306–10). The relatives *quās* and *quōs* (309–10), coming before their antecedents,
well express the bewilderment of Jupiter. What to do? He launches a lightning bolt, with
accompanying thunder, which smashes the chariot and quenches its fire with his own
superior fire (311–13). The startled horses at once leap apart and rip themselves free from
it (314–15: do not enquire too closely what now happens to the sun), and the pieces fall
to earth. Ovid envisages the bits lying scattered about the ground, horribly reminiscent
to us of pictures of crashed aeroplanes (316–18).

319–28: This is not, however, Phaethon's fate. Ovid pictures the boy like a comet, hair
flaming, in headlong descent ('comet' comes from Greek *komētēs* 'long-haired'; but he
should surely look more like a meteor, which does indeed look as if it could be falling,
322, unlike a comet). He lands nowhere near the chariot but in northern Italy (he has, of

excipit ∧Ēridanus fūmantiaque abluit ōra.
Nāides Hesperiae trifidā fūmantia flammā   325
corpora dant tumulō, signant quoque carmine saxum:
HĪC : SITUS : EST : PHAETHŌN : CURRŪS : AURĪGA : PATERNĪ
QUEM : SĪ : NON : TENUIT : MAGNĪS : TAMEN : EXCIDIT : AUSĪS

2.329–39: *Sol grieves, and Clymene scours the world to find the body*

nam pater obductōs,∧ luctū miserābilis aegrō,
condiderat ∧uultūs, et, sī modo crēdimus, ūnum   330
īsse diem sine sōle ferunt. incendia lūmen
praebēbant, aliquisque malō fuit ūsus in illō.
at Clymenē, postquam dīxit quaecumque∧ fuērunt
in tantīs ∧dīcenda malīs, lūgubris et āmēns
et laniāta sinūs, tōtum percēnsuit orbem,   335

324 *excipiō* 3/4 pick up, collect
Ēridan-us ī 2m. river Eridanus (the Greek
  name for the Po, in northern Italy – Latin
  Padus – about 3,000 miles from Phaethon's
  fatherland, Ethiopia)
abluō 3 wash, bath
325 *Hesperi-us a um* western, i.e. in Italy
trifid-us a um three-pronged (of forked
  lightning)
326 *tumul-us ī* 2m. tomb, burial
signō 1 mark, carve
carmen carmin-is 3n. epitaph
327 *sit-us a um* located, placed
328 *quem*: i.e. *currus*; *teneō* here means 'hold
  on track'
excidō 3 fall out (of the chariot), perish
aus-um ī 2n. bold deed/exploit
magnīs . . . ausīs: abl. of cause or 'attendant
  circumstances'

329 *obduct-us a um* veiled (*obdūcō*).
  Phaethon's father was the Sun
miserābil-is e pitiable
aeger aegr-a um sick, ill, painful
331 *isse*: perf. inf. of *eō*, in acc. and inf. after
  ferunt
332 *malō*: i.e. only the virtual destruction of
  the world!
333 *Clymenē*: Greek nom., Phaethon's
  mother
quaecumque: 'whatever [things/words]'
  (n. pl.)
334 *lūgubr-is e* grieving
āmēns āment-is distraught, maddened
335 *laniō* 1 tear
sin-us ūs 4m. breast. Here it is acc. of respect,
  i.e. '*laniāta* in respect of her *sinūs*' – the
  self-inflicted signs of grief, **RL**6(3)
percēnseō 2 roam

course, been travelling westwards with the Sun). Phaethon splashes down in the river Po,
which tenderly takes him in and cleans him (324), before he is buried with a sympathetic,
almost sentimental, inscription composed by the motherly Naiads (325–8). Nothing
about the destruction of much of the known world? But Ovid is not often interested in
pious lectures or distributing blame: there is little useful one can say, after all, about a
young man who learned too late the folly of his ways and met a ghastly death, wreaking
cosmic havoc in the process.

329–39: If Ovid remains cool about the fate of Phaethon, he shows us the grief of his
parents. Sol veils his face and refuses to shine for a day (329–31; note *crēdimus* and *ferunt*

exanimēsque artūs prīmō, mox ossa requīrēns.
repperit ossa tamen, peregrīnā condita rīpā,
incubuitque locō, nōmenque in marmore lēctum
perfūdit lacrimīs, et apertō pectore fōuit.

<table>
<tr><td>

336 *exanim-is is* lifeless
art-us ūs 4m. limb
requīrō 3 look for. Since Clymene does not
  know Phaethon has been buried, she looks
  first for his limbs, then (given that flesh will
  not last long) for his bones, and finally finds
  his grave

</td><td>

337 *peregrīn-us a um* foreign
338 *incumbō* 3 *incubuī* lie down
marmor -is 3n. marble
339 *perfundō* 3 *perfūdī* bathe, flood
aperiō 4 open (i.e. she bares her breast)
foueō 2 *fōuī* cherish, warm

</td></tr>
</table>

Learning vocabulary for Passage 4, Phaethon

aequor -is 3n. sea
aest-us ūs 4m. heat
ārid-us a um dry, parched
aurīg-a ae 1m. charioteer
careō 2 *caruī* lack, be lacking, do without
  (+ abl.)
cinis ciner-is 3m./f. ashes
curr-us ūs 4m. chariot
curu-us a um curved
frēn-um ī 2n. rein, control
fūmō 1 smoke
gemin-us a um twin, double
habēn-a ae 1f. rein
incendi-um ī 2n. fire, conflagration

indūcō 3 *indūxī inductum* draw X (acc.) over Y
  (dat.)
iug-um ī 2n. yoke
lōr-um ī 2n. rein
pondus ponder-is 3n. weight
praebeō 2 supply, provide
praeceps praecipit-is headlong
remittō 3 *remīsī remissum* let go of
rīm-a ae 1f. crack
rot-a ae 1f. wheel, i.e. chariot (cf. 'wheels')
ruō 3 *ruī rutum* run wild
spars-us a um scattered
stell-a ae 1f. star
super up, i.e. high, tall; *super* + acc., above

as Ovid goes into ironic 'historical' mode again). There is a typically amusing Ovidian paradox here: since the rising and setting of the sun *mark* the day, how can one tell that a day has passed? Still, it cannot have been all that bad, says the rational 'historian', because the earth was still on fire, so there was plenty of light about (331–2)! Clymene, saying all that can be said in the circumstances and exhibiting all the traditional signs of grief, roams the world in search of the remains and eventually finds the grave, where (again) her reaction is thoroughly typical. A son may have been guilty of folly, but he is still a son, and burial (the traditional job of the woman in the ancient world) was the least a mother could do for her beloved child.

Study section

1. Write out and scan ll.260–4, 314–18.
2. Trace the steps by which the chariot goes out of control and finally crashes.

3. How sympathetically characterised is Phaethon? Would you want to talk of 'the wild sexuality that runs out of control in the adolescent'? (Sharrock, in Hardie, 2002a, 97).

4. Identify some passages where it is not clear if Ovid is recounting facts or giving us a glimpse into human minds.

5. What contrasts of personnel and character do you find with the world-transforming event in passage 1?

6. Take any five lines, consecutive or not, and explain why they give you pleasure.

7. *Oxford Latin Dictionary* glosses *excidō* (328) as '(w.abl.) To be deprived or disappointed (of), fall short (of)'. Can this be right?

5   Diana and Actaeon, *Metamorphōsēs* 3.138–252

Background

So distraught were the daughters of the Sun, the Heliades, at Phaethon's death that they were turned into trees around his tomb and their tears into amber; while Cycnus (a grieving relative of Phaethon) was turned into a swan (Greek *kuknos*). The Sun was finally persuaded to return to his daily task, and Jupiter surveyed the damage to the world. While doing so, he had his way with the huntress Callisto, whom a furious Juno turned into a bear, but Jupiter re-transformed into a constellation. Various stories about gods' affairs, some told by a crow and a raven, ensue, and Book 2 ends with Jupiter, disguised as a bull, riding off with Europa.

Book 3 opens with Europa's father Agenor, who came from Phoenicia (Lebanon), ordering his son Cadmus to find Europa or go into exile. Cadmus chose the latter and consulted Apollo at Delphi, who told him to found a city (Thebes) in Greece, in Boeotia. Defeating a terrifying serpent there (which had killed all his companions), Cadmus was told by Athena/Minerva to sow its teeth in the ground. From these sprang armed warriors, who fought among themselves until the last five still standing agreed to stop and join Cadmus in founding the city. Cadmus married Harmonia, the daughter of Mars and Venus, and all seemed set fair for him. But Ovid goes on 'Yet a man should await his final day, and no one be called happy until he dies and his last rites are paid.' At this point, the story of Actaeon begins.

There were many myths associated with Thebes and Cadmus' family, the most famous probably being that of Pentheus and the Bacchant women, immortalised in Euripides' tragedy *Bacchae* (c. 407 BC). Ovid gives his version of this myth at the end of Book 3. This selection, however, offers the four preceding stories in their entirety – Diana and Actaeon, Juno and Semele, Tiresias, and Echo and Narcissus. They are glossed as separate stories, the only Latin omitted being a catalogue of dogs (3.207–27). They give a good idea of how inventively Ovid runs one story into another and develops broadly thematic subject-matter.

3.138–42: *Actaeon was an innocent victim*

prīma∧ nepōs – inter tot rēs tibi, Cadme, secundās –
∧causa fuit luctūs, aliēnaque cornua frontī
addita, uōsque, canēs, satiātae sanguine erīlī.   140
at bene sī quaerās, fortūnae crīmen in illō,
nōn scelus, inueniēs. quod∧ enim ∧scelus error habēbat?

3.143–54: *Actaeon calls for an end to the day's hunting*

mōns erat, īnfectus uariārum caede ferārum.
iamque diēs medius rērum contrāxerat umbrās,
et sōl ex aequō mētā distābat utrāque,   145
cum iuuenis∧ placidō* per dēuia lūstra uagantēs

138 *prima*: the first reason for Cadmus' grief, as Ovid
now explains, is that his grandson Actaeon grew
horns and was killed by his own dogs; the second
will involve his daughter Semele (next story). *nepōs,
cornua* and *uōsque* (*canēs*) (note the tricolon) are
complements of the subject, *prima . . . causa*
Cadme: note the 'apostrophe'
secundās: because, as Ovid has just explained,
Cadmus had won Harmonia (daughter of Mars
and Venus) as his bride, producing a glorious
dynasty of four daughters, each with at least one
son. Actaeon was son of Autonoe, who had
married Aristaeus. Is there a verbal joke here –
prima . . . secundās?
139 *aliēn-us a um* strange
frōns front-is 3f. forehead
140 *addō* 3 *addidī additum* add
satiō 1 glut, fill with
eril-is e master's, of one's master
141 *at*: strongly sympathetic, as is the coming apostrophe

quaerās: note subj.; the main clause is fut. ind.
(*inueniēs*), RLS2(c), W33
in illō: i.e. in Actaeon, applicable to Actaeon
142 *error-is* 3m. mistake. The word means basically
'wander', and Actaeon's 'mistake' will turn out to
be precisely that (175, *errāns*)
143 *infect-us a um* stained, darkened (*īnficiō*)
caed-ēs is 3f. slaughter
144 *rērum*: take with *umbrās*
contrahō 3 *contrāxī* shorten
145 *ex aequō* equally
mēt-a ae 1f. turning-point. This is a metaphor from
the chariot-racing track, which had two *mētae*,
one at either end of the central reservation round
which the teams raced. In the case of the sun, its
two *mētae* are the East and the West
distō 1 be distant from (+ abl.)
146 *placid-us a um* peaceful, friendly
dēui-us a um remote, out of the way
lūstr-um ī 2n. haunt
uagor 1 dep. wander, roam

138–42: This is a story with two morals: for Cadmus, call no man happy till he is dead (see **Background** above; 138–9 introduce the evidence for it); and for Actaeon, whose ghastly end is in Ovid's eyes entirely undeserved, life's (as it were) a bitch (141–2). These opening lines make up a teasing trailer for the story. Note the use of 'apostrophe' – first, to Cadmus, surely sympathetic (138); next, to the dogs (*uōsque, canēs*, 140), as if Ovid knew them (and therefore Actaeon) well, increasing the horror of *satiātae . . . erīlī*; and finally *quaerās . . . inueniēs* (141–2), presumably addressed to the reader rather than a consolation for Cadmus? Since Ovid himself was exiled for what he claimed as an unintended *error* on his part (see Introduction, p. 4), this seems particularly poignant.

143–54: Ovid sets the scene in two different locations: first, the *mōns* where the hunt has just finished (143–54), and second the *uallis* sacred to Diana into which Actaeon will

participēs operum compellat ∧Hyantius *ōre:
'līna madent, comitēs, ferrumque cruōre ferārum,
fortūnaeque∧ diēs habuit ∧satis. altera∧ lūcem
cum croceīs ∧inuecta rotīs ∧Aurōra redūcet,   150
prōpositum repetēmus opus. nunc Phoebus utrāque∧
distat idem ∧mētā, finditque uapōribus arua.
sistite opus praesēns, nōdōsaque tollite līna.'
iussa uirī faciunt, intermittuntque labōrem.

3.155–62: *A valley sacred to Diana is described*

uallis erat, piceīs et acūtā dēnsa cupressū,   155
nōmine Gargaphiē, succīnctae sacra Diānae,

147 *particeps particip-is* sharing in, partners in
compellō 1 call to
Hyanti-us a um offspring of Hyas (founder of the
   Hyantes, a Boeotian tribe) i.e. Actaeon
148 **lin-um ī* 2n. net, thread. Roman hunters staked
   out areas with nets, drove the beasts into them
   and killed them there
madeō 2 be soaked, wet
*comes comit-is 3m. comrade
*cruor-is 3m. gore
149 *altera*: begin translating this clause with *cum*
   'when' (150), which controls *redūcet*, **RLT**(d),
   W31
150 *croce-us a um* yellow
inuehō 3 *inuexī inuectum* ride, drive
rot-a ae 1f. wheel (Dawn rides a chariot; so does the
   Sun, but he appears on the horizon later than
   Dawn)
*Aurōr-a ae 1f. Dawn
151 *redūcō* 3 bring back
*repetō 3 repeat, take up again, seek again
Phoebus: here meaning 'sun' (*phoibos* in Greek
   means 'bright, shining')
152 *findō* 3 crack, split. The earth 'splitting' with the
   heat is a striking image
uapor-is 3m. heat, burning rays of the sun
153 *sistō* 3 stop

praesēns praesent-is present
nōdōs-us a um knotted
154 *intermittō* 3 lay off

Learning vocabulary
addō 3 *addidī additum* add
Aurōr-a ae 1f. Dawn
caed-ēs is 3f. slaughter
comes comit-is 3m. comrade
cruor-is 3m. gore
dēui-us a um remote, out of the way
distō 1 be distant from (+ abl.)
error-is 3m. mistake
frōns front-is 3f. forehead
īnfect-us a um stained, darkened
lin-um ī 2n. net, thread
mēt-a ae 1f. turning-point
repetō 3 repeat, take up again, seek again
satiō 1 glut, fill with
uagor 1 dep. wander, roam

155 *uall-is is* 3f. valley
pice-a ae 1f. spruce
acūt-us a um tapering
dēns-us a um thick, crowded
cupress-us ūs 4f. cypress
156 *Gargaphiē*: name of a spring near Plataea in
   Greece, here called a valley

innocently stray (155–62). Ovid sets the alarm-bells ringing at once: the *mōns* is already
blood-stained (143), and so too is the hunter's equipment (148); soon human blood will
be added. Actaeon, relaxed and agreeable (*placidō*) master of the hunt, thoughtfully calls
in his friends (146–7), since hunting has been good (148) and the heat is overwhelming
(152), and, tragically ignorant of what lies in store for him, says the day's *fortūna* is over
(cf. 141), and they will start again tomorrow (151). But it isn't, and he certainly won't.

155–62: Meanwhile, in another part of the mountain, there is a *locus amoenus* (see
Introduction, p. 8) – a thickly wooded vale at the end of which is a cave, tucked away

cūius in extrēmō est antrum^nemorāle^ recessū,
arte ^labōrātum nūllā: simulāuerat artem
ingeniō nātūra suō. nam pūmice uīuō
et leuibus tōfis nātīuum dūxerat arcum;   160
fōns^ sonat ā dextrā, tenuī ^perlūcidus undā,
margine grāmineō patulōs ^incinctus hiātūs.

3.163–72: *Diana is bathing there with her nymphs*

hīc dea siluārum, uēnātū fessa, solēbat
uirgineōs artūs liquidō perfundere rōre.
quō postquam subiit, nymphārum trādidit ūnī^   165
^armigerae iaculum pharetramque arcūsque retentōs,
altera dēpositae subiēcit brācchia pallae,
uincla duae pedibus dēmunt; nam, doctior illīs,
Ismēnis Crocalē sparsōs per colla capillōs

succinct-us a um girded up (i.e. gathered and tied at the waist, so as not to entangle her legs in the chase)
*Diān-a ae Diana (Artemis), goddess of virginity and the hunt
157 *cūius*: take with *in extrēmō . . . recessū*
nemorāl-is e wooded
recess-us ūs 4m. recess, corner
158 *labōrō* 1 work, construct
*simulō 1 imitate
159 *pūmex pūmic-is* 3m. pumice
uīu-us a um living
160 *dūxerat*: *nātūra* is the subject
tōf-us ī 2m. tufa
nātīu-us a um natural
*arc-us ūs 4m. arch; bow
161 **fōns font-is* 3m. spring, fountain
sonō 1 sound, tinkle
perlūcid-us a um transparent, clear
162 *grāmine-us a um* grassy
patul-us ī 2m. spreading
incinct-us a um surrounded (*incingō*)
hiāt-us ūs 4m. pool (acc. of respect after *incinctus*)
163 *uēnāt-us ūs* 4m. hunting
*fess-us a um tired

164 **uirgine-us a um* virgin
*art-us ūs 4m. limb
*liquid-us a um clear, fluid
*perfundō 3 soak, bathe (*fundō* 3 *fūdī fūsum* pour)
rōs rōr-is 3m. dew, i.e. water like dew
165 *subeō subīre subiī* enter
166 *armiger-a ae* 2f. armour-bearer, squire (here in apposition to *ūnī*)
iacul-um ī 2n. spear
retent-us a um unstrung, slackened (*retineō*)
167 *altera* (167) . . . *duae* (168): 'while another [nymph] . . . [and] two [others] . . .'
dēposit-us a um taken off, removed (*dēpōnō*)
subiciō 3/4 *subiēcī* place X (acc.) under Y (dat.)
pall-a ae 1f. cloak
168 *uincl-um ī* 2n. binding, thong
dēmō 3 remove
*nam moreover, again (indicating a transition)
169 *Ismēnis*: Greek nom. f., 'to do with the [unidentified] river Ismenus' near Thebes, i.e. Theban
Crocal-ē Greek nom., 'Crocale', the skilled *coiffeuse*
*spars-us a um loose, streaming; scattered (*spargō* 3 *sparsī sparsum* sprinkle, scatter)

(157) and natural (158–60). The idea of artless (*nūllā arte*) nature working like a living artist (*simulāuit*) is a typically Ovidian paradox. Romans were very keen on improving nature, but here nature has improved itself. The word-painting of 161–2 is especially effective – the tinkle of the water in 161, the broadening welcome of the grassy verges in 162. It is also *sacred to Diana* (156).

163–72: The *locus*, then, may be *amoenus* to her, but it will certainly not turn out to be so for Actaeon. Diana is the virgin (164) goddess of the woods and hunt (163), but she will

colligit in nōdum, quamuīs erat ipsa solūtīs.   170
excipiunt laticem Nephelēque Hyalēque Rhanisque
et Psecas et Phialē, funduntque capācibus urnīs.

3.173–85: *Actaeon comes onto the scene and the nymphs raise the cry*

dumque ibi perluitur solitā Tītānia lymphā,
ecce nepōs Cadmī, dīlātā parte labōrum,
per nemus ignōtum nōn certīs passibus errāns,   175
peruenit in lūcum; sīc illum fāta ferēbant.
quī simul intrāuit rōrantia fontibus antra,
sīcut erant, nūdae* uīsō^ sua pectora *nymphae
percussēre ^uirō, subitīsque ululātibus omne^

---

170 *nōd-us i* knot. This makes for a homely observation about the bathing habits of the mighty goddess

solūtīs: sc. *capillīs*, abl. of description referring to Crocale, **RLL**(f)3(i), **W**40; cf. Daphne at 1.497, 542

171 *latex latic-is* 3m. water, liquid

Nephelēque Hyalēque Rhanisque . . . Psecas . . . Phialē: Greek noms., names of Diana's nymphs (all suitably watery – 'Cloud', 'Crystal', 'Raindrop', 'Drizzle', 'Bowl')

172 *capāx capāc-is* large, capacious

urn-a ae 1f. urn, jug

Learning vocabulary
arc-us ūs 4m. arch; bow
art-us ūs 4m. limb
Diān-a ae Diana (Artemis), goddess of virginity and the hunt
fess-us a um tired
fōns font-is 3m. spring, fountain
liquid-us a um clear, fluid
nam moreover, again
perfundō 3 soak, bathe (*fundō* 3 *fūdī fūsum* pour)
simulō 1 imitate

spars-us a um loose, streaming; scattered (*spargō* 3 *sparsī sparsum* sprinkle, scatter)
uirgine-us a um virgin

173 *perluō* 3 wash

Tītāni-a ae 1f. Diana (grand-daughter of the Titan god Coeus)

lymph-a ae 1f. bath, water

174 *ecce* behold! look!

dīlāt-us a um put off, postponed (*differō*), i.e. Actaeon, after his rest (154), has not re-joined his friends to continue the *labor* of hunting but has wandered off on his own

175 *ignōt-us a um* unknown

176 *lūc-us ī* 2m. grove

177 *simul* as soon as, once

rōrō 1 be wet

178 *sīcut* just as

nūdae . . . uirō: heavy hyperbaton and suggestive interlacing of words here, with *uīsō* next to *sua pectora* and *percussēre* next to *uirō*; and is *sua pectora* acc. of respect after *nūdae* or object of *percussēre*? Logic and grammar make it clear, of course

179 *subit-us a um* sudden

ululāt-us ūs 4m. shriek, cry

---

turn out to be no friend of human hunters who accidentally trespass in her realm. Ovid strips her before our very eyes as she prepares for her bath (165–8). But it is not a bath. In the Roman fashion – the whole scene is amusingly reminiscent of a Roman aristocrat in her boudoir being attended by her slaves – she is in fact being washed down by her nymphs (171–2: note the brief epic-style catalogue of names). This is important. Were she in the pool, her nakedness would not be visible; but she is standing up, for all to see.

173–85: Enter the innocent Actaeon: 175 *ignōtum . . . nōn certīs passibus* and *errāns* (cf. *error* 142) all emphasise his innocence, and the reference to fate bringing him to the spot

implēuēre ∧nemus, *circumfūsaeque Diānam   180
corporibus tēxēre suīs. tamen altior illīs
ipsa dea est, collōque tenus superēminet omnēs.
quī color, īnfectīs∧ aduersī sōlis ab ictū
∧nūbibus, esse solēt, aut purpureae Aurōrae,
is fuit in uultū uīsae sine ueste Diānae.   185

3.186–97: *Diana turns Actaeon into a deer*

quae, quamquam comitum turbā est stīpāta suārum,
in latus oblīquum tamen astitit, ōraque retrō
flexit et, ut uellet prōmptās habuisse sagittās,

---

180 *circumfūs-us a um* surrounding (*circumfundō*)
182 *tenus* + abl. up to, by as much as (with *collō*)
superēmineō 2 be taller than
183 *quī color* . . . [185] *is fuit*: 'what colour/the
colour which . . . [185] this was [the colour]'
ict-us ūs 4m. impact, blow, strike
184 *solēt*: *-ēt* scans heavy. The final syllable of the 3rd
s. pres. ind. act. originally *did* scan heavy (such
scansion appears commonly in early Latin, e.g.
the comic poet Plautus), but later poets used that
scansion only rarely, usually when it was followed
by a strong pause
purpureae Aurōrae: 'rosy Dawn', gen. after *ictū*. Note
the metrical hiatus and rare (in Ovid) fifth-foot
spondee

186 *stīpō* 1 press round
187 *latus later-is* 3n. side, flank
oblīqu-us a um angled, sideways, i.e. Diana turns her
body away, so as to shield her front from Actaeon,
and then turns her head back to look at him
adstō 1 *adstitī* stand, turn
retrō back
188 *ut* . . . *sīc*: 'though . . . yet'
uellet: implying a wish on Diana's part, 'would that I
had my arrows..', i.e. 'much as she would have
liked . . .', **RL**153
prōmpt-us a um to hand, ready
sagitt-a ae 1f. arrow

---

(176) clinches it. The reaction of the naked nymphs as he enters the grove is instanta-
neous: breast-beating and shrieks signal their distress (178–80), and they hurry to protect
their mistress from human sight (180–1). But to no avail – the goddess, naturally, is taller
than they! (181–2: Ovid here plays amusingly with serious epic's affirmation of the gods'
stature and dignity, cf. e.g. *Aeneid* 1.501). Her blush – a charged emotional moment,
attracting a simile – is one of modesty (183–5: note *sine ueste* and cf. her protective action
at 186–8), but also of rage (cf. 252). What, however, can she in her nakedness do?

186–97: Ovid now looks into her thoughts: she wishes she had her arrows (188) – she
would have killed him at once if she had had them – but instead she sprinkles Actaeon's
face and hair with the water with which she is being washed down. At first glance this
looks like the panic reaction of a silly woman, but note *ultrīcibus* (190): vengeance is what
Diana wants, and the apparently harmless flicking of water will bring this about, as her
subsequent words make clear (191). Note that she justifies her action by claiming that
Actaeon would otherwise boast of seeing a goddess naked (192–3) – a feeble reason,
perhaps, but there is no answer to it. Actaeon is immediately transformed. His metamorphosis begins with the head and works down the body: horns (194), neck and ears
(195), arms becoming fore-legs (196–7) – his legs, presumably, become back legs, but we
are looking at the front of his body at the moment – and his whole body is veiled (197).
That last clause is significant. Actaeon's humanity is not completely destroyed by Diana's

quās habuit sīc hausit aquās, uultumque uirīlem
perfūdit, spargēnsque comās ultrīcibus undīs,   190
addidit haec clādis praenūntia uerba futūrae:
'nunc tibi mē positō uīsam uēlāmine nārrēs,
si poteris nārrāre, licet!' nec plūra mināta,
dat sparsō capitī uiuācis cornua ceruī,
dat spatium collō, summāsque cacūminat aurēs,   195
cum pedibusque manūs, cum longīs^ brācchia mūtat
^crūribus, et uēlat maculōsō uellere corpus.

3.198–206: *The terrified and helpless Actaeon flees*

additus et pauor est; fugit Autonoēius hērōs,
et sē tam celerem cursū mīrātur in ipsō.
ut uēro uultūs et cornua uīdit in undā,   200
'mē miserum!' dictūrus erat: uōx nūlla secūta est.
ingemuit: uōx illa fuit, lacrimaeque per ōra
nōn sua fluxērunt; mēns tantum prīstina mānsit.
quid faciat? repetatne domum et rēgālia tēcta

189 *quās . . . aquās*: take in order *hausit aquās quās habuit*. Ovid teases us again: it looks as if *quās* should pick up *sagittās* (188), but it refers forward to *aquās*
hauriō 4 *hausī* pour
uirīl-is e man's
190 **com-a ae* 1f. hair
ultrix ultric-is avenging. But how will mere *water* avenge Diana? We shall soon find out
191 *clād-ēs is* 3f. death, disaster
praenūnti-us a um prophetic of (+ gen.)
192 *tibi . . . nārrēs . . . licet*: 'it is permitted for you that (note: no *ut*) you tell of *mē . . . uīsam*'; for *licet* + subj., see **RLF2**
uelāmen uelāmin-is 3n. covering
193 *minor* 1 dep. threaten
194 *uiuāx uiuāc-is* long-lived, tenacious, vigorous
*ceru-us ī 2m. stag

195 *spati-um ī* 2n. length
cacūminō 1 bring to a point
*aur-is is 3f. ear
197 *crūs crūr-is* 3n. leg
maculōs-us a um dappled
uellus ueller-is 3n. hide
198 *pauor-is* 3m. fear
Autonoēius: (six syllables!), son of Autonoē, i.e. Actaeon; note the five speedy dactyls in this line
hērōs: Greek nom., hero
202 *ingemō* 3 *ingemuī* groan
uōx illa fuit: i.e. that was what passed for speech
203 *fluō* 3 *fluxī* flow
prīstin-us a um original
204 *faciat*: subj. of deliberative question
rēgāl-is e royal
tēct-um ī 2n. dwelling

action, merely veiled: he is still all too human underneath (cf. Io, passage 3, 1.632–50, 729–34).

198–206: Deers are fearful creatures, tuned to flight, and Diana injects fear into him; off he goes – note the bitterly ironic *Autonoēius hērōs* (198) – and Ovid looks into his mind for us. Not yet aware of his transformation, he is amazed at his speed (199), and it is only when he sees his reflection in the pool that he understands what has happened (200). Like Io (1.637), he tries to speak but cannot (201); all he can do is groan and weep (202–3). A deer he may be physically, but psychologically he is still human, thinking human thoughts (203). Ovid, who (like many other poets) enjoyed playing on this aspect of metamorphosis, reads these

an lateat siluīs? pudor hoc, timor impedit illud.   205
dum dubitat, uīdēre canēs . . .

[Ovid enumerates the catalogue of Actaeon's dogs and their names]

3.228–41: *Actaeon is caught by his dogs*

ille fugit per quae∧ fuerat ∧loca saepe secūtus,
hēu, famulōs fugit ipse suōs. clāmāre libēbat:
'Actaeōn ego sum! dominum cognōscite uestrum!'   230
uerba animō dēsunt; resonat lātrātibus aethēr.
prīma Melanchaetēs in tergō uulnera fēcit,
proxima Thēridamās, Oresītrophos haesit in armō
(tardius exierant, sed per compendia montis
anticipāta uia est). dominum retinentibus illīs,   235
cētera turba coit, cōnfertque in corpore dentēs.
iam loca uulneribus dēsunt; gemit ille, sonumque∧

205 *hoc . . . illud*: 'the one [option], the other
[option]', objects of *impedit*. We would expect
hoc (normally 'the latter'), i.e. *pudor*, to refer to
hiding in the woods, and *illud* (normally 'the
former'), i.e. *timor*, to going back home. Does this
make the better sense? Cf. notes on passage 2,
1.472 and 539)
impediō 4 prevent, stop

Learning vocabulary
aur-is is 3f. ear
ceru-us ī 2m. stag
com-a ae 1f. hair
ecce behold! look!
simul as soon as, once

228 *per quae . . . loca*: 'along what places', 'along the
places where'
229 **hēu* alas!
famul-us ī 2m. servants, helpers (i.e. the dogs that
had faithfully served him)
*clāmō 1 shout, cry out for
libet it pleases, there is a desire to

231 **dēsum dēesse* to be unforthcoming, offer no
access to, lack, fail (+ dat.)
uerba . . . aethēr: superb, chilling chiasmus.
Desperate to speak, all Actaeon can do is hear the
howling of dogs
resonō 1 echo, resound
lātrāt-us ūs 4m. barking
232 *Melanchaetēs . . . Thēridamās . . . Oresītrophos*:
Greek noms., names of dogs: 'Blackhair', 'Killer',
'Hill-bred'
233 *arm-um ī* 2n. shoulder
234 **exeō exīre exiī* set out
compendi-um ī 2n. short-cut
235 *anticipō* 1 occupy in advance
236 **coeō coīre* gather. Note the *c/qu* sounds in this
line – snapping teeth?
cōnferō 3 direct, aim
dēns dent-is 3m. tooth
237 *loca*: i.e. of his body
gemō 3 groan
son-us ī 2m. sound

thoughts for us: he is a *hērōs* (198), and 'heroic' shame and fear battle it out in his hero's
mind (204–5). The hesitation is fatal: his dogs spot him . . . (206).

228–41: As ever, Ovid picks up the horrible paradoxes and ironies of the situation,
Actaeon being pursued where he hunted (228), fleeing from his own dogs (229), wanting
to cry out but unable to (230–1), hearing no voice of his own but only the baying of the
chasing hounds (231). This crisply polarised line conveys a terrifying sense of human
helplessness (*animō* here means something like 'will-power': as a human he longs to

etsī nōn hominis – quem nōn tamen ēdere possit
ceruus – ^habet, maestīsque replet iuga nōta querēlīs,
et genibus prōnīs supplex similisque rogantī   240
circumfert tacitōs tamquam sua brācchia uultūs.

3.242–52: *Actaeon's friends urge the dogs on, wondering where Actaeon is*

at comitēs^ rapidum solitīs hortātibus agmen
^ignārī īnstigant, oculīsque Actaeona quaerunt,
et uelut absentem certātim Actaeona clāmant
(ad nōmen caput ille refert), et abesse queruntur   245
nec capere oblātae segnem spectācula praedae.
uellet abesse quidem, sed adest; uelletque uidēre,
nōn etiam sentīre canum fera facta suōrum.

---

238 *quem*: picks up *sonum*; subj. of characteristic, **RL**140.1, **RLQ**2(a), **W**38
ēdō 3 utter, make
239 **maest-us a um* anguished, unhappy
repleō 2 fill
iug-um ī 2n. ridge
querēl-a ae 1f. cry, complaint
240 *prōn-us a um* bending down
supplex supplic-is supplicating, entreating
241 *circumferō* 3 cast around, look round with (+ acc.)
tacit-us a um silent
brācchia: he has no arms to stretch out; all he can use is his face
242 *rapid-us a um* ferocious, ravening (*rapiō*)

hortāt-us ūs 4m. exhortation, cry of encouragement
agmen agmin-is 3n. pack (of dogs)
243 *īnstigō* 1 urge on
Actaeona: Greek acc. of Actaeon
244 *certātim* in competition
245 *referō* 3 turn back
abesse: 'that [he/Actaeon] is absent', acc. and inf. after *queruntur*; so *capere* (246)
246 *offeror offerrī oblātum* (pass.) come one's way unexpectedly, be heaven-sent
segn-is e slow, late (referring to Actaeon, understood subject of *capere*)
spectācul-um ī 2n. sight, spectacle
praed-a ae 1f. booty, prey
248 **fer-us a um* savage, wild

---

speak, as an animal he cannot). Three dogs, who knew where a deer would go in the circumstances and had taken a short cut, get him/it first, in the back and the side (232–5); and while they hold back 'their master' (235), the rest of the pack converges (236). Actaeon is still trying to communicate as a human with sounds (237–9) – his inarticulate cries now echo around like the dogs' barking (231) – and then tries to use a human gesture – supplication – to save himself (240). A suppliant kneeled before someone whose help he needed, stretching out his arms in appeal, to seize the knees and/or chin of the person he was supplicating. But what dog understands supplication? Besides, Actaeon has no hands with which (absurdly) to seize the canine knee (241) – as if that would have made any difference – and instead tries, pathetically, to appeal with his facial expression (Ovid exploits the same image with the equally helpless Io, passage 3, 1.729–33). As a deer, Actaeon is done for; but he still thinks as a human – and is done for no less. This scene is the stuff of nightmares.

241–52: Ovid saves the most dreadful irony till last: Actaeon's companions wonder where he is and call out for him to join the kill. Note the 'echoing' repetition of *Actaeona*

undique circumstant, mersīsque in corpore rōstrīs,
dīlacerant falsī dominum sub imāgine ceruī,   250
nec, nisi finītā^ per plūrima uulnera ^uītā,
īra pharetrātae fertur satiāta Diānae.

---

249 *undique* on all sides
circumstō 1 stand round
*mergō 3 *mersī mersum* plunge, bury, overwhelm
rōstr-um ī 2n. muzzle
250 *dīlacerō* 1 shred, rip apart
falsī . . . ceruī: note the repeated adj. + noun rhymes
  in this and the next two lines – to any particular
  effect?
*fals-us a um fake, counterfeit
*imāgō imāgin-is 3f. image, guise
252 *pharetrāt-us a um* bequivered. A powerful
  golden line ends the passage
fertur: is said [to be] *satiāta*; more ironical
  'historicising'

Learning vocabulary
clāmō 1 shout, cry out for
coeō coīre gather, come together; be united (often
  sexually)
dēsum dēesse to be unforthcoming, offer no access
  to, lack, fail (+ dat.)
exeō exīre exiī set out
fals-us a um fake, counterfeit
fer-us a um savage, wild
hēu alas!
imāgō imāgin-is 3f. image, guise
maest-us a um anguished, unhappy
mergō 3 *mersī mersum* plunge, bury, overwhelm

Learning vocabulary for Passage 5, Diana and Actaeon

addō 3 *addidī additum* add
arc-us ūs 4m. arch; bow
art-us ūs 4m. limb
aur-is is 3f. ear
Aurōr-a ae 1f. Dawn
caed-ēs is 3f. slaughter
ceru-us ī 2m. stag
clāmō 1 shout, cry out for
coeō coīre gather, come together; be united
  (often sexually)
com-a ae 1f. hair
comes comit-is 3m. comrade
cruor-is 3m. gore

dēsum dēesse to be unforthcoming, offer no
  access to, lack, fail (+ dat.)
dēui-us a um remote, out of the way
Diān-a ae Diana (Artemis), goddess of
  virginity and the hunt
distō 1 be distant from (+ abl.)
ecce behold! look!
error-is 3m. mistake
exeō exīre exiī set out, leave
fals-us a um fake, counterfeit
fer-us a um savage, wild
fess-us a um tired
fōns font-is 3m. spring, fountain

---

quaerunt/clamant 243–4 (looking for him *oculīs*, then shouting for him *absentem*). They
imagine it is *his* fault (*segnem*, 246) that he is not there to enjoy the spectacle (242–6). But
he *is* there, desperately wishing that he were not, or at any rate in different circumstances
(247–8). Ovid exploits this despairing paradox to the full, generating the most intense
pathos at Actaeon's fate: *uelut absentem* (244) and *ad nōmen . . . refert* (245) are especially
heart-rending. *dīlacerant falsī dominum sub imāgine ceruī* (250) makes a terrifying
climax. It is their own master the dogs actually rip apart. No deception there. The fact
that he is an *imāgō* (indeed, the real Actaeon is literally *sub imāgine*) makes no difference
to them. They cannot tell the real from the false. And that is *why* they rip him apart – were
he not an *imāgō*, were he not *falsus*, they would not. Only the helpless, *falsus* Actaeon
knows the truth of the matter. And so his dogs finish him off, and Diana's anger is satisfied (251–2).

Learning vocabulary for Passage 5, Diana and Actaeon (Continued)

frōns front-is 3f. forehead
fundō 3 *fūdī fūsum* pour
hēū alas!
imāgō imāgin-is 3f. image, guise
īnfect-us a um stained, tinged
līn-um ī 2n. net, thread
liquid-us a um clear, fluid
maest-us a um anguished, unhappy
mergō 3 *mersī mersum* plunge, bury,
    overwhelm
mēt-a ae 1f. turning-point

nam moreover, again (indicating a transition)
perfundō 3 bathe; *fundō* 3 *fūdī fūsum* pour
repetō 3 repeat, take up again, seek again
satiō 1 satisfy, fill with
simul as soon as, once
simulō 1 imitate
spars-us a um loose, streaming; scattered
    (*spargō* 3 *sparsī sparsum* sprinkle, scatter)
uagor 1 dep. wander, roam
uirgine-us a um virgin

Study section

1. Write out and scan ll.163–6, 242–6.
2. How does Ovid attempt to manipulate our feelings about Actaeon? Bring in
   the location as well as the portrayal of Diana and of Actaeon's comrades.
3. Take any five lines, consecutive or not, and explain why they give you pleasure (you can enjoy being chilled to the marrow).
4. How closely – or not – has Francesco Mosca been reading his Ovid?

Figure 1   Francesco Mosca, 'Diana and Actaeon'.

3.253–9: *The gods debate Diana's revenge, but Juno rejoices at it*

rūmor in ambiguō est: aliīs uiolentior aequō
uīsa dea est, aliī laudant, dignamque seuērā
uirginitāte uocant; pars inuenit utraque causās.   255
sōla Iouis coniunx nōn tam culpetne probetne
ēloquitur, quam clāde domūs^ ab Agēnore ^ductae
gaudet, et ā Tyriā collectum^ paelice trānsfert
in generis sociōs ^odium.

---

253 *ambigu-us a um* lit. 'going this way and that', i.e.
   marked by doubt
aliīs . . . aliī: 'to some . . . while others'
*uiolent-us a um savage, excessive
aequō: 'than was fair' (abl. of comparison after *uiolentior*)
254 *dignam*: referring to Diana (*uocant* [her]
   dignam)
seuēr-us a um strict, austere
255 *uirginitās uirginitāt-is* 3f. virginity (though
   Diana's virginity was never threatened by Actaeon)
256 *nōn tam . . . quam*: 'so far from *ēloquitur* . . . she
   gaudet'
. . . -ne . . . -ne: 'whether . . . or' (= *utrum . . . an*)
*culpō 1 blame, find fault
*probō 1 approve

257 *ēloquor* 3 dep. express a view
clād-ēs is 3f. disaster (abl. after *gaudet*)
Agēnōr -is 3m. Agenor, father of Cadmus and
   Europa. The latter was another of Jupiter's lovers
   (see Background to passage 5, Diana and
   Actaeon). Hence Juno's pleasure in the death of
   anyone connected with that line – in this case,
   Cadmus' grandson Actaeon (*generis sociōs*
   259)
258 *Tyri-us a um* Tyrian, from Tyre (in
   ancient Phoenicia, modern Lebanon),
   i.e. Europa
trānsferō trānsferre transfer
259 *generis sociōs*: i.e. Europa's relatives
odi-um i 2n. hatred
subeō take the place of, succeed (+ dat.)

253–9: Ovid makes the transition to the story of Semele by contrasting the debate that sprang up among the gods about the justifiability of Diana's revenge on Actaeon (253–5, cf. the river-gods visiting Peneus, **Background** to passage 3). Juno alone refuses judgement, because trouble for any member of Cadmus' family is fine by her (256–8). The reason for this is explained (Jupiter's affair with Cadmus' sister Europa, 258–9); but now Juno has found a *causa recēns* for anger – Jupiter's impregnation of a willing Semele, daughter of Cadmus (259–61). In this way, the thought-processes of Juno make the transition to Semele, and in the event will continue the theme of the previous story – ruthless divine revenge on mortals.

3.259–72: *Juno vows revenge on Jupiter's new lover Semele*

subit ecce priōrī

causa recēns, grauidamque∧ dolet dē sēmine magnī   260
esse Iouis ∧Semelēn; dum linguam ad iūrgia soluit,
'prōfēcī quid enim totiēns per iūrgia?' dīxit,
'ipsa petenda mihi est; ipsam, sī maxima Iūnō
rīte uocor, perdam, sī mē gemmantia∧ dextrā
∧scēptra tenēre decet, sī sum rēgīna Iouisque   265
et soror et coniunx, certē soror! at, puto, fūrtō est
contenta, et thalamī breuis est iniūria nostrī.
concipit (id dērat), manifestaque crīmina plēnō
fert uterō, et māter – quod uix mihi contigit – ūnō
dē Ioue uult fierī: tanta est fidūcia fōrmae.   270

---

260 *recēns recent-is fresh, new (*causa* = reason for grievance). By this device Ovid introduces the story of Cadmus' daughter Semele, who (for a change) is a willing lover of Jupiter

grauid-us a um pregnant

dolet: i.e. it rankles with Juno [that + acc. and inf.]

sēmen sēmin-is 3n. seed

261 *Semelēn*: Greek acc. of Semele

*iūrgi-um ī 2n. abuse, insult (to be directed at Jupiter)

*soluō 3 *soluī solūtum* unleash, release, let go

262 *prōficiō* 3/4 *prōfēcī* achieve

totiēns so many times, so often

263 *ipsa . . . ipsam*: i.e. Semele

sī: note the rising *sī* tricolon (263–6) with anaphora and asyndeton

264 *rīte* properly

gemmāns gemmant-is bejewelled

265 *scēptr-um ī* 2n. sceptre

decet it is right, fitting for X (acc.)

rēgin-a ae 1f. queen

266 *at*: introduces an objection from Semele's point of view ('But [I imagine she will say]'). *putō* is ironic: of course Juno knows Semele will not be content with what she has

fūrt-um ī 2n. theft, deception (i.e. the fact that Jupiter has deceived Juno to have an affair with Semele)

267 *content-us a um* fully satisfied

iniūri-a ae 1f. harm, wrong

268 *concipiō* 3/4 conceive, be pregnant

dērat: = *dēerat*, from *dēsum* 'be lacking'. The idea is 'that was the only thing that hadn't happened (but it had now)', i.e. 'that's all it needed!'

manifest-us a um obvious

269 *uter-us ī* 2m. womb

uix: Juno's children by Jupiter included Vulcan, the lame blacksmith god, Ares the war-god, Hebe, and the goddesses of childbirth

*contingō 3 *contigī* happen (to + dat.), come in touch/contact with

270 *fidūci-a ae* 1f. [Semele's] confidence, trust

259–72: The logic of Juno's justification for revenge goes: (i) 261–2, when I take it out on Jupiter for his affairs, it never makes any difference; (ii) 263–6, my authority as queen, wife and sister of Jupiter is at stake, and gives me the right to destroy Semele. The superb *sī* tricolon takes in Juno's reputation (*maxima . . . uocor*), her authority (*gemmantia . . . scēptra*) and her status as *rēgīna, soror, coniunx*, of Jupiter (a triplet in a tricolon), ending on the spitting fourth 'leg', *certē soror*, as if she were not Jupiter's wife at all. The whole suggests her rising sense of grievance at the insult done to her and justifies (in her own mind) her decision to act. Juno's anger (unlike Diana's in the last passage) seems impossible to assuage; (iii) 266–7, Semele may say she has all she wants (i.e. a child) and has done me little damage, but 268–70 (another tricolon) that is almost more than Jupiter has ever given me; (iv) 270, Semele is far too pleased with her looks anyway. This throwaway remark is a neat Ovidian touch, as if that is what *really* rankles with Juno; but in

fallat eam faxō; nec sum Sāturnia, sī nōn
ab Ioue^ mersa ^suō Stygiās penetrābit in undās.'

3.273–86: *Juno disguises herself and makes a suggestion to Semele*

surgit ab hīs soliō, fuluāque recondita nūbe
līmen adit Semelēs, nec nūbēs ante remōuit
quam simulāuit anum, posuitque ad tempora cānōs,   275
sulcāuitque cutem rūgīs, et curua^ trementī
^membra tulit passū. uōcem quoque fēcit anīlem,
ipsaque erat Beroē, Semelēs Epidauria nūtrīx.
ergō ubi, captātō sermōne diūque loquendō,
ad nōmen uēnēre Iouis, suspīrat et 'optō,   280

---

271 *fallat*: Jupiter is the subject; *fallat* is subj. after *faxō*

faxō: = *fēcerō*, i.e. before Semele has had Jupiter's child, 'I shall have brought it about [that + subj.; *ut* is rare with *faxō*] . . .', **RL**135

272 *mersa . . . undās*: a watery end promised for Semele – and all brought about by Jupiter! In fact Semele's end is a fiery one, but the end result is the same (cf. 290–1)

penetrō 1 sink (into). Cf. Cybele at 10.696–707 (passage 18)

273 *ab his*: = 'after this'

soli-um i 2n. throne

fulu-us a um yellow

recondit-us a um concealed (*recondō*)

274 *līmen līmin-is* 3n. threshold

Semelēs: Greek gen.

ante: take with *quam* 275

remoueō 2 *remōui* remove, disperse

275 *an-us ūs* 4f. old woman

tempor-a um 3n. pl. temples

cān-ī ōrum 2m. pl. grey hair

276 *sulcō* 1 furrow

cut-is is 3f. skin

rūg-a ae 1f. wrinkle

tremēns trement-is trembling

277 *anil-is e* old, quavering

Beroē: Greek nom., Beroē

Semelēs: Greek gen.

Epidauri-us a um from Epidaurus (in Greece)

nūtrix nūtric-is 3f. nurse

279 *loquendō*: lit. 'by talking', but effectively = 'after talking'

280 *suspīrō* 1 heave a sigh

optō 1 wish (that *ut* + subj.)

---

general, in a poem of transformation, no one should have confidence in their *fōrma* . . . even Jupiter, whose *fōrma* will prove Semele's undoing. Conclusion: three crisp words (271) – I shall make certain *Jupiter* destroys her (thus keeping Juno's hands 'clean' and multiplying Jupiter's hurt). Note that the purpose of Juno's complaint is to throw the whole blame for the affair on *Semele*. So Juno characterises what Semele has done as *fūrtum* (266), *iniūria* (267), *crīmina* (268). Since Semele is therefore to blame, she must be punished; and in punishing her, Juno will automatically punish Jupiter too (cf. her opening remarks: merely moaning about Jupiter's behaviour has never achieved anything in the past). There was a time when Juno dealt differently with Jupiter's *amours* (cf. Io, 1.622–4), but even so, sympathy for mortal sisters was never a strong suit among ancient goddesses when their own pride and status were at stake.

273–86: As Jupiter conducted his liaison with Io in a cloud to keep it secret from Juno (1.599–600), so Juno enclouds herself to keep her approach to Semele secret from Jupiter (273–4). Since she needs to win Semele's confidence if her plan is to work, she transforms

Iuppiter ut sit;' ait 'metuō tamen omnia. multī
nōmine diuōrum thalamōs iniēre pudīcōs.
nec tamen esse Iouem satis est. det pignus amōris,
si modo uērus is est: quantusque et quālis ab altā
Iūnōne excipitur, tantus tālisque rogātō   285
det tibi complexūs, suaque ante īnsignia sūmat!'

3.287–96: *Jupiter promises Semele to do whatever she wants – and regrets it*

tālibus^ ignāram Iūnō Cadmēida ^dictīs
fōrmārat: rogat illa Iouem sine nōmine mūnus.

---

281 *multī*: m. pl. – supply the appropriate noun
282 **ineō inīre iniī* enter
pudīc-us a um chaste, innocent
283 *det*: jussive subj., 'let . . .'; **RL**152, W28
pignus pignor-is 3n. proof, guarantee
284 *quantusque et quālis . . . tantus tālisque rogātō*:
'how tall and of what sort he [is when] *excipitur*
. . ., ask that so tall and of that sort he *det . . .*';
rogātō introduces two indirect commands
(*ut* understood)
285 *excipitur*: i.e. into her bed
rogātō: ancient 2s. (so-called 'future') imper. form,
RLA2(i)
286 *complex-us ūs* 4m. embrace
ante: adverbial, 'in your presence'
insigni-a um 3n. pl. regalia (including, inevitably, his
thunderbolt)

Learning vocabulary
contingō 3 *contigī* happen (to + dat.), come in
touch/contact with
culpō 1 blame, find fault
ineō inīre iniī enter
iūrgi-um i 2n. abuse, insult
optō 1 wish
probō 1 approve
recēns recent-is fresh, new
remoueō 2 *remōuī* remove, disperse
soluō 3 *soluī solūtum* unleash, release, let go
uiolent-us a um savage, excessive

287 *Cadmēida*: Greek acc., daughter of Cadmus, i.e.
Semele. This is a fine chiastic line, with Juno right
in the centre – mistress of all she surveys
288 *illa*: change of subject, Semele
sine nōmine: i.e. without naming/specifying what it was

---

herelf into Semele's old and trusted maid Beroē, Ovid picking out the physical features
that signal 'old' (274–8). Juno subtly steers the lengthy conversation (the deceiver must
not hurry things) towards the subject of Jupiter and Semele's pregnancy (279–80), and
plants the seeds of doubt in her mind: what if her lover were not Jupiter (280–2)? A
trusted friend carries conviction with a vulnerable young woman in this situation, and
Juno acts up to the part brilliantly – note the sympathetic *suspīrat* 280 and worried *metuō*
281. Note too the voice of experience at *multī . . . pudīcōs* (281–2): so easy for an innocent young thing to be caught unawares by exploitative males, Beroē/Juno implies. One
can almost hear Juno thinking: the little whore. Juno's suggestion of the proof Semele
should seek is full of irony. First, she herself (it would seem, 266, 269) rarely experienced
Jupiter as lover, but she knew *that* experience would be enough to kill Semele. Second,
with *excipitur* (passive) Beroē/Juno creates a picture of Jupiter as putty in *Juno*'s hands (if
only, Juno might be thinking to herself), hinting that anything Juno can do, surely the
gorgeous Semele could do so much better . . . This is brilliant characterisation.

287–96: In fact poor, *ignaram* (287) Semele is putty in Juno's hands (*fōrmārat* 288 makes
the point). Juno has brilliantly turned the tables on Jupiter by adopting Jupiter's tactic of

cui deus 'ēlige!' ait, 'nūllam patiēre repulsam.
quōque magis crēdās, Stygiī^ quoque cōnscia suntō   290
nūmina ^torrentis; timor et deus ille deōrum est.'
laeta malō, nimiumque potēns, peritūraque amantis
obsequiō, Semelē 'quālem Sāturnia' dīxit
'tē solet amplectī, Veneris cum foedus inītis,
dā mihi tē tālem!' uoluit deus ōra loquentis   295
opprimere: exierat iam uōx properāta sub aurās.

3.297–315: *Jupiter's appearance kills Semele, but he saves the baby*

ingemuit; neque enim nōn haec optāsse, neque ille
nōn iūrāsse potest. ergō maestissimus altum
aethera cōnscendit, uultūque sequentia trāxit
nūbila, quīs nimbōs immixtaque fulgura uentīs   300

289 *ēligō* 3 choose
patiēre: = *patiēris* (*patior* – tense?), RLC2
repuls-a ae 1f. rejection, rebuff
290 *quōque magis*: 'in order that *crēdās* the more . . .',
    RL148; contrast *quoque* (scansion!) later in the line
cōnsci-a um involved, witness
suntō: ancient 3pl. imper., RLE1
291 *torrēns torrent-is* 3m. torrent
timor et deus: the complement of *ille*, who is the river
    Styx (see note on 1.737)
292 *laeta . . . obsequiō*: a terrifying tricolon
*nimium too (much); too much of (+ gen.)
293 *obsequi-um i* 2n. compliance
quālem . . . tālem: see above on 284–5
294 **amplector* 3 dep. embrace
Veneris . . . foedus: pact of Venus, i.e. sexual
    intercourse

296 *exeō exīre exiī* come out, slip out
properāt-us a um hasty (*properō*)
297 *ingemō* 3 *ingemuī* groan
haec . . . ille: i.e. Semele . . . Jupiter
298 *iūrō* 1 swear
299 *cōnscendō* 3 ascend (to + acc.)
uultūque: all Jupiter needs is a facial expression –
    presumably, here, a dark one – for the clouds to
    obey and gather round
300 *quīs*: = *quibus*, dat. pl. after *addidit*, RLI3.
    Jupiter is here summoning the ingredients out of
    which he makes his thunderbolts
nimb-us i 2m. rain-cloud
immixt-us a um mixed with (+ abl.)
fulgur -is 3n. lightning-flash (produced by winds and
    clouds, as Romans believed, and harmless *by
    itself*)

disguise to 'get to' Semele in the first place, and then so arranging matters that (ironically) Jupiter's own undisguised *fōrma* as king of the gods will destroy his mortal lover.
Semele duly falls into the trap, and asks Jupiter to give her a present without telling him
what it is (288 – a typical ploy in ancient literature, the purpose of which is to see how far
the lover will go to demonstrate his love). Without thinking – blinded by passion and
self-importance? – Jupiter concedes the request, sealing it with an oath by the river Styx,
normally used only for oaths between deities (289–91). Juno knew her man. Ovid signals
the moment with a doom-laden, paradoxical tricolon (292–3, *laeta . . . obsequiō*) – con-
tradictions scarcely possible in a normal world, but in the world in which poor Semele
finds herself, all too dreadfully possible (the closing *obsequiō*, first word of 293, is especially powerful). And so Semele makes her fatal request (293–5). Even the king of the
gods could not stop her, much as he would have wished (295–6).

297–315: Jupiter groans, and Ovid hints at his thoughts: Semele wanted it, he swore to it,
but there is no going back now (297–8). No wonder Jupiter is *maestissimus* as he goes

addidit et tonitrūs et inēuītābile fulmen.
quā tamen usque potest, uīrēs sibi dēmere temptat
nec, quō^ centimanum dēiēcerat ^igne Typhōea,
nunc armātur ^eō: nimium feritātis in illō est.
est aliud leuius fulmen, cūi dextra Cyclōpum   305
saeuitiae flammaeque minus, minus addidit īrae:
'tēla secunda' uocant superī; capit illa, domumque
intrat Agēnoream. corpus mortāle tumultūs
non tulit aetheriōs, dōnīsque iugālibus arsit.
imperfectus adhūc īnfāns genetrīcis ab aluō   310
ēripitur, patriōque^ tener (sī crēdere dignum est)
īnsuitur ^femorī, māternaque tempora complet.

---

301 *tonitr-us ūs* 4m. thunder
inēuītābil-is e inescapable. The *fulmen* is the element
   that turns a harmless lightning-flash into a
   destructive thunderbolt
302 *quā . . . usque* as far as
sibi: dat. of loss, RL48.1
dēmō 3 remove, reduce
303 *centiman-us ūs* hundred-handed
dēiciō 3/4 *dēiēci* throw/hurl down
Typhōea: Greek acc. of Typhoeus, a giant who had
   once attempted to dethrone Jupiter
304 *armō* 1 arm
feritās feritāt-is 3f. ferocity
305 *Cyclōp-es um* 3m. Cyclopes, forgers of the thunderbolt
306 *saeuiti-a ae* 1f. savagery
308 *Agēnore-us a um* of Agenor, Semele's grandfather. It is odd to call Thebes 'Agenor's house'
   because Agenor lived in Phoenicia (Lebanon). It
   was Agenor's son Cadmus who founded Thebes
*mortāl-is e mortal, human

tumult-us ūs 4m. assault
309 *aetheri-us a um* ethereal, divine
*dōn-um ī 2n. gift (heavily ironical)
iugāl-is e of marriage. It is not uncommon in myth
   for marriage gifts to kill the bride; Medea sent
   such gifts to her husband's new wife Glauce
*ardeō 2 *ārsī* burst into flames
310 *imperfect-us a um* unformed
*adhūc so far
īnfāns īnfant-is 3m./f. infant, baby. This will turn out
   to be Dionysus/Bacchus, god of transformation,
   drink, etc.
genetrīx genetrīc-is 3f. mother
alu-us ī 2f. womb
311 **tener -a um* delicate
312 *īnsuō* 3 sew into (+ dat.)
femur femor-is 3n. thigh
mātern-us a um mother's. Ovid works the paradox
   of a child inserted *patriō . . . femorī* completing its
   mother's term
compleō 2 complete

---

back to the heavens (298); no wonder he summons his mists without enthusiasm (just a look, *uultū*, is enough), to which he adds the other ingredients that go to make up the devastating thunderbolt itself (298–301). But here Ovid faces a problem. Everyone knew that Semele was carrying the god Bacchus/Dionysus, and that Jupiter saved him from the blast. But if Jupiter is going to blast Semele to smithereens, how will he not destroy the child as well (presumably also part of Juno's plan)? Ovid, uniquely, explains at 302–7: there are different grades of thunderbolt, and Jupiter avoids the heavy-duty number by selecting a lower-grade version invested with less force by the Cyclopes (who forge them). This will kill Semele but allow the child to be saved. And so it happens: her mortal body cannot endure the assault of her marital 'gift' (308–9), but the foetus is saved, sewn into Jupiter's thigh till it comes to term (310–12) and then secretly reared by Semele's sister Ino (313–5) – secretly, because there was no knowing what the vengeful Juno might plan for it.

fūrtim illum prīmīs Īnō mātertera cūnīs
ēducat, inde datum nymphae Nȳsēides antrīs
occuluēre suīs, lactisque alimenta dedēre.   315

313 **fūrtim* secretly. Does this heavily spondaic line
  suggest a sense of conspiracy?
Īnō: Greek nom., Ino
māterter-a ae 1f. mother's sister
cūn-ae ārum 1f. pl. cradle, i.e. early years
314 *ēducō* 1 rear
datum: i.e. the baby
Nȳsēides: Greek nom. pl., 'from Nysa', located by the
  ancients in many parts of the world, e.g. Arabia,
  Libya, Ethiopia. Presumably 'Nysa' was supposed
  to explain Dio*nysus*' name (Greek *dios* means
  'divine')

315 *occulō* 3 *occuluī* hide
lac lact-is 3n. milk
aliment-um ī 2n. nourishment, food

Learning vocabulary
adhūc so far
amplector 3 dep. *amplexus* embrace
ardeō 2 *arsī arsum* burst into flames
dōn-um ī 2n. gift
fūrtim secretly
mortāl-is e mortal, human
nimium too (much) of + gen.
tener -a um delicate

Learning vocabulary for Passage 6, Juno and Semele

adhūc so far
amplector 3 dep. *amplexus* embrace
ardeō 2 *arsī arsum* burst into flames
contingō 3 *contigī* happen (to + dat.), come in
  touch/contact with
culpō 1 blame, find fault
dōn-um ī 2n. gift
fūrtim secretly
ineō inīre iniī initum enter
iūrgi-um ī 2n. abuse, insult

mortāl-is e mortal, human
nimium too (much); too much of +gen.
optō 1 wish
probō 1 approve of, prove
recēns recent-is fresh, new
remoueō 2 *remōuī remōtum* remove, disperse
soluō 3 *soluī solūtum* unleash, release, let go
tener -a um delicate
uiolent-us a um savage, excessive

Study section

1. Write out and scan ll.253–6.
2. Is Semele justly treated? If so, in whose eyes?
3. What do you make of Jupiter in this episode? Does he differ from the Jupiter
   of earlier stories?
4. '[Jupiter] knows that his *uīs*, his sexual power, will be too much for Semele.
   He tries to wear himself out first, by casting thunderbolts around' (Sharrock,
   in Hardie, 2002a, 96). Discuss.

3.316–23: *Jupiter wonders who gets more pleasure out of sex*

dumque ea per terrās fātālī lēge geruntur,
tūtaque bis genitī sunt incūnābula Bacchī,
forte Iouem memorant, diffūsum nectare, cūrās
sēposuisse grauēs, uacuāque∧ agitāsse remissōs
cum ∧Iūnōne iocōs, et 'māior uestra∧ profectō est,   320
quam quae contingit maribus', dīxisse '∧uoluptās.'
illa negat. placuit quae sit sententia doctī∧
quaerere ∧Tīresiae: Venus hūīc erat utraque nōta.

316 *ea*: n. pl. – supply appropriate noun	**319** *sēpōnō* 3 *sēposuī sēpositum* lay aside
fātāl-is e of fate, destiny, deadly. Though no 'law of fate' was involved in Semele's death, it must have been in Dionysus/Bacchus' birth, to which Ovid immediately turns	*agitō* 1 engage in
	remiss-us a um relaxed, casual
	320 *profectō* without doubt
	321 *mās mar-is* 3m. the male of the species
317 *bis genit-us a um* twice-born (i.e. from Semele and then again from Jupiter's thigh)	*uoluptās uoluptāt-is* 3f. pleasure (in love-making)
incūnābul-a ōrum 2n. cradle (i.e. infancy, early years)	**322** *placuit*: controls *quaerere*, introducing the indir. q. *quae sit*
*Bacch-us ī 2m. the god Dionysus/Bacchus	*quae*: refers to *uoluptās*
318 *memorō* 1 recall. Here it is followed by an acc. (*Iouem*) and inf. (*sēposuisse . . . agitāsse . . . dīxisse* 321); for perf. inf. form, see **RLA4**	**323** *Tīresiae*: gen. s. of Tiresias, the famous prophet-to-be, whose great-grandfather was the dragon killed by Cadmus (see **Background** to passage 5).
diffūs-us a um (*diffundō*) flushed, warmed	*Venus* = sex
nectar -is 3n. nectar (the drink of the gods; ambrosia is the food)	*utraque*: i.e. from a male and female point of view (this is about to be explained)

316–23: Destiny has taken its course and Bacchus is safe in his cradle (316–17). Now, 'they say' (more mock history?), Jupiter *cūrās sēposuisse grauēs*. But what 'cares' are these? The 'cares' of ruling the universe (Anderson)? Surely not. Jupiter has just given birth to Bacchus, a physically and mentally demanding enough time for a woman, let alone a man. It is the cares of childbirth he has just laid aside – a good Ovidian joke – with the help of a tot of nectar (318). Now, in party mood (320), Jupiter raises a not unrelated issue with Juno: who gets more pleasure out of sex (320–2)? Thus does Jupiter's reflection on the consequences of the Semele story smoothly effect the transition to the story of Tiresias who, being an expert on the matter of sexual pleasure (322–3), is summoned to give his verdict.

3.324–31: *The choice of Tiresias as judge is explained*

nam duo magnōrum∧ uiridī* coeuntia *siluā
corpora ∧serpentum baculī uiolāuerat ictū;   325
dēque uirō factus (mīrābile) fēmina, septem
ēgerat autumnōs. octāuō rūrsus eōsdem
uīdit, et 'est uestrae sī tanta potentia plāgae'
dīxit, 'ut auctōris sortem in contrāria mūtet,
nunc quoque uōs feriam.' percussīs anguibus īsdem,   330
fōrma prior rediit, genetīuaque uēnit imāgō.

3.332–8: *Juno punishes Tiresias, but Jupiter compensates*

arbiter hīc igitur, sūmptus dē līte iocōsā,
dicta Iouis firmat: grauius Sāturnia iūstō,

324 *duo . . . serpentum* (325): this long phrase, the object of *uiolāuerat* (325), is as long and as (grammatically) intertwined as the serpents
*uirid-is e green
325 **serpēns serpent-is* 3m./f. snake (*serpō* 3 crawl)
bacul-um ī 2n. stick
uiolō 1 hit, violate. Note the plupf. tense, identifying this as temporal background to the story; so *ēgerat* 327
ict-us ūs 4m. blow. This comes as a short, sharp thump, instantly concluding the lengthy intertwinings of 324–5
326 *factus . . . fēmina*: a witty agreement!
*mīrābil-is e wonderful, amazing
327 *autumn-us ī* 2m. autumn
octāuō: 'in the eighth [autumn]'

328 *plāg-a ae* 1f. blow. *uestrae . . . plāgae* construes with *potentia*, i.e. 'in hitting you'
329 *auctor -is 3m. originator (i.e. person who originally hit you)
in contrāria: 'to the opposite'
330 *feriō* 4 strike, hit
angu-is is 3.m./f. snake
331 *genetiu-us a um* original, with which X was born
332 *arbiter arbitr-ī* 2m. judge
līs līt-is 3f. quarrel, lawsuit
iocōs-us a um playful, jocular
333 *firmat*: in many versions of the story, Tiresias says that if there are ten units of pleasure in making love, the woman gets nine
iūstō: abl. of comparison after *grauius*

324–31: Tiresias' story – that he was changed into a woman when he beat two copulating snakes and changed back again when he repeated the trick seven years later (324–31) – was widely reported in ancient sources (in India and the Himalayas, it is thought to be very unlucky to see snakes copulating, and rituals are recommended to avoid the consequences). Ovid, sadly, does not go any more deeply into the reason for the change, nor the technicalities of it, nor does he expand on the new life Tiresias presumably led as a woman, but he is able to describe how Tiresias was restored to male form: he reasoned, logically, that beating copulating snakes changed the sex of the beater (328–30).

332–8: Tiresias' confirmation of Jupiter's view that women have more fun infuriates Juno (334) – a reaction judged at the time to be out of all proportion (*fertur*, 333), a view that apparently chimes with Ovid's view too (it was all a joke: *iocōsā*, 332). Why this reaction from Juno? Tiresias, after all, should know the answer (that was why he was called in to judge), and Juno does not deny his conclusion. Had Tiresias given away woman's great secret? (Greek and Roman males regularly claimed women were much keener on

nec prō māteriā, fertur doluisse, suīque
iūdicis aeternā damnāuit lūmina nocte.   335
at pater omnipotēns (neque enim licet irrita cūīquam∧
facta deī fēcisse ∧deō) prō lūmine adēmptō
scīre futūra dedit, poenamque leuāuit honōre.

---

334 *prō māteriā*: 'in proportion to the issue'
335 *iūdicis*: i.e. Tiresias, gen. after *lūmina*
aetern-us a um everlasting
damnō 1 condemn X (acc.) to Y (abl.)
336 *omnipotēns omnipotent-is* all-powerful

*irrit-us a um undone, vain; *irrita faciō* = 'make undone', 'nullify'
337 *adēmpt-us a um* removed (*adimō*)
338 *scire*: understand Tiresias as subject
*leuō 1 relieve, lighten, raise

---

sex than men.) Does it turn Jupiter's pursuit of women into a selflessly philanthropical exercise, since he gives them so much more pleasure than they him? Does Juno feel she is missing out, given how rarely she and Jupiter made love (see 3.266)? Or is it that she just hates anyone to do with Cadmus (see note on Agenor, 3.257)? Whatever the reason, Juno is bent on revenge for the smallest perceived slight. At least Jupiter, who is unable to undo another god's actions (336–7), is able to compensate Tiresias by other means. From now on, Tiresias may be blind, but not when it comes to seeing into the future – a great honour for any mere mortal (338).

Here, then, is another tale of a god's revenge on an innocent human, and an even less justified one, to judge by Ovid's comment on the 'amusing contest'. It is to be noted that the earlier Greek poet Callimachus offered a different explanation for Tiresias' blindness: he saw Athena/Minerva bathing naked on Mount Helicon and was struck blind (cf. Actaeon and Diana, passage 5). When Tiresias' mother objected to the punishment, Minerva explained that she had no hand in the matter – it was an immutable law of the gods – but agreed to give him the gift of prophecy and long life.

Learning vocabulary for Passage 7, Tiresias

auctor -is 3m. originator
Bacch-us ī 2m. the god Dionysus/Bacchus
irrit-us a um undone, vain
leuō 1 relieve, lighten, raise

mirābil-is e wonderful, amazing
serpēns serpent-is 3m./f. snake
uirid-is e green

Study section

1. Write out and scan ll.316–19.
2. Use previous metamorphoses to compose an Ovidian-style 'what if', describing how Tiresias changed into a woman (or back into a man).
3. Is Tiresias punished as a sign that he 'woefully lacks basic knowledge about men, women and sex' (Anderson)? Or because he 'clearly believed the

privileges of masculinity outweighed these (unexplained) pleasures [sc. that women got from sex]' (Fantham, 2004, 61)? Or does Ovid not tell us? And if so, why not?

4. You are a Roman woman. Respond to the stories of Actaeon, Semele and Tiresias.

5. Speculate why Ovid changes Callimachus' version of the story so radically.

3.339–50: *Liriope gives birth to Narcissus; Tiresias' strange prophecy*

ille, per Aoniās fāmā celeberrimus urbēs,
irreprehēnsa^ dabat populō ^respōnsa petentī.   340
prima^ fidē uōcisque ratae temptāmina sūmpsit
^caerula ^Līriopē, quam quondam flūmine curuō
implicuit clausaeque suīs Cēphīsos in undīs
uim tulit. ēnīxa est uterō pulcherrima^ plēnō
īnfantem ^nymphē, iam tunc quī posset amārī,   345
Narcissumque uocat. dē quō cōnsultus, an esset
tempora^ mātūrae uīsūrus ^longa senectae,
fātidicus uātēs 'sī sē nōn nōuerit' inquit.
uāna diū uīsa est uōx auguris. exitus illam
rēsque probat lētīque genus nouitāsque furōris.   350

---

339 *ille*: i.e. Tiresias
Aoni-us a um from Boeotia (the *Aones* being an abo-
  riginal Boeotian tribe)
celeber celebr-is e thronged, famous
340 *irreprehēns-us a um* faultless
341 *fidē*: archaic gen. s. of *fidēs*
rat-us a um authoritative, trusted
temptāmina sūmō 3 make a trial (of)
342 *caerul-us a um* sea-green
Liriopē: Greek nom., Liriope, mother of Narcissus by
  Cephisus; *caerula Liriopē* makes for a lovely,
  liquid sound
*quondam once (upon a time)
343 *implicō* 1 *implicuī* enfold, wrap round (the
  subject is Cephisus)
*claudō 3 *clausī clausum* enclose, trap. *clausaeque*
  (dat.) refers to Liriope and depends on *uim tulit*
Cēphīsos: Greek nom., Cephisus, a river (god) in
  Boeotia
344 *uim ferō* bring force to bear on, rape (+ dat.)
ēnītor 3 dep. *ēnīxus* give birth to

uter-us ī 2m. womb
345 *īnfāns īnfant-is* 3 m./f. infant, baby (to be picked
  up by *quī*)
posset: generic subj. after *quī*, 'the sort of baby that
  . . .', **RL**140.1, **RLQ**2(a), **W**38
346 **Narciss-us ī* 2m. Narcissus
cōnsulō 3 *cōnsuluī cōnsultum* consult (the subject is
  Tiresias, *fātidicus uātēs* 348)
347 *mātūr-us a um* ripe, mellow; an optimistic,
  expansive golden line
senect-a ae 1f. old age
348 *fātidic-us a um* oracular
*uāt-ēs is 3m. prophet, seer
349 *uān-us a um* hollow, foolish
augur -is 3m./f. prophet
exit-us ūs 4m. outcome
illam: = *uōcem*
350 *rēs*: i.e. the subject-matter of the prophecy
  (nom.)
lēt-um ī 2n. death
nouitās nouitāt-is 3f. novelty

339–50: Ovid makes the transition to the story of Narcissus by stating that Teiresias'
new-found prophetic powers brought him tremendous fame (339–40), and giving an
example. Liriope, Ovid says, was the first to put Tiresias to the test (341–2) after she had
been raped by a river-god (341–4) and borne Narcissus. Even as a tiny baby, he was

3.351–61: *Narcissus rejects all lovers; then Echo falls for him*

namque ter ad quīnōs ūnum Cēphīsius annum
addiderat, poteratque puer iuuenisque uidērī.
multī illum iuuenēs, multae cupiēre puellae;
sed fuit in tenerā tam dūra superbia fōrmā,
nūllī illum iuuenēs, nūllae tetigēre puellae.   355
adspicit hunc trepidōs agitantem in rētia ceruōs
uōcālis nymphē, quae nec reticēre loquentī
nec prior ipsa loquī didicit, resonābilis Ēchō.
corpus adhūc Ēchō, nōn uōx erat; et tamen ūsum∧
garrula nōn ∧alium, quam nunc habet, ∧ōris habēbat,   360
reddere dē multīs ut uerba nouissima posset.

---

351 *ter ad quīnōs*: to the three-times five, i.e. fifteen (years)
Cēphīsius: son of Cephisus, i.e. Narcissus
352 *addiderat*: note the 'background' plupf.; there will be perfs. in 353–5; in 356 we come to the present
354 *tenerā tam dūra*: a clever antithesis
superbi-a ae 1f. pride
356 **adspiciō* 3/4 *adspexī adspectum* observe, catch sight of, see
trepid-us a um frightened
agitō 1 drive
rēt-e is 3n. net

357 *uōcāl-is e* talkative
reticeō 2 stay silent (in the presence of + dat.). *reticēre* and *loquī* are infs., dependent on *didicit* 358
358 *discō* 3 *didicī* learn how to (+ inf.)
resonābil-is e able [only] to repeat sounds
Ēchō: Greek nom. s., Echo
360 *garrul-us a um* chatty
nōn alium quam: 'no different from that [*ūsum . . . ōris*] which'
361 *ut*: 'namely, that [she] . . .'; the 'explanatory' *ut* clause enlarges on *ūsum*
dē multīs: supply *uerbīs*
nouissima: i.e. 'the very last/final'

---

lovable (345; note that Liriope is *pulcherrima* herself, 344) – and it is that capacity to *be* loved which will undo him, because of his unwillingness to love in return. Teiresias' reply to Liriope's understandably infatuated maternal request (346–7) is incomprehensible as it stands (often the nature of prophecy) (348–9), since, usually, it is *not* knowing oneself that leads to disaster (cf. Oedipus; does 'know' here have a sexual sense too? It can carry that meaning in Latin). But in this case it is the only thing that will save Narcissus. Ovid teases us further: Narcissus' death will be of an especially strange and novel type (349–50). In both these ways, Ovid whets the reader's appetite for the story ahead. Observe that, if Ovid has wandered somewhat off-theme here – Narcissus is not a member of Cadmus' family – his subject-matter (disastrous sexual engagements) will remain broadly on-theme, even if avenging deities feature only marginally (406).

351–61: To be attractive to both men and women, Narcissus needs to be poised on the edge of manhood: aged sixteen (351), he is man enough for the females, but still boy enough for the males (the pattern of attraction that holds in the ancient world). So, as *puer* and *iuuenis* (352) Narcissus attracts both sexes equally (note the equal balance of 353), but because of the pride and hardness (*dūra*) of character that goes with his *tenerā* form (354) – a typically sharp Ovidian antithesis – he also keeps them at bay equally (355). *superbia* has strong overtones of Greek *hubris*, that proud, self-willed arrogance that always leads to disaster: Narcissus is his own worst enemy, and his *superbia* will be his undoing. All this

3.362–9: *How Juno had punished Echo for aiding Jupiter's affairs*

(fēcerat hoc Iūnō, quia, cum dēprendere posset
sub Ioue saepe suō nymphās in monte iacentēs,
illa deam longō prūdēns sermōne tenēbat,
dum fugerent nymphae. postquam hoc Sāturnia sēnsit,   365
'hūius' ait 'linguae, quā sum dēlūsa, potestās
parua tibi dabitur, uōcisque breuissimus ūsus,'
rēque minās firmat. tantum haec in fine loquendī
ingeminat uōcēs audītaque uerba reportat.)

3.370–8: *Echo's silent passion for Narcissus*

ergō ubi Narcissum per dēuia rūra uagantem   370
uīdit et incaluit, sequitur uestīgia fūrtim;

---

362 *Iūnō*: as usual, she blames the women whom
Jupiter seduces as much as Jupiter (cf. **Comment**
on Semele, passage 6, second para., pp. 103–4)
363 *sub Ioue . . . suō*: literally!
364 *illa*: i.e. Echo
365 *prūdēns prudent-is* deliberate(ly), i.e. Echo was
acting in the interests of her fellow-nymphs (and,
whether intentionally or not, of Jupiter too)
fugerent: note the subj. with *dum*, **RL**165.2
366 *dēlūs-us a um* tricked (*dēlūdō*)

potestās potestāt-is 3f. power. It controls *hūius . . .*
linguae
368 *rēque*: 'and by action' (*rēs*)
min-a ae 1f. threat
tantum only
haec: Echo, subject
369 *reportō* 1 repeat
370 *rūs rūr-is* 3n. countryside
371 **(in)calēscō 3 incaluī* become hot, excited (with
desire)

---

is highly reminiscent of the erotic love-poetry Ovid had written in his early career, when
obstinacy and jealousy were always making 'true love' impossible to find. Note the
balance of 353 and 355, a sort of linguistic 'mirror image' of what Narcissus will see in the
water, while *cupiēre* and *tetigēre* foreshadow precisely the conflict Narcissus will himself
experience. Like most young men in *Metamorphōsēs*, Narcissus spends his days in hunting
(356, though Narcissus will turn out to be strangely pale for a hunter, 419, 423), and this
is how the nymph Echo spots him (356–7). Ovid at once indicates her disability – she can
only reply to what others say – and points out that at this stage she has a body (357–61).
Ovid here lays the ground for future developments. She will act in one respect as a sort of
alter-Narcissus, since they both have a limited capacity to respond (she only to what she
has heard, he only to himself); but sexually her outlook is quite different.

362–9: How did Echo's plight come about? At 362–9, Ovid tells her story, cleverly insert-
ing another transformation. When Jupiter was seducing nymphs in the mountains, she
would delay Juno by engaging her in lengthy conversations (362–5). When Juno realised
what was going on, she reduced her speech to the ability only to repeat the last words of
anything she heard another person say (366–9). We have already met Juno vengefully
exacting cruel punishments on those who cross her (e.g. Io, Semele and Tiresias).

370–92: What if a nymph, falling madly in love with a human (370–2 + fire simile 373–4),
wanted to make her feelings felt but could only repeat what *he* said? She would feel

quōque magis sequitur, flammā propiōre calēscit,
nōn aliter quam cum, summīs circumlita∧ taedīs,
admōtās rapiunt ∧uīuācia ∧sulphura flammās.
ō quotiēns uoluit blandīs accēdere dictīs   375
et mollēs adhibēre precēs! nātūra repugnat,
nec sinit incipiat sed, quod sinit, illa parāta est
exspectāre sonōs, ad quōs sua uerba remittat.

3.379–92: *Echo fails to seduce Narcissus when he does speak*

forte puer, comitum sēductus ab agmine fīdō,
dīxerat: 'ecquis adest?' et 'adest' responderat Ēchō.   380
hīc stupet, utque aciem partēs dīmittit in omnēs,
uōce 'uenī!' magnā clāmat; uocat illa uocantem.
respicit et, rūrsus nūllō ueniente, 'quid' inquit
'mē fugis?' et totidem, quot dīxit, uerba recēpit.

372 *quō-que magis*: + ind., 'by how much the more',
'the more'; *quō* is abl. of difference, **RL**100B.5,
WSuppl.syntax
373 *circumlit-us a um* smeared, daubed onto (+ dat.)
taed-a ae 1f. torch
374 *uīuāx uīuāc-is* tenacious, lively
sulphur -is 3n. sulphur (subject), i.e. when a flame is
brought near a torch smeared with sulphur, the
sulphur immediately catches fire
375 **quotiēns* how often
bland-us a um winning
376 *adhibeō* 2 apply, use
377 *sinō* 3 allow (*sc.* 'her') to + subj.
incipiō 3/4 begin, initiate (the conversation)
quod sinit: i.e. what her *nātūra* does allow
illa: she, i.e. Echo
378 **son-us ī* 2m. sound (i.e. words)
*remittō 3 send back, return. This is subj. because the
ad quōs clause indicates the purpose that Echo has
in mind

Learning vocabulary
adspiciō 3/4 *adspexī adspectum* observe, catch sight
of, see

claudō 3 *clausī clausum* enclose, trap
(in)calēscō 3 *incaluī* become hot, excited (with
desire)
Narciss-us ī 2m. Narcissus
quondam once (upon a time)
quotiēns how often
remittō 3 send back, return
son-us ī 2m. sound
uāt-ēs is 3m. prophet, seer

379 *sēduct-us a um* separated (*sēdūcō*). Note the
prefix *sē-*, 'apart'
agmen agmin-is 3n. line, column
fid-us a um trusty, loyal
380*ecquis*: '[Is] anyone?'; note the effective chiastic
line – A *dīxerat*/B *adest*/B *adest*/A *responderat*,
helping create an 'echo' effect
381 *stupeō* 2 be amazed, startled
382 *uōce* . . . *uocantem*: note the cleverly 'responding' play on *uōx*/ *uocō*
383 *respiciō* 3/4 look back
*rūrsus again
384 **totidem* the same number of [*uerba*]

dreadfully frustrated, obviously (375–6), but all she could do would be to wait for him to
speak (377–8), and try to turn it to her advantage. And so it happens. Ovid constructs a
situation in which Narcissus has become separated from his companions and calls out if
there is anyone present (*ecquis adest?*). The nymph replies *adest* ('There is [someone]
present', 380). This initial exchange is conducted in the pluperfect *dīxerat* . . . *responderat*
(379–80), but now Ovid zooms us right into the present (381 *stupet*). And so the play on
words goes on (note how 385 *dēceptus imāgine uōcis* foreshadows Narcissus' own fate,
'looks' replacing 'voice'), till the *double entendre* of *coeāmus* (386) meets with a joyous

perstat et, alternae dēceptus imāgine uōcis,   385
'hūc coeāmus' ait; nūllīque^ libentius umquam
respōnsūra* ^sonō, 'coeāmus!' rettulit *Ēchō,
et uerbīs fauet ipsa suīs, ēgressaque siluā
ībat, ut iniceret spērātō brācchia collō.
ille fugit, fugiēnsque 'manūs complexibus aufer!   390
ante' ait 'ēmoriar, quam sit tibi cōpia nostrī.'
rettulit illa nihil nisi 'sit tibi cōpia nostrī!'

3.393–401: *Rejected Echo fades away into a voice*

sprēta latet siluīs, pudibundaque frondibus ōra
prōtegit, et sōlis ex illō uīuit in antrīs.
sed tamen haeret amor crēscitque dolōre repulsae.   395
extenuant uigilēs corpus miserābile cūrae,
addūcitque cutem maciēs, et in āera sūcus

---

385 *perstō* 1 persist
altern-us a um alternating, reciprocating
386 **hūc* (to) here
libentius more willingly
388 *faueō* 2 back up, act in support of (+ dat.)
siluā: i.e. *from* the wood ('true' ablative, **RL**100A,
   survey of uses [a])
389 *iniciō* 3/4 throw X (acc.) round Y (abl.). Note
   that *in-* scans heavy because it is treated as if it is
   iniiciō (i.e. *in* + *iaciō*, whose first *i* is consonantal)
390 *complex-us ūs* 4m. embracing
391 *ante . . . quam*: take these two words together,
   controlling the result-type clause beginning *sit*,
   RL165.3
ēmorior 3/4 dep. die. Is this subj. here or fut.? What
   would be the difference in meaning?
*cōpi-a ae 1f. control over, use of (X gen.) for sexual

purposes. Note how Echo cleverly turns the *sit* of
Narcissus' *antequam* clause into a wish (**RL**153)
by omitting the *antequam*
393 *sprēt-us a um* rejected (*spernō*)
pudibund-us a um embarrassed
frōns frond-is 3f. leaf
394 *prōtegō* 3 cover
ex illō: 'from then on'
395 **haereō* 2 cling on; stay put
repulsa-a ae 1f. rejection
396 *extenuō* 1 make thin
uigil -is keeping [her] awake
*miserābil-is e pitiful
397 *addūcō* 3 tighten, shrink, contract
cut-is is 3f. skin
maci-ēs -ēī 5f. thinness
sūc-us ī 2m. juice

---

coeāmus! from Echo (387), who launches herself at him (388–9). Even his verbal efforts
to shake her off only encourage her the more (391–2). Poor Echo! She thinks they are
speaking the same language, and so they are, but not in the sense she imagines. Note that
Narcissus says he will die before he has sex (391). Ironically, he will indeed.

393–401: Which leads to another transformation: Echo now fades away, leaving only
sound and rocks behind. Ovid tracks the emotional and physical stages. Emotionally
Echo feels the rejection and the shame and hides in caves (393–4), but her love for
Narcissus merely grows because of her rejection (395, a typical Ovidian paradox).
Physically, she seems to be decomposing, like a dead body: sleepless, she becomes emaci-
ated (397); her flesh shrivels as its moisture dissipates into the air, leaving only a voice
and bones (397–8), and even then her bones turn into what looks like stone (399, cf.

corporis omnis abit. uōx tantum atque ossa supersunt:
uōx manet, ossa ferunt lapidis trāxisse figūram.
inde latet siluīs, nūllōque in monte uidētur,   400
omnibus audītur; sonus est, quī uīuit in illā.

3.402–6: *Narcissus is cursed by a rejected lover*

sīc hanc, sīc aliās∧ undīs aut montibus ∧ortās
lūserat hīc ∧nymphās, sīc cōetūs ante uirilēs;
inde manūs aliquis dēspectus ad aethera tollēns
'sīc amet ipse licet, sīc nōn potiātur amātō!'   405
dīxerat: adsēnsit precibus Rhamnūsia iūstīs.

---

399 *manet*: i.e. *only* her voice remained unaltered
lapis lapid-is 3f. stone
400 *latet*: i.e. she *remains* hidden there (where she
had taken refuge at 393)
401 *omnibus*: dat. of agent ('by everyone',
RLL(e)(iv), W24), or locative (RLL(g), W37) 'in
all [mountains]'? The latter has much to be said
for it
402 *hanc*: 'her', i.e. Echo, object (like *aliās nymphās*
and *cōetūs*) of *lūserat*, of which the subject is
Narcissus
undīs aut montibus: i.e. river- and mountain-
nymphs
403 *hīc*: i.e. Narcissus
sīc . . . ante: 'so [too as he had] previously'
cōet-us ūs 4m. crowd; sexual relations
uiril-is e of/with men
404 *dēspect-us a um* despised (*dēspiciō*). Observe that
it is a man who is speaking

405 *licet*: + subj. (no *ut*, cf. RLF2) effectively
expresses a wish here, 'let him', 'may he'; *amō*
here = fall in love
potiātur: jussive subj.; *sīc . . . sīc* of 405 echoes the
triple *sīc* of 402–3. Narcissus' deceitful (403)
behaviour is about to reap its own reward
406 *adsentiō* 4 *adsēnsi* assent to (+ dat.)
Rhamnūsi-a ae 1f. Nemesis, goddess of vengeance.
She had a temple at Rhamnus (in Attica)

Learning vocabulary
cōpi-a ae 1f. control over, use of (X gen.) for sexual
purposes
ecquis: '[Is] anyone?'
haereō 2 cling on; stay put
hūc (to) here
miserābil-is e pitiful
rūrsus again
totidem the same number of

1.409). The bones do this, presumably, not in skeleton form but as a rock formation, it
being in rocky territory particularly that one hears echoes. In this form, sound + rocks,
she stays hidden in the woods where she had earlier taken refuge (393), and that is why,
Ovid explains, you never see her in the mountains; you only hear her (400–1). All that
(paradoxically) 'lives' in her is *sonus*.

402–6: Narcissus, who treats everyone like this (402–3), is riding for a fall, and eventually
one of his would-be male lovers despairingly curses him, praying that he may experience
what he inflicts on others (404–5: the five repeated *sics* of 402–5 is especially effective).
The goddess of vengeance, Nemesis, is listening to these *iūstīs* prayers (406). We may
ask – *iūstīs* in whose eyes? Nemesis'? (Yes, surely); Ovid's as well? Anyway, Nemesis now
has all that she needs in order to act, and is never mentioned again. But this throws up a
serious challenge for the poet: given that Narcissus automatically rejects all advances,
how can he possibly suffer at the hands of others in the way others have suffered because
of him?

3.407–14: *Narcissus comes across a cool, clear spring*

fōns erat illīmis, nitidīs argenteus undīs,
quem neque pāstōrēs neque pāstae monte capellae
contigerant aliudue pecus, quem nūlla uolucris
nec fera turbārat, nec lāpsus ab arbore rāmus.   410
grāmen erat circā, quod proximus ūmor alēbat,
siluaque sōle locum passūra tepēscere nūllō.
hīc puer, et studiō uēnandī lassus et aestū,
prōcubuit, faciemque locī fontemque secūtus.

3.415–26: *Narcissus sees himself in the pool and is amazed*

dumque sitim sēdāre cupit, sitis altera crēuit,   415
dumque bibit, uīsae correptus imāgine fōrmae,
spem sine corpore amat, corpus putat esse, quod umbra est.
adstupet ipse sibī, uultūque immōtus eōdem
haeret, ut ē Pariō fōrmātum marmore signum;

---

407 *fōns erat*: the typical start for the description of a *locus amoenus* (and therefore trouble; see Introduction, p. 8)
illīmis slime-free
nitid-us a um glittering
argente-us a um silvery
408 *pāst-us a um* grazing (*pāscor*)
monte: abl. of place, **RL**100A(b)
capell-a ae 1f. goat
409 *pecus pecor-is* 3n. herd, animals
uolucr-is is 3f. bird
410 *turbō 1 disturb. *turbā(ue)rat* is plupf.
rām-us ī 2m. branch
411 *grāmen grāmin-is* 3n. grass
ūmor -is 3m. water
alō 3 feed, nourish
412 *passūra*: 'always ensuring that'; this is a calm,

changeless world
tepēscō 3 grow warm
413 *uēnor* 1 dep. hunt
lass-us a um tired
414 *prōcumbō* 3 *prōcubuī* lie down
secūtus: i.e. attracted by
415 *sit-is is 3f. thirst
sēdō 1 slake
416 *corrept-us a um* fascinated, arrested (*corripiō*)
fōrmae: i.e. his own *fōrma*
418 *adstupeō* 2 be amazed at, enthralled by (+ dat.)
immōt-us a um motionless. *uultū . . . eōdem* indicates another motionless feature
419 *Pari-us a um* from Paros (an island in the Aegean, famous for its superb marble used only in the finest statues)
marmor -is 3n. marble

407–14: Ovid sets the scene for Narcissus' demise in the typical *locus amoenus* – cool, shady, grassy and so on (see Introduction, p. 8), the whole grammatically ordered with great skill to emphasise the untouched 'virginity' of the landscape. Ovid gives the water-feature top billing with a four-line description emphasising its purity, seclusion and stillness (407–10), and draws attention to Narcissus' thirst (413–14) – important preparation for what is to come. Note also *faciem* (413): appearances will play a large part in subsequent events.

415–26: From here on Ovid is in literary heaven: a young man looks into the water in which he is slaking his thirst and gradually falls in love with what he sees – himself (one can imagine him watching the surface as it clears, and then ruffling it as he drinks, then

spectat, humī positus, geminum – sua lūmina – sīdus,   420
et dignōs∧ Bacchō, dignōs et Apolline ∧crīnēs,
impūbēsque genās, et eburnea colla, decusque
ōris, et in niueō mixtum candōre rubōrem;
cūnctaque mīrātur, quibus est mīrābilis ipse.
sē cupit imprūdēns et, quī probat, ipse probātur;   425
dumque petit, petitur; pariterque accendit et ardet.

3.427–36: *Vainly, Narcissus tries to kiss and embrace the image*

irrita fallācī quotiēns dedit ōscula fontī,
in mediīs∧ quotiēns uīsum captantia* collum

---

421 *et Apolline*: 'of Apollo as well' – Apollo having
   much more celebrated locks than Bacchus
422 *impūb-is* beardless
gen-a ae 1f. cheek
eburne-us a um ivory
decus decor-is 3n. glory, distinction, grace
423 *niue-us a um* snowy
*mixt-us a um mixed (*misceō*)

*candor -is 3m. radiance, whiteness
424 **mīrābil-is e* admirable
425 *imprūdēns imprūdent-is* ignorant, unaware
426 **pariter* equally
accendō 3 set on fire
427 *fallāx fallāc-is* deceitful, spurious
428 **captō* 1 try to get hold of

---

seeing it clear again, while self-love slowly grows, 415–16, cf. 475–86). We must presume that this is the first time Narcissus has *ever* seen himself. Ovid is laying the ground for a series of brilliantly ingenious ironies and paradoxes on the subject of Narcissus' unconscious self-admiration, active matching passive, subject and object becoming one and the same thing. Such a scenario offers the poet full scope for playing with both the emotion (love) and the verbal possibilities (reflexive action/behaviour, paradox, antithesis, irony) that seem to give him most pleasure. Off he goes, pen exploding with possibilities: *sitis . . . sitis altera* (415), *uīsae . . . imāgine* (416), *corpore . . . corpus, spem . . . umbra* (417), *ipse sibi* (418). At 419, Narcissus is as motionless as a masterpiece of the sculptor's art – Ovid suggesting the way Narcissus sees himself in the water? Note that this image tells us nothing about Narcissus' pallor: ancient statues were painted. The self-admiration continues at 420–3 – one can almost see Narcissus checking off each feature and thoroughly approving of his eyes like constellations, hair like the gods', etc. *mīrātur . . . mīrābilis* (424) brings the sequence to a climax, and at 425 we turn to the disastrous consequences (marked by *imprūdēns*) – *sē cupit, probat . . . probātur* (425), *petit . . . petitur*, and finally *accendit et ardet* (426). He is done for. This is a brilliant *tour de force*, prevented (just) from becoming a *tour de farce* because of the pathos and human sympathy that Ovid evokes: Narcissus' love looks perfect because it is so symmetrical, so exactly matched and returned, but that is why it is impossible. The exquisite irony underlying it all is that Narcissus himself is suffering at his *own* hands, in precisely the same way that others have suffered at his own hands too. It is pay-back time, and it is Narcissus who pays back himself as he gazes down on the image lying beneath him in the pool (452, *resupīnō*).

427–36: Admiration leads to action: Narcissus attempts to kiss and embrace his image, but finds he cannot (427–9: lovely irony in *nec sē dēprendit*). At this, all the positives of

*brācchia mersit ^aquīs, nec sē dēprendit in illīs!

quid uideat, nescit; sed quod uidet, ūritur illō,   430

atque oculōs īdem, quī dēcipit, incitat error.

crēdule, quid frūstrā simulācra fugācia captās?

quod petis, est nūsquam; quod amās, āuertere, perdēs!

ista repercussae, quam cernis, imāginis umbra est.

nīl habet ista suī; tēcum uēnitque manetque;   435

tēcum discēdet, sī tū discēdere possīs!

3.437–53: *Narcissus cannot tear himself away and mourns his fate*

nōn illum Cereris, nōn illum cūra quiētis

abstrahere inde potest sed, opācā fūsus in herbā,

spectat inexplētō mendācem lūmine fōrmam,

perque oculōs perit ipse suōs; paulumque leuātus   440

---

430 *quid uideat . . . quod uidet*: enjoy the contrast between the (vague) subj. and (definitive) ind. here

431 *incitō* 1 spur on

432 *crēdul-us a um* naïve

*simulācr-um ī 2n. image, likeness

*fugāx fugāc-is fleeting

433 *āuertor* 3 dep. turn away. *āvertere* is imper., virtually a conditional clause, with *perdēs* the main verb

434 *repercuss-us a um* reflected (*repercutiō*)

*cernō 3 *crēuī crētum* discern, perceive

435 *nīl . . . suī*: lit. 'nothing of itself/its own', i.e. no real substance of its own; *ista* (i.e. *umbra*) is the subject

Learning vocabulary

candor -is 3m. radiance, whiteness

captō 1 try to get hold of

cernō 3 *crēuī crētum* discern, perceive

fugāx fugāc-is fleeting

mirābil-is e admirable

mixt-us a um mixed (*misceō*)

pariter equally

simulācr-um ī 2n. image, likeness

sit-is is 3f. thirst

turbō 1 disturb

437 *illum*: i.e. Narcissus

Cerēs Cerer-is 3f. Ceres, god of harvest, i.e. bread. *Cereris*, like *quiētis*, depends on *cūra*

438 *abstrahō* 3 drag away

opāc-us a um shady

fūs-us a um spread out (*fundō*)

439 *inexplēt-us a um* insatiable

mendāx mendāc-is deceptive, lying

440 *paulum* a little

---

the previous lines turn negative, starting with *irrita fallācī* (427): his eyes deceive him (*nescit, dēcipit, error* 430–1); and as Ovid apostrophises the situation, appealing to Narcissus in the second person to abandon the task (432–6), the hopelessness of his situation is emphasised by further words of negative connotation (*frūstrā . . . fugācia . . . nūsquam . . . perdēs . . . imāginis umbra . . . nīl . . . discēdet . . . discēdere*). The key word is the first, from which all else stems – *crēdule*, an appeal full of pity for the young man (432).

437–53: As with Echo, nothing can be done for him: lack of food and sleep prepare us for the worst (437–8; cf. *perit* 440, *tābuerit* 445). *oculōs* (440) is significant: ancient lovers are often said to be captivated by the eyes of the beloved (*Cynthia prīma suīs miserum mē cēpit ocellīs*, says Propertius in the first line of his first Elegy). Narcissus' eyes of love will kill him. The appeal to nature (*iō siluae*) to observe and sympathise, as if it were a friendly bystander

ad circumstantēs tendēns sua brācchia siluās
'ecquis, iō siluae, crūdēlius' inquit 'amāuit?
scītis enim et multīs latebra opportūna fuistis.
ecquem, cum uestrae tot agantur saecula uītae,
quī sīc tābuerit, longō meministis in aeuō?   445
et placet et uideō; sed quod uideōque placetque,
nōn tamen inuēnī; tantus tenet error amantem.
quōque magis doleam, nec nōs mare sēparat ingēns,
nec uia, nec montēs, nec clausīs moenia portīs.
exiguā prohibēmur aquā! cupit ipse tenērī: 450
nam quotiēns liquidis porrēximus ōscula lymphīs,
hīc totiēns ad mē resupīnō nītitur ōre.
posse putēs tangī; minimum est, quod amantibus obstat.'

3.454–62: *Narcissus tries to address the image*

'quisquis es, hūc exī! quid mē, puer ūnice, fallis?
quōue petītus abīs? certē nec fōrma nec aetās   455

441 *circumstō* 1 stand round
442 *iō*: an emotional exclamation
443 *latebr-a ae* 1f. hiding-place
opportūn-us a um convenient.
444 *ecquem*: obj. of *meministis* (445)
agantur: *agō* here is used of passing time
saecul-um ī 2n. generation, century (subject)
445 *tābēscō* 3 *tabuī* waste away. Why subj.?
446 *et placet et uideō*: note the chiastic repetition in
the second half of the line
448 *quōque magis*: here + subj., 'in order that *doleam*
the more'; **RL**148, cf. on 372
sēparō 1 keep apart

449 *moeni-a um* 3n. pl. walls
port-a ae 1f. gate
450 **exigu-us a um* narrow
451 **porrigō* 3 *porrēxi* offer, stretch
lymph-a ae 1f. water
452 *totiēns* so often
resupīn-us a um turned upwards
nītor 3 dep. reach out
453 *putēs*: conditional subj.; understand 'that he'
obstō 1 get in the way of (+ dat.)
454 *ūnic-us a um* matchless
455 *nec . . . est mea*: 'it is not *mea fōrma nec aetās
quam*'

(*circumstantēs* 441), is typical: there is no one else to turn to anyway, but lovers always feel that their love is unique (442–5) and therefore engages the interest of even the inanimate world. *opportūna* (443) is richly ironic: here is Narcissus in just such a place but unable to take any advantage of it. Narcissus is baffled why nature is so obdurate (446–7: that *error* is teasing – his fault or not?) and life so painful (448): first, because nature has placed no vast boundaries between him and the object of his desire – just a little water (448–50) – and, second, because their desire for each other appears to be mutual (450–2). He cannot understand what can be getting in the way, he ends (453: note *tangī*: anyone can touch, but poor Narcissus wants to *be* touched; cf. *tenērī* 450). The answer is, ironically, nature – reflections in water being natural. It is to be noted that by this stage (beginning with *nōs* 448; cf. the neutral *quod* at 446), Narcissus has begun clearly to articulate the idea that the image is a real, other person.

454–62: Nature having failed to respond, Narcissus expands on the last point (453) and, turning back from the wood to the image in the water itself, makes an appeal to it, the

est mea, quam fugiās, et amārunt mē quoque nymphae!
spem mihi nescioquam uultū prōmittis amīcō.
cumque ego porrēxī tibi brācchia, porrigis ultrō;
cum rīsī, adrīdēs; lacrimās^ quoque saepe notāuī,
mē lacrimante, ^tuas; nūtū quoque signa remittis   460
et, quantum mōtū fōrmōsī suspicor ōris,
uerba refers aurēs nōn peruenientia nostrās!'

3.463–73: *Narcissus realises the image is – himself*

'iste ego sum; sēnsī, nec mē mea fallit imāgō.
ūror amōre meī; flammās moueōque ferōque.
quid faciam? roger anne rogem? quid dēinde rogābō?   465
quod cupiō mēcum est; inopem mē cōpia fēcit.
ō utinam ā nostrō sēcēdere corpore possem!
uōtum in amante nouum, uellem quod amāmus abesset.

---

456 *fugiās*: subj. of characteristic
amārunt: = *ama(uē)runt*
457 *nescioquī/quae/quod* of some sort or other, some measure of
prōmittō 3 promise
amīcō: here an adj., 'friendly'
458 *cumque* and whenever (note the ind. *porrēxī*)
ultrō willingly, eagerly
459 *rīdeō* 2 *rīsī* smile, laugh
adrīdeō 2 smile/laugh back
notō 1 observe
460 *lacrimō* 1 weep
nūt-us ūs 4m. nod (i.e. when I nod)
461 *quantum* in as far as
mōt-us ūs 4m. movement
fōrmōs-us a um beautiful

suspicor 1 dep. gather, conclude
462 *aur-is is* 3f. ear
463 *iste*: *iste* means 'that (belonging to you/of yours)'
465 *faciam*: deliberative subj., like *roger* and *rogem*, **RL152**
anne: = *an* + *ne* = *an*, 'or'
466 *inops inop-is* poor
467 *ō*: note the (despairing) hiatus; see on passage 1, 1.363
sēcēdō 3 withdraw
468 *uōtum*: understand *est*
in amante: i.e. 'for a lover [to make]'
uellem: the object of Narcissus' *uōtum*, 'that I should wish'
abesset: object of Narcissus' wish, 'that *quod amāmus* (subject) *abesset*', **RLL-V(a)4**

---

burden of which is that the image's actions suggest 'he' desires union as much as Narcissus does (457–62). By this time, the reader might begin to feel that it is all becoming rather unlikely. Narcissus cannot be *that* dim, can he? Two points. First, Narcissus inhabits a world full of water- and mountain-nymphs (Echo, and cf. 402). That there should be a desirable spirit-like form under the water reaching out for him is not a surprise: the woods and rivers are full of spirits (cf. Arethusa's plight, passage 10, 5.597–8), and many of them have already tried to seduce him. Second – and this is the crucial point – he is being punished by the god Nemesis; his punishment is to fall in love with himself, and to do that he has to be blinded to the true nature of what he is seeing.

463–73: With *iste ego sum* the truth finally strikes home: Narcissus realises he cannot say *tū* because that would imply the reflection is a real *other* person. He is looking at himself, is himself the cause of his feelings (463–4), and it is far too late for him to do anything

iamque dolor uīrēs adimit, nec tempora∧ uītae
∧longa meae superant, prīmōque exstinguor in aeuō.   470
nec mihi∧ mors grauis est ∧positūrō morte dolōrēs;
hīc, quī dīligitur, uellem diuturnior esset.
nunc duo concordēs animā moriēmur in ūnā.'

3.474–93: *Vainly Narcissus calls on his reflection, and slowly withers away*

dīxit, et ad faciem rediit male sānus eandem,
et lacrimīs turbāuit aquās, obscūraque mōtō∧   475
reddita fōrma ∧lacū est; quam cum uīdisset abīre,
'quō refugis? remanē nec mē, crūdēlis, amantem
dēsere!' clāmāuit; 'liceat, quod tangere nōn est,
adspicere, et miserō praebēre alimenta furōrī!'
dumque dolet, summā uestem dēdūxit ab ōrā   480

469 *adimō* 3 remove
470 *exstinguō* 3 put out, destroy
471 *morte*: abl. of means, **RL**100A(b), **W**14
472 *dīligō* 3 love
uellem: 'I should wish that' *hīc . . . diuturnior esset*
diuturn-us a um long-lasting, permanent (*sc.* 'than I am')
473 *concors concord-is* in harmony, together
474 *sān-us a um* healthy
475 **obscūr-us a um* obscured, dark, opaque
476 *reddita . . . est*: i.e. his *fōrma* came back to him *obscūra*

lac-us ūs 4m. lake
abīre: understand *fōrmam* as subject of the acc. and inf.
478 **dēserō* 3 *dēseruī dēsertum* desert, abandon
nōn est: = it is not possible
479 *praebeō* 2 offer
aliment-um ī 2n. sustenance (cf. the 'thirst' of his love at 415)
480 *dēdūcō* 3 *dēdūxī* remove, pull down and off (as a more dramatic gesture of grief, rip down and off)
ōr-a ae 1f. hem, edge

about it. Having fallen so hopelessly in love, he cannot suddenly fall out again: the irony of *nec mē mea fallit imāgō* is apparent. The scintillating paradoxes of his position ring out, reversing all the clichés about excluded and thwarted lovers that feature so large in ancient love-poetry – because it is himself he is excluding, and against his most heartfelt desires. As Tiresias warned (348), he now knows himself, and that knowledge will doom him, since his love can never be requited, even though he acknowledges that it must (by definition) be unfulfillable (465–8). Observe the brilliant oxymoron at 466. Narcissus has all he wants because what he wants (*cupiō*) is *mēcum*; but this very 'wealth' (*cōpia*) – wonderful news in any other circumstances for a lover – leaves him *inopem*. Death alone awaits (469–72), the sole consolation being that they will 'both' die together, united in body and spirit (473). Even now, knowing what he does, Narcissus cannot believe there is not a distinct, separate person there.

474–93: He is, indeed, *male sānus* (474), as he recognises (*furōrī* 479), and in his deranged state seems to think his lover has deserted him when the surface of the water is disturbed by his tears (475–8; cf. his earlier drinking, before he developed these feelings 415–16). He can now only feed his delusion (*alimenta*, 479; cf. his earlier *sitis*,

nūdaque marmoreīs percussit pectora palmīs.
pectora trāxērunt roseum percussa rubōrem,
nōn aliter quam pōma solent quae, candida parte,
parte rubent, aut ut uariīs solet ūua^ racēmīs
dūcere purpureum nōndum ^mātūra colōrem.   485
quae simul adspexit liquefactā rūrsus in undā,
nōn tulit ulterius, sed ut intābēscere flāuae
igne leuī cērae mātūtīnaeque pruīnae
sōle tepente solent, sīc attenuātus amōre
līquitur et tēctō paulātim carpitur ignī.   490
et neque iam color est mixtō candōre rubōrī,
nec uigor et uīrēs et quae modo uīsa placēbant,
nec corpus remanet, quondam quod amāuerat Ēchō.

481 *marmore-us a um* white, marble
palm-a ae 1f. palm. Note the emphatic alliteration of *percussit pectora palmīs* in this golden line; 482 is almost golden too, the repeated *pectora . . . percussa* preparing for the simile
482 *rose-us a um* rose-coloured
483 *pōm-um ī* 2n. apple
parte . . . parte: abl. of respect, **RLL**(f)4(vi)
484 *rubeō* 2 blush
ūu-a ae 1f. grape (here abl. of place, 'in', 'among')
racēm-us ī 2m. bunch, cluster
485 *purpure-us a um* reddish (these grapes are not yet a fully ripened purple)
mātūr-us a um ripe (cf. 347!)
*color -is 3m. colour, tinge, hue
486 *quae*: i.e. his *pectora*
liquefact-us a um clear, calm

487 *ulterius* any longer
intābēscō 3 melt (inf. after *solent*, 489)
*flāu-us a um yellow
488 **cēr-a ae* 1f. wax
mātūtīn-us a um early-morning
pruīn-a ae 1f. frost
489 *tepeō* 2 grow warm
attenuāt-us a um weakened, made thin (*attenuō*)
490 *līquō* 3 melt away
paulātim slowly, gradually
*carpō 3 *carpsī carptum* pick, harvest; plunder, devour; weaken, consume
491 *mixtō candōre*: abl. of description (his previous *color* is being described, in comparison with its colourlessness now – the first sign that he is fading away)
492 *uigor -is* 3m. energy, vigour

415–16). Ripping one's clothes is a typical gesture of anguish (cf. Byblis in passage 15, 9.636–7), as is beating one's breast (480–2), and this allows Ovid a pretty image involving the colour of apples and grapes to picture the bruising of Narcissus' white skin (483–5). This image of himself inflames Narcissus all the more when he sees it in the now cleared water (486–7), and another double simile involving the gently (*leuī*) melting wax and morning frost (487–9) pictures and 'explains' by analogy with the physical world his slow physical demise, as he wastes away with frustrated desire (489–93), just like poor Echo earlier (396–401). Frustrated Roman lovers in elegy are always talking about 'perishing' for their love. Here Narcissus actually does. Ovid's mention of Echo's previous love for him (493) creates the transition to the part she plays in his final hours, appropriately enough, given that their 'elegiac' fates – wasting away for love of the same person – are so similar. Nemesis is, then, doubly avenged. Not only is Narcissus unable to master his beloved (cf. 405), he also meets the same fate as one of his rejected lovers.

3.494–510: *Echo pities the boy; but all that remains of him is a flower*

quae tamen ut uīdit, quamuīs īrāta memorque,
indoluit, quotiēnsque puer miserābilis 'ēheu'   495
dīxerat, haec resonīs iterābat uōcibus 'ēheu';
cumque suōs manibus percusserat ille lacertōs,
haec quoque reddēbat sonitum plangōris eundem.
ultima uōx∧ solitam fuit ∧haec spectantis in undam:
'heu frūstrā dīlecte puer!', totidemque∧ remīsit   500
∧uerba locus, dictōque 'ualē', 'uale' inquit et Ēchō.
ille caput uiridī fessum submīsit in herbā,
lūmina mors clausit dominī mīrantia fōrmam.
tum quoque sē, postquam est īnfernā sēde receptus,
in Stygiā spectābat aquā. planxēre sorōrēs   505
Nāides, et sectōs frātrī posuēre capillōs,

494 *quae*: i.e. Echo (subject); understand 'him' after *uīdit*
495 *indoleō* 2 grieve
*ēheu (cf. *heu*): a cry of anguish
496 *reson-us a um* echoing
iterō 1 repeat
498 *sonit-us ūs* 4m. sound
plangor -is 3m. grief, distress
499 *spectantis*: refers to Narcissus, 'of him gazing'
500 *dīlect-us a um* beloved
501 *ualē, uale*: the second *uale* is in hiatus with *inquit* and its *e* scans light; it is permitted (though very rare) for a vowel to be lightened in such instances. Here, the effect is of *uale* fading away . . .

502 *uiridī*: the fresh, lively green contrasts with Narcissus' deathly pallor
submittō 3 *submīsī* lower
503 *dominum*: Narcissus is enslaved to the beauty of his 'master'
504 *infern-us a um* in the underworld
sēd-ēs is 3f. seat, home, residence
505 **plangō* 3 *planxī* mourn. The Naides are water-nymphs, presumably daughters of the river-god Cephisus; the repetition of the word in different forms in 505–7 (polyptoton) gives a sense of the repeated cries of grief
506 *sect-us a um* cut. Cutting the hair was a common sign of mourning

494–510: Echo, despite her memories of the past (494), grieves at Narcissus' fate, echoing both his cries (495–6) and the sound from his beating of his upper arms (497–8, cf. 481). When Echo originally 'replied' to Narcissus, she picked up words that rejected her and turned them into words of love. Now, they just repeat each other, hopelessly. Narcissus' words of farewell to the image are, ironically, Echo's words of farewell to him (500–1). She was a real 'other', but he had rejected her in favour of the empty image (note the moving *solitam*, 499). Finished now with gazing at his reflection, he slumps on the grass (502) and, still admiring his *dominus* (himself/the image) at the end of his life (503), he carries on gazing at it even in death (505) – one *umbra* gazing hopelessly at another; and those who had loved him in life, even the Dryades presumably rejected by him (402–3), mourn his passing (505–7). The *flōs croceus* that is found in place of his body (509–10) is (perhaps) the daffodil-like mountain species known as *Narcissus poeticus* (Ovid wisely refrains from detailing how *that* transformation took place). Many daffodils have a yellow flower and white leaves; and many of them bow over, as if staring at their own reflection.

(On this episode, see Nuttall in Martindale, 1988, 141–6.)

planxērunt Dryades; plangentibus adsonat Ēchō.
iamque rogum quassāsque facēs feretrumque parābant –
nūsquam corpus erat. croceum prō corpore flōrem
inueniunt, foliīs medium cingentibus albīs.   510

Dryas Dryad-is 3f. wood-nymph
adsonō 1 sound along with (+ dat.). Echo responds
   to the Dryades because she can no longer respond
   to Narcissus
508 *rog-us ī* 2m. funeral-pyre
quass-us a um for brandishing (*quatiō*) (lit. 'brandished', used here proleptically, i.e. they were
   going to be brandished)
fax fac-is 3f. torch
feretr-um ī 2n. bier
509 *nūsquam* nowhere. The absence of e.g. *sed* (asyndeton) creates a sense of surprise
*croce-us a um yellow
*flōs flōr-is 3m. flower
510 *foli-um ī* 2n. leaf
alb-us a um white

Learning vocabulary
carpō 3 *carpsī carptum* pick, harvest; plunder,
   devour; weaken, consume
cēr-a ae 1f. wax
color -is 3m. colour, tinge, hue
croce-us a um yellow
dēserō 3 *dēseruī dēsertum* desert, abandon
ēheū (cf. *heū*) a cry of anguish
exigu-us a um narrow
flāu-us a um yellow
flōs flōr-is 3m. flower
obscūr-us a um obscured, dark
plangō 3 *planxī* mourn
porrigō 3 *porrēxī porrēctum* offer, stretch

Learning vocabulary for Passage 8, Echo and Narcissus

adspiciō 3/4 *adspexī adspectum* observe, catch
   sight of, see
candor -is 3m. radiance, whiteness
captō 1 try to get hold of
carpō 3 *carpsī carptum* pick, harvest, take;
   plunder, devour; weaken, consume
cēr-a ae 1f. wax
cernō 3 *crēuī crētum* discern, perceive
claudō 3 *clausī clausum* enclose, trap
color -is 3m. colour, tinge, hue
cōpi-a ae 1f. control over, use of (X gen.) for
   sexual purposes; plenty
croce-us a um yellow
dēserō 3 *dēseruī dēsertum* desert, abandon
ecquis: '[Is] anyone?'
ēheū (cf. *heū*) a cry of anguish
exigu-us a um narrow
flāu-us a um yellow
flōs flōr-is 3m. flower
fugāx fugāc-is fleeting
haereō 2 cling on; stay put
hūc (to) here

(in)calēscō 3 *incaluī* become hot, excited (with
   desire)
mīrābil-is e admirable
miserābil-is e pitiful
mixt-us a um mixed (*misceō*)
Narciss-us ī 2m. Narcissus
obscūr-us a um obscured, dark
pariter equally
plangō 3 *planxī* mourn
porrigō 3 *porrēxī porrēctum* offer, stretch
quondam once (upon a time)
quotiēns how often
remittō 3 send back, return
rūrsus again
simulācr-um ī 2n. image, likeness
sit-is is 3f. thirst
son-us ī 2m. sound
totidem the same number of
turbō 1 disturb
uāt-ēs is 3m. prophet, seer

Study section

1. Write out and scan ll.365–9, 499–503.
2. 405 *iūstīs*: in Ovid's or Nemesis' eyes? Does it make any difference?
3. Do you feel pity for Narcissus? Or was he justly punished?
4. What purpose does Echo serve in the story?
5. Does Ovid push the paradoxes and ironies too far for credibility? Or does credibility not matter?
6. What would one mean if one were to say that the story has all been done by mirrors?
7. 'Narcissus' final dissolution is triggered by the sight of his blushing flesh compared in the simile at 483–5 to apples and grapes. The ultimate fruitlessness of Narcissus' desire is signalled by his attempt to feed on a literary *simulacrum*, or simile' (Hardie, 2002, 163). Discuss.
8. What are the parallels between the Narcissus story and the following passage (John Milton, *Paradise Lost* 4.449–76)? What is the big difference? How does Milton 'christianise' it? (See Burrow in Hardie, 2002a, 316–17.)

Eve, who was formed out of a rib from Adam's side, is talking to Adam of the moment she awakened and 'came to life':

That day I oft remember, when from sleep
I first awaked, and found myself reposed
Under a shade of flow'rs, much wond'ring where
And what I was, whence thither brought, and how.
Not distant far from thence a murmuring sound   5
Of waters issued from a cave and spread
Into a liquid plain, then stood unmoved
Pure as th' expanse of heav'n; I thither went
With unexperienced thought, and laid me down
On the green bank, to look into the clear   10
Smooth lake, that to me seemed another sky.
As I bent down to look, just opposite,
A shape within the wat'ry gleam appeared
Bending to look on me: I started back,
It started back, but pleased I soon returned,   15
Pleased it returned as soon with answering looks
Of sympathy and love; there I had fixed
Mine eyes till now, and pined with vain desire,
Had not a voice thus warned me, 'What thou seest,
What there thou seest fair creature is thyself,   20
With thee it came and goes: but follow me,

And I will bring thee where no shadow stays
Thy coming, and thy soft embraces, he
Whose image thou art, him thou shalt enjoy
Inseparably thine, to him shalt bear   25
Multitudes like thyself, and thence be called
Mother of human race'. What could I do,
But follow straight, invisibly thus led?

9   Pyramus and Thisbe, *Metamorphōsēs* 4.55–166

From now on there is only a minimal learning vocabulary. It will consist of words that occur more than once in the passage in question, but do not occur in the *Total Learning Vocabulary*. All these words will be listed in the section *Learning Vocabulary* at the end of the passage (as usual), *but they will not be re-listed* in the *Total Learning Vocabulary*. Consequently, if they recur in later passages, they will be glossed there again.

As a result, you can read passages 9–16 in any order and still find fully glossed all words that do not appear in the *Total Learning Vocabulary*. See p. 20 n.4.

Background

The daughters of Minyas, refusing to partake in Bacchant rites, tell each other stories instead. The first sister tells the following tale, its purpose being to explain how the mulberry's berries, once white, changed to dark red.

4.55–64: *Pyramus and Thisbe are in love but cannot marry*

'Pȳramus et Thisbē, iuuenum pulcherrimus alter,   55
altera, quās Oriēns habuit, praelāta puellīs,
contiguās tenuēre domōs, ubi dīcitur altam^

---

55 *Oriēns Orient-is* 3m. the East
56 *altera*: take in order *altera praelāta puellīs . . . quās*
praelāt-us a um exalted over (+ dat.) (*praeferō*)
57 *contigu-us a um* adjacent

dīcitur: subject is *Semiramis*, the founder and queen of Babylon (60 miles south of modern Baghdad; Herodotus, *Histories* 1.184). She was the widow of Ninus (88), after whom Nineveh was named

---

Warning note

This tale, as we have seen, is told by a daughter of Minyas, and from now on, most of the tales will be stories within stories. It may, therefore, have been composed by Ovid to convey something about the teller of the story. But without reading the stories in their full context, it is not helpful to discuss this possible angle. I therefore say nothing about it.

55–64: Ovid at once establishes the location of the story: in the East (56), in Babylon (58). Its walls of baked mud (58) caused some comment in countries like Greece and Italy,

[130]

coctilibus mūrīs cīnxisse Semīramis ^urbem.
nōtitiam prīmōsque gradūs uīcīnia fēcit,
tempore crēuit amor; taedae quoque iūre coissent,   60
sed uetuēre patrēs. quod nōn potuēre uetāre,
ex aequō captīs ardēbant mentibus ambō.
cōnscius omnis abest; nūtū signīsque loquuntur,
quōque magis tegitur, tēctus magis aestuat ignis.'

4.65–80: *They communicate through a shared garden wall*

'fissus erat tenuī rīmā, quam dūxerat ōlim   65
cum fieret, pariēs^ domuī ^commūnis utrīque.
id uitium, nūllī per saecula longa notātum,
(quid nōn sentit amor?) prīmī uīdistis amantēs
et uōcis fēcistis iter, tūtaeque^ per illud
murmure ^blanditiae minimō trānsīre solēbant.   70

---

58 *coctil-is e* built of baked (mud) bricks (Herodotus, *Histories* 1.179)
59 *nōtiti-a ae* 1f. acquaintance
grad-us ūs 4m. approach (i.e. steps towards each other)
uīcīni-a ae 1f. proximity
60 *taed-a ae* 1f. marriage (torch). Take with *iūre*
coissent: note the conditional plupf. subj.
61 *quod*: 'the thing which', explained in 62. There is an amusing jingling sound to 61
62 *ex aequō* equally
63 *cōnsci-us a um* complicit, who knows about it
nūt-us ūs 4m. nod
64 *quōque magis . . . magis*: + ind., 'by how much the more . . . the more', **RL**100B.5, **WSuppl.**syntax. Note the polyptoton of *tegitur, tēctus* and chiasmus with *magis*
aestuō 1 blaze up
65 *findō* 3 *fidī fissum* split (the subject of *fissus erat* is *pariēs*)

rīm-a ae 1f. crack
ōlim long ago
66 *cum fieret*: i.e. when the wall was being built
*pariēs pariet-is 3m. wall (separating the two properties). This scans as two syllables, the first heavy, as though the *i* were consonantal
commūn-is e shared, common to (+ dat.)
domuī: dat. of *domus*
67 *uiti-um ī* 2n. fault
nūllī: dat. of agent
saecul-um ī 2n. age
notō 1 notice
68 *uīdistis*: Ovid drops into the 2nd pl. here ('apostrophe'), addressing the two lovers
69 *illud*: i.e. the crack in the wall
70 *murmur -is 3n. whisper
blanditi-a ae 1f. sweet nothing, endearment
trānseō trānsīre 3 cross, pass

---

where there was plenty of stone for building. The lovers live in adjacent properties (57), and Ovid describes how their young love, beginning so innocently, grew over time (59–60); but parental disapproval drove them 'underground', making the whole 'affair' all the more exciting (61–4). All this is sweetly stereotypical. Ovid well understands the clichéd thrills of private youthful infatuation – he sees into their minds and produces a delightfully sympathetic and amusing account of young 'lurve'.

65–80: In this new situation, the pair are at first able to communicate only through signs to each other when they just happen to meet (63). But there is a hole in the garden-wall that separates the properties (not an internal house-wall; 79, 91–2 make it clear the wall is outside, because they have to leave it when night falls). This *pariēs . . . commūnis* both

saepe, ubi cōnstiterant hinc Thisbē, Pȳramus illinc,
inque uicēs fuerat captātus anhēlitus ōris,
"inuide" dīcēbant "pariēs, quid amantibus obstās?
quantum erat, ut sinerēs tōtō nōs corpore iungī,
aut, hoc sī nimium est, uel ad ōscula danda patērēs?   75
nec sumus ingrātī: tibi nōs dēbēre fatēmur,
quod datus est uerbīs ad amīcās trānsitus aurēs."
tālia dīuersā nēquīquam sēde locūtī
sub noctem, dīxēre "ualē", partīque^ dedēre
ōscula quisque ^suae nōn peruenientia contrā.'   80

4.81–92: *They decide to run away and agree a meeting place*

'postera nocturnōs Aurōra remōuerat ignēs,
sōlque pruīnōsās radiīs siccāuerat herbās;

---

71 *hinc . . . illinc*: chiasmus
72 *in uicēs* in turn
anhēlit-us ūs 4m. breath. The two are breathing each
   other's breath in turn through the chink in the
   garden wall
73 *inuid-us a um* envious
obstō 1 get in the way of (+ dat.)
77 *quantum erat*: 'how much would it be [for you to,
   ut + subj.]', i.e. how little it would cost you to . . . ;
   cf. **RLS2**(c)Notes(6)
sinō 3 allow
75 *pateō* 2 open up
76 *ingrāt-us a um* ungrateful
fateor 2 dep. admit
77 *quod*: explains what the lovers owe – 'the fact that
   . . .'

amīcās: here used as an adjective
trānsit-us ūs 4m. way of communicating, pathway
78 *nēquīquam* in vain
sēd-ēs is 3f. position, house
79 *noctem*: note acc. with *sub*
80 *peruenientia*: stress the *per* – the *ōscula* could not
   get *through* the wall
81 *poster-us a um* the next (a golden line)
nocturn-us a um of the night
ignēs: i.e. the stars
82 *pruīnōs-us a um* frosty
radi-us i 2m. ray
siccō 1 dry

---

separates them and allows them to communicate privately with each other – love picks
up everything, Ovid charmingly puts it, as he drops into a complicitous apostrophe with
uīdistis (68) – and they are thus enabled to pour out their sweet nothings without anyone
else hearing (*tūtae*, 69–70). If they cannot hold each other, they can at least try to catch
each other's breath – a delightful conceit (72). They personify the wall, accusing it of
getting in the way (73–7, cf. Narcissus at 3.448–50); not that they wish to offend it . . .
(76–7). Note that innocent first love has now become a passionate desire for intercourse
(*tōtō . . . corpore*, 74). They stop talking this sort of juvenile drivel (*tālia . . . nēquīquam*
78) only when night falls, when they part with unavailing kisses (79–80). Ovid here brilliantly recreates the intensely introspective world of adolescent love, which means so
much to the young lovers and is the source of such innocent amusement for everyone
else.

81–92: Next day the young lovers decide to act. Spurred by their whispered (83) despair
at their situation (84), they agree to break out. Breathlessly, they plot the escapade. The

ad solitum coiēre locum. tum murmure paruō
multa prius questī, statuunt ut, nocte silentī,
fallere custōdēs foribusque excēdere temptent,   85
cumque domō exierint, urbis quoque tēcta relinquant;
nēue sit errandum lātō spatiantibus aruō,
conueniant ad busta Ninī, lateantque sub umbrā
arboris: arbor ibī niueīs ūberrima pōmīs –
ardua mōrus – erat, gelidō contermina fontī.   90
pacta placent; et lūx, tardē discēdere uīsa,
praecipitātur aquīs, et aquīs nox exit ab īsdem.'

4.93–104: *Thisbe sees a lion, runs, but leaves a cloak behind*

'callida per tenebrās, uersātō cardine, Thisbē
ēgreditur, fallitque suōs, adopertaque uultum

---

84 *multa*: n. pl. object of *questī*
statuō 3 decide to/that they should (*ut* + subj. –
   temptent, relinquant, conueniant, lateant)
silēns silent-is quiet, silent
85 *for-ēs ium* 3f. pl. doors
excēdō 3 depart
86 *tēct-um ī* 2n. building
87 *nēue*: 'and lest'
errandum: impersonal gerundive, 'it is to be got lost
   by (dat.) them *spatiantibus . . .*', 'they should get
   lost as they . . .', **RLO**(2)
88 *conueniō* 3/4 meet (subj. after *statuunt*)
bust-um ī 2n. tomb. When the romance of Ninus
   and Semiramis had passed into legend, we are
   told this modest monument was a mile high and a
   mile wide
Nin-us ī 2m. Ninus (legendary founder of Ninevah
   and husband of Semiramis)
89 *niue-us a um* snowy (white)
ūber -is fertile
*pōm-um ī 2n. fruit
90 **mōr-us ī* 2f./*mōr-um ī* 2n. mulberry-tree. Ovid
   brings in the mulberry, reminding us that the

apparent purpose of this story was to explain how
   its fruit changed colour
contermin-us a um next to (+ dat.). The location
   next to a *fōns* is important: it is the *fōns* that will
   attract the lion
91 **pact-um ī* 2n. agreement; *pact-us a um* agreed
92 *praecipitor* 1 dep. plunge headlong. There is a neat
   chiastic balance to this line
aquīs: i.e. dip below the horizon. The sun is pre-
   sumed to disappear under the sea in the West,
   and at night to emerge from it in the East (it is
   irrelevant that it is quite difficult to *see* the sea
   from Babylon, the Mediterranean being about
   500 miles west, the Persian gulf about 300 south-
   east)
93 *callid-us a um* skilful
tenebr-ae ārum 2f. pl. shadows, darkness
uersō 1 manipulate, turn
cardō cardin-is 3m. door(-hinge). A tense moment –
   will it creak?
94 *adopert-us a um* covered, veiled (presumably with
   the *uēlāmen*, 101: preparation for what will follow)
uultum: acc. of respect, **RL6.3**

---

absurdly detailed 84–6 (which boils down to 'step one: leave town') captures their excited
sense of planning, 87 their sense of danger; 88–90 finally gets to the practical point. Given
that they met soon after dawn (81–2; ah, young love!), 91–2 suggests it has taken much of
the day to come up with this exciting adventure. *tardē* is a neat touch. Time usually flies
for lovers, but because they are in such a haste to escape together, now it drags.

93–104: 'Skilful' (93) Thisbe carefully opens the door and follows the plan to the letter,
obediently sitting down under the tree (95), covering her face in addition (94), and
terribly excited by the daring of it all (96). But when the moon (99, cf. *tenebrās* 93)

peruenit ad tumulum, dictāque sub arbore sēdit.   95
audācem faciēbat amor. uenit ecce recentī
caede leaena boum, spūmantēs oblita rictūs,
dēpositūra sitim uīcīnī fontis in undā;
quam procul ad lūnae radiōs Babylōnia Thisbē
uīdit, et obscūrum timidō pede fūgit in antrum;   100
dumque fugit, tergō uēlāmina lāpsa relīquit.
ut lea saeua sitim multā compescuit undā,
dum redit in siluās, inuentōs^ forte sine ipsā
ōre cruentātō ^tenuēs laniāuit ^amictūs.'

4.105–27: *Pyramus finds the cloak, fears the worst and commits suicide*

'sērius ēgressus, uestīgia^ uīdit in altō   105
puluere ^certa ferae, tōtōque expalluit ōre
Pȳramus. ut uērō uestem quoque sanguine tīnctam

95 *tumul-us i* 2m. tomb, mound, hill
96 *audācem*: understand 'her'
97 *leaen-a ae* 1f. lioness
boum: gen. pl. of *bōs*, 'bull, cow', dependent on *recentī caede*
spūmō 1 foam
oblit-us a um smeared (*oblinō*)
rict-us ūs 4m. jaw (acc. of respect after *oblita*)
98 *dēpōnō* 3 quench
99 *quam*: i.e. the lioness (connecting relative, RL107)
Babylōni-us a um Babylonian
100 *fūgit . . . fugit* (101): note the difference between these two forms

101 *tergō*: 'true' abl., **RL100A**, Survey(a)
*uēlāmen uēlāmin-is 3n. any sort of clothes or covering (cf. 94, which argues for headgear of some sort, and *uestem* 107)
102 *le-a ae* 1f. lioness
compescō 3 *compescuī* allay, quench
104 *cruentāt-us a um* bloody
*laniō 1 tear at
amict-us ūs 4m. cloak, garment
105 *sērius* later (*Pȳramus* 107 is subject)
106 *puluis puluer-is* 3m. dust
expallēscō 3 *expalluī* turn pale
107 *tingō* 3 *tīnxī tīnctum* tinge

conveniently reveals a lioness appearing fresh from the kill, *Babylōnia* Thisbe – note the epic 'heroic' epithet – retreats, *timidō pede*: not so heroic after all (96–100). Indeed, so quickly does she run for it that her *uēlāmen* falls off (101). The lioness gives it a thoughtful gnaw (*sine ipsā* amusingly suggests it was hoping to find someone inside) and disappears back into the woods (103–4).

105–27: Pyramus arrives *sērius* on the scene (105) – Ovid does not explain why, but the story demands it – and even *sērior* in the sentence (107). He sees (presumably by the light of the moon) the lion's tracks, and his worst fears are confirmed by the bloody *uēlāmen* (105–8). Pyramus did not actually 'order' Thisbe to come to the spot (111) – they agreed it together (84 ff.) – but he heroically takes responsibility for her (as he thinks) death because of his late arrival (112). Absurdly, he challenges the lions to eat him too (112–14), imagining a whole pride living in the cave where Thisbe is currently sheltering (presumably that is what *sub hāc rūpe* refers to, 114, cf. *antrum* 100), but then chooses the more heroic, and certain, option. All this is announced in high rhetorical style.

repperit, "una duōs" inquit "nox perdet amantēs,
ē quibus illa fuit longā dignissima uītā.
nostra nocēns anima est. ego^ tē, miseranda, perēmī,   110
in loca plēna metūs ^quī iussī nocte uenīrēs,
nec prior hūc uēnī. nostrum dīuellite corpus,
et scelerāta ferō cōnsūmite uīscera morsū,
ō quīcumque sub hāc habitātis rūpe leōnēs!
sed timidī est optāre necem." uēlāmina Thisbēs   115
tollit, et ad^ pactae sēcum fert arboris ^umbram,
utque dedit nōtae^ lacrimās, dedit ōscula ^uestī,
"accipe nunc" inquit "nostrī quoque sanguinis haustūs!"
quōque erat accīnctus, dēmīsit in īlia ferrum.
nec mora; feruentī moriēns ē uulnere trāxit.   120
ut iacuit resupīnus humō, cruor ēmicat altē,
nōn aliter quam cum uitiātō fistula plumbō
scinditur, et tenuēs^ strīdente forāmine longē
ēiaculātur ^aquās, atque ictibus āera rumpit.
arboreī fētūs, adspergine caedis, in ātram   125

108 *ūna . . . amantēs*: a fine antithesis, at such an
  agonising moment
110 *nocēns nocent-is* guilty
miserand-us a um pitiable
perimō 3 perēmī kill, destroy
111 *uenīrēs*: *iussī* here is followed by the subj.
112 *dīuellō 3* tear apart
113 *scelerāt-us a um* accursed (a ringing golden line)
cōnsūmō 3 eat up
uiscera-um 3n. pl. entrails
mors-us ūs 4m. bite
114 *ō quīcumque*: take with *leōnēs*
habitō 1 live
rūp-ēs is 3f. rock
leō leōn-is 3m. lion
115 *timidī est*: 'it is [the characteristic] of the *timidus*
  . . .', cf. RLL(d)1
optāre: i.e. only/merely to *wish* for death
nex nec-is 3f. death
Thisbēs: Greek gen. s.
118 *haust-us ūs* 4m. draught
119 *quōque*: refers to *ferrum*

accingō 3 accīnxī accīnctus gird oneself, put round
  oneself
dēmittō 3 dēmīsī sink
īli-a um 3n. pl. groin
120 *feruēns feruent-is* fresh, hot
121 *resupīn-us a um* on one's back
ēmicō 1 leap, spurt
122 *quam cum*: + ind., 'than when'
uitiāt-us a um faulty
fistul-a ae 1f. (water-)pipe
plumb-um ī 2n. lead
123 *scindō 3* split
strīdēns strīdent-is hissing
forāmen forāmin-is 3n. hole
124 *ēiaculor 1* dep. pump out
ict-us ūs 4m. impact, blow
rumpō 3 rip through, break
125 *arbore-us a um* of a tree
*fēt-us ūs 4m. fruit
adspergō adspergin-is 3f. spattering
*āter ātr-a um black

Addressing a grand farewell to the veil, as if that were Thisbe herself (115–18: note the
kisses and tears and the charming *nōtae* 117: it was clearly a favourite garment of hers),
he plunges the sword into his groin (119), 'where death in battle comes most painfully for
wretched mortals' (Homer, *Iliad* 13.568–9, Rieu–Jones). Heroic wounds are always
feruēns, and so is this (120). But why does Pyramus pull the sword out so quickly? This is
a heroic gesture (Pallas tries it at *Aeneid* 10.486–7), however misplaced for a suicide, but

uertuntur faciem, madefactaque sanguine rādīx
purpureō tingit pendentia mōra colōre.'

4.128–46: *Thisbe finds the dying Pyramus*

'ecce, metū nōndum positō, nē fallat amantem,
illa redit, iuuenemque oculīs animōque requīrit,
quantaque^ uītārit nārrāre ^perīcula gestit.   130
utque locum et uīsā cognōscit in arbore fōrmam,
sīc facit incertam pōmī color: haeret, an haec sit.
dum dubitat, tremebunda uidet pulsāre cruentum
membra solum, retrōque pedem tulit, ōraque buxō
pallidiōra gerēns, exhorruit aequoris īnstar,   135
quod tremit, exiguā cum summum stringitur aurā.

126 *madefact-us a um* soaked	*haec*: i.e. the (proper) tree
rādix rādic-is 3f. root. A root soaked in blood would not from then on deliver a dark red tinge to the berries, but it makes a good story	133 *tremebund-us a um* trembling
	pulsō 1 writhe on (+ acc.)
	cruent-us a um bloody
127 *purpure-us a um* purple (almost a golden line)	134 *sol-um ī* 2n. ground (contrast *sōlus* and *sōl*)
tingō 3 tinge	*retrō* back
130 *uītō* 1 avoid. *uītārit = uītāuerit* (RLA4), subj. in an indirect question after *nārrāre*	*bux-um ī* 2n. box-wood (here abl. of comparison)
gestiō 4 desire keenly (to + inf.)	135 *pallid-us a um* pale
131 *fōrmam*: i.e. the shape of the tree where they had agreed to meet	*exhorreō* 2 shudder
	īnstar like (+ gen.)
132 *incertam*: i.e. Thisbe – she cannot understand why the tree has changed colour	136 *tremō* 3 tremble
	summum: i.e. the surface
	stringō 3 ruffle

there is obviously another reason: Pyramus' blood must spatter the mulberry, and Ovid imagines the sword needs to be removed for that to happen (125–7). In one of the funniest similes in *Metamorphōsēs* (which has generated much tut-tutting about 'lapse of taste'), Ovid uses the image of a burst and hissing lead water-pipe to describe how the blood shot up all over the bush (121–4; in epic a simile often accompanies a great hero's death). This is medically accurate: Pyramus' sword would have hit the femoral artery, whence the blood would have shot out many a mile. It is also anachronistic (ancient Babylonians did not have water delivered by lead pipe), but that never worried Ovid: it merely adds to the fun. It is also appropriate: the mulberry is extremely squishy and juicy.

128–46: Which leaves Thisbe. Fear and duty/love fight it out in her (128), not without an eager desire to share all her exciting adventures with her beloved (130) – a nice touch – but out she comes (129), to be bewildered by what she finds: a very differently coloured mulberry tree (131–2: wonderful bathos – no laughing, now). Her gaze moves from the mulberry tree to the ground – where limbs writhing on the bloody soil greet her. High emotions regularly attract a simile, and here she is likened to a breeze rippling over waters (135–6, cf. *tremebunda* 133); and when she sees who it is, she goes into full mourning ritual (138–9), apparently replacing Pyramus' blood with her tears (cf. 118!), and getting only cold comfort from her kisses (140–1, cf. 117). Her cries are enough to rouse him for

sed postquam remorāta suōs cognōuit amōrēs,
percutit indignōs clārō plangōre lacertōs,
et laniāta comās, amplexaque corpus amātum,
uulnera supplēuit lacrimīs, flētumque cruōrī   140
miscuit, et gelidīs in uultibus ōscula fīgēns
"Pȳrame," clāmāuit, "quis tē mihi cāsus adēmit?
Pȳrame, respondē! tua tē, cārissime, Thisbē
nōminat; exaudī, uultūsque attolle iacentēs!"
ad nōmen Thisbēs, oculōs iam morte grauātōs   145
Pȳramus ērēxit, uīsāque recondidit illā.'

4.147–66: *Thisbe laments and commits suicide too*

'quae postquam uestemque suam cognōuit, et ēnse
uīdit ebur uacuum, "tua tē manus" inquit "amorque
perdidit, īnfēlīx! est et mihi fortis∧ in ūnum

137 *remoror* 1 dep. wait	**146** *ērigō* 3 *ērēxī* open
138 *indign-us a um* blameless	*uīsāque . . . illā*: abl. abs., 'her having been seen', 'and
plangor -is 3m. blow	when he had seen her'
140 *suppleō* 2 *supplēuī* fill	*recondō* 3 *recondidī* shut again (*sc. oculōs*)
flēt-us ūs 4m. tears	**147** *quae*: i.e. Thisbe. Her ensuing speech is full of
141 *misceō* 2 *miscuī* mingle	emotional doublets and antitheses (see e.g.
142 *adimō* 3 *adēmī* remove, take away	148–50 *manus/amor*, 152 *causa/comes*, 152–3
143 *cār-us a um* beloved, dear	*possum + reuellī*, 156, 159)
144 *nōminō* 1 name, call on	*uestemque*: the *que* anticipates *et*, 'both . . . and'
exaudiō 4 listen, hear	*ēns-is is* 3m. sword
attollō 3 raise up	**148** *ebur -is* 3n. ivory (sheath)
145 *Thisbēs*: gen. s. of Thisbe	**149** *in ūnum hoc*: 'for this one [*sc.* purpose]', i.e.
grauō 1 weigh down	suicide

one last time. He responds, touchingly, to her name, not his (145), looks up at her, and dies (142–6). This is all gloriously melodramatic stuff, worthy of a 1920s silent movie.

147–66: Thisbe now recognises her *uēlāmen* and sees the empty scabbard (147: an important observation, for it proves Pyramus committed suicide) and draws the correct conclusion (148–9). Summoning up all her physical and mental strength (149–50), she decides to seek the heroic reputation (*dīcar*) of one who joined her lover in death (151–2 – note that she too takes the blame for it, *causa*, as he had at 110), emphasising that death could have been the one thing that separated them, but will not be allowed to now (152–3). She ends by calling on (i) her parents, who forbade their union, to allow them to be joined in death (154–7), and (ii) the mulberry (stop giggling) always to bear fruit the colour of blood in memory of their suicides (158–61). That said, she falls on Pyramus' still warm sword (162–3). Her prayers move both gods and parents; not that the gods had anything to do with the story, but it makes a suitably tearful conclusion, heightened by the sentimental *ūnā – urnā* word-play (164–6): the two are finally united, but only in death, and as ashes. Thisbe's self-dramatised posturing, embracing in the name of love a supreme self-sacrifice for no particular purpose, is very well done.

hoc ^manus, est et amor: dabit hīc in uulnera uīrēs.   150
persequar exstinctum, lētīque miserrima dīcar
causa comesque tuī; quīque a mē morte reuellī
hēū sōlā poterās, poteris nec morte reuellī.
hoc tamen ambōrum uerbīs estōte rogātī,
ō multum miserī meus illiusque parentēs,   155
ut, quōs certus amor, quōs hōra nouissima iūnxit,
compōnī tumulō nōn inuideātis eōdem.
at tū^ quae rāmīs ^arbor miserābile corpus
nunc tegis ūnīus, mox es tēctūra duōrum,
signa tenē caedis, pullōsque et luctibus aptōs   160
semper habē fētūs, geminī monimenta cruōris."
dīxit, et aptātō pectus mucrōne sub īmum
incubuit ferrō, quod adhūc ā caede tepēbat.
uōta tamen tetigēre deōs, tetigēre parentēs;
nam color in pōmō est, ubi permātūruit, āter,   165
quodque rogīs superest, ūnā requiēscit in urnā.'

---

150 *in uulnera*: '(in)to my wounds', i.e. the wounds I intend to deal myself in order to die
151 *exstinct-us a um* dead; understand *tē*
lēt-um ī 2n. death
152 *quīque*: 'and you [note *poterās*] who' (i.e. Pyramus)
reuellō 3 pluck, tear from (+ abl.)
153 *nec*: 'not *even*'; i.e. death alone *could* have plucked Pyramus from me; now not *even* death will pluck him from me
154 *ambōrum*: i.e. both of us
estōte rogātī: 'be asked', 'you must be asked' (the subject is *meus* [*parēns*] *illiusque parentēs*, 155); *hoc* is the (effective) object. For *estōte*, see **RLE1**
156 *ut*: this introduces the request to be made of their parents
157 *compōnō* 3 place together

158 *tū*: the *arbor* is being addressed
160 *signa*: Thisbe is referring to the reddened mulberries
pull-us a um sombre
apt-us a um appropriate for (+ dat.)
161 *moniment-um ī* 2n. memorial
162 *aptō* 1 fit
mucrō mucrōn-is 3m. sharp point (of sword)
īm-us a um lower (part of)
163 *incumbō* 3 *incubuī* lean on (+ dat.)
ferr-um ī 2n. blade
tepeō 2 grow warm
165 *permātūrēscō* 3 *permātūruī* ripen
166 *rog-us ī* 2m. funeral pyre
requiēscō 3 rest, lie
urn-a ae 1f. urn

In this tale Ovid beautifully mixes narrative and soliloquy and combines the innocent, the juvenile, the ludicrous and the rather sweet, with a good dose of high rhetoric too. It certainly makes an agreeable change from the destructive and cynical *amōrēs* of the gods.

But there is more than that: there is parody – of romance (parents forbidding marriage; lovers escaping, then losing each other; mistaken suicides; together with all the overblown language); and of Roman love-elegy, in which the lover laments his inability to be with his beloved. Typical of such literature is the 'excluded lover', trying to get into his beloved's room – a situation parodied here by reversal, as Pyramus and Thisbe have to *leave* their houses to be together (e.g. Thisbe silently opening the door is a regular feature of such poetry).

Learning vocabulary for Passage 9, Pyramus and Thisbe

āter ātr-a um black
fēt-us ūs 4m. fruit
laniō 1 tear at
mōr-us ī 2f./mōr-um ī 2n. mulberry-tree
murmur -is 3n. whisper
pact-um ī 2n. agreement

pact-us a um agreed
pariēs pariet-is 3m. wall
pōm-um ī 2n. fruit
radi-us ī 2m. ray
tumul-us ī 2m. tomb, mound, hill
uēlāmen uēlāmin-is 3n. cloak

Study section

1. Write out and scan ll.142–6.
2. Does *tremebunda* (133) agree better with Thisbe (understood subject) or *membra* (134)?
3. If the text at 143 read *cārissima* with no commas, what would it mean? Which do you prefer?
4. In what senses would you call this story 'romantic'?
5. 'Pyramus and Thisbe wish to move away from "nods and signs" with which their love was first formulated to a real presence, in which the barriers of language are effaced and they can be truly together . . . Their failure is therefore inevitable, because there can be no such escape from language' (Fowler, 2000, 161). Discuss.
6. What do you make of Arthur Golding's translation of ll.93–163? Is it fair to the spirit of Ovid?

   1 As soon as darkness once was come, straight Thisbe did devise   93
     A shift to wind her out of doors, that none that were within
     Perceive her. And, muffling her with clothes about her chin
     That no man might discern her face, to Ninus' tomb she came
   5 Unto that tree and sat her down there underneath the same.   95
     Love made her bold. But see the chance: there comes besmeared with blood
     About the chaps a lioness all foaming from the wood
     From slaughter lately made of kine, to staunch her bloody thirst
     With water of the foresaid spring. Whom Thisbe spying first
  10 Afar by moonlight, thereupon with fearful steps gan fly   100
     And in a dark and irksome cave did hide herself thereby.
     And as she fled away for haste, she let her mantle fall,
     The which for fear she left behind, not looking back at all.
     Now when the cruel lioness her thirst had staunched well,
  15 In going to the wood she found the slender weed that fell
     From Thisbe, which with bloody teeth in pieces she did tear.
     The night was somewhat further spent ere Pyramus came there;   105
     Who, seeing in the subtle sand the print of lion's paw,

Waxed pale for fear. But when also the bloody cloak he saw
20 All rent and torn, 'One night', he said, 'shall lovers two confound,
Of which long life deservèd she of all that live on ground.
My soul deserves of this mischance the peril for to bear;   110
I, wretch, have been the death of thee, which to this place of fear
Did cause thee in the night to come and came not here before.
25 My wicked limbs and wretched guts with cruel teeth therefore
Devour ye, O ye lions all that in this rock do dwell!
But cowards use to wish for death.' The slender weed that fell   115
From Thisbe up he takes and straight doth bear it to the tree
Which was appointed erst the place of meeting for to be.
30 And when he had bewept and kissed the garment which he knew,
'Receive thou my blood too,' quoth he. And therewithal he drew
His sword, the which among his guts he thrust, and by and by
Did draw it from the bleeding wound, beginning for to die,   120
And cast himself upon his back. The blood did spin on high
35 As, when a conduit-pipe is cracked, the water, bursting out,
Doth shoot itself a great way off and pierce the air about.
The leaves that were upon the tree, besprinkled with his blood,   125
Were dyèd black. The root also, bestainèd as it stood,
A deep dark purple colour straight upon the berries cast.
40 Anon, scarce ridded of her fear with which she was aghast,
For doubt of disappointing him comes Thisbe forth in haste
And for her lover looks about, rejoicing for to tell
How hardly she had scaped that night the danger that befell.   130
And as she knew right well the place and fashion of the tree
45 (As which she saw so late before), even so when she did see
The colour of the berries turned, she was uncertain whether
It were the tree at which they both agreed to meet together.
While in this doubtful stound[1] she stood, she cast her eye aside
And there beweltered in his blood her lover she espied
50 Lie sprawling with his dying limbs. At which she started back
And lookèd pale as any box; a shuddering through her strake,
Even like the sea which suddenly with whizzing noise doth move   135
When with a little blast of wind it is but touched above.
But when, approaching nearer him, she knew it was her love,
55 She beat her breast, she shriekèd out, she tare her golden hairs
And, taking him between her arms, did wash his wounds with tears.
She ment[2] her weeping with his blood and, kissing all his face   140
(Which now became as cold as ice), she cried in woeful case,

1. *stound* = amazement
2. *ment* = mixed

'Alas! What chance, my Pyramus, hath parted thee and me?
60 Make answer, O my Pyramus! It is thy Thisb, even she
Whom thou dost love most heartily that speaketh unto thee.
Give ear and raise thy heavy head.' He, hearing Thisbe's name,   145
Lift up his dying eyes and, having seen her, closed the same.
But when she knew her mantle there and saw his scabbard lie
65 Without the sword, 'Unhappy man, thy love hath made thee die.
Thy love', she said, 'hath made thee slay thyself. This hand of mine
Is strong enough to do the like. My love no less than thine   150
Shall give me force to work my wound. I will pursue the dead
And, wretched woman as I am, it shall of me be said
70 That like as of thy death I was the only cause and blame,
So am I thy companion eke and partner in the same.
For death which only could, alas, asunder part us twain
Shall never so dissever us but we will meet again.
And you, the parents of us both, most wretched folk alive,   155
75 Let this request that I shall make in both our names belive[3]
Entreat you to permit that we, whom chaste and steadfast love
And whom even death hath joined in one, may as it doth behove
In one grave be together laid. And thou, unhappy tree,
Which shroudest now the corse of one and shalt anon through me
80 Shroud two, of this same slaughter hold the sicker signs for aye:
Black be the colour of thy fruit and mourning-like alway,   160
Such as the murder of us twain may evermore bewray.'
This said, she took the sword yet warm with slaughter of her love
And, setting it beneath her breast, did to her heart it shove.
7. It is worth comparing the rude mechanicals' version of this story in Shakespeare's *Midsummer Night's Dream* (Act 5, scene 1). Shakespeare knew Ovid through Golding.

3. *belive* = at once

10   Arethusa *Metamorphōsēs* 5.572–641

Background

Minerva is in conversation with the Muses, goddesses of the arts, who tell of the challenge to their skills thrown down by the mortal daughters of Pierus (the Pierides). In the ensuing contest of song, the Muses choose Calliope to represent them. First, one of the Muses says, Calliope sings of Pluto's (Hades') abduction of Proserpina (Persephone), daughter of Ceres (Demeter). Ceres scoured the world for her lost child, and eventually the Sicilian river-goddess Arethusa told her that she had seen her in the underworld. The incensed Ceres went to Jupiter, who negotiated a settlement – Proserpina was to spend six months with Hades in the underworld, and six months with Ceres on earth.

The Muse now relates how Calliope described Ceres, relieved at her daughter's return, asking Arethusa how she had arrived in Sicily and become a sacred spring. The *mise-en-scène* is Arethusa's spring in Sicily, where Arethusa had given Ceres the news about her daughter.

5.572–84: *Arethusa describes how she never paid much attention to her looks*

'exigit alma Cerēs, nātā sēcūra receptā,
quae tibi causa fugae, cūr sīs, Arethūsa, sacer fōns.
conticuēre undae, quārum dea sustulit altō

---

572 *exigō* 3 ask
alm-us a um kindly
Cerēs Cerer-is 3f. Ceres
nātā: i.e. Proserpina
sēcūr-us a um free of care, relieved
573 *tibi*: in this part of Calliope's reported song, Ceres is envisaged to be chatting away with Arethusa

causa fugae [*sit*]: in her earlier encounter with Arethusa (5.487–508), Ceres had learned that Arethusa, though born in Greece, now regarded Sicily as her home
574 *conticeō* 2 fall silent. The *undae* = the waters of Arethusa's spring

---

572–84: Calliope reports how Ceres, relieved at the return of her daughter, asked Arethusa about her flight and transformation into a *fōns* (572–3). It will emerge that, as a young girl from the region of Elis in Greece, Arethusa had been pursued by the local river-god Alpheus and ended up in Sicily as a spring (goddess). It is interesting that

fonte caput, uiridēsque manū siccāta capillōs,   575
flūminis Ēleī ueterēs nārrāuit amōrēs.
"parsʌ ego nymphārum, quae sunt in Achāide," dīxit
"ʌūna fuī, nec mē studiōsius altera saltūs
lēgit, nec posuit studiōsius altera cassēs.
sed quamuīs fōrmae numquam mihi fāma petīta est,   580
quamuīs fortis eram, fōrmōsae nōmen habēbam,
nec mea mē faciēs nimium laudāta iuuābat.
quāque aliae gaudēre solent, ego rūstica dōte
corporis ērubuī, crīmenque placēre putāuī." '

5.585–98: *One day after hunting she stripped to bathe in a stream*

'lassa reuertēbar (meminī) Stymphālide siluā.   585
aestus erat, magnumque labor gemināuerat aestum.
inueniō sine uertice aquās, sine murmure euntēs,
perspicuās ad humum, per quās numerābilis altē

---

575 *siccō* 1 remove excess moisture from, dry
capillōs: acc. of respect after *siccāta*
576 *Ēlē-us a um* of Elis (in Greece, through which
   the river Alpheus ran)
577 *Achāis Achāid-is* 3f. Achaea, the Peloponnese
   (southern Greece)
578 *studiōs-us a um* keen, eager (here a comp. adv.;
   note *mē*, abl., and the clever verbal balancing of
   578–9)
salt-us ūs 4m. glade
579 *cass-is is* 3m. hunting-net
581 *fōrmōs-us a um* beautiful; (noun) a beauty. Note
   the word-play with *fortis*, *fāma* and *fōrma* in
   580–1
582 *iuuō* 1 please

583 *rūstic-us a um* from the country
dōs dōt-is 3f. gift, dowry (of beauty). Here it is abl.
   expressing cause, RL108.2, WSuppl.syntax
584 *ērubēscō* 3 *ērubuī* blush, feel shame
crīmen: supply *esse*, 'it to be a crime to . . .'
585 *lass-us a um* tired, exhausted
reuertor 3 dep. turn back from (+ abl.)
Stymphālis Stymphālid-is 3 of Stymphalus (in the
   Peloponnese)
586 *gerninō* 1 double
587 *uertex uertic-is* 3m. eddy, swirl. The description
   of a *locus amoenus* begins (see Introduction, p. 8)
*murmur -is 3n. low noise, murmur
588 *perspicu-us a um* clear
numerābil-is e able to be counted

Arethusa describes Alpheus' attempted rape as *amōrēs* (see Introduction, pp. 9–10).
Arethusa/her spring falls silent as she rises from its waves, wrings the water out of her
hair – a homely touch: no nymph can tell her story with wet hair – and prepares to tell the
tale of what happened to her long ago (574–6).

   Arethusa's situation is typical of a number of Ovid's heroines: a country (583) girl, part
of a gang (577–8), with an enthusiasm for and skill in hunting (578–9, cf. *fortis* 581),
known for her beauty but having no interest in it. Indeed, she thought it wrong to be
attractive in this way – that was for others (580–4). She is, in other words, a simple,
modest girl. We know what happens to such girls in Ovid.

585–98: She goes hunting; it is summer; she gets hot and tired (585–6) – no surprise, since
Stymphalus, from which she is returning, is sixty miles from her home in the Elis region.
Lo, she comes across a *locus amoenus*: clear, still, silent water (587–9 – note how she elicits

calculus omnis erat, quās tū uix īre putārēs.
cāna salicta dabant nūtrītaque pōpulus undā   590
sponte suā nātās rīpīs dēclīuibus umbrās.
accessī, prīmumque pedis uestīgia tīnxī,
poplite dēinde tenus; neque eō contenta, recingor
molliaque impōnō salicī uēlāmina curuae,
nūdaque mergor aquīs. quās dum feriōque trahōque   595
mīlle modīs lābēns excussaque brācchia iactō,
nescioquod mediō sēnsī sub gurgite murmur,
territaque īnsistō propiōris margine rīpae.'

5.599–617: *The river (god) Alpheus calls out to her, and the chase begins*

' "quō properās, Arethūsa?" suīs Alphēus ab undīs,
"quō properās?" iterum raucō mihi dīxerat ōre.   600

589 *calcul-us ī* 2m. pebble
īre: i.e. flow, move (*aquās* still subject)
putārēs: note conditional subj. and 'apostrophe'. Do the spondees of *quās tū uix īre putārēs* imitate the sluggishness of the river?
590 *cān-us a um* white
salict-um ī 2n. willow
nūtriō 4 feed
pōpul-us ī 2f. poplar tree
591 *sponte suā* of its own accord
nātās . . . umbrās: object of *dabant*; *nāt-us* here means 'natural'
rīpīs: dat. pl.
dēclīu-is e sloping
592 *tingō* 3 *tīnxī* dip
593 *poples poplit-is* 3m. knee
tenus + abl. up to, so far as

content-us a um satisfied
recingor 3 (pass.) strip
594 *impōnō* 3 place X (acc.) on Y (dat.). Nearly a golden line
salix salic-is 3f. willow
uēlāmen uēlāmin-is 3n. clothes
595 *feriō* 4 strike
596 *excutiō* 3/4 *excussī excussum* shake (out)
iactō 1 throw
597 *gurges gurgit-is* 3m. stream, flood, eddy. A sinister golden line
598 *insistō* 3 stand
propior -is nearer
599 *Alphē-us ī* 2m. god of the river Alpheus, who lives in its streams
600 *rauc-us a um* husky, hoarse

the listener's sympathy with *putārēs*, 589), and overhanging trees (willows and poplars, common beside rivers), fed by the stream, giving shade to the banks (590–1). She takes all her clothes off and plunges in, and Ovid lingers over the strip show – she dabbles the toes, goes in up to the knees, finds it all irresistible (*neque eō contenta*), then off with the clothes (carefully hanging them from a willow-tree, 594 – a nice touch) and in she glides (592–5). Then what happens? Enter a river-god. Ovid motivates his entrance by making Arethusa splash around a lot (595–6) – more horizontal drowning than swimming, but the ancients were not renowned for their interest in the activity – and in such a normally peaceful spot it is not surprising Alpheus notices. But Arethusa too senses something is wrong, and *territa* – this is such a quiet spot – immediately hops out onto the nearer bank (597–8). But are her clothes within reach . . . ? One's thoughts race at the delightful vision, all the more agreeable for being left to the imagination. The answer is, of course, no (601–2).

599–617: Alpheus twice bellows the same question roughly at her (599–600: subtlety is not his strength), and that is enough to put Arethusa to flight (see 573), naked too, for

sīcut eram, fugiō sine uestibus (altera uestēs
rīpa meās habuit): tantō magis īnstat et ardet,
et quia nūda fuī, sum uīsa parātior illī.
sīc ego currēbam, sīc mē ferus ille premēbat,
ut fugere accipitrem pennā trepidante columbae,   605
ut solet accipiter trepidās urgēre columbās.
usque sub Orchomenon Psōphīdaque Cyllēnēnque
Maenaliōsque sinūs gelidumque Erymanthon et Ēlin
currere sustinuī, nec mē uēlōcior ille.
sed tolerāre diū cursūs ego uīribus impār   610
nōn poteram, longī patiēns erat ille labōris.
[But even through plains, mountains covered with trees,
and rocks and crags and where there was no way, I ran.]
sōl erat ā tergō: uīdī praecēdere longam
ante pedēs umbram, nisi sī timor illa uidēbat;   615

602 *īnstō* 1 press forward, be urgent
603 *parāt-us a um* ready, prepared
605 **accipiter accipitr-is* 3m. hawk. Note the verbal
  balance and variety of 604–6
trepidō 1 tremble
*columb-a ae 1f. dove
606 *trepid-us a um* terrified
urgeō 2 chase
607 *Orchomenon*: Greek acc. of Orchomenos; the
  first of a list of six Greek locations, in the order
  three towns, two mountain areas and a region.
  The three towns of 607 are given their locations in
  the three areas of 608

Psōphīda: Greek acc. of Psophis
Cyllēnēn: Greek acc. of Cyllene (note the rare fifth-
  foot spondee)
608 *Maenali-us a um* of Maenalos
sin-us ūs 4m. hollow, gulf
Erymanthon: Greek acc. of Erymanthus
Ēlin: Greek acc. of Elis
610 *tolerō* 1 sustain
impār -is unequal in (+ abl.)
611 *patiēns* able to put up with (+ gen.)
[But even . . . I ran]: a later addition to the text
614 *praecēdō* 3 move ahead
615 *nisi sī timor*: 'unless it was my fear that . . .'

reasons she explains, making Alpheus all the more enthusiastic, as she well understands (601–3). One cannot blame him (she certainly does not seem to). He is a pagan god. In his eyes, what are beautiful naked women in woods *for*? Especially ones who have been frolicking about in *his* river? The chase is accompanied by an image adapted from Homer: 'As a mountain hawk, the fastest thing on wings, effortlessly swoops after a timid dove; under and away the dove dives off, and the hawk, shrieking close behind, strikes at it again and again . . .' (*Iliad* 22.139–42, Rieu–Jones). Arethusa sees the chase from both sides – the pursuer and the pursued, the terrifying and the terrified – and in language that closely mirrors the opposing points of view (604–6). The length of the chase is ludicrous: to interleave 607–8, Alpheus to Orchomenus (near the plain of Maenalus) is thirty-five miles; from there to Psophis (near Mount Erymanthus) is twenty-five miles; and from there to Cyllene (on the coast in Elis) is forty-five miles – a grand total of 105 miles. Fit girl, Arethusa, especially when you realise that her day's hunting had already taken her to Stymphalus (sixty miles from home) and then back to the Alpheus (say, fifty miles) where she had (briefly) enjoyed her cooling dip. But this is what people in myth can do. Arethusa is going well, but the god's stamina is superior and, whether she imagines seeing his shadow or not (a nice touch, 615), she hears his feet and feels his panting breath on

sed certē sonitusque pedum terrēbat, et ingēns∧
crīnālēs uittās adflābat ∧anhēlitus ōris.'

5.618–41: *Arethusa calls on Diana for help, who turns her into a stream*

'fessa labōre fugae "fer opem, dēprendimur," inquam
"armigerae, Diāna, tuae, cūi saepe dedistī
ferre tuōs arcūs inclūsaque tēla pharetrā!"   620
mōta dea est, spissīsque ferēns ē nūbibus ūnam
mē super iniēcit. lūstrat cālīgine tēctam
amnis, et ignārus circum caua nūbila quaerit,
bisque locum, quō mē dea tēxerat, īnscius ambit,
et bis "iō Arethūsa, iō Arethūsa" uocāuit.   625

616 *sonit-us ūs* 4m. sound	*lūstrō* 1 survey, scan
617 *crīnāl-is e* in my hair	*cālīgō cālīgin-is* 3f. mist
uitt-a ae 1f. band	*tēctam*: supply *mē*
adflō 1 breathe on	**623** *amn-is is 3m. river (god)
anhēlit-us ūs 4m. gasping	*cau-us a um* hollow
619 *armiger -a -um* armour-bearer	*nūbil-um ī* 2n. cloud
620 *inclūs-us a um* enclosed	**624** *bis twice
621 *spiss-us a um* dense, thick	*īnsc-us a um* ignorant
*nūb-ēs is 3f. cloud	*ambiō* 4 go round, skirt
ūnam: i.e. of the clouds	**625** *iō* hey! Note the three hiatuses involving *iō* (see
622 *iniciō* 3/4 *iniēcī* throw	passage 1, 1.363)

her hair (609–17) – a vivid, Homeric touch. In the funeral games for Patroclus, Odysseus races against Ajax son of Oileus and keeps hard behind him: 'So close was Odysseus behind Ajax, his feet falling in Ajax's tracks before the dust had settled down again; and he kept up so well that his breath fanned Ajax's head. He was desperate to win, and all the Greeks cheered him on, shouting encouragement to a man who was doing all he could already' (*Iliad* 23.763–7, Rieu–Jones). In Homer, our eyes are on Odysseus, the pursuer: in Ovid, on the pursued. Arethusa does not, of course, see the terrifying, unseen predator: she has no time to look round.

618–41: As an enthusiastic huntress, Arethusa (we now learn) had served the virgin goddess Diana as her armour-bearer; to her, therefore, she calls for help (618–20). The goddess responds, hiding Arethusa in thick cloud. This leaves Alpheus baffled, and he stalks around this cloud, repeatedly calling out for her (622–5: after a 105-mile chase, one might have expected Alpheus to register that he was not wanted, but obviously not). Arethusa now turns the spotlight on her feelings which, in an unexpected way, will be the key to her fate. Two apt epic images occur to her: first, 627, sheep hearing wolves howling round a sheepfold (Turnus prowls round the Trojan camp 'like a wolf in the dead of night, lying in wait in all the wind and rain by a pen full of sheep, and growling at the gaps in the fence, while the lambs keep up their bleating, safe beneath their mothers', Virgil, *Aeneid* 9.59–63, West); second, 628–9, a hare cowering under a bush in sight of the hunting dogs'

quid mihi∧ tunc animī ∧miserae fuit? anne quod agnae est,
si qua lupōs audit circum stabula alta frementēs;
aut leporī, quī, uepre latēns, hostīlia cernit
ōra canum, nūllōsque audet dare corpore mōtūs?
nōn tamen abscēdit; neque enim uestīgia cernit   630
longius ūlla pedum: seruat nūbemque locumque.
occupat obsessōs sūdor mihi frīgidus artūs,
caeruleaeque cadunt tōtō dē corpore guttae,
quāque pedem mōuī, mānat locus, ēque capillīs
rōs cadit et, citius quam nunc tibi facta renārrō,   635
in laticēs mūtor. sed enim cognōscit amātās
amnis aquās, positōque uirī, quod sūmpserat, ōre
uertitur in propriās, ut sē mihi misceat, undās.

---

626 *quid animī*: lit. 'what [of] mind', i.e. what thoughts (subject of *fuit*), RLL(d)2, W15
anne quod agnae est: lit. 'whether [my *animus* is] what it is for a lamb' (gen. of characteristic)
627 *lup-us ī* 2m. wolf
circum + acc., around
stabul-um ī 2n. sheepfold, pen
fremō 3 howl
628 *lepus lepor-is* 3m. hare
uepr-is is 3m. thorn-bush
hostīl-is e hostile
629 *can-is is* 3m./f. dog
mot-us ūs 4m. movement
630 *abscēdō* 3 leave (the god is the subject)
631 *longius*: i.e. further on

632 *obsideō* 2 *obsessī obsessum* besiege
sūdor -is 3m. sweat
frigid-us a um cold
633 *caerule-us a um* blue-green (because she is a water-nymph)
gutt-a ae 1f. drop
634 *mānō* 1 drip
635 *rōs rōr-is* 3m. dew
citius more quickly
renārrō repeat, tell
636 *latic-ēs um* 3m. pl. water
637 *quod*: refers to *ōre*
638 *propri-us a um* own
misceō 2 mix X (acc.) into Y (dat.), i.e. have intercourse with

---

jaws, terrified of moving (Menelaus leaves the battlefield, looking all round him 'like an eagle, which is said to have the sharpest sight of any bird in the sky: however high in the air, it still spots the swift hare crouching under a leafy bush and swoops down, seizes it and takes its life', *Iliad* 17.674–8, Rieu–Jones). But, dim and baffled (623, 624) as Alpheus is, he does not give up – after all, he sees no footprints leading away from the cloud, so she must still be in there – so he just keeps watching and waiting (630–1). Back to Arethusa, on whom the pressure is beginning to tell: she starts to sweat, drops fall, the ground under her feet gets soaked, it pours from her hair – and lo, she is gradually and almost naturalistically liquefying (632–6! – though we are not told that Diana brought this about). At this point Arethusa presumably starts trickling her way out of the cloud; at any rate, Alpheus, who may be dim in some respects but knows a thing or two about water, realises the stream must be her and immediately reverts to liquid form himself in order to mate with her (636–8). But Diana now intervenes to anticipate him. She splits the earth, Arethusa pours into it before Alpheus can do anything about it and, swept due west along an underground tunnel under the sea, surfaces about 250 miles away on Ortygia, an island off Syracuse in Sicily (639–41). Virtue triumphant! It is rare for a nymph in *Metamorphōsēs* to escape the attentions of a rampant god.

Dēlia rūpit humum, caecīsque ego mersa cauernīs
aduehor Ortygiam quae^ mē, cognōmine dīuae*   640
^grāta *meae, superās ēdūxit ^prīma sub aurās.'

639 *Dēli-a ae* 1f. Delia (lit. 'born on Delos'), i.e.
    Diana
rumpō 3 *rūpī* break, cleave
caec-us a um blind, dark
cauern-a ae 1f. cavern
640 *aduehor* 3 pass. be carried off
641 *Ortygi-a ae* 1f. Ortygia, an island at the entrance
    to the harbour of Syracuse. Arethusa was carried

along an underground river from Greece to this
island in Sicily, where she finally emerged into the
upper air again and became a spring
cognōmine dīuae . . . meae: i.e. because it bore the
    name of my [patron] goddess. Ortygia ('Quail
    island') was the original name of the Greek island
    of Delos, where Diana (Artemis) and Apollo were
    born

Learning vocabulary for Passage 10, Arethusa

accipiter accipitr-is 3m. hawk
amn-is is 3m. river (god)
bis twice

columb-a ae 1f. dove
murmur -is 3n. low noise, murmur
nūb-es is 3f. cloud

    This is a splendid story. The theme may be commonplace but the telling, in the mouth
of the woman who experienced it all, is not. It is full of vivid, pacy, narrative action and
sharp, engaging observations.

Study section

1. Write out and scan ll.593–8.
2. What picture of Arethusa emerges from this story? How is it different from
   e.g. that of Daphne (passage 2) and Io (passage 3), and why? (Bear in mind
   who the narrator is.)
3. Account for the changes Ovid has made to the two epic similes at 626–9.
4. Does Arethusa express any resentment at her treatment by Alpheus? Why
   not?

11   Minerva and Arachne, *Metamorphōsēs* 6.1–145

Background

The Arethusa story (passage 10) was one of the contributions made by the Muse Calliope (as reported by another Muse) in the singing contest to which the Muses had been challenged by the proud (mortal) daughters of Pierus. The Muses, naturally, won, and the Pierides were turned into chattering magpies. These stories were being told to Minerva; and in this story, Minerva (who thoroughly approved of the Muses' revenge) remembered that she had been challenged to a weaving contest by the mortal Arachne. This leads Ovid to tell the story of Minerva's action against her.

6.1–13: *Minerva looks for revenge on the lowly but brilliant weaver Arachne*

praebuerat dictīs Trītōnia tālibus aurēs,
carminaque Āonidum iūstamque probāuerat īram.
tum sēcum: 'laudāre parum est, laudēmur et ipsae,
nūmina∧ nec spernī sine poenā ∧nostra sināmus.'
Maeoniaeque animum fātīs intendit Arachnēs,   5

---

1 *praebuerat*: note the string of plupfs. (2, 7, 10, 11, 12), laying out the background to the story
Trītōni-a ae 1f. Minerva/Athena (said to be connected with Lake Tritonis in Greece)
2 *carmen carmin-is* 3n. song
Āonid-es um 3f. pl. the Muses (Mount Helicon, home of the Muses, was situated in Aonia, a part of Boeotia in Greece)
iram: i.e. at the daughters of Pierus for challenging the Muses to a singing contest, for which the Muses subsequently punished them
3 *laudāre*: understand 'Muses' as the object
parum too little, not enough

laudēmur: note the jussive subj., like *sināmus*, 4. Minerva uses the royal 'we' here, meaning 'I' (hence *ipsae*, nom. pl. f.)
4 **spernō* 3 *sprēuī sprētum* spurn, despise
sinō 3 allow
5 *Maeoni-us a um* from Maeonia, another name for Lydia (central western Turkey)
fātīs: i.e. the fate that Minerva ought to deal out to her
intendō 3 direct, turn
Arachnēs: Greek gen. s. of *Arachnē* (the Greek for 'spider')

1–13: Minerva thoroughly approves of the Muses' treatment of the Pierides who had had the temerity to challenge the Muses to a singing contest (1–2). Nevertheless, her praise for them reminds her that she needs to be praised too (ancient gods were never modest about their demands or needs), and she remembers that her own godhead is currently

[149]

quam sibi lānificae^ nōn cēdere laudibus ^artis
audierat. nōn illa locō nec orīgine gentis
clāra, sed arte, fuit. pater hūīc Colophōnius Idmōn
Phōcaicō bibulās tingēbat mūrice lānās;
occiderat māter, sed et haec dē plēbe suōque   10
aequa uirō fuerat. Lȳdās tamen illa per urbēs
quaesierat studiō nōmen memorābile quamuīs,
orta domō paruā, paruīs habitābat Hypaepīs.

6.14–25: *Everyone came to see Arachne's work, which looked like Minerva's*

hūīus ut adspicerent opus admīrābile, saepe
dēseruēre suī nymphae uīnēta Timōlī,   15
dēseruēre suās nymphae Pactōlides undās.

6 *quam . . . audierat*: '[Arachne] whom [Minerva]
    had heard'
lānific-us a um to do with wool-working, weaving
cēdere: i.e. Arachne did not yield *sibi* (i.e. to
    Minerva) in *laudibus artis lānificae*
7 *illa*: i.e. Arachne (subject) *fuit clāra nōn . . . nōn
    . . . sed . . .* (all abl. explaining *in what/why* she
    was [not] famous, **RLL**(f)4(iii), **WSuppl.**syntax)
8 *Colophōni-us a um* from Colophon (in Ionia,
    central western Turkey)
Idmōn -is 3m. Idmon, Arachne's father
9 *Phōcaic-us a um* from Phocaea (a coastal town
    north of Colophon). Observe the golden line to
    describe the work of Arachne's humble father
bibul-us a um thirsty, absorbent
tingō 3 dye, tint
mūrex mūric-is 3m. (very expensive) purple dye
    (extracted from shellfish)

*lān-a ae 1f. wool
10 *occiderat*: meaning? Note scansion
sed et haec but she too
plēbs plēb-is 3f. common citizen, member of rank-
    and-file
suō . . . uirō: dat. after *aequa* (they are equal in
    humble origin)
11 *Lȳd-us a um* of Lydia
illa: i.e. Arachne
12 *memorābil-is e* memorable
13 *Hypaep-a ōrum* 2n. Hypaepa, a town in Lydia
14 *admīrābil-is e* wonderful
15 *uinēt-um ī* 2n. vineyard
Timōl-us ī 2m. Timolus (also Tmolus), a mountain
    in Lydia
16 *Pactōlis Pactōlid-is* 3f. of the river Pactolus, whose
    source lay in T(i)molus. It was supposed to run
    with gold (see **Comment** on passage 19, 11.137)

being insulted (3–4) by the mortal Arachne, who (Minerva had heard) reckoned she was
just as good a weaver as Minerva herself (5–7). And so, with a somewhat lumpy thematic
transition, Ovid moves on to the next story. Arachne's humble origins – her father a mere
pleb who worked with dye, her dead mother his equal in this (7–11) – make her trans-
gression all the more galling, and Ovid emphasises Arachne's active desire for almost
heroic fame (*nōmen memorābile*) in spite of her background (12–13: *parua paruīs* reinforces our sense of the 'small-town' girl keen to make good). Ovid, having told us that
Minerva was wondering what to do about Arachne (5), prompts us (as often) to see this
account of Arachne's activities through Minerva's eyes, as if 6–13 were her reflections on
the matter.

14–25: Further – and even worse – Arachne had actually won the fame she sought, since
crowds of nymphs came from miles not only to admire the finished product but even to

nec factās sōlum uestēs, spectāre iuuābat

tum quoque cum fierent: tantus decor adfuit artī.

sīue rudem prīmōs lānam glomerābat in orbēs,

seu digitīs subigēbat opus, repetītaque^ longō*   20

^uellera mollībat nebulās ^aequantia *tractū,

sīue leuī teretem uersābat pollice fūsum,

seu pingēbat acū – scīrēs ā Pallade doctam.

quod tamen ipsa negat, tantāque offēnsa magistrā

'certet' ait 'mēcum: nihil est quod uicta recūsem!'   25

17 *spectāre iuuābat*: controls *factās uestēs* (the finished product) and *uestēs* (understood)

18 *tum quoque cum . . . fierent*: i.e. the actual processes; just watching Arachne prepare her material was an experience by itself, as Ovid goes on to explain

19 **sīue . . . seu* whether . . . or

rud-is e raw. The raw wool, sheared or pulled off the sheep, was first formed into a ball (19); the ball was fixed onto a stick (distaff); from this 'cloud' (as Ovid calls it, 21) of wool a thread was teased out between finger and thumb of the left hand (20–1), and fixed on to a spindle (spinning stick) which one twirled with the right hand (22). The left hand continued to feed the thread on to the spindle, round which the thread wrapped itself. The finished thread was then ready to be woven on the loom

glomerō 1 gather, form

20 *subigō* 3 work

repetīt-us a um set on again, worked with again (i.e. repeatedly)

21 *uellus ueller-is* 3n. fleece

nebul-a ae 1f. cloud

aequō 1 resemble (+ acc.)

tract-us ūs 4m. drawing-out (into threads)

22 *teres teret-is* smooth, rounded. A golden line

uersō 1 turn

pollex pollic-is 3m. thumb

fūs-us ī 2m. spindle

23 **pingō* 3 *pinxī pictum* embroider, depict, paint

ac-us ūs 4f. needle

scīrēs: main verb after *sīue . . . seu . . . sīue . . . seu*. Note conditional subj. and apostrophe, drawing the reader in to agree with Ovid's compliment, which he repeats at 104. Nevertheless, we do not actually *witness* Minerva teaching her; we have to assume that Minerva, being goddess of weaving, must automatically have given her the skills she had

*Pallas Pallad-is 3f. Pallas [Athena], i.e. Minerva. 'Pallas' is a Greek word of mysterious derivation; it may mean 'mistress'

doctam [*esse*]: sc. 'that she had been . . .'

24 *quod*: 'a suggestion which', as if someone had on some occasion made such a remark and she had vehemently denied it. In so doing, Arachne was effectively denying the existence of Minerva as goddess of weaving

offēns-us a um annoyed at (+ abl.)

magistr-a ae 1f. teacher (i.e. Minerva)

25 *certō* 1 compete (note: subj.)

nihil: i.e. no penalty/punishment

uicta: participle with conditional force, **RLP4**

*recūsō 1 refuse (to pay)

Figure 2   Spinning on Ithaca.

watch her work (14–18). The balanced repetitions of 15–16, especially the forceful *dēseruēre* (not just 'left') and repeated *suī, suās*, emphasise that whatever people's attachments to their homes, they still came. Ovid now expands on Arachne's manual skill, covering everything from forming the raw wool into balls and drawing it out in threads, to turning the spindle and embroidering (19–23). The climax comes at 23–5: she must have been taught by Minerva herself (note the 2nd s. *scīrēs*, drawing the reader into agreement).

6.26–33: *Minerva, disguised as an old woman, tells Arachne to be humble*

Pallas anum simulat, falsōsque in tempora cānōs
addit et īnfirmōs, baculō quōs sustinet, artūs.
tum sīc orsa loquī: 'nōn omnia grandior aetās,
quae fugiāmus, habet; sērīs uenit ūsus ab annīs.
cōnsilium nē sperne meum. tibi fāma^ petātur   30
inter mortālēs faciendae ^maxima lānae.
cēde deae, ueniamque tuīs, temerāria, dictīs
supplice uōce rogā: ueniam dabit illa rogantī.'

6.34–52: *Arachne refuses and accepts Minerva's challenge to a contest*

adspicit hanc toruīs, inceptaque fila relinquit,
uixque manum retinēns, cōnfessaque uultibus īram,   35

---

26 *an-us ūs* 4f. old woman
tempus tempor-is 3n. side of the forehead, temple
cān-us a um grey (hair)
27 *īnfirm-us a um* weak
artūs: take in order *īnfirmōs artūs quōs baculō sustinet*
bacul-um ī 2n. stick
28 *grand-is e* old
29 *quae fugiāmus*: picks up *omnia*, i.e. 'not everything that older age has [is the sort of thing]' *quae
   fugiāmus* (generic subj., **RL**140, **W**38)
*sēr-us a um late(r)

30 *nē sperne*: for *nē* + imp. 'don't' (common in
   poetry), see **RLL-V**(a)3
petātur: note subj.
32 **ueni-a ae* 1f. pardon, forgiveness
temerāri-us a um rash
33 *supplex supplic-is* humble
34 *adspicit*: Arachne is subject
*toru-us a um grim, unyielding (supply *oculīs*)
*incept-us a um begun (*incipiō*); *incept-um ī* 2n.
   beginning, plan
fīl-um ī 2n. thread

Nonsense, says Arachne, *offēnsa* at the idea that her skill was anyone's but her own – let Minerva challenge me and find out! One can sense Minerva's bile rising as she goes through all this in her mind (cf. 30–3). This narrative so far is all background to the story proper, which will begin at 26. Observe how Ovid's careful use of tense marks it off: plu-perfects *audierat* (7), *occiderat* (10), *fuerat* (11), *quaesierat* (12), followed by perfects and imperfects (15–23). Then, in 24–5, Ovid switches to the present – the situation as it is now, with which Minerva is about to deal.

26–33: Disguising herself as an old woman (26–7), Minerva argues that, since old age has some uses, Arachne should be prepared to take advice from her (28–30; note *sperne*, cf. 4) – do not challenge the gods but ask forgiveness for daring to do so (30–3). Note *cēde*, *ueniam* (twice), *temerāria*, *supplice*, and *rogō* (twice). Will a proud woman like Arachne listen to that? It is almost as if Minerva is inviting Arachne to fall into the trap.

34–52: It is Arachne's last chance. She fluffs it. Furious, she puts down her work, only just prevents herself from hitting the old woman and, turning on her (34–6), accuses her of being senile (37–8) and bossy (38–9), and expresses confidence in her own

tālibus obscūram resecūta est Pallada dictīs:
'mentis inops longāque uenīs cōnfecta senectā,
et nimium uīxisse diū nocet. audiat istās∧,
sī qua tibī nurus est, sī qua est tibi fīlia, ∧uōcēs.
cōnsiliī satis est in mē mihi, nēue monendō   40
prōfēcisse putēs, eadem est sententia nōbīs.
cūr nōn ipsa uenit? cūr haec certāmina uītat?'
tum dea 'uēnit!' ait, fōrmamque remōuit anīlem
Palladaque exhibuit. uenerantur nūmina nymphae
Mygdonidesque nurūs; sōla est nōn territa uirgō.   45
sed tamen ērubuit, subitusque∧ inuīta notāuit
ōra ∧rubor rūrsusque ēuānuit, ut solet āēr
purpureus fierī, cum prīmum Aurōra mouētur,
et breue post tempus candēscere sōlis ab ortū.
perstat in inceptō, stolidāque cupīdine palmae   50

36 *resequor* 3 *resecūtus* reply to (golden line, with chiasmus)
37 *inops inop-is* deficient in (+ gen.)
cōnfect-us a um worn out (*cōnficiō*)
senect-a ae 2f. old age
38 *nimium . . . diū*: i.e. too long
nocet: used here impersonally, 'it harms [you] to have . . .'
audiat: note subj. The subject is any *nurus* or *fīlia* the old woman (as Arachne thinks she is) may have; obj. is *uōcēs* (39), i.e. keep your advice for your own family
39 *tibī . . . tibi*: note different scansions
*nur-us -ūs 4f. daughter-in-law, wife
40 *nēue* 'or in case'
41 *prōficiō* 3/4 *prōfēcī* achieve anything, do some good (supply *tē* as subject of the acc. and inf. after *putēs*)
eadem: i.e. I have not changed my mind
ipsa: i.e. Minerva herself
42 **certāmen certāmin-is* 3n. contest
uītō 1 avoid

43 *uēnit*: cf. *uenit*, 42
anīl-is e of an old woman
44 *Pallada*: Greek acc. of Pallas
exhibeō 2 reveal (oneself as)
ueneror 1 venerate, worship
45 *Mygdonis Mygdonid-is* of the Mygdones, Phrygian (Phrygia is next to Lydia), i.e. everyone who has come to admire Arachne's work (cf. 14–16)
46 *ērubēscō* 3 *ērubuī* blush
subit-us a um sudden
notō 1 mark
47 *ēuānēscō* 3 *ēuānuī* disappear
ut: introduces a simile
48 *purpure-us a um* crimson
49 *candēscō* 3 grow white
ort-us ūs 4m. rising; *ab* = 'after'
50 *perstō* 1 persist
stolid-us a um stupid, crass
cupīdō cupīdin-is 3f. desire
palm-a ae 1f. prize, victory

judgement (40–1). Not knowing that she is addressing Minerva, she challenges Minerva to a show-down (42) – who reveals herself and accepts (43–4). Everyone else, naturally, falls down to venerate the goddess, but not Arachne (44–5). Ovid dwells on the unwitting (*inuīta*) blush that quickly fades from her cheek (simile, 46–9). Does Arachne realise she has gone too far? Does she feel she should back down? No! Ovid-as-narrator emphasises that she brings her own punishment upon herself, generated by obstinacy (*perstat*) and short-sighted greed (*stolidā cupīdine*, 50–1: cf. *fāta* with *fātīs* 5). As for Minerva, no more warnings from her, but down to business (51–2). This is what she has been waiting for all along. Revenge, and praise, will be hers – or at least, the first.

in sua fāta ruit; neque enim Ioue nāta recūsat,
nec monet ulterius, nec iam certāmina differt.

[53–8: Ovid describes how the looms were set up and prepared for weaving]

The two of them get down to business, robes hitched up to the girdle,
Experienced hands hard at it, enthusiasm making light of the work.   60
Threads dipped in Tyrian purple are being woven here
And lighter shades, imperceptibly merging.
Imagine a rainbow when the sun has broken through after a shower:
It paints the length of the sky with its great curving arc,
Gleaming with a thousand different hues,   65
But impossible to tell where one becomes another.
Adjacent colours look the same; at the edges, distinctions are clear.
And here gold threads are being worked into the cloth,
As ancient tales are woven on the loom.

6.70–82: *Minerva puts at the centre her ancient contest with Poseidon*

Cecropiā Pallas scopulum Māuortis in arce   70
pingit et antīquam dē terrae nōmine lītem.
bis sex caelestēs, mediō Ioue, sēdibus altīs,
augustā grauitāte, sedent. sua^ quemque deōrum
īnscrībit ^faciēs: Iouis est rēgālis imāgō;
stāre deum pelagī longōque ferīre tridente   75

---

51 *Ioue nāta*: lit. 'born from Jove', i.e. Minerva
52 *ulterius* any more
differō 3 put off
70 *Cecropi-us* in Athens (lit. 'of Cecrops', an ancient king of Athens)
scopul-us ī 2m. rock
Māuors Māuor-tis 3m. Mars. The 'rock of Mars' is the Areopagus, 'Ares' hill', just below the Acropolis, i.e. citadel (*arce*), of Athens
71 **antīqu-us a um* ancient
līs līt-is 3f. quarrel, dispute. Poseidon (Neptune) and Athena (Minerva) both wanted to be patrons of Athens. Poseidon, god of the sea, struck a rock and produced a stream of (salt) water; Athena made an olive-tree shoot up. She was adjudged the winner, and the town was called after her. Ovid now describes what Minerva is depicting;

hence e.g. *īnscrībit* 74, *facit* 76, *dat* 78, *simulat* 80 all have Minerva as subject
72 *bis* twice
mediō . . . grauitāte: a fine rising tricolon, with asyndeton; the first an abl. abs.; the second an abl. of place, **RL**100A(b); the third an abl. of description, **RLL**(f)3(i), **W**40
sēdēs sēd-is 3f. seat, throne
73 *august-us a um* solemn, venerable. Is this a nod to the emperor Augustus?
74 *īnscrībō* 3 identify, mark
rēgāl-is e royal, regal
75 *stāre*: depends on *facit* 'she makes X [*to*] *stand* . . .'; so too *ferīre* and *exsiluisse* 77
pelag-us ī 2n. sea
feriō 4 strike
tridēns trident-is 3m. trident

70–82: *ekphrasis* (the Greek for 'description') is the technical term used for the detailed *literary* description of a real or imaginary work of art (it is a subject that generates much excitement among literary scholars). Faced with describing a work of art in words, the

aspera saxa facit, mediōque ē uulnere saxī
exsiluisse fretum, quō pignore uindicet urbem;
at sibi dat clipeum, dat acūtae cuspidis hastam,
dat galeam capitī, dēfenditur aegide pectus,
percussamque suā simulat dē cuspide terram   80
ēdere cum bācīs fētum cānentis olīuae;
mīrārīque deōs; operis Victōria fīnis.

6.83–102: *In the corners, Minerva depicts mortals who challenged the gods*

ut tamen exemplīs intellegat aemula laudis
quod pretium spēret prō tam furiālibus ausīs,

76 *uulnere*: i.e. where the trident struck
77 *exsiliō* 4 *exsiluī* gush, leap out
*fret-um ī 2n. sea-water, sea
pignus pignor-is 3n. token, sign, pledge
uindicō 1 lay claim to (subj. of purpose)
78 *sibi*: Minerva now refers to how she depicted
   herself
clipe-us ī 2m. shield
acūt-us a um sharp
* cuspis cuspid-is 3f. point
hast-a ae 2f. spear
79 *gale-a ae* 1f. helmet
aegis aegid-is 3f. aegis (a breastplate or shield of some
   sort)
80 *percutiō* 3/4 *percussī percussum* strike
81 *ēdō* 3 produce, give forth (inf. after *simulat*, 'she
   simulated X *to happen . . .*')
bāc-a ae 1f. berry

*fēt-us ūs 4m. fruit, offspring
cāneō 2 be grey
olīu-a ae 1f. olive
82 *mīrārīque*: inf. after *simulat* again, *deōs* being the
   subject
Victōria: i.e. a picture of the goddess Victory, to celebrate Minerva's triumph
83 *exempl-um ī* 2n. example (here abl., 'by means
   of')
aemula laudis '[Minerva's] rival for praise' (i.e.
   Arachne, subject)
84 *preti-um ī* 2n. price, i.e. punishment (obj. of
   spēret)
spēret: i.e. 'hope for', 'could expect [to pay]' (subj.
   after *intellegat*)
furiāl-is e frenzied, mad
aus-um ī 2n. recklessness, criminal outrage

author unsurprisingly turns the static picture into a story, saying who is who and what
they are doing. Ovid now gives us thorough *ekphraseis* (plural) of Minerva's and
Arachne's imaginary tapestries: first, Minerva's. The centre of her tapestry is a picture of
herself defeating Poseidon in a contest to become the patron of Athens. The location is
explained (the Areopagus – 'Ares/Mars' rock' – near the Acropolis, 70–1); the gods are
present, with special emphasise on Jupiter, each identifiable by look (72–4, including a
fine rising tricolon); Poseidon is shown striking a rock from which water pours out
(75–7); Minerva depicts herself in full regalia (78–9), producing the (winning) olive
(80–1), while all the gods look on in wonder; and the work is finished off with a repre-
sentation of the goddess Victory (82), a god popular with the army (the emperor
Augustus had erected an altar to Victory in the Senate house in 29 BC) and therefore with
a military figure such as Minerva. Self-praise could hardly go further. Nor could the hint
to Arachne: that Minerva is a winner.

83–102: In the four corners of her tapestry, however, Minerva depicts what happens to
those who cross the gods – and Ovid leaves us in no doubt that she has Arachne in mind
here (83–4). Most of the stories attached to these sinners are not known to us: Rhodope

quattuor in partēs certāmina quattuor addit,   85
clāra colōre suō, breuibus distīncta sigillīs.
Thrēiciam Rhodopēn habet angulus ūnus et Haemum,
nunc gelidōs montēs, mortālia corpora quondam,
nōmina summōrum sibi quī tribuēre deōrum.
alterā^ Pygmaeae fātum miserābile mātris   90
^pars habet; hanc Iūnō uictam certāmine iussit
esse gruem populīsque suīs indīcere bellum.
pinxit et Antigonēn, ausam contendere quondam
cum magnī cōnsorte Iouis, quam rēgia Iūnō
in uolucrem uertit; nec prōfuit Īlion illī   95
Lāomedōnue pater, sūmptīs quīn candida pennīs
ipsa sibi plaudat crepitante cicōnia rōstrō.
quī superest sōlus, Cinyrān habet angulus orbum;
isque gradūs templī, nātārum membra suārum,
amplectēns saxōque iacēns lacrimāre uidētur.   100

85 *partēs*: 'corners' (cf. *angulus* 87, 98)
86 *distīnct-us a um* embellished, picked out
sigill-um ī 2n. figure
87 *Thrēici-us a um* from Thrace
Rhodopēn: Greek acc. s. of Rhodope
*angul-us ī 2m. corner
Haem-us ī 2m. Haemus, lover (some say brother) of Rhodope. We know nothing of the background to this story. Did they proclaim themselves happier than Jupiter and Juno?
88 *nunc . . . quondam*: the line is structured A BC BC A
89 *quī*: refers back to Rhodope and Haemus; begin translating this line with it
tribuō 3 *tribuī* assign
90 *Pygmae-us a um* of the Pygmies. Again, we know no detail of a Pygmy woman defeated in a contest
92 *grus gru-is* 3m./f. crane
indīcō 3 *bellum* (+ dat.) bring war on
93 *Antigonēn*: Greek acc. of Antigone. She was daughter of Laomedon, a Trojan king of Ilium (95), and boasted that her hair was more beautiful than Juno's (nothing to do with the Antigone of Sophocles' famous play)
contendō 3 fight
94 *cōnsors cōnsort-is* 3f. wife

95 **uolucr-is is* 3f. bird
Ilion: Greek nom., Ilium, the city attacked by the Greeks in the Trojan war (Ilium is usually called 'Troy', but that technically is the name of the region, not the city)
illī: i.e. Antigone
96 *Lāomedōn Lāomedont-is* 3m. Laomedon (father of Antigone, a king of Ilium)
quīn 'so as to prevent [it coming about] that [she] . . .' + subj., RL174.2
97 *plaudō* 3 applaud (+ dat.). Even as a stork, Antigone continues boasting
crepitō 1 clatter
cicōni-a ae 2f. stork (in apposition to Antigone, RL17B, W3)
rōstr-um ī 2n. beak
98 *quī*: refers to *angulus*, with which begin the translation of this line
Cinyrān: Greek acc. of Cinyras. Did Cinyras' daughters boast in a temple that they were lovelier than the gods, to be punished by being turned into temple steps?
orb-us a um bereaved
99 *grad-us ūs* 4m. step
100 *lacrimō* 1 cry, weep

and Haemus are a mystery (87–9), as is the female Pygmy (90–2); Antigone apparently boasted about the beauty of her hair and was turned into a stork (93–7); and we can only guess at what Cinyras' daughters did (98–100). Minerva ends by bordering the tapestry with a further self-reference – her very own olive (101–2). This is a tapestry with a message for mortals like Arachne: never cross a god like Minerva.

circuit extrēmās oleīs pācālibus ōrās
(is modus est) operisque suā facit arbore finem.

6.103–14: *Arachne depicts Jupiter's disguises and various affairs*

Maeonis ēlūsam dēsignat imāgine taurī
Eurōpam; uērum taurum, freta uēra putārēs.
ipsa uidēbātur terrās spectāre relictās   105
et comitēs clāmāre suās tāctumque uererī
adsilientis aquae timidāsque redūcere plantās.
fēcit et Asteriēn aquilā luctante tenērī,
fēcit olōrīnīs Lēdam recubāre sub ālīs;
addidit ut, satyrī cēlātus imāgine, pulchram^   110
Iuppiter implērit geminō ^Nyctēida fētū,
Amphitryōn fuerit cum tē, Tīrynthia, cēpit,

---

101 *circu(m)eō* 4 *circui* encircle, surround (Minerva is the subject)
ole-a ae 1f. foliage from the olive
pācāl-is e of peace. The olive branch has long been used as a sign of peace
ōr-a ae 1f. edge
102 *suā . . . arbore*: Athena's tree was the olive
103 *Maeonis* 3f. (nom.) woman from Maeonia, i.e. Arachne
ēlūdō 3 *ēlūsī ēlūsum* trick, deceive
dēsignō 1 depict
104 *Eurōp-a ae* 1f. Europa. Jupiter, disguised as a bull, tricked her into climbing on to his back; he then swam off with her (see the **Background** to passage 5)
taur-us ī 2m. bull
106 *tāct-us ūs* 4m. touch
uereor 2 dep. fear
107 *adsiliō* 4 leap up
plant-a ae 1f. foot
108 *fēcit*: Arachne is subject; verbs describing what she 'made happen' are in the inf., e.g. *tenērī*, 108
Asteriēn: Greek acc. of Asterie. She was seduced by

Jupiter in the form of an eagle (in some versions she escaped)
aquil-a ae 1f. eagle
luctor 1 dep. struggle
109 *olōrīn-us a um* of a swan
Lēd-a ae 1f. Leda. She was seduced by Jupiter in the form of a swan, and gave birth to (some say) Clytemnestra, Helen, Castor and Pollux
recubō 1 lie back
āl-a ae 1f. wing
110 *ut* how + subj. (after *addidit* and at 113; and implied at 112 [*ut*] *Amphitryōn*)
satyr-us ī 2m. satyr
cēlō 1 hide
111 *Nyctēida*: Greek acc. of Nycteis, 'daughter of Nycteus', otherwise known as Antiope
112 *Amphitryōn*: husband of Alcmena who came from Tiryns in Southern Greece
fuerit: i.e. how Jupiter turned himself into Amphitryon; Alcmena subsequently gave birth to Hercules (Latin name)/Heracles (Greek name)
cum 'at the time when'
Tīrynthi-us a um from Tiryns (i.e. Alcmena)

103–14: Arachne takes a quite different tack: gods in disguise, who deceive helpless females into sexual submission. At once Ovid points to the superiority of Arachne's work: it really did look like the real thing (104). Europa, being carried far out to sea on the back of the bull-Jupiter, really did seem to be gazing at the retreating shore (105), and her companions to be shouting (106, how does one picture a shout?) and afraid of following her as the sea leapt up at them and they withdrew their feet (106–7). In other words, Arachne is a master at depicting emotion, movement and sound; there is nothing as complex in Minerva's work. Next, Asterie and Leda struggle against Jupiter in the form of an eagle and swan (108–9); disguised as a satyr, Jupiter impregnates Antiope (110–11);

aureus ut Danaēn, Asōpida lūserit ignis,
Mnēmosynēn pāstor, uarius Dēōida serpēns.

6.115–28: *She depicts Neptune, Apollo, Dionysus and Saturn in disguise*

tē quoque mūtātum toruō, Neptūne, iuuencō   115
uirgine in Aeoliā posuit; tū uīsus Enīpeus
gignis Alōīdās, ariēs Bīsaltida fallis,
et tē flāua comās frūgum mītissima māter
sēnsit equum, sēnsit uolucrem crīnīta colubrīs
māter equī uolucris, sēnsit delphīna Melanthō.   120
omnibus hīs faciemque suam faciemque locōrum
reddidit. est illīc agrestis imāgine Phoebus,

---

113 *aure-us a um* golden. In this and the next line we get a string of adjectives and nouns (in the nom.) referring to Jupiter (*aureus, ignis, pāstor, uarius . . . serpēns*, to be prefaced with 'disguised as') and the different women he seduced (in the acc.). The verb *cēpit* is to be understood where no other verb is available
Danaēn: Greek acc. of Danae; producing Perseus
Asōpida: Greek acc. of Asopis, otherwise Aegina, producing the hero Aeacus
114 *Mnēmosynēn*: Greek acc. of Mnemosyne, producing the nine Muses
Dēōida: Greek acc. of Deois (= daughter of Demeter) i.e. Proserpina, herself a daughter of Jupiter – an incestuous end to the list of Jupiter's seductions
115 *Neptūn-us ī* 2m. Neptune, god of the sea. Arachne now pictures his affairs
116 *Aeoli-us a um* daughter of Aeolus. This *uirgō* is Canace, who produced five offspring. Note the string of 'apostrophes' in 115–20 (cf. 112)
posuit: understand 'Arachne' as subject
uīsus: 'seen as', 'in the guise of'; this controls Enipeus and *ariēs* 117

Enīpeus: a river (god) in Thessaly
117 *gignō* 3 father, sire
Alōīdās: acc. pl. of Aloidae, the giants Otus and Ephialtes
ariēs ariēt-is 3m. ram
Bīsaltida: Greek acc., daughter of Bisaltes (Theophane, otherwise unknown)
118 *tē*: i.e. Neptune, whom three subjects (*māter* = Demeter 118, *māter* = Medusa 120, *Melanthō* 120) experience (*sēnsit* three times) as a horse, bird and dolphin
frūx frūg-is 3f. fruit
mīt-is e mild, gentle
119 *crīnīt-us a um* coiffeured (with + abl.)
coluber colubr-ī 2m. snake
120 *equī*: i.e. Pegasus
uolucer uolucr-is e fast
delphīna: Greek acc. s. of *delphin*, a dolphin
122 *reddidit*: the subject is Arachne
agrest-is is 3m. countryman, peasant. For a time Apollo was forced to serve king Admetus. The reasons for his disguises as a hawk and lion are a mystery to us

---

he takes Alcmena in the guise of her husband Amphitruo (112); descending in a gold shower, he takes Danae, and as fire, shepherd and a snake, other women. The sheer variety and complexity of the scenes on offer elevate Arachne's tapestry far above Minerva's comparatively mundane effort.

115–28: And Arachne is not finished yet (does Ovid's use of a string of apostrophes (115–20) introduce a note of wonder, perhaps, at Arachne's brilliance or her foolhardy courage?). She turns from Jupiter to other gods. Neptune (Poseidon) is depicted on the pull in various guises, and all perfectly rendered in look and location (115–22); so too Apollo (122–4), Bacchus/Dionysus (125) and Saturn (126). While Minerva bordered her

utque modo accipitris pennās, modo terga leōnis
gesserit, ut pāstor Macarēida lūserit Issēn,
Līber ut Ērigonēn falsā dēcēperit ūuā,   125
ut Sāturnus equō geminum Chīrōna creārit.
ultima pars tēlae, tenuī circumdata limbō,
nexilibus flōrēs hederīs habet intertextōs.

6.129–45: *The furious Minerva drives Arachne to suicide, but then turns her into a spider*

nōn illud∧ Pallas, nōn illud∧ carpere Līuor
possit ∧opus. doluit successū flāua uirāgō,   130
et rūpit pictās, caelestia crīmina, uestēs,

---

123 *utque* 'and how [he] . . .'. *ut* is used in the same
way at 124, 125 and 126
modo . . . modo now . . . now . . .
accipiter accipitr-is 3m. hawk
leō -nis 3m. lion
124 *pāstor*: i.e. *as* a shepherd; we know nothing
about his deception of Isse
Macarēida: Greek acc. of Macareis, daughter of
Macareus
Issēn: Greek acc. of Isse
125 *Liber*: Arachne finishes off her work by depicting the affairs of two other gods – Liber (another
name for Bacchus/Dionysus, god of drink) and
Saturn. Little or nothing is known about either of
these affairs
Ērigonēn: Greek acc. of Erigone
ūu-a ae 1f. grape. Presumably Liber/Bacchus disguised himself as a grape?
126 *Sāturn-us ī* 2m. Saturn, a very ancient god (presumably disguised as a horse, *equō*)

geminum: i.e. double-natured, half-man, half-horse
Chīrōna: Greek acc. of Ch(e)iron, a centaur famous
for his wisdom (in one story he raised the young
Achilles, Homer *Iliad* 11.832)
creō 1 create, produce
127 **tēl-a ae* 1f. tapestry, weaving
limb-us ī 2m. border, edge
128 *nexil-is e* twining
heder-a ae 1f. ivy
intertext-us a um interwoven. A rare double spondee
ends the almost golden line and Arachne's work
129 *carpō* 3 carp at, criticise, pick to pieces (note the
weaving metaphor)
Līuor -is 3m. Envy, Spite (personified as a god)
130 *success-us ūs* 4m. (good) result, success (here abl.
of cause, **RL**108.2, **RLL**(f)4(iii), **W**Suppl.syntax)
uirāgō uirāgin-is 3f. warlike woman, i.e. Minerva.
She was a martial goddess (hence her gear at
78–9), and now she is about to show it
131 *rumpō* 3 *rūpī* smash, rip up

---

tapestry with olives, Arachne surrounds hers with flowers intertwined with ivy, a much
more complex creation. So Arachne's 'take' on the gods in her tapestry is of a quite different order from Minerva's. In Minerva's effort, grandiose divinities bring blessings to a city
but punish any who dare to challenge them by transforming them (i.e. mortals transformed by divine hatred); in Arachne's, all the gods, without exception, transform themselves into various undignified forms, human, animal, vegetable and mineral, to indulge
what seems to be their sole purpose in life, sex with mortal females (i.e. gods transformed
by mortal lust).

129–45: There is no official judging, but it is clear who has won. Arachne's tapestry
cannot be faulted (129–30); and Minerva's *dolor* at Arachne's *successū* ends any possible
doubts on the matter. Minerva had wanted to be praised (3): and she has failed. Her rage

utque Cytōriacō radium dē monte tenēbat,
ter quater Idmoniae frontem percussit Arachnēs.
nōn tulit infēlīx, laqueōque animōsa ligāuit
guttura; pendentem Pallas miserāta leuāuit,   135
atque ita 'uīue quidem, pendē tamen, improba' dīxit,
'lēxque^eadem poenae, nē sīs sēcūra futūrī,
^dicta tuō generī sērīsque nepōtibus estō!'
post ea discēdēns, sūcīs Hecatēidos herbae
sparsit; et extemplō trīstī medicāmine tāctae   140
dēfluxēre comae, cum quīs et nāris et aurēs,
fitque caput minimum, tōtō quoque corpore parua est;
in latere exīlēs digitī prō crūribus haerent,
cētera uenter habet, dē quō tamen illa remittit
stāmen, et antīquās exercet arānea tēlās.   145

---

132 *Cytōriac-us a um* from Mount Cytorus in Turkey, where boxwood – a hard wood – was grown
radi-us ī 2m. shuttle
133 *ter* three times
quater four times
Idmoni-a ae 2f. daughter of Idmon (Arachne)
134 *infēlix*: i.e. Arachne
laque-us ī 2m. noose
animōs-us a um proud, spirited
ligō 1 tie, bind
135 *guttur -is* 3n. throat
miseror 1 dep. take pity on
136 *improb-us a um* presumptuous
137 *lēxque*: subject of *estō* 138
sēcūr-us a um care-free (about + gen.)
futūr-um ī 2n. the future
138 *estō*: 3rd person imper. of *sum*, RLE1
139 *suc-us ī* 2m. juice

Hecatēidos: Greek gen. of *Hecatēis*, 'belonging to Hecate' (goddess of the underworld); Hecate is a witch, and expert in witchcraft
herb-a ae 1f. herb
140 *sparsit*: cf. Diana flicking water at Actaeon, passage 5, 3.189–90
extemplō immediately
medicāmen medicāmin-is 3n. drug
141 *dēfluō* 3 *dēfluxi* drop off
quīs = *quibus*
nār-is is 3f. nose
143 *latus later-is* 3n. side
exil-is e thin
crūs crūr-is 3n. leg, shin
144 *uenter uentr-is* 3m. stomach
145 *stāmen stāmin-is* 3n. thread
antiquās: i.e. what she used to practise as a human
exerceō 2 practise
arāne-a ae 1f. spider (in apposition to Arachne)

---

is instant and terrible. Now *uirāgo*, emphasising her warlike nature (130), Minerva reacts at once, ripping into Arachne's masterpiece, tearing it to pieces (131) in surely one of the most terrifying lines in Ovid, with its brilliantly ambiguous *caelestia crīmina*: the canvas both depicts the scandals of the gods and is itself a scandal against the gods, because it is so clearly superior to Minerva's efforts. She then ferociously attacks Arachne herself (132–3). A mortal does not cross a god; even less does one defeat a divinity in a contest. Gods do not lose to mortals. But Ovid does not construct Arachne's inner thoughts for us. We can, perhaps, try. She thought (perhaps) this was to be a fair fight. Her whole life was given to her art. She knew she had won. Why carry on, if this was the divine response? So in pride (*animōsa*, 134) and despair (*infēlix*), she hangs herself (appropriately, for someone who has used thread all her life). Minerva has pity on her (*miserāta*, 135), holds her up to stop her hanging (*leuāuit*, 135) and allows her to live (*uiue*, 136). But it does not stop Minerva from ensuring that Arachne understands the implications of victory (*improba*, 136) and does not get above herself in the future (the implication of *sēcūra futūrī*, 137). The price Arachne pays for life is still a *poena* (137) for her and her descendants – the life of a humble spider (Ovid aetiologising again; see the **Glossary of Technical Literary Terms**). To effect the transformation Minerva scatters Arachne with witch's juice (139–40), and Ovid rises brilliantly to the challenge of transforming a young woman into a spider. He starts with the head: that must lose hair, nose and ears (141). Then size: everything shrinks (142). Legs become fingers, located along her side (143), and everything else (arms, neck, trunk and so on) becomes belly (144), from which the thread issues that enables her to carry on a travesty of her former activity (144–5) – for every spider's web is the same as every other (and very easy to destroy).

Learning vocabulary for Passage 11, Minerva and Arachne

angul-us ī 2m. corner
antīqu-us a um ancient
certāmen certāmin-is 3n. contest
cuspis cuspid-is 3f. point
fēt-us ūs 4m. fruit, offspring
fret-um ī 2n. sea-water, sea
incept-us a um begun (*incipiō*); *incept-um ī* 2n. beginning, plan
lān-a ae 1f. wool
nur-us -ūs 4f. daughter-in-law, wife
Pallas Pallad-is 3f. Pallas [Athena], i.e. Minerva

pingō 3 *pinxī pictum* embroider, depict
recūsō 1 refuse (to do)
sēr-us a um late(r)
seu whether, or
siue whether, or
spernō 3 *sprēuī sprētum* spurn, despise
tēl-a ae 1f. tapestry, weaving
toru-us a um grim, unyielding
ueni-a ae 1f. pardon, forgiveness
uolucr-is is 3f. bird

Study section

1. Why did Minerva bother to challenge Arachne to a contest?
2. How would you define the functions of the two tapestries?
3. Do you admire Arachne? Or did she get what was coming to her? How does your answer affect your view of Minerva?
4. Weaving is regularly likened to writing in the ancient world. So is 'the episode of Arachne and Minerva . . . an essay on narrative technique, a discourse on the partiality and ideology of the point of view of the producer of a text'? (Rosati, in Hardie et al. 1999, 252; cf. Farrell, 'Minerva first assaults Arachne physically and then unravels her text as well', ibid. 137.)

12 Cephalus and Procris, *Metamorphōsēs* 7.694–756, 796–862

Background

Androgeos, son of Minos, king of Crete, had been raised in Athens. When he grew up, he took part in the All-Athenian games and won everything. The king of Athens, Aegeus, already suspicious of the young man's ambitions, sent him to kill the bull of Marathon – and the bull duly killed him. His father Minos decided to take his revenge and set out to attack Athens. He approached king Aeacus on the island of Aegina (opposite Athens in the Saronic gulf) for help, but Aeacus decided to side with Athens, a decision much welcomed by the Athenians in the person of their envoy to Aegina, Cephalus. In the course of his stay on Aegina, Aeacus' son Phocus asks Cephalus about the spear he is carrying. Cephalus agrees to tell its story, explaining that it caused the death of his beloved wife (Procris).

7.694–9: *Cephalus describes his superlative wife*

'Procris^ erat, sī forte magis peruēnit ad aurēs*
Orīthȳīa *tuās, raptae ^soror Orīthȳīae.   695
sī faciem mōrēsque uelīs cōnferre duārum,
dignior ipsa rapī. pater hanc mihi iūnxit Erechtheus,
hanc mihi iūnxit Amor; fēlīx dīcēbar eramque.
(nōn ita dīs uīsum est, aut nunc quoque forsitan essem.)'

---

694 *Procris* (Greek acc. *Procrin*) Procris
sī forte magis: in case his listeners do not know who Procris was, Cephalus politely explains by reference to her famous sister, Oreithyia
695 *Orīthȳī-a ae* 1f. Oreithyia (abducted by the god Boreas, the North Wind). Note the double spondee ending to the line

696 *cōnferō cōnferre* compare (cf. 'cf.')
697 *ipsa*: i.e. Procris
rapī: see discussion at Introduction, pp. 8 ff.
Erechtheus: Greek nom. s., Erechtheus, a very early king of Athens (the Erechtheum, a sanctuary on the Acropolis, was named after him)
699 *forsitan* perhaps (often with subj.)

694–9: Cephalus praises his wife by contrasting her with Oreithyia and arguing that, had looks and loyalty been Boreas' priority (696), Boreas would have shown far better judgement had he abducted Procris (697). Cephalus goes on to say that his was a love-marriage and a happy one (697–8), but then drops a stark warning of what is to come by revealing that the *gods* saw things differently (699). Certainly Aurora seemed to threaten that Cephalus would have problems (712–13), and even disguised Cephalus to help him

7.700–13: *Cephalus is warned by the goddess Aurora, whose advances he rejected*

'alter agēbātur post sacra iugālia mēnsis   700
cum mē, cornigeris tendentem rētia ceruīs,
uertice dē summō semper flōrentis Hymettī
lūtea∧ māne uidet pulsīs ∧Aurōra tenebrīs
inuītumque rapit. liceat mihi uēra referre,
pāce deae: quod sit roseō spectābilis ōre,   705
quod teneat lūcis, teneat cōnfinia noctis,
nectareīs quod alātur aquīs – ego Procrin amābam,
pectore Procris erat, Procris mihi semper in ōre.
sacra torī coitūsque nouōs thalamōsque recentēs
prīmaque dēsertī referēbam foedera lectī.   710
mōta dea est, et "siste tuās, ingrāte, querēlās!
Procrin habē!" dīxit; "quod sī mea prōuida mēns est,
nōn habuisse uolēs", mēque illī īrāta remīsit.'

700 *agēbātur*: used here of the passing of time
*iugāl-is e to do with marriage; *iugāl-ia ium* 3n. pl. marriage
mēns-is is 3m. month
701 *cum* when
mē: agrees with *tendentem* and object of *Aurōra uidet* (703)
corniger -a -um horned
*rēt-e is 3n. net
ceru-us ī 2m. stag
702 *uertex uertic-is* 3m. peak
flōreō 2 flower
Hymett-us ī 2m. Hymettus (a hill near Athens famous for its honey: hence the reference to flowers)
703 *lūte-us a um* saffron
māne early in the morning
pellō 3 *pepulī pulsum* banish
tenebr-a ae 1f. shadow
704 *inuītum*: supply *mē* (Cephalus)
705 *quod* + subj.: tends to express other people's view of the matter 'on the grounds that (as people say) . . .', **RLR4, WSuppl.syntax**

sit: Aurora is the subject
rose-us a um rosy
spectābil-is e easy on the eye
706 *lūcis*: like *noctis*, take with *cōnfinia*
cōnfini-um ī 2n. boundary
707 *nectare-us a um* tinged with nectar (which only divinities drank)
709 *sacra*: n. pl. adj. used as a noun, **RL14.7, W4.** Note the emotional rising tricolon, to be concluded with a fourth 'leg' at 710
coit-us ūs 4m. sexual intercourse
710 *dēsertī*: because Cephalus had now left it. A golden line
referēbam: i.e. I kept on talking about all this to Aurora
*foedus foeder-is 3n. bond, obligation
711 *sistō* 3 stop
ingrāt-us a um ungrateful
querēl-a ae 1f. complaint
712 *prōuid-us a um* prophetic
713 *illī* i.e. to Procris

catch out his wife (721), while the goddess Diana was the source of the spear that never missed, given by Procris to Cephalus with disastrous consequences (756, 841). But whether these divine interventions turn out to justify Cephalus' claim is a question for debate.

700–13: Cephalus' story begins with his abduction *inuītum* by Aurora, goddess of the dawn (703–4). Cautiously, perhaps for fear of inviting retribution from the goddess (704–5), he concedes Aurora's beauty, authority and divinity, all reasons for yielding to

7.714–22: *Cephalus returns home, suspecting Procris of infidelity*

'dum redeō mēcumque deae memorāta retractō,
esse metus coepit nē iūra iugālia coniunx   715
nōn bene seruāsset. faciēs aetāsque iubēbat
crēdere adulterium, prohibēbant crēdere mōrēs;
sed tamen āfueram, sed et haec erat, unde redībam,
crīminis exemplum, sed cūncta timēmus amantēs.
quaerere quod doleam statuō dōnīsque pudīcam   720
sollicitāre fidem; fauet hūīc Aurōra timōrī,
immūtatque meam (uideor sēnsisse) figūram.'

714 *memorō* 1 mention (cf. *sacra* above). *deae* is dat. of agent
retractō 1 reconsider
717 *adulteri-um ī* 2n. adultery
718 *sed tamen . . . sed . . . sed*: three reasons why Cephalus persuaded himself that his wife had committed adultery
haec: i.e. Aurora
unde: i.e. from whom
719 *exempl-um ī* 2n. example (referring to Aurora, a goddess not known for her modesty)

720 *quod doleam*: note subj., 'the sort of thing that I was grieving over'; what difference would *quid* make?
statuō 3 decide (+ inf.)
*pudīc-us a um honourable, chaste
721 **faueō* 2 (+ dat.) encourage
timōrī: i.e. my fears about Procris' fidelity
722 *immūtō* 1 alter

her (705–7). But Procris, he says, dominates his thoughts (707–8: note the repetition of her name), and the only topic he can talk about to Aurora is how much his marriage bed means to him (709–10: note the fine rising tricolon of 709, becoming a tetracolon in 710). Aurora angrily dismisses him, warning him that he will wish he had never married Procris in the first place (711–13). One remembers Cephalus' gloomy introduction to the story (699).

714–22: As Cephalus returns home to Procris, he mulls over what Aurora has told him (714), presumably asking himself why on earth he should wish never to have married Procris. Ovid shows his thoughts wavering – has she been unfaithful? She has the looks, but what about her loyalty? But he had been away; look at Aurora's behaviour (since Aurora's behaviour proved men's suspicions that women were sexually voracious, Procris 'must' have had the desire); lovers always fear the worst (Cephalus appeals to human nature to justify his fears) (715–19). So he decides to put Procris to the test and see if he can lure her into adultery with gifts (720–1). But adultery with whom, where and how? The answer Ovid adopts is – with himself, in his own house. If this is to happen, however, Cephalus must be made unrecognisable. Eschewing the 'false beard' option, Ovid solves the problem by saying that Aurora encouraged his fears and herself disguised his features – a transformation that Cephalus claims himself to have felt taking place (721–2). By Ovid's high standards this is a pretty feeble device; and since the whole plan will ultimately turn out to be a flop, it does not say much for Aurora's *prōuida mēns* (712) either. But Aurora wanted revenge on Cephalus and therefore did what she could to try to get it.

7.723–42: *Disguised, Cephalus finally 'proves' that Procris is unfaithful*

'Palladiās ineō nōn cognōscendus Athēnās,
ingrediorque domum; culpā domus ipsa carēbat,
castaque signa dabat, dominōque erat anxia raptō.   725
uix aditus per mīlle dolōs ad Erechthida factus.
et uīdī, obstipuī, meditātaque paene relīquī
temptāmenta fidē; male mē quīn uēra fatērer
continuī, male quīn, ut oportuit, ōscula ferrem.
trīstis erat (sed nūlla tamen fōrmōsior illā^   730
esse potest ^trīstī) dēsīderiōque dolēbat
coniugis abreptī. tū collige quālis^ in illā*,
Phōce, ^decor fuerit, *quam sīc dolor ipse decēbat!
quid referam, quotiēns temptāmina nostra pudīcī^
reppulerint ^mōrēs, quotiēns "ego" dīxerit "ūnī   735
seruor; ubīcumque est, ūnī mea gaudia seruō"?
cuī^ nōn ista fidē satis experientia ^sānō
magna foret? nōn sum contentus, et in mea pugnō

723 *Palladi-us a um* belonging to Pallas
    (Athena)
Athēn-ae ārum 2f. pl. Athens
724 *ingredior* 3 dep. enter
*careō 2 lack, be free of (+ abl.)
725 *cast-us a um* chaste
dominō [i.e. Cephalus] . . . *raptō*: abl. of cause,
    RL108.2, **RLL**(f)4(iii), **W**Suppl.syntax
anxi-us a um worried
726 *uix . . . factus*: i.e. it was virtually impossible
    even to *see* Procris
adit-us ūs 4m. entrance
dol-us ī 2m. trick
Erechthida: Greek acc. of *Erechthis*, daughter of
    Erechtheus (Procris)
727 *obstupēscō* 2 *obstipuī* be amazed, dumbstruck
paene almost
728 *temptāment-um ī* 2n. test
fidē: archaic form of the gen. *fideī*; so too at 737
    (after *satis*)
*male hardly, scarcely

quīn but that [I] + subj. (after *mē . . . continuī*;
    'from', 'without' is often the best translation);
    RL174.2
*fateor 2 dep. confess, admit (to)
729 *contineō* 2 restrain
730 *erat*: '*she* was'
731 *dēsīderi-um ī* 2n. loss
732 *abripiō* 3/4 *abripuī abreptum* kidnap, steal
tū: Cephalus here turns to Phocus, the person to
    whom he is telling the story
colligō 3 imagine, infer
733 *deceō* 2 be fitting for, suit X (acc., here *quam*)
734 *temptāmen temptāmin-is* 3n. test
735 *repellō* 3 *reppulī* rebuff, reject
736 *ubīcumque* wherever
737 *experienti-a ae* 1f. proof
738 *foret*: imperf. subj. of *sum*, **RLE**1
content-us a um satisfied
in mea . . . uulnera: i.e. 'to hurt myself', cf. Oscar
    Wilde 'Yet each man kills the thing he loves'
    (*Ballad of Reading Gaol*, I.vii)

723–42: Unrecognised, then, Cephalus returns home to Athens and finds no sign of any infidelity whatsoever. Indeed, the whole household is deeply worried about its master's absence, and it takes an enormous effort for him even to see Procris (723–6). He contemplates abandoning his test, and is hardly able to restrain himself from revealing who he is there and then (727–9); and Procris' sadness at the loss of her husband makes her all the more beautiful, proving how beautiful she was in real life (730–3: Cephalus makes this point personally to Phocus, adding greatly to our sense of his sincerity). Time and

uulnera, dum cēnsūs dare mē prō nocte pacīscor,
mūneraque augendō tandem dubitāre coēgī.   740
exclāmō male uictor: "ego en, ego fictus adulter
uērus eram coniunx; mē, perfida, teste tenēris!" '

7.743–56: *Cephalus admits his error to Procris, who gives him a hunting-dog and spear*

'illa nihil; tacitō tantummodo uicta pudōre
īnsidiōsa malō cum coniuge līmina fūgit,
offēnsāque meī genus omne perōsa uirōrum   745
montibus errābat, studiīs operāta Diānae.
tum mihi dēsertō uiolentior ignis ad ossa
peruenit; ōrābam ueniam, et peccāsse fatēbar
et potuisse datīs^ similī succumbere culpae
mē quoque ^mūneribus, sī mūnera tanta darentur.   750
haec mihi cōnfessō, laesum prius ulta pudōrem,
redditur et dulcēs concorditer exigit annōs.

---

739 *cēns-us ūs* 4m. personal fortune
prō nocte: i.e. for a night of love
pacīscor 3 dep. agree
740 *augeō* 2 increase
741 *exclāmō* 1 cry, shout out
en look! there!
*fict-us a um false, disguised
adulter -ī 2m. adulterer
742 *perfid-us a um* disloyal
test-is is 3m. witness. Here it is abl. abs. with *mē*,
    'with me as witness'
743 *illa nihil*: supply *dīxit*
tacit-us a um silent
tantummodo simply
744 *īnsidiōs-us a um* treacherous
cum: = 'and also', rather than 'in company with'

līmen līmin-is 3n. hearth
745 *offēns-a ae* 1f. resentment (*meī* 'of/at me'). Here
    it is abl. of cause
perōs-us a um hating
746 *operor* 1 dep. busy oneself (with)
747 *ignis*: i.e. of love
748 *ueni-a ae* 1f. pardon
peccō 1 make a mistake. Both *peccāsse* and *potuisse*
    have *mē* (750) as subject after *fatēbor*
749 *succumbō* 3 yield to
751 *haec*: object of *cōnfessō*
cōnfiteor 2 dep. *cōnfessus* admit, confess
ulcīscor 3 dep. *ultus* be avenged for (+ acc.)
752 *concorditer* in harmony
exigō 3 pass

---

again she repeats her loyalty to her husband (734–6); but Cephalus, admitting his insanity, carries on until he does just enough to make her hesitate. This is sufficient for him to reveal his disguise and claim 'victory' over her (737–42).

743–56: Procris is dumbstruck and overcome with inexpressible shame (743) – outrage that her husband should impugn her honour so wrongly and (perhaps) guilt that she *did* hesitate over his gifts (740: we must remember that this is a woman of the very highest standards of moral probity). But her primary feeling is one of deep resentment at Cephalus' behaviour (745) – as Cephalus' own commentary on himself admits: *īnsidiōsa, malō* 744 – and she runs from the house, not to find another man (she hates them all 745) but to take up hunting (744–6: there is a narrative point here, as will

dat mihi praetereā, tamquam sē parua dedisset
dōna, canem mūnus, quem cum sua^ trāderet illī
^Cynthia, "currendō superābit" dīxerat "omnēs."   755
dat simul et iaculum manibus quod (cernis) habēmus.'

[Cephalus first tells the story of the hunting-dog, which he unleashed to pursue a wild beast that was terrorising Thebes. The beast kept just out of the dog's reach, and Cephalus was about to hurl his spear at it when the two animals were turned to marble, as if the god did not want either of them to lose. Phocus, the son of Aeacus to whom Cephalus is telling the story, now enquires about the spear.]

7.796–803: *Cephalus describes the love he and Procris had for each other*

'gaudia prīncipium nostrī sunt, Phōce, dolōris;
illa prius referam. iuuat ō meminisse beātī
temporis, Aeacidā, quō prīmōs rīte per annōs
coniuge eram fēlix, fēlix erat illa marītō!
mūtua cūra duōs et amor sociālis habēbat,   800

753 *praetereā* in particular
parua . . . dōna: in apposition to *sē*
754 *mūnus*: in apposition to *canem*
sua . . . Cynthi-a ae 1f. her . . . Diana (goddess of
    Mount Cynthus and of hunting, see 746)
illī: i.e. to Procris
756 **iacul-um i* 2n. hunting spear

796 *prīncipi-um i* 2n. beginning
797 *beāt-us a um* blessed, joyful
798 *Aeacidā*: Greek voc. of Aeacides, son of Aeacus,
    i.e. Phocus
rīte rightly
800 *mūtu-us a um* shared, mutual
sociāl-is e in partnership

shortly become clear, but see Introduction, p. 7 for this sign of the man-hating woman). This instant reaction of a transparently honest woman at last brings Cephalus to his senses, and he begs forgiveness, admitting his folly and agreeing that he too could have been similarly tempted (747–50; the *culpa* of 749 primarily refers to his own self-confessed weakness – he exonerates *her* completely). Her *pudor* finally satisfied by this confession (751, cf. 743), she comes back to him, and life resumes its perfect harmony for the couple (752). She even gives Cephalus some gifts from her hunting days (746), which can now be assumed to be over – a speedy dog given her by Diana and a hunting-spear that never misses (753–6: we have been told this by Ovid in a passage not in the selection).

796–803: To introduce the story of Procris' death, Cephalus recapitulates and expands on 752 (especially *concorditer*), sketching the loving and harmonious existence they enjoyed: *gaudia* (796), *beātī* (797) and *fēlix* (twice, 799) describe the result, which is explained by their *mūtua cūra* and *amor sociālis* (800). Sexually (801 *thalamōs*), even gods like Jupiter and Venus would have failed to lure them away (801–2; cf. Cephalus' earlier

nec Iouis illa meō^ thalamōs praeferret ^amōrī,
nec mē quae caperet, nōn sī Venus ipsa uenīret,
ūlla erat; aequālēs ūrēbant pectora flammae.'

7.804–20: *Cephalus explains that, after hunting, he would call on the breeze to refresh him*

'sōle ferē radiīs feriente cacūmina prīmīs,
uēnātum in siluās iuuenāliter īre solēbam,   805
nec mēcum famulī nec equī nec nāribus ācrēs^
īre ^canēs nec līna sequī nōdōsa solēbant;
tūtus eram iaculō. sed cum satiāta ferīnae^
dextera ^caedis erat, repetēbam frīgus et umbrās
et quae dē gelidīs exībat uallibus auram.   810
aura petēbātur mediō mihi lēnis in aestū,
auram exspectābam, requiēs erat illa labōrī.
"aura," (recordor enim) "ueniās" cantāre solēbam,
"mēque luēs intrēsque sinūs, grātissima, nostrōs,
utque facis, releuāre uelīs quibus ūrimur aestūs."   815

801 *praeferō praeferre* 3 prefer X (acc.) to Y (dat.).
  Note the conditional subj., and cf. 802 *caperet . . .
  ueniret*
802 *nec mē . . . erat*: take in the order *nec ūlla erat
  quae mē*
803 *aequāl-is e* equal
804 *radi-us ī* 2m. ray
  feriō 4 strike
  cacūmen cacūmin-is 3n. peak
805 *uēnātum*: supine of *uēnor* 1 dep. 'hunt', expressing purpose, RL118(2)
  iuuenāliter as a young man will
806 *famul-us ī* 2m. attendant
  nār-is is 3f. nose
807 *nōdōs-us a um* knotty
808 *iaculō*: Cephalus hunted alone and was 'safe with

his spear' because it never missed and automatically came back to the sender (7.683–4)
  satior 1 dep. have enough of (+ gen.)
  ferīn-us a um of wild animals
809 *frīgus frīgor-is* 3n. cool
810 *et quae*: take in order *et auram quae*
  uall-is is 3f. valley
811 *lēn-is e* gentle
812 *requiēs requiēt-is* 3f. relaxation from (+ dat.)
813 *recordor* 1 dep. recall
  ueniās: jussive subj., like *luēs, intrēs* (814), and *uelīs*
    (815); RL152, W28
  cantō 1 sing
814 *luō* 3 wash
  sin-us ūs 4m. breast, chest
815 *releuō* 1 relieve

brush with Aurora). *aequālēs . . . flammae* (803) summarises the shared, mutual nature
of such feelings for each other.

804–20: Cephalus now describes his early-morning hunting routine. He did not hunt
with the crowd but, going solo, put his trust in the magic hunting-spear which Procris
had given him (804–8, cf. 756). Satisfied with the morning's exertions, he would then
seek the cool and the shade and the breeze (808–10) – especially the breeze, *aura*, which
he waited for to cool him down and bring him rest (810–12). Cephalus remembers
summoning the breeze aloud for this purpose (813–15); he remembers adding playful

forsitan addiderim (sīc mē mea fāta trahēbant)
blanditiās plūrēs, et "tū mihi magna uoluptās,"
dīcere sim solitus, "tū mē reficisque fouēsque,
tū facis ut siluās, ut amem loca sōla, meōque^
spīritus iste tuus semper captātur ab ^ōre."'   820

7.821–34: *Cephalus' words are reported to Procris, who thinks he is being unfaithful*

'uōcibus ambiguīs dēceptam praebuit aurem
nescioquis, nōmenque aurae tam saepe uocātum
esse putat nymphae, nympham mē crēdit amāre.
crīminis extemplō fictī temerārius index
Procrin adit, linguāque refert audīta susurrā.   825
crēdula rēs amor est; subitō conlāpsa dolōre
(ut mihi nārrātur) cecidit, longōque^ refecta
^tempore sē miseram, sē fātī dīxit inīquī,
dēque fidē questa est, et crīmine concita uānō

---

817 *blanditi-a ae* 1f. endearment
uoluptās uoluptāt-is 3f. pleasure
818 **reficiō 3 refēcī refectum* refresh, revive
foueō 2 caress
819 *facis ut*: + subj., indicating result ('bring it about that . . .'), **RL**135
820 *spīrit-us ūs* 4m. breath
captō 1 draw in
821 *ambigu-us a um* double-edged
822 **nescio-quis/quae quid* some(one) or other
823 *esse . . . nymphae*: 'to be of a . . .', i.e. to belong to

824 *extemplō* at once
temerāri-us a um thoughtless, hasty
index indic-is 3m. informer
825 *susurr-us a um* whispering
826 *crēdul-us a um* gullible
conlābor 3 dep. *conlāpsus* collapse
827 *ut mihi nārrātur*: i.e. after the events described in this story
828 *inīqu-us a um* cruel, unjust. *fātī . . . inīquī* is gen. of description, **RL**101, **W**40
829 *concit-us a um* stirred, provoked
uān-us a um empty, groundless

---

blandishments, addressing *aura* almost as if it were human in its ability to respond to his needs and look after him (816–20) – something he now realises was fatal (*fāta*, 816). Orders like *intrēs sinus* (814) and words like *releuāre*, *ūrō*, *uoluptās*, *foueō*, *spīritus* + *ōs* all have alternative, quasi-amorous connotations, as do sentiments about *aura*'s ability to make him love woods and lonely places.

821–34: *uōcibus ambiguīs* indeed (821): someone hears him, thinks he is in love with a woman called Aura (is the fact that Aur(or)a earlier abducted him significant?), and reports it to Procris (821–5). Love is gullible (826, cf. 719) and Procris' first reaction is physical collapse (826–7), followed by recovery, lament, and fear of the consequences (827–30). Nevertheless, she is not wholly convinced: doubt, hope and mistrust play their part (*spēratque miserrima fallī* is a brilliant description of a state of mind) and she decides the evidence of her own eyes is needed before she will condemn her husband (832–4). We are in the same situation as in the first half of the story, only with different players: there

quod nihil est metuit, metuit sine corpore nōmen   830
[and the unhappy woman grieved as if over a real mistress].
saepe tamen dubitat spēratque miserrima fallī,
indiciōque fidem negat et, nisi uīderit ipsa,
damnātūra suī nōn est dēlicta marītī.'

7.835–50: *Procris spies on Cephalus at the hunt, and is mistakenly killed by his spear*

'postera dēpulerant Aurōrae lūmina noctem;   835
ēgredior, siluāsque petō uictorque per herbās,
"aura, uenī," dīxī "nostrōque medēre labōrī!"
et subitō gemitūs^ inter mea uerba uidēbar
^nescioquōs audīsse; "uenī," tamen "optima" dīxī.
fronde leuem rūrsus strepitum faciente cadūcā,   840
sum ratus esse fēram, tēlumque uolātile mīsī;
Procris erat, mediōque tenēns in pectore uulnus
"ēī mihi!" conclāmat. uōx est ubi cognita fidae
coniugis, ad uōcem praeceps āmēnsque cucurrī;
sēmianimem et sparsās foedantem sanguine uestēs   845
et sua (mē miserum!) dē uulnere dōna trahentem
inueniō, corpusque meō mihi cārius ulnīs
mollibus attollō, scissāque ā pectore ueste
uulnera saeua ligō, conorque inhibēre cruōrem,
neu mē morte suā scelerātum dēserat, ōrō.'   850

833 *indici-um* ī 2n. information, story
fidem: i.e. credence, belief in
834 *damnō* 1 condemn
dēlict-um ī 2n. crime
835 *poster-us a um* [of the] next [day]
dēpellō 3 *dēpulī* drive off, dispel
837 *medeor* 2 dep. (+ dat.) ease, alleviate (the effects of)
838 *gemitūs*: this word is used of animal as well as human noises. Cephalus ignores it at first, but when he also hears leaves rustling (840), he draws the 'obvious' conclusion
840 *strepit-us ūs* 4m. sound, rustle
cadūc-us a um falling
841 *reor* 2 dep. *ratus* think
uolātil-is e flying
843 *ēī* alas

conclāmō 1 cry out
fid-us a um faithful
844 *āmēns āment-is* distraught
845 *sēmianim-is e* dying
foedō 1 stain
846 *dōna*: i.e. the *iaculum* (756)
847 *meō*: i.e. *meō corpore*, abl. of comparison after *cārius*
cār-us a um dear
uln-a ae 1f. (outstretched) arms
848 *attollō* 1 raise up, lift
scindō 3 *scissī scissum* cut
849 *ligō* 1 bind
inhibeō 2 stop
850 *neu*: + subj., after *ōrō*
scelerāt-us a um wicked

Cephalus was suspicious, sought personal evidence and was proved wrong; now it is Procris' turn, but her search for personal evidence will prove fatal.

835–50: Next morning (835: is the mention of Aurora here significant?), Cephalus goes through the same routine: hunt, rest (836) and summoning of *aura* (837). But Procris

7.851–62: *Procris' dying words reveal her misunderstanding*

'uīribus illa carēns et iam moribunda, coēgit
haec^ sē ^pauca loquī: "per nostrī foedera lectī,
perque deōs supplex ōrō superōsque meōsque,
per sī quid meruī dē tē bene, perque manentem^
nunc quoque cum pereō, causam mihi mortis, ^amōrem: 855
nē thalamīs Auram patiāre innūbere nostrīs."
dīxit, et errōrem tum dēnique nōminis esse
et sēnsī et docuī. sed quid docuisse iuuābat?
lābitur, et paruae fugiunt cum sanguine uīrēs.
dumque aliquid spectāre potest, mē spectat et in mē   860
infēlīcem animam nostrōque exhālat in ōre;
sed uultū meliōre morī sēcūra uidētur.'

851 *moribund-us a um* on the point of death
853 *supplex supplic-is* pleading, as a suppliant
854 *mereō* 2 *bene dē* deserve well of/have a claim on
 X (abl.)
856 *nē . . . patiāre*: 'do not allow', **RLL-V(a)3**, **W28**
innūbō 3 marry into (+ dat.)

859 *lābor* 3 dep. slip away (in death) (Procris is
 subject)
861 *exhālō* 1 breathe out
sēcūr-us a um relieved of care, at peace

is in hiding, listening; she makes a noise which could be interpreted as that of an animal, Cephalus summons *aura* again, hears leaves rustling, thinks it is a wild beast and lets fly, hitting his wife (838–43). Distraught, he runs to her cries: he finds her nearly dead, bloodied, and pulling his 'gift' out of her body, a line full of pathos (844–7). Frantically, he lifts her up, cuts away her clothes, binds the wound, tries to stop the bleeding, curses himself and begs her to live (847–50). All this is told in pacy, urgent, narrative style.

851–62: Procris' last plea makes for moving reading: in the name of their marriage vows, the gods, her deserts and their love – four passionate appeals – she calls on Cephalus not to marry Aura (851–6). So Cephalus is brought to realise what he has done. But it is all too late; his only, scant, consolation is that he is able to tell her the truth before she dies (857–8), and that she breathes her last in his arms, at peace (859–62).

This is a tale of the misunderstandings to which, because of human weakness, a certain type of 'true love' is subject: the greater one's 'love', the more one is subject to jealousy and fear of betrayal. It is constructed in a quasi-tragic form. 'Tragedy' is popularly used nowadays to mean 'someone dying young or in unusual circumstances'. This is a sad corruption of a literary concept, which is generally characterised by a number of typical – though not necessarily exclusive – markers. These include divine prophecies, ignorance of the true state of affairs (generating irony), self-delusion, misunderstanding and understanding too late to avoid disaster, all of which are present here. But this tale stops short of full-blown tragedy because of the character of the suspicious and somewhat self-regarding Cephalus, who is not exactly that 'great man' capable of eliciting our full sympathies.

Learning vocabulary for Passage 12, Cephalus and Procris

careō 2 lack, be free of (+ abl.)
fateor 2 dep. *fassus* confess, admit (to)
faueō 2 *fauī fautum* (+ dat.) encourage
fict-us a um false, disguised
foedus foeder-is 3n. bond, obligation
forsitan perhaps (often + subj.)
iacul-um ī 2n. hunting spear
iugāl-is e to do with marriage; *iugāl-ia ium* 3n.
  pl. marriage

male hardly, scarcely
nescio-quis/quae/quid some(one) or other
pudic-us a um honourable, chaste
Procris (Greek acc. *Procrin*) Procris
reficiō 3 *refēcī refectum* refresh, revive
rēt-e is 3n. net

Study section

1. No serious transformations occur in this story – or do they? And if so, of what sort are they?
2. 'It seems Cephalus had learnt nothing from his early experiences and, despite great happiness with Procris, persisted in going out alone to hunt' (Fantham, 2004, 84). Do you agree with this analysis?
3. Does Aurora get her revenge in the end?
4. There are four other versions of the Cephalus and Procris story (below). How has Ovid modified them, and with what effect on his version of the story? Consider in particular the themes of mutual love, guilt, and the role of the narrator. How is the homosexual motif dealt with? (Ovid himself reworks the story at *Ars Amātōria* 3.684–746, as a lesson to girls not to jump to conclusions about their menfolk.)

Pherecydes (fifth century BC)

Cephalus tries to 'prove' Procris' virtue by an eight years' absence and returning in a disguised form. He successfully seduces her with gifts and reveals his true identity, but is reconciled to her. Later Procris suspects that, while out hunting, he is having an affair with another woman. She questions a servant, who tells her that Cephalus has been heard to ask 'cloud' (Greek *Nephelē*) to come to him. She investigates and runs towards him when she hears him so talking. Cephalus panics and accidentally kills her with the spear.
Scholium on Homer's *Odyssey* 11.321

Apollodorus (third century BC)

Cephalus married Procris, but Dawn fell in love with him and carried him off.
Library 1.9.5

. . . the dog that Procris had been given by Minos and brought over from Crete.
Library 2.4.7

Procris sleeps with Pteleon in return for a golden crown. When Cephalus discovers this, she flees to Minos in Crete, who has a fairly serious problem. His wife Pasiphae, envious of his numerous lovers, has cast a spell on him so that he ejaculates harmful beasts, killing any woman who sleeps with him. Procris gives him a magic drink that clears the problem, and sleeps with him. A grateful Minos gives her the magic dog and spear but, fearful of Pasiphae, Procris returns to Athens. She is reconciled to Cephalus and, a keen huntress, joins him in the chase. But she is killed by Cephalus, who throws his spear into the bush where, unknown to him, she is pursuing an animal.
Library 3.15.1

Antoninus Liberalis (second century AD?, probably drawing on Nicander, c. 130 BC)

Cephalus marries Procris, but Eos (Aurora), falling for his looks, abducts and seduces him . . . [gap in the text here]. Cephalus, testing to see if Procris intends to remain faithful to him, pretends to go hunting, and tells a messenger to give her gold from a stranger who wants to sleep with her. When the amount is doubled, Procris agrees. Cephalus reveals the truth, and the shamed Procris flees to stay with Minos on Crete. Minos has a problem: he is childless because he ejaculates snakes, scorpions and millipedes, killing any woman who sleeps with him. Procris tells him to ejaculate into a goatskin bag before having intercourse with his wife Pasiphae. This he does, and when Pasiphae produces children, he rewards Procris with the magic spear and dog. She returns to Cephalus, having disguised herself as a young man, hunts with him and says she will give him the dog and spear only if he sleeps with her/him. He agrees, she reveals her true identity, and upbraids him for behaving even worse than she had. [There is nothing about Procris' death.]
Metamorphōsēs 41

Hyginus (second century AD)

Cephalus and Procris pledge loyalty to each other, so that when Aurora abducts Cephalus, he rejects her advances. Aurora, saying that she does not want him to break his pledge unless Procris does first, changes his shape and sends him as a guest with gifts to seduce Procris. Procris yields, Aurora undoes the disguise and Procris flees to Crete, where she hunts with Diana, who gives her the magic spear and dog. Diana then disguises her as a young man and she returns to Cephalus, matching him in hunting with the spear and dog. Cephalus, desperate to get the spear and dog, agrees to her/his demand to sleep with her/him – where he discovers that the 'boy' is his wife. They are reconciled. But, still fearful of Aurora, Procris hides in the bushes to watch him hunting and is killed by the javelin when the bushes move and he takes her for a wild animal.

Genealogiae 189

13 Minos, Ariadne, Daedalus and Icarus, *Metamorphōsēs* 8.152–235

Background

While Minos was attempting to take Athens (see the **Background** to passage 12), he had left trouble back home in Crete – the Minotaur, the product of a union between his wife Pasiphae and a bull with whom she had fallen in love (Minos-*taurus*: Minos-bull). Minos now returns to Crete and decides to rid the family of this blot. For this he turns to the world-famous inventor Daedalus, who had taken refuge in, or been exiled to, Crete after murdering his nephew (and had helped Pasiphae achieve union with the bull).

8.152–68: *Minos arrives home and tells Daedalus to construct the winding labyrinth*

uōta Iouī Mīnōs taurōrum corpora centum
soluit, ut ēgressus ratibus Cūrētida terram
contigit, et spoliīs decorāta est rēgia fixīs.
crēuerat opprobrium generis, foedumque patēbat   155

152 *taur-us ī* 2m. bull. Minos promised the sacrifice to Jupiter if he was successful in his campaign to punish the Athenians for the death of his son Androgeos. The sacrifice of one hundred oxen is a hecatomb (Greek *hekaton* 100, *bous* ox)
taurōrum corpora centum: in apposition to *uōta*
153 *rat-is is* 3f. boat
Cūrētida: Greek acc. of *Cūrētis* 'belonging to the Curetes', agreeing with *terram*; it means 'Cretan', the Curetes being an ancient C(u)retan people who worshipped Zeus by beating shields, etc. (they saved the baby Zeus from death at the hands of his father Cronus by beating their shields and so drowning the infant cries that would have given him away)

154 *spoli-a ōrum* 2n. pl. spoils (arms, equipment etc.)
decorō 1 adorn
rēgi-a ae 1f. palace
fix-us a um hung up (*figō*). Hanging up spoils of war at home – rather than in a temple – was a particularly Roman thing to do
155 *opprobri-um ī* 2n. shame, disgrace (referring to the Minotaur; the point is that the Minotaur has now grown up and cannot be ignored or hidden any longer)
foed-us a um disgusting
pateō 2 be exposed, come to light; be open

152–68: Minos returns home to Crete, remembers his vows to his father Zeus/Jupiter (a hecatomb is a gigantic offering) and commemorates his local successes in the war against Athens (152–4). But he needs to do something about the Minotaur. *crēuerat* indicates

mātris adulterium mōnstrī nouitāte bifōrmis;
dēstinat hunc Minōs thalamō remouēre pudōrem,
multiplicīque domō caecīsque inclūdere tēctīs.
Daedalus, ingeniō fabrae celeberrimus artis,
pōnit opus, turbatque notās, et lūmina flexā∧   160
dūcit in errōrem uariārum ∧ambāge uiārum,
nōn secus ac liquidīs Phrygius Maeandrus in aruīs
lūdit, et ambiguō lāpsū refluitque fluitque,
occurrēnsque sibī uentūrās aspicit undās,
et nunc ad fontēs, nunc ad mare uersus apertum   165
incertās exercet aquās: ita Daedalus implet
innumerās errōre uiās, uixque ipse reuertī
ad līmen potuit. tanta est fallācia tēctī.

156 *mātris*: i.e. Pasiphae, mother of the Minotaur
adulteri-um i 2n. adultery
*mōnstr-um i 2n. monstrosity
nouitās nouitāt-is 3f. phenomenon
bifōrm-is e two-formed (i.e. man and bull)
157 *dēstinō* 1 determine
thalamō: i.e. from his marriage
158 *multiplex multiplic-is* complex
caec-us a um dark, treacherous
inclūdō 3 shut up
*tēct-um i 2n. building (the 'labyrinth')
159 *Daedal-us i* 2m. Daedalus
faber fabr-a um of the craftsman
celeber celebr-is e famous
160 *opus*: i.e. the labyrinth
not-a ae 1f. sign, marker (to help get one's bearings)
flex-us a um tortuous
161 *ambāge-s* 3f. twists and turns

162 *nōn secus ac*: 'not otherwise than', 'just as',
    introducing a simile
Phrygi-us a um in Phrygia
Maeandr-us i 2m. Maeander, a winding river in
    Roman Asia (modern Turkey)
163 *ambigu-us a um* uncertain
lāps-us ūs 4m. course. Note the prevalence of *l* in this
    line
(re)fluō 3 flow (back)
164 *occurrō* 3 meet up with (+ dat.)
165 *uersus*: from *uertor*
166 *exerceō* 2 keep in motion, ply
167 *innumer-us a um* myriad
ipse: i.e. Daedalus
reuertor 3 dep. return, find one's way back
168 *līmen limin-is* 3n. entrance
fallāci-a ae 1f. deceptiveness

how the problem *had* grown (one could, as it were, keep such a monster swaddled in baby-clothes only for so long); *patēbat* indicates what the situation now *was* (155), with *opprobrium*, *foedum* (155) and *mōnstrī* (156) all emphasising the shame Minos feels for his family. Daedalus, then, is summoned to get rid of this *pudor* (157), and Minos tells him what to do – construct a treacherous, complex building in which the monster can be hidden away (158). One would have thought killing it, or locking it up in a perfectly simple building, would have done the trick: but this is myth. The result is the labyrinth, a building after Ovid's heart – all sign(-post)s confused (160, cf. 167), eyes deceived, and routes full of twists and turns (160–1, cf. 167). A brilliant simile likens the labyrinth to the river Maeander (no less meandering today) and its god at the same time: that too deceives and is uncertain in its course (163, 166, cf. 167), turning back on itself (164, cf. 167), going now one way, now another (165, cf. 167) – the whole thing such a master-piece of deception (168, cf. 160–1, 166) that even Daedalus could hardly find his way out (167–8). The simile is as complex in its tortuous, sinuous twists and turns as the labyrinth it describes.

8.169–82: *Theseus kills the Minotaur with the help of Ariadne, whom he later deserts*

quō postquam geminam taurī iuuenisque figūram
clausit, et Actaeō bis pāstum sanguine mōnstrum   170
tertia sors annīs domuit repetīta nouēnīs,
utque ope uirgineā nūllīs iterāta∧ priōrum
iānua∧difficilis filō est inuenta relectō,
prōtinus Aegīdēs raptā Mīnōide Dīam
uēla dedit, comitemque suam crūdēlis in illō   175
lītore dēstituit. dēsertae et multa querentī
amplexūs et opem Līber tulit, utque perennī

---

169 *geminam . . . figūram*: = the Minotaur
170 *Actae-us a um* to do with Attica (Athens' territory). When Minos found that he could not take
Athens, he had prayed to his father Zeus/Jupiter
for revenge on the city. Athens was immediately
hit by a plague, and its people were told that it
would be lifted only when they had given satisfaction to Minos. Minos demanded that a sacrifice of
seven men and seven girls be sent to feed the
Minotaur in its labyrinth every nine years. Time
has now moved on, and the Minotaur has tasted
Attic blood twice (*bis*), but the third youth con-
signment (*tertia sors* 171) is to cause its death
bis twice
pāscō 3 *pāui pāstum* feed
171 *domō* 3 *domuī* overcome. Theseus volunteered
for the third group, killed the Minotaur and with
the help of thread (*filō . . . relectō* 173) supplied by
Minos' daughter Ariadne (*uirgineā* 172) found his
way out of the labyrinth. Theseus sailed off with
Ariadne back to Athens but subsequently aban-

doned her on the island of Naxos (176)
nouēn-ī ae a every nine
172 *uirgine-us a um* of a virgin (Ariadne)
iterō 1 visit a second time
priōrum: i.e. the Athenians in the first two consign-
ments; gen. after *nūllīs*
173 *fil-um ī* 2n. thread
relect-us a um re-wound, wound up (*relegō*)
174 *Aegīdēs*: Greek nom., 'son of Aegeus', i.e.
Theseus
Mīnōis Mīnōid-is 3f. 'daughter of Minos' i.e. Ariadne
Dī-a ae 1f. Naxos (a Greek island)
175 *uēl-um ī* 2n. sail; *uēla dare* set sail
lītus lītor-is 3n. shore
176 *dēstituō* 3 *dēstituī* abandon
dēsert-us a um deserted. Here it is dat. s. f., referring
to Ariadne, as is also *querentī*
177 *amplex-us ūs* 4m. embrace, love. Note the syllepsis of *amplexūs et opem*
Līber -ī 2m. Bacchus/Dionysus
perenn-is e perennial

169–82: And so the Minotaur is led into the labyrinth. It has its first taste of human flesh
with the first consigment of Athenian youth, and nine years later its second (169–70). Nine
years after that comes Theseus. Ovid, for some reason, compresses the whole story into a
few lines. If one did not know about Minos' daughter Ariadne falling in love with Theseus
and giving him the thread with which to mark his trail into and out of the labyrinth where
he killed the Minotaur, it would be very hard to see what was behind 172–3. Ovid further
compounds the problem by naming the couple by their father's names (patronymic) in
174; Theseus' desertion of Ariadne on Naxos (175–6) is called *crūdēlis*, but is otherwise
unexplained, though 176 makes Ariadne's distress clear enough; and why did Dionysus
come to her rescue? There was a sexual motive (*amplexūs*), but, given Dionysus' elevation
of her, or at least her crown, to stardom (in another tradition, Ariadne herself was placed
among the stars), one would have appreciated a little more detail. Since Ovid gives nearly

sīdere clāra foret, sūmptam dē fronte corōnam
immīsit caelō. tenuēs uolat illa per aurās,
dumque uolat, gemmae nitidōs uertuntur in ignēs,   180
cōnsistuntque locō, speciē remanente corōnae,
quī medius Nīxīque genu est Anguemque tenentis.

8.183–7: *Daedalus decides that he and his son shall escape from Crete by flight*

Daedalus intereā, Crētēn longumque perōsus
exilium, tāctusque locī nātālis amōre,
clausus erat pelagō. 'terrās licet' inquit 'et undās   185
obstruat, at caelum certē patet; ībimus illāc!
omnia possideat, nōn possidet āera Mīnōs.'

---

178 **corōn-a ae* 1f. crown. Bacchus took this from Ariadne's forehead, to turn into the constellation called the Northern Crown. Placing people or objects among the stars is called 'catasterism' (from the Greek prefix *kata* + *astereō*, 'en-star', cf. *astēr* 'star'). Bacchus throws the crown up into the sky as he and Ariadne race through the air in his chariot
179 *immittō* 3 *immīsī* launch
*uolō 1 move through the air, fly
180 *gemm-a ae* 1f. jewel
nitid-us a um shining, glittering
ignēs: i.e. stars
181 *speci-ēs speci-ēī* 5f. appearance
182 *quī*: picks up *locō*
medius: here + gen., controlling *Nīxī genu* and

Anguem tenentis, both constellations
Nīx-us (*-a um*) *genu*: 'One-who-bends the knee', i.e. the Kneeler
Anguem tenēns tenent-is: 'One-who-holds the snake', i.e. Ophiuchus
183 *Crētēn*: Greek acc. of Crete
longumque: at least eighteen years, to calculate from this passage alone (170–1)
perōs-us a um hating
184 *nātāl-is e* of one's birth (for Daedalus, this means Athens)
185 *pelag-us ī* 2n. sea. Minos at this time ruled the waves
licet although (+ subj.), **RLV**
186 *obstruō* 3 close off. Minos is the subject
illāc by that route

---

six lines to the transformation of Ariadne's crown into a constellation (177–82) – and the same number to the whole of the rest of the story (172–7) – it is clearly this metamorphosis which interests him: but even so, it does not interest him much. This episode, though a masterpiece of compression, does not show Ovid at his imaginative best; but if nothing else, it serves to highlight the brilliance with which he develops character and plot elsewhere. Had he revised *Metamorphōsēs*, perhaps this passage would have attracted his attention. (Ovid's *Heroides* 10 is a letter from Ariadne to Theseus.)

183–7: Daedalus is doubly motivated to leave Crete (183–4), but 185–7 make it clear that Minos rules earth and sea. That leaves only the air – but also (the fourth element) fire . . .

188–202: The transformation which forms the centre-piece of the Daedalus story, then, is ornithological: Daedalus is to use his brilliance as an inventor to turn himself and his son Icarus into birds. Normally, only gods can engineer metamorphosis: here a human

8.188–202: *Daedalus makes and tests the wings; Icarus is thrilled*

dīxit, et ignōtās animum dīmittit in artēs,
nātūramque nouat. nam pōnit in ōrdine pennās
ā minimā coeptās, longam breuiōre sequentī,   190
ut clīuō crēuisse putēs. sīc rūstica∧ quondam
∧fistula disparibus paulātim surgit auēnīs.
tum linō mediās et cēris alligat īmās
atque ita compositās paruō curuāmine flectit,
ut uērās imitētur auēs. puer Īcarus ūnā   195
stābat et, ignārus sua sē tractāre perīcla,
ōre renīdentī modo quās uaga mōuerat aura,
captābat plūmās, flāuam modo pollice cēram
mollibat, lūsūque suō mīrābile∧ patris
impediēbat ∧opus. postquam manus ultima coeptō   200
imposita est, geminās opifex lībrāuit in alās
ipse suum corpus, mōtāque pependit in aurā.

---

188 *ignōt-us a um* unknown
189 *nouō* 1 innovate in, alter
190 *ā . . . sequentī*: '[feathers] beginning from the
  smallest, with the shorter coming behind the
  long', i.e. short feathers first, then the long feathers (see Figure 3). For the problem of how the
  wings work, see **Comment** *ad loc.*
191 *crēuisse*: understand *pennās* as the subject of this
  inf.
clīu-us ī 2m. slope (here, ablative of place)
rūstic-us a um rustic, country
192 *fistul-a ae* 1f. pan-pipe (see 1.709–12)
dispar -is unequal
paulātim gradually
auēn-a ae 1f. reed
193 *mediās*: i.e. the *pennās* in the *mediās* and *īmās*
alligō 1 bind
īm-us a um at the bottom

194 *compōnō* 3 *composuī compositum* put together,
  construct
curuāmen curuāmin-is 3n. curve
195 *Īcar-us ī* 2m. Icarus, Daedalus' son
ūnā alongside
196 *tractō* 1 handle
perīcla = perīcula
197 *renīdeō* 2 smile
modo . . . modo . . . now . . . now . . .
quās: take in order *captābat plūmās quās*
uag-us a um wandering
198 *plūm-a ae* 1f. feather
pollex pollici-is 3m. thumb
199 *mollibat*: = archaic form of *molliēbat*
lūs-us ūs 4m. play
201 *impōnō* 3 *imposuī impositum* place, put on
opifex opific-is 3m. craftsman
lībrō 1 balance, suspend

---

will try to. Ovid emphasises the daring and novelty of what this entails – the equivalent of interfering with nature itself (188–9) – and turns his own inventive capacities to describing first how he built the wings.

What if . . . ? Herewith a digression on a problem:

1. The feathers are laid side by side (189), and Ovid says that they are graded in length, shorter ones following behind longer ones (190); the image of a slope (Ovid invites his audience to imagine it with *putēs*) and of pan-pipes is used to illustrate it (191–2).
2. But how do the feathers cohere into wings? Ovid tells us that the feathers are bound

8.203–9: *Daedalus instructs Icarus on how to fly*

īnstruit et nātum, 'mediō' que 'ut līmite currās,
Īcare,' ait 'moneō, nē, sī dēmissior ībis,
unda grauet pennās, sī celsior, ignis adūrat.   205
inter utrumque uolā! nec tē spectāre Boōtēn
aut Helicēn iubeō strictumque Ōrīonis ēnsem;

---

203 *īnstruō* 3 instruct
līmes līmit-is 3m. track, route
204 *dēmiss-us a um* low (note the comparative here
    meaning 'too')
205 *grauō* 1 weigh down
cels-us a um high
adūrō 3 scorch

206 *Boōtēn*: Greek acc. of Bootes, a constellation (the
    Ox-driver)
207 *Helicēn*: Greek acc. of Helice, a constellation
    (the Great Bear); Bootes and Helice together indi-
    cate the North, Orion the South
strict-us a um drawn (*stringō*)
Ōrīōn -is 3m. Orion, a constellation
ēns-is is 3m. sword

---

together down the middle with thread: so that keeps them together. But where does
the wax come into it? The wax is *īmās*, 'at the base/end/bottom'. Do we then imagine a
row of feathers, held together with twine, with the quills stuck into (as it were) a long
bar or arm of wax? If so, the finished wing could certainly then be curved slightly, like
a real bird's (194–5).

3. How then, and where on the body, are the wings fitted? Along the arms would be the
obvious place, but 201–2 tells us that Daedalus fits his *body into* the wings (as if into a
harness of some sort), and at 209 Ovid tells us the wings are attached to Icarus' *shoulders*. This squares with their depiction in Pompeian art (see Figure 3).

4. But how do the wings work? Are they flapped? Possibly: they are certainly moved
(216). But to judge from 202, where Daedalus hangs in the wind ('moved breeze'), 212
where he is elevated on the wings, and 228, their purpose seems to be to catch the
breezes: i.e. the escapees are gliding. They would need to adjust their wings to do that
efficiently, and that accounts for *mouet* of 216; note that the wings have already been
given a slight curve at 194. Note also that *uolō* means 'move through the air' (cf. 179);
it does not necessarily imply 'flapping one's wings'. If this is what Ovid had in mind,
then when the long bar of wax melts (226–7), the wings (whose feathers are held
together by twine) free themselves from the wax *as a whole* and drop away completely
(again, see fig. 3, where Icarus lies on the shore with one wing still attached, the other
in one piece next to him). The desperate and terrified Icarus then tries to use his arms
as wings, but since arms do not have feathers (*nūdōs* 227) and 'lack oarage' (228:
because they have never *had* 'oarage'), they are useless. This seems to me the best way
of interpreting how Ovid imagined the scene (the appended passage in the **Study
section** should also be consulted on the matter).

5. But to end with a *caveat*: Daedalus is not a god but a real human being, altering his own
and his son's body so that they can fly. Fantasy and reality, in other words, collide
starkly here. Ovid can see how wings could be made, but how they could actually *work*
– how a human body could be adapted so that one could fly using them – is a serious
problem. The static-wing gliding theory (rather like a sailing ship, with which Ovid
contrasts an oared ship at 228) is the easiest solution.

mē duce, carpe uiam!' pariter praecepta uolandī
trādit, et ignōtās umerīs accommodat ālās.

208 *pariter . . . et* at the same time as
praecept-um ī 2n. instruction

209 *ignōt-us a um* unfamiliar
accommodō 1 fit

Figure 3   Daedalus and Icarus. Wall-painting from Pompeii.

Back to the text. Icarus is with his father, watching (195). We picture the sort of boy he
is by what he is *doing*; with shining face (197), clearly captivated by the present miracle
his father is working (*mirābile*, 199), he gets in the way all the time by playing with feathers and wax (197–200). The picture moves onto a quite different level with the narratorial comment *ignārus* – what Icarus does not *realise* is that he is in fact handling the means
of his death. Job done, Daedalus fits himself into the wings, and hangs there in the breeze.

203–9: Time to lecture his son (Ovid is very good on the 'generation gap' in this episode).
Daedalus imagines Icarus running ahead (203) – he knows what small boys are like,
always rushing about – and urges on him the middle way no less than three times: *mediō
līmite* (203) . . . not *dēmissior* or *celsior* (204–5) . . . *inter utrumque* (206). He warns his
son not even to look at the constellations (206–7: Icarus, like Phaethon, may regard them
as real horrors in the sky, 2.198–200), but to follow his lead (208). As he speaks, he fits the
ignōtās wings on him. The warning signs are already out.

8.210–35: *Icarus flies too close to the sun and plunges to his death*

inter opus monitūsque genae maduēre senīlēs,	210
et patriae tremuēre manūs; dedit ōscula∧ nātō*	
nōn iterum ∧repetenda *suō, pennīsque leuātus	
ante uolat comitīque timet, uelut ālēs, ab altō∧	
quae teneram prōlem prōdūxit in āera ∧nīdō,	
hortāturque sequī, damnōsāsque ērudit artēs,	215
et mouet ipse suās et nātī respicit ālās.	
hōs, aliquis tremulā dum captat harundine piscēs,	
aut pāstor baculō stīuāue innīxus arātor,	
uīdit et obstipuit, quīque aethera carpere possent,	
crēdidit esse deōs. et iam Iūnōnia laeuā	220
parte Samos (fuerant Dēlosque Parosque relictae),	
dextra Lebinthos erat fēcundaque melle Calymnē,	

210 *monit-us ūs* 4m. advice, warning
gen-a ae 1f. cheek
madeō 2 *maduī* be wet
senil-is e of the old man
211 *tremō* 3 *tremuī* tremble
213 *ālēs ālit-is* 3m./f. bird
214 *prōl-ēs is* 3f. offspring, race
prōdūcō 3 *prōdūxī* lead out
nid-us i 2m. nest
215 *damnōs-us a um* ruinous, pernicious
ērudiō 4 teach, train in
216 *respiciō* 3/4 look back at
217 *tremul-us a um* trembling
harundō harundin-is 3f. reed, rod
***pisc-is is* 3m. fish
218 *bacul-um i* 2n. stick, crook
stiu-a ae 1f. shaft of a plough-handle
innix-us a um leaning on (*innītor*)
arātor -is 3m. ploughman
219 *obstupēscō* 2 *obstipuī* be amazed
quīque . . . possent: translate after *crēdidit . . . deōs*
220 *Iūnōni-us a um* belonging to Juno

laeu-us a um left
221 *Samos . . . Dēlos . . . Parosque*: all nom. s. of the Greek islands Delos, Paros, Samos. One would have expected Daedalus, whose native land was Athens (cf. 184), to be flying north-west from Minos' palace in Knossos, but now they turn north-east to Lebinthos and Calymne – though Ovid has little option because that is the area where the isle of Icaros and the Icarian sea, named after Icarus, actually are. How come? We know that there was an Attic deme called Icaria – perhaps because in the 'original' version of the myth Icarus fell into the sea near it. If so, was the name then somehow transferred (by colonists?) to the present island, and later tradition gradually forgot about the obscure Attic connection? See Rudd in Martindale (1988, 24).
222 *Lebinthos*: nom. s. of the Greek island Lebinthos
fēcund-us a um fertile
mel mell-is 3n. honey
Calymnē: nom. s. of the Greek island Calymne

210–35: It is clear that Daedalus is full of fear for his exuberant young son. Ovid again realises Daedalus' *inner* terror (210–12) by movingly describing Daedalus' *physical* reactions as he fits on the wings – tears, trembling hands, kisses (*nōn repetenda* – the last he will ever give him, another moving narratorial shift), and fear (*timet*) as he flies ahead, leading the way (213, cf. 208). A simile decorates the moment: a mother bird leads its *teneram* young from its *altō* (and therefore dangerous) nest into the air, presumably for the first time (214–15). Daedalus is taking his 'young' high *up* into the air, for the first time. Clearly young Icarus is not obeying orders, so Daedalus has to urge him to stay close, teaching him (215: that *damnōsās* is telling: in whose eyes? A regretful Daedalus', or is it Ovid's comment? Cf. 188–9), and watching him closely (216). Now a brilliant change of focus: we

cum puer audācī coepit gaudēre uolātū
dēseruitque ducem, caelīque cupīdine tractus
altius ēgit iter. rapidī uīcīnia sōlis   225
mollit odōrātās, pennārum uincula, cērās;
tābuerant cērae; nūdōs quatit ille lacertōs,
rēmigiōque carēns nōn ūllās percipit aurās,
ōraque caeruleā^ patrium clāmantia nōmen
excipiuntur ^aquā, quae nōmen trāxit ab illō.   230
at pater īnfēlīx, nec iam pater, 'Īcare,' dīxit,
'Īcare,' dīxit 'ubi es? quā tē regiōne requīram?'
'Īcare' dīcēbat: pennās aspexit in undīs,
dēuōuitque suās artēs, corpusque sepulcrō
condidit, et tellūs ā nōmine dicta sepultī.   235

223 *uolāt-us ūs* 4m. flight
224 *cupīdō cupīdin-is* 3f. desire
225 *rapid-us a um* scorching, consuming
uīcīni-a ae 1f. proximity
226 *odōrāt-us a um* sweet-smelling
uincul-um ī 2n. binding
227 *tābēscō* 3 *tābuī* melt
quatiō 3/4 beat
228 *rēmigi-um ī* 2n. oarage
percipiō 3/4 acquire, catch

229 *caerule-us a um* blue
231 *Īcare*: Daedalus repeats his son's name three
times. It was traditional at Roman funerals to call
out the name of the dead person three times
232 *regiō regiōn-is* 3f. area
233 *aspiciō = adspiciō*
234 *dēuoueō* 2 *dēuōuī* abjure
235 *sepult-us a um* buried (*sepeliō*) – on the island
named after Icarus (another Ovidian aetiology)

move from the feelings and actions of the fliers to spectators on the ground – a fisherman, shepherd, ploughman (217–18) – suddenly freezing, amazed at what they see (219) and imagining them to be gods (219–20). What an achievement! But they are human – *damnōsās artēs*? Since gods do not career incompetently across the sky, Daedalus and his son must by now have learned the skill; indeed, they have made rather good progress (about 200 miles if they are passing Samos, 221). But now young Icarus lets this flying/gliding business go to his head (note *audācī* 223), regarding it as fun (*gaudēre*, as boys will, cf. 195–200). He wants to explore, like all boys, to reach for the skies (224–5). He abandons his father and starts to climb. As for Daedalus, one can imagine him still plodding boringly on, ignorant of what is now unfolding above him, assuming his son is following (cf. 196: *damnōsās artēs*?). What if . . . ? The sun (= fire) is scorching (225); the softened wax (cf. 199), releasing its perfumes (226: *odōrātās* is an exquisite change of focus – does Icarus smell it?), loosens the feathers and melts. Vainly Icarus tries to grip the air – but there is nothing to grip it with (228), his arms being useless (227). Ovid, true artist, spares imposing on us his emotionalising insights into the boy's thoughts as he plunges to the sea (no modern novelist could possibly resist); the boy merely, uselessly, poignantly calls out *pater*! But even Daedalus cannot save him now (229–30). Indeed, Daedalus (no longer a father, as Ovid poignantly reminds us, 231) has no idea where Icarus is. How could he? His own panic-stricken cries (232–3) reflect his frantic searching (note the contrast between single cries, *dīxit*, and continued cries, *dīcēbat*) – and then he sees the feathers. Again, Ovid appends no narratorial comment to that bald statement: but Daedalus' instant disavowal of his (*damnōsās*?) *artēs* – trying to alter nature and challenge the gods (188–9, 220)? – tells us everything we need to know about what *Daedalus* thinks of his invention.

Learning vocabulary for Passage 13, Minos, Ariadne, Daedalus and Icarus

corōn-a ae 1f. crown
mōnstr-um ī 2n. monstrosity
pateō 2 be exposed, come to light; be open
pisc-is is 3m. fish

taur-us ī 2m. bull
tēct-um ī 2n. building
uolō 1 move through the air, fly

Study Section

1. What image does Ovid present to us of Daedalus? Is it condemnatory in any sense?
2. Compare Icarus with Phaethon (passage 4).
3. How does Ovid generate pathos in this story?
4. Compare this passage with Ovid's alternative and in interesting ways very different version of the story in his *Ars Amātōria* 2.19–98, where Ovid uses the myth to illustrate that one cannot restrain or pin down any creature with wings, e.g. *Amor*!
5. What moral would you care to draw from this story? Do not aspire too high? The dangers of new technologies? Always obey father? Or would you rather avoid moralising from it?

14   Baucis and Philemon, *Metamorphōsēs* 8.626–724

Background

Theseus' conquest of the Minotaur brings him fame throughout Greece, and he is invited to join the expedition to kill the Calydonian boar. Mission accomplished, he is on his way back to Athens when he accepts an invitation from the river-god Achelous to stay for a while, Achelous' river being in flood. Over dinner, one of the guests invited by Achelous suggests that the gods do not have the power to transform the shapes of Nature. The company is shocked, and one of them, the hero Lelex (described as 'ripe in years and wisdom'), tells the story of Baucis and Philemon (who apparently lived in 'Hellespontine' Phrygia, northern Turkey: see on 719) to refute the idea. As often in Ovid, this mythical couple are thoroughly Romanised.

8.626–36: *Jupiter and Mercury find a humble cottage to stay in*

'Iuppiter hūc speciē mortālī cumque parente
uēnit Atlantiadēs positīs cādūcifer ālis.
mīlle domōs adiēre, locum requiemque petentēs,
mīlle domōs clausēre serae. tamen ūna∧ recēpit,
∧parua quidem, stipulīs et cannā ∧tēcta palūstrī,   630

626 *hūc*: i.e. the marshy land in the Phrygian hills where the couple once lived
speci-ēs ēi 5f. disguise (here abl. of description, **RLL**(f)3(i), **W**40)
parente: i.e. his father Jupiter
627 *Atlantiadēs*: Greek nom., 'grandson of Atlas', i.e. Mercury (Hermes), god of heralds
cādūcifer ī 2m. staff-bearer. The *cādūceum* was the staff carried by heralds as a token of peace. Mercury is not carrying it here, because he is dis-

guised as a human; but *cādūcifer* is still his official title. Wittily, Ovid sets *positīs ālis* – the part of his gear Mercury *has* dispensed with – on either side of the word
628 *requi-ēs ēi* 5f. rest
629 *ser-a ae* 1f. bolt, bar
630 *stipul-a ae* 1f. straw
cann-a ae 1f. reed
palūstr-is e from the marsh

626–36: Lelex, who had himself seen the place in Phrygia where the miracle which he is about to describe took place, relates how Jupiter and Mercury came 'here' (626), Mercury having taken off the wings normally to be found on his ankles (627). The reason why they came and what they were doing in disguise does not emerge till the end; but it is a common literary theme that gods wander the earth disguised as humans in order to

[185]

sed ^pia. Baucis anus parilīque aetāte Philēmōn
illā^ sunt annīs iūnctī iuuenālibus, ^illā
cōnsenuēre ^casā, paupertātemque fatendō
effēcēre leuem nec inīquā mente ferendō.
nec rēfert, dominōs illīc famulōsne requīrās: 635
tōta domus duo sunt, īdem pārentque iubentque.'

8.637–50: *The old couple make the gods comfy and prepare food*

'ergo ubi caelicolae paruōs tetigēre penātēs,
submissōque humilēs intrārunt uertice postēs,

631 **an-us ūs* 4f. old woman
paril-is e equal, like
632 *illā . . . illā . . . casā*: the grand rhetorical repetitions amusingly describe – a little cottage
iuuenāl-is e youthful
633 *cōnsenēscō* 3 grow old together
*cas-a ae 1f. hut. This is the word used of Romulus'
cottage which was preserved on the Palatine hill
in Rome: Baucis and Philemon are 'good old
Romans'
paupertās paupertāt-is 3f. poverty
fateor 2 dep. admit
634 *leuem*: i.e. their poverty
nec: introduces the second reason for their ability to
endure poverty

iniqu-us a um resentful
635 *rēfert* it matters (whether + subj., impersonal
verb, **RLF2**)
famul-us ī 2m. slave
636 *pāreō* 2 obey
637 *caelicol-a ae* 1m. heaven-dweller. This is a grand,
dignified term for the gods, in contrast to the
humble surroundings
penāt-ēs um 3m. household gods
638 *submiss-us a um* lowered. 638 is a sonorous
golden line, describing the gods' entrance into the
little hut
humil-is e humble, lowly, poor
uertex uertic-is 3m. head
post-is is 3f. door-post

identify good and bad behaviour (cf. *Odyssey* 17.483–7, where some of the suitors warn
Antinous not to abuse the beggar-Odysseus: 'Antinous, you did not do well but very
badly to hit that wandering wretch, if he was some god from the skies. Gods disguise
themselves as strangers from far-off places in all sorts of ways, and move from city to city,
observing whether men behave justly or savagely'). The two gods knock on a thousand
doors looking for somewhere to stay, drawing blanks until they come to the cottage of
Baucis and her husband Philemon (628–9: note the repetition of *mīlle domōs*). *parua . . .
sed pia* (630–1) immediately summarises the world of this delightful couple: material
poverty, but religious devotion and sense of duty. They had been in this poor, thatched
(630) cottage ever since they were newly married (632), and had grown old in it (633).
They had handled poverty by unselfconsciously admitting it and refusing to grumble
about it (633–4); and they had no slaves but were happy to act as both servant and master
to each other, sharing between them the giving and obeying of orders (635–6). These are
shrewd observations by Ovid into the conditions underpinning a happy marriage,
however straitened the circumstances. Observe the rhymes *illā . . . illā* (632), *cōnsenuēre
. . . effēcēre* (633–4), *fatendō . . . ferendō* (633–4), *dominōs . . . famulōs* (635), *pārentque
iubentque* (636), increasing, perhaps, our sense of the simple unity of the couple's lives.

637–50: But this self-sufficient couple are not thereby unresponsive to the needs of
others: their *pietās* sees to that. Their *penātēs* (Roman household gods) may be tiny

membra senex positō iussit releuāre sedīlī,
cūī superiniēcit textum rude sēdula Baucis.   640
inde focō tepidum cinerem dīmōuit, et ignēs∧
suscitat ∧hesternōs, foliīsque et cortice siccō
nūtrit, et ad flammās animā prōdūcit anīlī;
multifidāsque facēs rāmāliaque ārida tēctō
dētulit et minuit, paruōque admōuit aēnō;   645
quodque∧ suus coniunx riguō collēgerat hortō,
truncat ∧holus foliīs. furcā leuat ille bicornī
sordida terga suis nigrō pendentia tignō,

639 *releuō* 1 rest	*rāmāl-ia ium* 3n. pl. twigs
sedīl-e is 3n. seat	*ārid-us a um* dry
640 *superiniciō* 3/4 *superiniēcī* throw X (acc.) over Y (dat.)	**tēct-um ī* 2n. roof, house
text-um ī 2n. cloth	**645** *dēferō dēferre dētulī* bring down from (abl.)
rud-is e rough	*minuō* 3 *minuī* chop up
sēdul-us a um busy	*admoueō* 2 *admōuī* put X (acc.) under Y (dat.)
641 **foc-us ī* 2m. hearth	*aēn-us ī* 2m. bronze pot
*tepid-us a um warm	**646** *quodque*: 'and the *holus quod . . .*'
dīmoueō 2 *dīmōuī* move around	*rigu-us a um* well-watered
642 *suscitō* 1 stir up	*hort-us ī* 2m. garden
hestern-us a um yesterday's	**647** *truncō* 1 strip X (acc.) of its Y (abl.)
*foli-um ī 2n. leaf	*holus holer-is* 3n. cabbage
cortex cortic-is 3m. bark	**furc-a ae* 1f. (two-pronged) fork, house support
sicc-us a um dry	*bicorn-is e* with two prongs
643 *nūtriō* 4 feed	**648** *sordid-us a um* grimy
prōdūcō 3 help on [the ashes] *ad*	*sūs su-is* 3m./f. pig, sow
anīl-is e old woman's	*tign-um ī* 2n. beam. Meat was smoked in order to help it dry out and thus preserve it, since bacteria can live only in liquids. Smoking also flavoured the meat
644 *multifid-us a um* split	
fax fac-is 3f. kindling	

(637) and the gods have to stoop to get into the cottage (note the golden line 638 *submissō . . . humilēs*), but the welcome is warm and busy (*sēdula*, 640) and its detail is delightful: the bench where the gods are to sit is spruced up with a rough cloth (639–40); yesterday's fire is revived (the old ash is cleared away first), fed with light kindling and puffed into flame (642–3), not for warmth but to cook over (the careful couple do not keep a fire going when it is not needed); then larger pieces of wood for the fire are brought down from the roof where they had been put to dry (*ārida*, 644), and economically split up (*minuit*, 645) before being placed under a *paruō* cooking pot (645). Baucis then prepares for boiling a cabbage picked from the *riguō* garden (the cabbage is a very humble vegetable in Roman eyes, but Philemon is a conscientious gardener), while Philemon brings down a side of pork from the roof-beams, where it had been placed to be 'smoked' by the fire (the beams where it was lodged are black, 648). Though Philemon cuts off only a small portion for cooking (650), this is a generous act. A side of pork, however *sordida*, was precious and expensive fare for this poor couple – it had been saved up for a long time, making it even more *sordida* (649) – but Philemon does not hesitate to share it. These are special measures for a special occasion.

seruātōque diū resecat dē tergore partem^
^exiguam, ^sectamque domat feruentibus undīs.'   650

8.651–78: *All is made ready for the feast and the food is served*

'intereā mediās fallunt sermōnibus hōrās,
sentīrīque moram prohibent. erat alueus^ illīc
^fāgineus, dūrā clāuō suspēnsus ab ānsā;
is tepidīs implētur aquīs, artūsque fouendōs
accipit. in mediō^ torus* est dē mollibus uluīs   655
*impositus ^lectō, spondā pedibusque salignīs.
uestibus hunc uēlant, quās nōn nisi tempore festō
sternere cōnsuērant, sed et haec uīlisque uetusque
uestis erat, lectō nōn indignanda salignō.
accubuēre deī. mēnsam succīncta tremēnsque   660
pōnit anus, mēnsae sed erat pēs tertius impār.

---

649 *resecō* 1 cut off
tergore: = *tergō*
650 *sect-us a um* cut, sliced
domō 1 soften, cook
ferueō 2 bubble, boil
652 *alue-us ī* 2m. tub
653 *fāgine-us a um* of beechwood (a water-resistant wood)
clāu-us ī 2m. nail
suspēns-us a um hung (*suspendō*)
āns-a ae 1f. handle
654 *foueō* 2 soothe
655 *ulu-a ae* 1f. sedge (marsh grass)
656 *impōnō* 3 *imposuī impositum* place over

spond-a ae 1f. bed-frame
**salign-us a um* of willow (a cheap wood)
657 *fest-us a um* of (religious) holidays
658 *sternō* 3 spread
cōnsuēscō 3 *cōnsuēuī* be accustomed
uīl-is e cheap
659 *indignor* 1 dep. be unworthy of
660 *accumbō* 3 *accubuī* recline
succīnct-us a um girt up (*succingō*)
tremēns trement-is trembling
661 **mēns-a ae* 1f. table; course of a meal
impār -is unequal. A three-legged table can stand securely, however rough the ground, but only if its three legs are of equal length

---

651–78: Like good hosts, the couple engage their guests in conversation and prevent any awkwardness at the wait for food (651–2); they bathe the gods' feet in a wooden tub (652–4); and so that the gods can recline to eat (as aristocratic Romans did), they use their bed for the purpose, placing on it a mattress stuffed with sedge, lacking anything more luxurious like down (655). This they cover with cheap cloth brought out only on festal occasions, i.e. when the gods are celebrated – a pleasant irony (657–9). Willow (656, 659) was a poor man's wood – so the cheap cloth was appropriate. The gods recline, but not the hosts: it is their job to serve. Baucis girds herself up for action and brings up a table (660), but it is wobbly and needs fixing with a piece of pot under one of the legs. That done, she wipes it down, not with a fine cloth but some fresh mint from the garden (661–3). The first course is simple and also from the garden – olives, wild cherries preserved in wine, endive, radish, cheese, egg – and served on earthenware dishes (664–8). Wine is served in ancient beechwood cups, the cracks plugged with wax (668–70), and then comes the main course (the pork, and cabbage from the hearth, 671). The same (young) wine is brought back again – no extensive, expensive cellar for this couple – and

testa parem fēcit, quae postquam subdita clīuum
sustulit, aequātam mentae tersēre uirentēs.
pōnitur hīc bicolor sincērae bāca Mineruae,
conditaque in liquidā corna autumnālia faece,   665
intibaque et rādīx et lactis massa coāctī,
ōuaque nōn ācrī leuiter uersāta fauīllā,
omnia fictilibus. post haec caelātus^ eōdem*
sistitur *argentō ^crātēr fabricātaque^ fāgō
^pōcula, quā caua sunt, flāuentibus ^illita cērīs.   670
parua mora est, epulāsque focī mīsēre calentēs,
nec longae rūrsus referuntur uīna^ senectae
dantque locum mēnsīs paulum ^sēducta secundīs.
hīc nux, hīc mixta est rūgōsīs cārica palmīs,

662 *test-a ae* 1f. piece of pot
subdit-us a um placed under (*subdō*)
*clīu-us ī 2m. slope, incline
663 *aequāt-us a um* levelled (*aequō*)
ment-ae ae 1f. mint
tergeō 2 *tersī* wipe off, clean
uireō 2 be green
664 *bicolor -is* of two colours (i.e. green and black
   and therefore not ripe; *bicolor* is a politely epic
   way of putting it)
sincēr-us a um unblemished
bāc-a ae 1f. berry
Mineruae: her *bāca* was the olive. The phrase
   sincērae . . . Mineruae is a grandly epic way of
   saying 'olive', perhaps incongruously amusing in
   the humble setting
665 *corn-um ī* 2n. wild cherry
autumnāl-is e of autumn
faex faec-is 3f. the lees of wine
666 *intib-um ī* 2n. chicory, endive
rādīx rādīc-is 3f. radish
lac lact-is 3n. milk
mass-a ae 1f. lump
coāct-us a um curdled (i.e. cheese)
667 *ōu-um ī* 2n. egg. *ab ōuō usque ad māla*, lit. 'from
   egg right up to apples' (675), 'from start to finish',
   was a proverb drawn from the courses of a typical
   Roman meal – which this is
uersō 1 turn
fauīll-a ae 1f. ash

668 *fictil-e is* 3n. earthenware (here 'in earthenware')
*caelō 1 engrave, emboss
669 *sistō* 3 place, set down
argent-um ī 2n. silver. Note the Ovidian irony – the
   dishes were in fact all made of pottery, which
   (unlike silver) was not usually engraved. Silver
   would have been on show only in wealthy house-
   holds
*crātēr -is 3m. bowl in which wine was mixed
fabricāt-us a um made of (+ abl.)
fāg-us ī 2f. beechwood
670 *pōcul-um ī* 1n. cup
cau-us a um hollow
flāuēns flāuent-is yellow
illit-us a um smeared (*illinō*)
671 *epul-ae ārum* 2f. pl. feast, banquet
caleō 2 be warm
672 *senect-ae ae* 1f. old age (describing the wine). It is
   not vintage (*nec longae*), and is here brought back,
   not replaced with something else
673 *dō locum*: 'give place', i.e. were taken away
paulum for a while
sēdūcō 3 *sēdūxī sēductum* move away, apart
mēnsīs . . . secundīs: this followed the main course,
   and usually consisted of fruit and nuts
674 *nux nuc-is* 3f. nut
rūgōs-us a um wrinkled
cāric-a ae 1f. lit. 'from Caria' (southern Turkey), i.e.
   the cheapest dried fig
palm-a ae 1f. date

then put on one side (it is a small table) to make room for the last course (672–3) – nuts,
figs, dates, plums, apples, grapes and honeycomb. Since the couple live in Phrygia, these
are all local goods. But the style of food, and the order in which it is served, is thoroughly
Roman; and, for all its simplicity, there is, above all else (677), no resentment or lack of
good will about the couple's pleasure in service (677–8). It makes for a heart-warming
scene. What the gods make of it all, Ovid has not told us – yet.

prūnaque et in patulīs redolentia māla canistrīs,   675
et dē purpureīs collectae uītibus ūuae.
candidus in mediō fauus est; super omnia, uultūs
accessēre bonī, nec iners pauperque uoluntās.'

8.679–94: *The gods work a miracle and tell the couple to escape impending disaster*

'intereā totiēns haustum crātēra replērī
sponte suā, per sēque uident succrēscere uīna.   680
attonitī nouitāte pauent, manibusque supīnīs
concipiunt Baucisque precēs timidusque Philēmōn,
et ueniam dapibus nūllisque parātibus ōrant.
ūnicus ānser erat, minimae custōdia uīllae,
quem dīs hospitibus dominī mactāre parābant.   685
ille celer pennā tardōs aetāte fatīgat
ēlūditque diū, tandemque est uīsus ad ipsōs
cōnfūgisse deōs. superī uetuēre necārī

675 *prūn-um ī* 2n. plum	*supīn-us a um* upturned. Palms of the hands were
patul-us a um wide, flat	turned up to heaven in prayers and appeals (espe-
redoleō 2 give off a smell, be fragrant	cially supplication)
māl-um ī 2n. apple	**682** *concipiō* 3/4 utter
canistr-um ī 2n. basket	*prex prec-is* 3f. prayer
676 *purpure-us a um* purple	**683** *ueni-a ae* 1f. pardon
uīt-is is 3f. vine	*daps dap-is* 3f. feast
ūu-a ae 1f. grape	*parāt-us ūs* 4m. preparation, utensils
677 *candid-us a um* white	**684** *ūnic-us a um* one, single
fau-us ī 2m. honeycomb	*ānser -is* 3m. goose
uultūs: i.e. the looks on the faces of the old couple	*custōdi-a ae* 1f. guard. There was a famous story of
678 *iners inert-is* sluggish, lazy	the geese that guarded the Capitol, the main fort
679 *totiēns* so many times	of early Rome, and warned of an impending
hauriō 4 *hausī haustum* empty, drain	attack by the Gauls around 390 BC (the date is dis-
crātēra: Greek acc. of *crātēr*	puted)
repleō 2 refill	*uīll-a ae* 1f. dwelling
680 *sponte suā* of its own accord	**685** *mactō* 1 sacrifice
succrēscō 3 be re-supplied	**686** *fatīgō* 1 exhaust
681 *attonit-us a um* amazed	**687** *ēlūdō* 3 elude
nouitās nouitāt-is 3f. phenomenon	**688** *cōnfugiō* 3 *cōnfūgī* seek refuge with (+ acc.)

679–94: He does now: a miracle occurs (679–80, cf. the widow's cruse, 1 Kings 17.10–24, a story with many parallels to this one). Being pious, the couple are terrified of the implications and immediately offer up prayers, presuming that these divinities are offended by the simplicity of the meal (681–3); and to show they mean it, they immediately set off to chase, catch and sacrifice the goose who guards their little cottage (684–7). In a scene of gentle farce, the goose is too quick and slippery for the slow old pair, and takes refuge with the gods – who finally reveal who they are and their purpose in coming: justly (*meritās*) to punish the wicked (687–90). Far from being angry with the couple, they indicate their pleasure by inviting them to flee with them up the mountain before disas-

"dī" que "sumus, meritāsque luet uīcīnia∧ poenās
∧impia" dīxērunt; "uōbīs immūnibus hūius∧   690
esse ∧malī dabitur. modo uestra relinquite tēcta,
ac nostrōs comitāte gradūs, et in ardua montis
īte simul!" pārent ambō, baculīsque leuātī
nītuntur longō uestīgia pōnere clīuō.'

8.695–710: *The flood engulfs everything, but their cottage becomes a temple*

'tantum aberant summō, quantum semel īre sagitta   695
missa potest. flexēre oculōs, et mersa∧ palūde
∧cētera prōspiciunt, tantum sua tēcta manēre.
dumque ea mīrantur, dum dēflent fāta suōrum,
illa uetus dominīs etiam casa parua duōbus
uertitur in templum: furcās subiēre columnae,   700
strāmina flāuēscunt, aurātaque tēcta uidentur
caelātaeque forēs, adopertaque marmore tellūs.
tālia tum placidō Sāturnius ēdidit ōre:

689 *merit-us a um* justified	*suōrum*: i.e. their neigbours
luō 3 pay	**699** *etiam*: with *duōbus*, i.e. 'even for just the two of
uīcīni-a ae 1f. neighbourhood	them'
690 *impi-us a um* disrespectful	**700** *subeō subīre subiī* replace
immūn-is e exempt from (+ gen.)	*column-a ae* 1f. column
691 *dabitur*: 'it will be granted *uōbis esse immūnibus*'	**701** *strāmen strāmin-is* 3n. straw
692 *comitō* 1 accompany	*flāuēscō* 2 turn yellow
grad-us ūs 4m. step	*aurāt-us a um* golden, gilded
ardua: n. pl., used as a noun	**702** *for-is is* 3f. door
693 *bacul-um i* 2n. stick	*adopert-us a um* covered, paved
694 *nītor* 3 dep. struggle	*marmor -is* 3n. marble
695 *sagitt-a ae* 1f. arrow	**703** *placid-us a um* kindly. A grand and dignified line
696 *palūs palūd-is* 3f. swamp	*Sāturnius*: i.e. Jupiter
697 *prōspiciō* 3/4 see	*ēdō* 3 *ēdidī* issue
698 *dēfleō* 2 weep for	

ter strikes (690–3). Seizing their walking-sticks, the couple struggle on up the hill (693–4). Virtue has been rewarded. The gods are just – in this episode, at least.

695–710: But there is more to come. Flood-waters (cf. Deucalion and Pyrrha, passage 1) submerge everything but their own little hut (695–7). Kind-hearted as they are, they are lamenting the fate of their neighbours (however wicked in the gods' eyes) when they see their little cottage turned into a temple (698–700), the first of the speaker Lelex's transformations. The wooden external supports of the house become pillars, the house and thatch turn golden, the doors become engraved (metal), and the ground on which the hut is set is paved with marble (700–2) – all indications of the most luxurious and expensive temple imaginable, worthy of divine handiwork, in strong contrast to what it had been before. When Jupiter asks the pair what they want – note that he sees them both as

"dīcite, iūste senex, et fēmina coniuge iūstō
digna, quid optētis." cum Baucide pauca locūtus,   705
iūdicium superīs aperit commūne Philēmōn:
"esse sacerdōtēs dēlūbraque uestra tuērī
poscimus, et, quoniam concordēs ēgimus annōs,
auferat hōra duōs eadem, nec coniugis∧ umquam
busta ∧meae uideam, neu sim tumulandus ab illā."'   710

8.711–24: *The couple's prayers are answered; the speaker confirms the story*

'uōta fidēs sequitur: templī tūtēla fuēre,
dōnec uīta data est. annīs aeuōque solūtī
ante gradūs sacrōs cum stārent forte, locīque
nārrārent cāsūs, frondēre Philēmona Baucis,
Baucida cōnspexit senior frondēre Philēmōn.   715
iamque super geminōs crēscente cacūmine uultūs,
mūtua, dum licuit, reddēbant dicta, "ualē" que
"ō coniunx" dīxēre simul, simul abdita∧ tēxit

---

706 *iūdici-um i* 2n. judgement
aperiō 4 reveal
707 *sacerdōs sacerdōt-is* 3m./f. priest(ess)
dēlūbr-um i 2n. shrine
tueor 2 dep. guard, oversee
quoniam since, because
708 *concors concord-is* of one mind
709 *auferat*: note subj., expressing a wish; cf. *uideam, sim tumulandus*, **RL**153, **RLL**-V(a)4
710 *bust-um i* 2n. pyre, tomb
tumulō 1 bury
711 *fidēs*: i.e. fulfilment; the gods show their good faith by honouring the couple's wishes

tūtēl-a ae 1f. guardian
714 *frondeō* 2 sprout leaves. It had been revealed earlier that the trees were a linden (Baucis) and an oak (Philemon)
Philēmona: Greek acc. s. of Philemon
715 *Baucida*: Greek acc. s. of Baucis
senior -is elderly
716 *cacūmen cacūmin-is* 3n. tree-top
717 *mūtu-us a um* corresponding, reciprocal
718 *abdit-us a um* hidden

---

equals (704) – it is typical of their relationship that Philemon immediately consults his wife (703–6). They agree that they want to return to the home that has served them so well – and they must therefore become priests of what is now a shrine. In the spirit of *concordia* (708) that has characterised their whole life, they also wish, when the time comes, to be joined in death (709–10).

711–24: And so it happens. Time passes, and one day they are chatting about everything that has happened to them when they both simultaneously sprout leaves (711–15). They have time only to bid farewell to each other (naturally, in identical words) before Lelex's second divine transformation is complete (716–19): the gods are also loyal to their promises. Lelex proves the story by saying that an inhabitant of the area still shows off the trees, and that he himself has seen the garlands that hang there – indeed, he has even added one of his own, with a suitable observation (or is it a prayer?) about the consequences for those who take care of the gods.

^ōra frutex. ostendit adhūc Thȳnēius^ illīc
^incola dē geminō uīcīnōs corpore truncōs.   720
haec mihī nōn uānī^ (neque erat, cūr fallere uellent)
nārrāuēre ^senēs; equidem pendentia uīdī
serta super rāmōs, ponēnsque recentia dīxī
"cūra deum dī sunt, et, quī coluēre, coluntur."'

719 *frutex frutic-is* 3m. bush. Enjoy the rustling *s, x*
and *t* of 718–19
ostendit: Ovid now switches to the present and gets
Lelex to quote evidence from a local inhabitant,
before recording his own (722–4)
Thȳnēi-us a um from Bithynia, here meaning
(Hellespontine) Phrygia in the north of modern
Turkey
720 *incol-a ae* 1m. inhabitant
trunc-us ī 2m. tree-trunk
721 *uān-us a um* unreliable
erat: supply e.g. 'reason'

722 *equidem* personally speaking
723 *sert-um* ī 2n. garland, wreath
rām-us ī 2m. branch
recentia: i.e. garlands which I myself placed (*pōnēns*)
724 *cūra deum* (= *deōrum*): a compressed phrase,
meaning 'those who take care of the gods'
sunt . . . coluntur: most texts print *sint . . . colantur*
(both jussive subj.). This turns an observation or
statement of fact into something like a prayer.
Which suits Lelex's argument better (see
Background)?

Learning vocabulary for Passage 14, Baucis and Philemon

an-us ūs 4f. old woman
caelō 1 engrave, emboss
cas-a ae hut
clīu-us ī 2m. slope, incline
crātēr -is 3m. bowl in which wine was mixed
foc-us ī 2m. hearth
foli-um ī 2n. leaf

furc-a ae 1f. (two-pronged) fork; house-
support
mēns-a ae 1f. table; course of a meal
salign-us a um of willow
tēct-um ī 2n. roof, house
tepid-us a um warm

Study section

1. Pick out the means by which Ovid characterises Baucis and Philemon (their
   hut and its contents are also relevant here). How do their characters differ
   from that of another couple, Deucalion and Pyrrha (passage 1)?
2. Identify some of the comic elements in this story. Some argue that these mock
   or patronise the couple. What is your view?
3. Does this story 're-establish the gods' power and morality impressively'?
4. We do not know the source of this story. Compare it with the following Jewish
   tale from the Bible, in which God sends two angels to punish the cities of
   Sodom and Gomorrah for their evil-doing (c. 2000 BC, when a major earth-
   quake does seem to have obliterated the area). The translation is from the
   New Revised Standard version:

The two angels came to Sodom in the evening, and Lot was sitting in the gateway of Sodom. When Lot saw them, he rose to meet them, and bowed down with his face to the ground. He said, 'Please, my lords, turn aside to your servant's house and spend the night, and wash your feet; then you can rise early and go on your way.' They said, 'No; we will spend the night in the square.' But he urged them strongly; so they turned aside to him and entered his house; and he made them a feast, and baked unleavened bread, and they ate. But before they lay down, the men of the city, the men of Sodom, both young and old, all the people to the last man, surrounded the house; and they called to Lot, 'Where are the men who came to you tonight? Bring them out to us, so that we may know them.' Lot went out of the door to the men, shut the door after him, and said, 'I beg you, my brothers, do not act so wickedly. Look, I have two daughters who have not known a man; let me bring them out to you, and do to them as you please; only do nothing to these men, for they have come under the shelter of my roof.' But they replied, 'Stand back!' And they said, 'This fellow came here as an alien, and he would play the judge! Now we will deal worse with you than with them.' Then they pressed hard against the man Lot, and came near the door to break it down. But the men inside reached out their hands and brought Lot into the house with them, and shut the door. And they struck with blindness the men who were at the door of the house, both small and great, so that they were unable to find the door.

Then the men said to Lot, 'Have you anyone else here? Sons-in-law, sons, daughters, or anyone you have in the city – bring them out of the place. For we are about to destroy this place, because the outcry against its people has become great before the LORD, and the LORD has sent us to destroy it.' So Lot went out and said to his sons-in-law, who were to marry his daughters, 'Up, get out of this place; for the LORD is about to destroy the city.' But he seemed to his sons-in-law to be jesting.

When morning dawned, the angels urged Lot, saying, 'Get up, take your wife and your two daughters who are here, or else you will be consumed in the pun-ishment of the city.' But he lingered; so the men seized him and his wife and his two daughters by the hand, the LORD being merciful to him, and they brought him out and left him outside the city. When they had brought them outside, they said, 'Flee for your life; do not look back or stop anywhere in the Plain; flee to the hills, or else you will be consumed.' And Lot said to them, 'Oh, no, my lords; your servant has found favour with you, and you have shown me great kindness in saving my life; but I cannot flee to the hills, for fear the disaster will overtake me and I die. Look, that city is near enough to flee to, and it is a little one. Let me escape there – is it not a little one? – and my life will be saved!' He said to him, 'Very well, I grant you this favour too, and will not overthrow the city of which you have spoken. Hurry, escape there, for I can do nothing until you arrive there.' . . .

Then the LORD rained on Sodom and Gomorrah sulphur and fire from the LORD out of heaven; and he overthrew those cities, and all the Plain, and all the inhabitants of the cities, and what grew on the ground. But Lot's wife, behind him, looked back, and she became a pillar of salt.
Genesis 19.1–26

If there are enough similarities between this story and Ovid's tale, would that demonstrate that Ovid's tale is of Jewish origin?

15   Byblis, *Metamorphōsēs* 9.517–665

Background

Conversation over Achelous' dinner table turns to other examples of metamorphosis, and Achelous admits he can change into a (limited) number of different shapes at will. This leads him to tell the story of his losing battle with Hercules, and when the party breaks up Ovid continues the Hercules theme with tales of his death and birth. Alcmene, Hercules' mother, is told the story of Dryope who picked a plant to amuse her baby and was turned into a lotus tree. The next stories concern Hercules' nephew Iolaus, who has been restored to youth, and of Callirhoe, who will win a concession from Jupiter to increase the age of her sons. They raise among the gods the question of getting old.

The gods are less than enthusiastic about this idea, but Jupiter tells them that fate cannot be avoided and points to various of his own sons, Minos included, who are bowed down in years. Ovid now tells how the power of the aged Minos was being threatened by the youthful son of Apollo and Deione, Miletus (after whom the powerful city on the coast of Asia Minor was named); and this leads Ovid to tell the story of the twins born to Miletus by Cyanee, daughter of the river-god Maeander. Their names are Byblis and Caunus, and Byblis has conceived a more than ordinary love for her handsome brother. Consumed with desire, she wrestles desperately with her conscience but finally decides she can hide her feelings for him no longer; she must communicate them, somehow, to him. This is where the extract begins.

Internal debates of this sort had long been a standard literary form in Ovid's time. They are found in Homer (one famous example is Hector's soliloquy as Achilles charges at him, *Iliad* 22.99–130), continue down through Greek tragedy (e.g. Medea's debate whether to kill her children, Euripides *Medea* 1021–55) and are taken up by Roman authors such as Virgil (e.g. Dido's debate about whether to commit suicide, *Aeneid* 4.534–52). One of the finest soliloquies about the effects of passion on the female heart occurs in the *Argonautica* by Apollonius Rhodius, when Medea, who is on fire for Jason, wonders whether to help him get the Golden Fleece and then escape with him (3.744–801).

9.517–29: *Byblis finally decides to compose a letter to her brother, admitting her love*

hoc placet, haec dubiam uīcit sententia mentem.
in latus ērigitur, cubitōque innīxa sinistrō
'uīderit: īnsānōs' inquit 'fateāmur amōrēs!
ēi mihi, quō lābor? quem mēns mea concipit ignem?'   520
et meditāta manū compōnit uerba trementī.
dextra tenet ferrum, uacuam tenet altera cēram.
incipit et dubitat, scrībit damnatque tabellās,
et notat et dēlet, mūtat culpatque probatque,
inque uicem sūmptās pōnit positāsque resūmit.   525
quid uelit ignōrat; quicquid factūra uidētur,
displicet. in uultū est audācia mixta pudōrī.
scrīpta 'soror' fuerat; uīsum est dēlēre sorōrem,
uerbaque corrēctīs incīdere tālia cērīs:

Note

From now on, Latin words that you have not met, but which have an obvious English meaning or are based on known compounds, are given their dictionary form in the vocabulary but are not translated. They are marked with an asterisk *after* the word in question, thus: *dubi-us a um**.

Note that *-cipiō* derives from *capiō*, *-ficiō* from *faciō*, *-pliceō* from *placeō*, *-cidō* from *-cadō*, *-cīdō* from *caedō*, *-iciō* from *iaciō*, *-ripiō* from *rapiō*.

517 *hoc placet*: i.e. her decision to write to Caunus and reveal all
dubi-us a um*
518 *latus later-is* 3n. side
ērigor 3 pass. prop oneself up
cubit-um ī 2n. elbow
innītor 3 dep. *innīxus* lean
sinister sinistr-a um left. She will hold the writing tablet in her left hand, the stylus in the right (522)
519 *uīderit*: *uideō* here has the meaning 'see to it',

'make what one will of it', casting the responsibility for action on the subject (in this case, Caunus); *uīderit* is a jussive perf. subj., **RL**152, **W**28
insan-us a um*
*fateor 2 dep. *fassus* confess, admit to
520 *ēi mihi* alas for me
lābor: note the long *ā*
concipiō 3/4 catch (as in 'catch fire')
quem: take with *ignem*
521 *meditāt-us a um* (pass.)*. Note the golden line
compōnō 3*
522 *ferrum*: lit. iron, i.e. the metal stylus; a finely balanced line
523 *incipiō* 3/4 begin
damnō 1 condemn
524 *notō 1 write; realise; mark, notice
525 *in uicem* in turns
resūmō 3*
527 *displicet* 2* (impersonal)
529 *corrēctīs* (*corrigō* 3)*. Note the golden line
incīdō 3 cut (in the wax)

517–29: At the moment, Byblis has *done* nothing wrong: she is merely harbouring terrible feelings and thoughts. So her mind is in turmoil about the action she has decided to take because she knows her desires will have dreadful consequences; even now that she has made up her mind (she thinks), she acknowledges her feelings are madness (519–20). Such self-contradictions are meat and drink to Ovid. The trembling hand that takes up the tablet (521) cannot decide what to write (522–7 – a marvellous evocation of a stalled brain: might it be significant that *ferrum* [522] can also mean 'sword'?), because her outrageous *audācia* (determination to tell all) clashes with her *pudor* (her desire to keep it all secret, 527), a moment dramatised by her inability to write to Caunus as *soror* (528). The

9.530–46: 'My looks should tell you everything; I have fought my feelings, but now surrender'

'quam, nisi tū dederis, nōn est habitūra salūtem,   530
hanc tibi mittit amāns: pudet, ā, pudet ēdere nōmen,
et sī quid cupiam quaeris, sine nōmine^ uellem
posset agī mea causa ^meō, nec cognita Byblis
ante forem, quam spēs uōtōrum certa fuisset.
esse quidem laesī poterat tibi pectoris index –   535
et color et maciēs et uultus et ūmida saepe
lūmina nec causā suspīria mōta patentī
et crebrī amplexūs, et quae, sī forte notāstī,
ōscula sentīrī nōn esse sorōria possent.
ipsa tamen, quamuīs animō graue uulnus habēbam,   540

530 *quam . . . amāns*: take in the order *amāns mittit tibi hanc salūtem quam nōn est habitūra, nisi tū dederis*
salūtem: 'good health!' will translate this ambiguously enough both as a greeting and as an indication of Byblis' problem; for the significance of this word at the start of a letter, see **Comment**
531 *pudet**: impersonal verb; cf. *pudor*
ēdō 3 publish, announce
532 *uellem*: 'I should wish [that]' + subj. (*mea causa posset agī* and *cognita forem*), **RLL-V(a)3–4**
534 *ante forem quam*: take in the order *forem, antequam*, **RLE1**, **RL165**

535 *index indic-is* 3m. evidence
536 *maciēs maci-ēī* 5f. loss of weight
ūmid-us a um wet
537 *suspīri-um ī* 2n. sigh
patēns patent-is obvious
538 *amplex-us ūs* 4m.*
quae: take in order *et ōscula quae, sī forte notāstī, nōn possent sentīrī esse sorōria*
notāstī: = *notāuistī*, **RLA4**
539 *sorōri-us a um**
540 *ipsa*: i.e. *ego ipsa*
uulnus: cf. her battle against her feelings, 543

wax tablet is a mess of deletions (529) before she finally starts. The whole passage is a fine example of Ovid's power of depicting a mental state – in this case, a mind in turmoil – by its physical manifestations, naturally whetting our appetite for what Byblis will eventually say.

530–46: Roman letters always begin with a formulaic greeting, a common one being 'The sender [nom.] to the recipient [dat.] *SPD*' = *salūtem plūrimam dat* 'gives very much *salūs*', where *salūs* means 'good luck, good health' (cf. *saluē* 'hullo, greetings'). Here the sender is an *amāns*, who turns out to be female (*habitūra*, 530), sending a *salūtem* (531) which she immediately says she cannot expect to enjoy herself unless the recipient of the letter reciprocates it (530). She is after something – but what? She goes on to admit that *pudor* prevents her from naming herself (531), but lets her name emerge after all (533) in a convoluted expression of her desire to do no such thing unless her hopes are met (534). Not that the name tells the recipient of the letter anything – yet: Caunus may be surrounded by legions of girls named Byblis willing him into their arms. But at all events, this is a strange beginning to a letter: the recipient will surely wonder what the problem is with the sender. It immediately emerges: her wounded heart (535, cf. 540, 543–4), expressed in terms of a number of physical symptoms of inner feelings culminating in

quamuīs intus erat furor igneus, omnia fēcī
(sunt mihi dī testēs), ut tandem sānior essem,
pugnāuīque diū uiolenta Cupīdinis arma
effugere īnfēlīx, et plūs quam ferre puellam
posse putēs, ego dūra tulī. superāta fatērī   545
cōgor, opemque tuam timidīs exposcere uōtīs.'

9.547–63: 'I want to be closer to you; forget convention; no one need know'

'tū seruāre potes, tū perdere sōlus amantem:
ēlige, utrum faciās. nōn hōc inimīca precātur,
sed quae, cum tibi sit iūnctissima, iūnctior esse
expetit, et uinclō tēcum propiōre ligārī.   550
iūra senēs nōrint, et quid liceatque nefāsque
fāsque sit, inquīrant, lēgumque exāmina seruent.
conueniēns Venus est annīs temerāria nostrīs.
quid liceat, nescīmus adhūc, et cūncta licēre

541 *intus* inside	*nōn inimīca*: 'no [female] enemy [of yours]' – Byblis
furor: an admission of irrationality, cf. *sānior* 542	refers to herself
igne-us a um*	**549** *iūnctissima** (*iungō*)
542 *test-is is* 3m. witness	**550** *expetō* 3*
sān-us a um*	*uinc(u)l-um ī* 2n. bond, tie
543 *Cupīdō Cupīdin-is* 3f. the god Cupid (Desire)	*propior -is* closer
545 *putēs*: subj. 'you would think'	*ligō* 1 bind
dūra: n. pl. used as a noun, **RL**14.7, **W**4	**551** *nō(ue)rint*: (very dismissive) jussive subj. of
546 *exposcō* 3 implore, beg for	*nōscō* (so *inquirant* and *seruent* 552)
547 *tū . . . amantem*: fine verbal and emotional	**552** *inquīrō* 3*
balance – *sōlus amantem* is a very powerful word-	*exāmen exāmin-is* 3n. balance, niceties
placement at the end of the line	**553** *conueniēns conuenient-is* fitting, appropriate
548 *ēligō* 3 choose	*temerāri-us a um rash

excessively physical actions (embraces, kisses) – and the forbidden word, *sorōria*, finally emerging (535–9, cf. 528). The truth is now out for Caunus. At once, Byblis offers the classic defence: she admits she has been wounded (i.e. by love) and is mad (540–2) and claims she has done all she can to fight back against it, but to no avail (543–5; note the self-pitying *īnfēlīx* 544). Under compulsion therefore (*cogor*: it is always someone else's fault), she can only, timidly (appealing to the masculine in him), beg Caunus' help (546). This is the argument of self-pitying exploitation: 'I can't help what I am doing: therefore you must.'

547–63: Having boxed the wholly innocent Caunus into a corner, Byblis turns the guilt screw – it's now all your responsibility (not mine), and my fate is in your hands (547–8). That sounds threatening, so she hastens to assure Caunus that she is doing all this as a friend, who just wishes to be bound (note the helpless passive, as if it is none of her doing)

crēdimus, et sequimur magnōrum exempla deōrum.   555
nec nōs aut dūrus pater aut reuerentia fāmae
aut timor impediet (tantum sit causa timendī!);
dulcia frāternō sub nōmine fūrta tegēmus.
est mihi lībertās tēcum sēcrēta loquendī,
et damus amplexūs, et iungimus ōscula cōram;   560
quantum est, quod dēsit? miserēre fatentis amōrem,
et nōn fassūrae, nisi cōgeret ultimus ardor,
nēue merēre meō subscrībī causa sepulchrō.'

9.564–73: *Sealing the tablets, she tells a slave to deliver them*

tālia nēquīquam perarantem plēna relīquit
cēra manum, summusque in margine uersus adhaesit.   565

555 *exempl-um ī* 2n.*
556 *reuerenti-a ae* 1f.*
557 *tantum sit*: lit. 'let there only be . . . !', 'if only
   there were . . . !'
558 *frātern-us a um**
fūrt-um ī 2n. theft
559 *sēcrēt-us a um**
560 *amplexus -ūs* 4m.*
cōram publicly
561 *quantum est quod*: 'how much is there that . . .'
misereor 2 dep. have pity on (+ gen., here *fatentis* 'the
   one who . . .')
562 *nōn fassūrae*: 'and would not confess [it]' –
   'would', because of the subj., *cōgeret*, in the *nisi*
   clause 'unless *ultimus ardor* were to . . .'

ardor -is 3m.*
563 *nēue* and don't (+ imper.)
merēre: 2s. pass. imper. of *mereō* 2, think worthy to
   (+ inf.), **RLB1** (pres. imper. pass.)
subscrībō 3 inscribe
causa: '[as] the reason for' + dat. (in apposition to
   understood *tū*, **RL17B, W3**)
564 *nēquīquam* in vain
perarō 1 furrow (as a metaphor of the stylus plough-
   ing through the wax on the tablet)
plēna relīquit cēra: 'the full wax/tablet left her hand',
   i.e. the tablet was full when she put it down
565 *margō margin-is* 3m./f. edge
adhaereō 2 *adhaesi* cling on

by closer ties (548–50). Byblis dismisses arguments about right and wrong: they are for old men to argue about (551–2), she says, while we are of an age for rash adventure (553), and are prepared to believe anything is permitted, especially since this is the example the gods set (554–5: it tells us all we need to know about Byblis' state of mind that at 542 she called on the gods to witness her heroic struggle against her feelings, and at 555 cites them as justification for yielding to them!). She dismisses arguments about conventional pro-prieties: strict fathers, desire for fame, or fear cannot stop us, since we (note the use of 'we' and 'our' throughout: Caunus is automatically assumed to be a willing partner) make physical contact anyway, and can therefore go all the way without attracting suspi-cion (558–61). Finally, she appeals for pity (561–2) and ends with a threat (563). The whole brilliant speech is straightforward blackmail: in what other terms can Byblis couch it?

564–73: At once Ovid tell us this packed epistle (the last line squeezed into the margin) will not work (*nēquīquam*, 564) – or is Ovid telling us what Byblis feels? (The same ques-tion can be asked of *sua crīmina*, 566.) Physical symptoms again indicate emotional state (567 and *pudibunda* 568); and for a second time Byblis has difficulty in articulating her

prōtinus impressā signat sua crīmina gemmā,
quam tīnxit lacrimīs (linguam dēfēcerat ūmor);
dēque suīs ūnum famulīs pudibunda uocāuit,
et paulum blandīta 'fer hās, fidissime, nostrō'
dīxit, et adiēcit longō post tempore 'frātrī.'   570
cum daret, ēlāpsae manibus cecidēre tabellae.
ōmine turbāta est, mīsit tamen. apta minister
tempora nactus adit, trāditque latentia uerba.

9.574–84: *The slave tells Byblis of Caunus' appalled reaction*

attonitus subitā iuuenis Maeandrius īrā
prōicit acceptās lectā sibi parte tabellās,   575
uixque manūs retinēns trepidantis ab ōre ministrī,
'dum licet, ō uetitae scelerāte libīdinis auctor,
effuge!' ait 'quī, sī nostrum tua fāta pudōrem
nōn traherent sēcum, poenās mihi morte dedissēs.'

---

566 *imprīmō* 3 *impressī impressus**
signō 1*
gemm-a ae 1f. signet-ring. The two sides of the tablet are closed and sealed with a blob of hot wax, which is then impressed with the signet ring (the ring was usually moistened to prevent the wax sticking to it, 567). If anyone subsequently interfered with the tablets, the impress made by the signet would be destroyed
567 *tingō* 3 *tīnxī* moisten
dēficiō 3/4 *dēfēcī* fail, leave
ūmor -is 3m. moisture. Note the tears vs. dry tongue antithesis
568 *famul-us ī* 2m. slave
pudibund-us a um blushing, shame-faced
569 *paulum* a little
blandior 4 ingratiate oneself (with + dat.)
fīd-us a um*
570 *adiciō* 3/4 *adiēcī* add. Note the lovely delay to the word *frātrī*
post: here used adverbially 'later', 'after', how *much*

later being expressed by the abl., **RL**100B5, **W**Suppl.syntax
571 *ēlābor**
572 **ōmen ōmin-is* 3n. omen, sign
*apt-us a um suitable, proper
*minister ministr-ī 2m. slave
573 *nanciscor* 3 dep. *nactus* find, get
574 *attonit-us a um* astonished
subit-us a um*
Maeandrius i.e. Caunus, grandson of the river (god) Meander
575 *prōiciō* 3/4*
576 *trepidō* 1 be terrified
577 *scelerāt-us a um* wicked
*libīdō libīdin-is 3f. lust
auctor -is 3m. agent, initiator
578 *nostrum . . . pudōrem*: i.e. shame on me
579 *sēcum*: reflexive, referring to *tua fāta* (the slave's death)
poenās dō: lit. 'give a penalty to' (+ dat.), i.e. be punished by (dat.) with (abl.)

---

relationship with her brother in terms of a sibling (570, cf. 528). An omen accompanies her handing over of the tablets. She knows it is an omen. She ignores it (571–2). *latentia uerba* surely has a double meaning – the words are indeed hidden inside the tablets, but they also carry a secret (573), which is about to be revealed.

574–84: Caunus' reaction is predictable (574–6) – he does not even need to read the whole thing (575) – and his threat to 'shoot the messenger' is withdrawn only because of his sense of *pudor* (578). That is all we need to know about him to realise that Byblis will

ille fugit pauidus, dominaeque ferōcia Caunī   580
dicta refert. pallēs audītā, Bybli, repulsā,
et pauet obsessum glaciālī frīgore corpus.
mēns tamen ut rediit, pariter rediēre furōrēs,
linguaque uix tālēs ictō dedit āere uōcēs:

9.585–600: 'Fool! I should have tested his feelings first!'

'et meritō! quid enim temerāria uulneris hūius   585
indicium fēcī? quid, quae cēlanda fuērunt,
tam cito commīsī properātīs uerba tabellīs?
ante erat ambiguīs animī sententia dictīs
praetemptanda mihī. nē nōn sequerētur euntem,
parte aliquā uēlī, quālis foret aura, notāre   590
dēbueram, tūtōque marī dēcurrere, quae nunc
nōn explōrātīs implēuī lintea uentīs.
auferor in scopulōs igitur, subuersāque tōtō
obruor ōceanō, neque habent mea uēla recursūs.
quid quod et ōminibus certīs prohibēbar amōrī   595

580 *ferōx ferōc-is**
581 *palleō* 2 grow pale. Note the 'apostrophe'
Bybli: voc. of Byblis
repuls-a ae 1f.*
582 *obsideō* 2 *obsēdī obsessum* beset, assail
glaciāl-is e*
*frigus frigor-is 3n. chill
584 *uix*: take with *ictō . . . āere* (i.e. barely audible)
585 *meritō* deservedly, naturally
quid: here and 586, 'why?'
586 *indici-um ī* 2n. disclosure, revelation
quae: refers to *uerba* 587
cēlō 1 hide
587 *cito* quickly
588 *ante*: adverbial use, 'before that', 'first'
ambigu-us a um*
589 *praetemptō* 1 test, try out in advance
nē nōn sequeretur euntem: supply *aura* (590) as

understood subject, and *mē* with *euntem* as
object; *nē nōn* i.e. 'in case . . . not'; the image here
is naval, of testing out a breeze to make sure it is
favourable before setting off
590 *uēl-um ī 2n. sail
quālis: indirect question after *notāre dēbueram*
591 *dēcurrō* 3*
quae: '[I] who . . .'
592 *explōrō* 1*
linte-um ī 2n. sail
593 *scopul-us ī* 2m. rock
subuertō 3 *subuersī subuersum* overwhelm
594 *obruor* 3 pass.*
ōcean-us ī 2m.*
recurs-us ūs 4m. return, way back
595 *quid quod* 'what of the fact that . . . ?'
ōminibus: see 571–2

never get her way. Byblis' physical reaction on hearing the news briefly freezes her (581–2: note the apostrophe), but when she gathers herself, her old madness returns (583).

585–600: She now regrets her haste in committing herself to a written message in which all was revealed (cf. 564, 573); before that, she now thinks, she should have tested Caunus out face to face *ambiguīs dictīs* (588), and gauged the wind before launching out on the high seas (589–92) and finding herself shipwrecked (593–4). This nautical image may sit strangely in the mouth of a woman; but Byblis is no ordinary woman, and she is now in full (male)

indulgēre meō, tum cum mihi ferre iubentī
excidit et fēcit spēs nostrās cēra cadūcās?
nōnne uel illa diēs fuerat, uel tōta uoluntās,
sed potius mūtanda diēs? deus ipse monēbat
signaque certa dabat, sī nōn male sāna fuissem.'   600

9.601–12: 'Had I told him personally, I could have persuaded him'

'et tamen ipsa loquī, nec mē committere cērae
dēbueram, praesēnsque meōs aperīre furōrēs.
uīdisset lacrimās, uultum uīdisset amantis;
plūra loquī poteram, quam quae cēpēre tabellae.
inuītō potuī circumdare brācchia collō,   605
et, sī rēicerer, potuī moritūra uidērī
amplectīque pedēs, adfūsaque poscere uītam.
omnia fēcissem, quōrum sī singula dūram^
flectere nōn poterant, potuissent omnia, ^mentem.
forsitan et missī sit quaedam culpa ministrī: 610

---

596 *indulgeō* 2* (+ dat.)
597 *excidō* 3* (*cēra* is subject of both *excidit* and *fēcit*)
cadūc-us a um fallen
598 *diēs*: i.e. the day/time at which I sent the
  tablets
fuerat: *mūtanda* (599) completes *fuerat*
600 *signaque certa*: see 571–2
*sān-us a um**
602 *praesēns praesent-is**
aperiō 4 reveal
604 *plūra . . . quam quae* more than what

poteram: note the ind. with *possum* in a conditional
  sense 'I would have been able'; so *potuī*, 605, 606;
  RLS2(c)Notes(6)
606 *rēiciō* 3/4 reject
607 *adfūs-us a um* prostrate
poscō 3 beg for
609 *flectō* 3 bend
poterant, potuissent: observe the distinction between
  ind. and subj. here
mentem: Caunus', of course
610 *forsitan* perhaps (+ subj.)

'heroic' mode (compare e.g. the 'masculinised' figure of Medea in Euripides' *Medea*).
Besides, she goes on, she was warned by the omen not to go ahead (595–600, cf. 571–2); not
that the omen meant she was wrong, only that she had chosen the wrong day (598–9)! This
is significant: Byblis is not repenting of what she hoped to achieve (she cannot believe her
uoluntās should have been changed), but rather lamenting over the bad timing that led to
her failure. In this sense alone, she admits she had been *male sāna* (600): but her failure to
think straight related not to the wrong she knew she was doing but her inability to achieve it.

601–12: Summarising her unsuccessful tactics (601–2), she fantasises about what would
have happened had she spoken to Caunus face to face (fantasy, because of the evidence of
574–9 and because she admits her feeling are *furōrēs*). She imagines that her tears, looks
(603), words (604), embraces (605), threats to commit suicide and self-prostration (606–7)
would have succeeded as a package, whereas individual elements of it might not (608–9).
When Byblis wonders if the slave was to blame for not handing over the tablets at a suitable
moment (610–12, cf. 572–3), it is clear she has taken delusion and excuses to new heights.

nōn adiit aptē, nec lēgit idōnea, crēdō,
tempora, nec petiit hōramque animumque uacantem.'

9.613–19: *'But my brother can still be won over!'*

'haec nocuēre mihī. neque enim est dē tigride nātus
nec rigidās silicēs solidumue in pectore ferrum
aut adamanta gerit, nec lac bibit ille leaenae.   615
uincētur! repetendus erit, nec taedia coeptī
ūlla meī capiam, dum spīritus iste manēbit.
nam prīmum, sī facta mihī reuocāre licēret,
nōn coepisse fuit: coepta expugnāre secundum est.'

9.620–9: *'If I give up now, he will think I did not mean it; I am guilty anyway'*

'quippe nec ille potest, ut iam mea uōta relinquam,   620
nōn tamen ausōrum semper memor esse meōrum.

---

611 *adiit*: note heavy *-it*. In some perfect verbs, too, the 3rd s. originally scanned heavy. See the note on *solēt*, 3.184
lēgit: note the long *ē*
idōne-us a um suitable
612 *petiit*: see on *adiit* above
uacō 1 be free, undistracted (referring to both *hōram* and *animum*)
613 *tigris tigrid-is* 3f.*
614 *rigid-us a um**
silex silic-is 3m./f. flint
*solid-us a um**
615 *adamas adamant-is* 3m. steel
lac lact-is 3n. milk
leaen-a ae 1f. lioness

616 *nec taedia . . . manēbit*: a promise she will be forced to fulfil (649 ff.)
taedi-um i 2n. weariness
617 *spirit-us ūs* 4m.*
618 *primum . . . fuit*: 'my first choice . . .', cf. *secundum* 619; note *fuit* 'would have been', cf. on *possum* above, 604–6
619 *expugnō* 1 succeed in, achieve (the image is one of successful siege warfare)
620 *quippe* the reason is that, for
ut: here used to mean 'even supposing that'; cf. 628
621 *nōn*: remember the *nec* of 620, 'it is impossible for him *not* to . . .'
aus-um i 2n. daring deed

613–19: But the past is past; now she must look to the future. She argues that, since Caunus is not a wild animal or entirely inanimate, i.e. congenitally unsusceptible to human charms (613–15), she must continue to hammer away at him while life remains in her (616–17). She obviously does not know her man: he *is* congenitally unsusceptible to her charms by the very fact that he is human and her desires so *non*-human. Repeating the point that it would have been better not to have started the way she did (i.e. with the letter), she affirms she now has no option but to go on and win through. Note *expugnāre*, an image taken from laying siege to and storming a town – the 'heroic' Byblis again (cf. the nautical image at 589–92).

620–9: But what will *Caunus* make of all this? Surely, she thinks, he will admire her (male heroic?) daring (620–1); but if she gives up now, he will assume she was not really serious,

et, quia dēsierim, leuiter uoluisse uidēbor,
aut etiam temptāsse illum īnsidiīsque petīsse,
uel certē nōn hōc^, quī plūrimus urget et ūrit
pectora nostra, ^deō, sed uicta libīdine crēdar;   625
dēnique iam nequeō nīl commīsisse nefandum.
et scrīpsī et petiī: reserāta est nostra uoluntās;
ut nihil adiciam, nōn possum innoxia dīcī.
quod superest, multum est in uōta, in crīmina paruum.'

9.630–40: *Caunus flees from her advances; she follows him*

dīxit, et (incertae tanta est discordia mentis),   630
cum pigeat temptāsse, libet temptāre. modumque
exit, et īnfēlix committit saepe repellī.
mox ubi fīnis abest, patriam fugit ille nefāsque,

---

622 *quia*: this means 'because'. Byblis is reflecting on how Caunus would react if she gave up her approach to him
dēsinō 3 *dēsiī* give up, stop (*sc.* wooing him)
uoluisse: *sc.* to woo and win him
623 *temptāsse*: i.e. that I was not serious about him
īnsidi-ae ārum 2f. pl. traps, tricks
624 *uel certē nōn*: the main clause for these two lines is *uicta* [sc. *esse*]. . . *crēdar*, 'I shall be believed [to have been] conquered' 625
625 *urgeō* 2 assault
626 *nequeō* 4 be unable, be impossible (for someone)
nefand-us a um unspeakable, wicked, evil
627 *reserō* 1 reveal, lay bare
ut: see 620 above
628 *adiciō* 3/4 add (i.e. carry on in the same way)

innoxi-us a um guiltless
629 *quod*: 'as for what . . . '
multum in: i.e. there is much [to be gained] in . . . , but *paruum in . . .*
crīmina: i.e. *further* wrongdoing (she has done so much already)
630 *discordi-a ae* 1f.*
631 *cum* whereas, though
piget (impersonal) it irks, pains
temptāsse: contrast the tense with *temptāre*
libet (impersonal) it brings pleasure
632 *committit*: *sc.* 'herself'
repellō 3*
633 *fīnis abest*: i.e. there was no end to what Byblis tried to do or say

---

but merely overcome by lust rather than by the god who is responsible for her feelings (622–5)! She has a high opinion of the persuasive power of her 'sincerity' if she thinks Caunus would be moved by *that* argument (he could not care less whether she was moved by a god or not: he just wants her to stop). But Byblis is desperate. She realises she is trapped, since she knows she *has* done wrong already (626), her wishes are now out in the open (627) and therefore she is (already) guilty whatever she does (628). So, having committed all the *crīmina* she has, she may as well plough on and at least hope to have her wishes fulfilled (629) – which would, of course, add another *crīmen*, incest. But Byblis is not thinking straight.

630–40: Indeed, she is hardly thinking at all, as Ovid makes clear: *discordia mentis* says it all (630), as she decides the only thing to do now is what she regrets having done in the past (631). So if there was once a moral issue at stake for her, there is no longer. There is a simply a tactical issue – how do I get my way, at whatever cost? Abandoning all restraint, the *īnfēlix* girl (a touch of sympathy here) willingly lays herself open to a life of permanent

inque peregrīnā pōnit noua moenia terrā.
tum uērō maestam tōtā Mīlētida mente   635
dēfēcisse ferunt, tum uērō ā pectore uestem
dēripuit, planxitque suōs furibunda lacertōs.
iamque palam est dēmēns, inconcessaeque fatētur
spem Veneris, siquidem patriam inuīsōsque penātēs
dēserit, et profugī sequitur uestīgia frātris.   640

9.641–8: *Byblis' journey across Asia*

utque tuō mōtae, prōlēs Semelēia, thyrsō
Ismariae celebrant repetīta triennia bacchae,
Byblida nōn aliter lātōs ululāsse per agrōs
Būbasides uīdēre nurūs. quibus illa relictīs
Cāras et armiferōs Lelegas Lyciamque pererrat.   645

634 *peregrīn-us a um* foreign
moen-ia ium 3n. pl. walls
635 *Mīlētida*: Greek acc. s. of *Mīlētis*, 'daughter of
  Miletus' i.e. Byblis
636 *dēficiō 3/4 *dēfēcī* fail in, lose control of (+ abl.);
  fade out, come to an end
ferunt: Ovid in 'historical' mode again
637 *dēripiō* 3/4 *dēripuī* pull X (acc.) down from (*ā*) Y
furibund-us a um*
638 *dēmēns dēment-is**
inconcess-us a um forbidden
639 *sīquidem* since (this clause provides the evidence
  that she is now mad)
inuīs-us a um hated
penāt-ēs -um 3m. pl. household gods
640 *profug-us a um* exiled
641 *utque*: introducing a simile
tuō: refers to the 'offspring of Semele' (Bacchus)
  (apostrophe)
prōl-ēs is 3f. offspring
Semelēi-us a um of Semele (mother of Bacchus)

thyrs-us ī 2m. thyrsus (a wand carried by worship-
  pers of Bacchus)
642 *Ismari-us a um* from Mount. Ismarus in Thrace
  (the scene of Bacchic orgies)
celebrō 1 throng, crowd into
trienni-um ī 2n. two-yearly festival/rites (Romans
  counted inclusively)
bacch-ae ārum 1f. pl. female Bacchic revellers,
  Bacchae
643 *Byblida*: Greek acc. s. of Byblis (take after *nōn
  aliter*)
aliter otherwise
ululō 1 shriek, howl
644 *Būbas-is Būbasid-is* (female) from Bubassus (a
  town in Caria, South-Western Turkey)
nur-us ūs 4f. young woman
645 *Cāras*: Greek acc. pl. of *Cāres*, Carians
armifer -a um*
Lelegas: Greek acc. pl. of *Leleges*, a Carian people
Lyci-a ae 1f. Lycia (an area south east of Caria)
pererrō 1*

rejection (631–2; for *repellī*, cf. *repulsā* 581), with the result that Caunus leaves Miletus
for foreign parts (633–4: he founds, as one would, the town of Caunus, on the south-west
coast of modern Turkey). At this, Byblis goes into the equivalent of mourning, ripping
her clothes, beating her arms (635–7). Now openly deranged and freely admitting to her
feelings (638–9), she too abandons Miletus and sets out after the brother she has effectively driven into exile (*profugī*, 640).

641–8: She is like a maddened bacchant as she wanders howling across Asia (641–4), first
going south to Bubassus (644), then north through Caria to the Leleges (645), then back to
the south coast again (further east) into Lycia (645) and the three towns/mountains/rivers

iam Cragon et Limyrēn Xanthīque relīquerat undās,
quōque Chimaera iugō mediīs in partibus ignem,
pectus et ōra leae, caudam serpentis habēbat.

9.649–65: *Byblis collapses and, consumed with tears, changes into a fountain*

dēficiunt siluae, cum tū lassāta sequendō
concidis, et dūrā positīs tellūre capillīs,   650
Bybli, iacēs, frondēsque tuō premis ōre cadūcās.
saepe illam nymphae^ tenerīs ^Lelegēides ulnīs
tollere cōnantur, saepe ut medeātur amōrī
praecipiunt, surdaeque adhibent sōlācia mentī.
mūta iacet, uiridēsque suīs tenet unguibus herbās   655
Byblis, et ūmectat lacrimārum grāmina rīuō.
Nāidas hīs uēnam, quae numquam ārēscere posset,

646 *Cragon*: Greek acc. s. of Cragos, a town/mountain range in Lycia
Limyrēn: Greek acc. s. of Limyrē, a town/mountain range in Lycia
Xanth-us ī 2m. Xanthus (a river and town in Lycia)
647 *quōque . . . iugō*: 'and what ridge', 'and the ridge where'
Chimaer-a ae 1f. Chimaera, a fabled monster (his constituent body parts are now described)
partibus: i.e. of its body
648 *le-a ae* 1f. lioness
649 *lassāt-us a um* exhausted
650 *concidō* 3*
651 *Bybli*: voc. of Byblis
frōns frond-is 3f. leaf
652 *Lelegēis Lelegēid-is* (woman) of the Leleges
uln-a ae 1f. arms

653 *ut*: how (introducing an indirect question)
medeor 2 dep. cure (+ dat.)
654 *praecipiō* 3/4 instruct
surd-us a um deaf
adhibeō 2 offer
sōlāci-um ī 2n. comfort, relief, consolation
655 *mūt-us a um**
ungu-is is 3m. finger-nail
656 *ūmectō* 1 moisten
grāmen grāmin-is 3n. grass
rīu-us ī 2m. river, stream
657 *Nāidas*: Greek acc. pl., Naiads (acc. and inf. after *ferunt*)
hīs: (abl.) i.e. her tears
uēn-a ae 1f. water-course, channel
ārēscō 3 dry up

there (646–8) before (apparently) winding up again with the Leleges. This is a crazed itinerary indeed; to be pedantic, about 700 miles (if the Leleges are as far north as the Troad).

649–65: No surprise, then, that she finally collapses – Ovid moves sympathetically into the second person with *tū* (apostrophe) – and, using leaves as a pillow against the hard ground, she indicates that she has had enough (649–51). Her search has been in vain, as it would have been even if she had found Caunus. All efforts to stir her or to help her fail (652–4). She is past human reach – dumb, inert, gripping the earth, weeping copiously. Time, then, for her transformation. The Naiades feed a channel under her to draw her tears away – they are water-nymphs: that is their job (658) – and gradually Byblis, grandchild of Apollo, is 'naturalistically' turned into a spring (663–5; the presence of an *īlex* hints that it is an agreeable spot; cf. Arethusa at 5.632–6). If this is her 'punishment', it could perhaps have been a lot worse. It is clear that, by now, she can take no more anyway

subposuisse ferunt. quid enim dare māius habēbant?
prōtinus, ut sectō piceae dē cortice guttae,
utue tenāx grauidā mānat tellūre bitūmen;   660
utue, sub aduentū spīrantis lēne Fauōnī,
sōle remollēscit quae frīgore cōnstitit unda;
sīc, lacrimīs cōnsūmpta suīs, Phoebēia Byblis
uertitur in fontem, quī nunc quoque uallibus illīs
nōmen habet dominae, nigrāque sub īlice mānat.   665

658 *subpōnō* 3 place X (acc.) under Y (abl.)
659 *ut*: introducing a simile
secō 1 *secuī sectum* cut
pice-us a um of pitch
cortex cortic-is 3m. bark
gutt-a ae 1f. drop, drip
660 *tenāx tenāc-is* clinging (a golden line)
grauid-us a um pregnant, fertile
*mānō 1 ooze, drip, flow
bitūmen bitūmen-is 3n. tar
661 *aduent-us ūs* 4m. arrival
spīrō blow, breathe

lēne gently
Fauōni-us ī 2m. West wind
662 *sōle . . . unda*: take in order *unda quae . . .*
    remollēscit sōle
remollēscō melt
663 *cōnsūmō* 3*
Phoebēi-us a um grandchild of Phoebus/Apollo.
    Compare Arethusa (passage 10, 5.636), who like-
    wise 'dissolves' into a stream
664 *uall-is is* 3f. valley
665 *ilex ilic-is* 3f. holm-oak, ilex

(cf. 616–17), and Ovid's comment on the intervention of the Naiads (658) suggests he sees it that way too (Ovid gives us an alternative version at *Ars Amatōria* 1.283–4 in a passage emphasising women's lust for sex on any terms, where he says that Byblis atoned by bravely (*fortiter*) hanging herself). The three naturalistic similes that accompany the metamorphosis – pitch from cut pines, tar oozing from the ground and melting ice (659–62) – attempt to show how she was consumed by her tears (663). With the exception of the last, it is not at all obvious how these are meant to work.

Learning vocabulary for Passage 15, Byblis

apt-us a um suitable, proper
cadūc-us a um fallen
dēficiō 3/4 *dēfēcī* fail in, lose control of (+ abl.);
    fade out, come to an end
fateor 2 dep. *fassus* confess, admit to
frigus frigor-is 3n. chill
libīdō libīdin-is 3f. lust

mānō 1 ooze, drip, flow
minister ministr-ī 2m. slave, attendant
notō 1 write; realise; mark, notice
ōmen ōmin-is 3n. omen, sign
temerāri-us a um rash
uēl-um ī 2n. sail

Study section

1. At 522, Ovid uses *ferrum* to denote Byblis' stylus. *ferrum* can also mean 'sword'. Brown writes ' . . . in carving her confessional letter she seals her doom as surely as though she had stabbed herself' (2005, 17–18). Do you agree? Does she seal her doom with this act?

2. At 569 *paulum* is printed. Some editors prefer *pauidum*. To whom would that refer, and what would it mean? Should *pauidum* be in the acc.? If it were an adverbial acc. (**RLL**(c)6), what would it mean? Line 580 may – or may not – be relevant.

3. At 584, should we read *mox* in place of *uix*?

4. At 627, *temerāta* (from *temerō* 1 violate, pollute) is preferred by some editors to *reserāta*. Your choice?

5. Trace the stages by which Byblis' resistance to her feelings collapses.

6. Do you feel sympathy for Byblis? Does that sympathy wane at any stage?

7. How important was realism to Ovid?

16 Orpheus, *Metamorphōsēs* 10.8–63, 11.1–66

Background

The story of Byblis is followed by a happier story of sexual crisis. Iphis, born a girl, is brought up as a boy to mollify her father. When Iphis grows up and (to her horror) is given a bride, a god intervenes, turns Iphis into a boy, and everyone lives happily ever after. The god of marriage, Hymen, who has been attending Iphis' wedding, is then summoned to oversee the marriage of the famous Thracian singer Orpheus to Eurydice, but the omens that attend the ceremony are not good. Orpheus was renowned for his ability to charm with his singing all humanity, living or dead, and all nature, animate or inanimate.

10.8–17: *Orpheus makes his way to Hades after Eurydice is bitten by a snake*

exitus auspiciō grauior; nam nūpta per herbās
dum noua Nāiadum turbā comitāta uagātur,
occidit, in tālum serpentis dente receptō.   10
quam satis ad superās postquam Rhodopēius^ aurās
dēflēuit ^uātēs, nē nōn temptāret et umbrās,

Book 10

8 *exit-us ūs* 4m. outcome
auspici-um ī 2n. omens (the bad omens that attended Orpheus' wedding)
nūpta . . . noua: 'the new bride' (subject), i.e. Eurydice
per herbās: take with *uagātur*
9 *Nāiadum*: gen. pl. of Naiads (take with *turbā*)
comitor 1 dep. accompany (+ abl.)

10 *tāl-us ī* 2m. ankle
dēns dent-is 3m. tooth
11 *quam*: i.e. Eurydice; begin with *postquam*
*Rhodopēi-us ī 2m. (man from) Mount Rhodope in Thrace (i.e. Thracian)
12 *dēfleō* 2*
nē nōn: 'in case he should not', 'in case he should fail to'. Orpheus will try anything to get Eurydice back

---

8–17: The story of Orpheus and Eurydice was very well known. Ovid rapidly gets out of the way the details that do not interest him – Eurydice's death (8–10), Orpheus' despair (11–12: he sings to the upper air above and then to the shades below) and his descent to the underworld (14–17). There is none of the usual stuff about Cerberus the dog, the ferryman, the souls of the dead and so on. One might have thought this last item would rather appeal to Ovid, but Homer had done it in *Odyssey* 11 and Virgil in *Aeneid* 6 and

[210]

ad Styga Taenariā est ausus dēscendere portā,
perque leuēs populōs simulācraque fūncta sepulcrō
Persephonēn adiit, inamoenaque rēgna tenentem^   15
umbrārum ^dominum, pulsīsque ad carmina neruīs,
sīc ait:

10.17–24: *'I have come here for my wife and nothing else'*

'ō positī sub terrā nūmina mundī,
in quem reccidimus, quicquid mortāle creāmur,
sī licet, et falsī positīs ambāgibus ōris
uēra loquī sinitis, nōn hūc, ut opāca uidērem   20
Tartara, dēscendī, nec utī uillōsa colubrīs
terna Medūsaeī uincīrem guttura mōnstrī.
causa uiae est coniunx, in quam calcāta uenēnum
uīpera diffūdit crēscentēsque abstulit annōs.'

13 *Styga*: Greek acc. of Styx, the underworld river
Taenari-us a um of Taenarus. This is in the far south of Greece where it was believed there was an entrance to the underworld
port-a ae 1f. gate
14 *fungor* 3 dep. *fūnctus* experience (+ abl.)
15 *Persephonēn*: Greek acc. of Persephone (Proserpina), goddess of the underworld
adiit: note heavy *-it*; compare *solēt*, 3.184
inamoen-us a um charmless
*rēgnum i 2n. kingdom
16 *dominum*: i.e. Pluto
pellō 3 *pepulī pulsum* pluck, strike
*carmen carmin-is 3n. music, song
*neru-us i 2m. string (of a lyre)
17 *ō*: appealing to *nūmina*
18 *recidō* 3 sink, fall back
quicquid: 'whatever [of us] are . . . ', 'whatever we are who are . . . '
creō 1 create
19 *ambāg-ēs um* 3f. pl. deceptions

ōris: from *ōs*, 'mouth' i.e. speech
20 *sinō* 3 allow
opāc-us a um*
21 *Tartar-a ōrum* 2n. pl. Tartarus, the underworld
utī: = *ut*
uillōs-us a um rough, shaggy (with + abl.)
coluber colubr-ī 2m. snake
22 *tern-us a um* triple
Medūsae-us a um Medusa-like. The *mōnstrum* is the three-headed dog Cerberus, which had snakes for hair, like Medusa
uinciō 4 bind. Hercules had bound Cerberus and brought him to the upper world as the last of his twelve labours
guttur -is 3n. throat
23 *calcō* 1 tread on
uenēn-um i 2n. poison
24 *uiper-a ae* 1f. viper
diffundō 3 *diffūdī* pour, spread

Georgics 4. Ovid here has a different target in his sights, which no one had previously attempted: the song that Orpheus sang to appeal for his wife's return.

17–24: Orpheus, appealing in a grandly sonorous opening to the lords of the world below (17–18), explains to the underworld gods why he has come. He says that, if he is allowed to tell the truth (19–20: he must impress his absolute sincerity on the gods below, as if poets were renowned for their falsehoods), he has descended to the depths not to view the monsters (21–2, which Ovid has indeed not done, though he gets in a quick description of Cerberus at this point) but to save his wife (23–4).

10.25–39: *'Love drove me on; since we are all yours eventually, give her back'*

'posse patī uoluī, nec mē temptāsse negābō: 25
uīcit Amor. superā deus hīc bene nōtus in ōrā est;
an sit et hīc, dubitō. sed et hīc tamen auguror esse,
fāmaque sī ueteris nōn est mentīta rapīnae,
uōs quoque iūnxit Amor. per ego haec loca plēna timōris,
per Chaos hoc ingēns uastīque silentia rēgnī,   30
Eurydicēs, ōrō, properāta retexite fāta.
omnia dēbēmur uōbīs, paulumque morātī
sērius aut citius sēdem properāmus ad ūnam.
tendimus hūc omnēs, haec est domus ultima, uōsque
hūmānī generis longissima rēgna tenētis.   35
haec quoque, cum iūstōs mātūra perēgerit annōs,
iūris erit uestrī: prō mūnere poscimus ūsum;
quodsī fāta negant ueniam prō coniuge, certum est
nōlle redīre mihī: lētō gaudēte duōrum.'

27 *auguror* 1 dep. guess
28 *mentit-us a um* untrue, false
rapin-a ae 1f. abduction, seizure. The reference is to Pluto abducting Persephone down to the underworld
30 *Chaos* n.: Greek acc. s. of Chaos, 'Gaping Void'
*silenti-um ī 2n. silence
31 *Eurydicēs*: Greek gen. s.
retexō 3 unweave, reverse
32 *omnia*: either acc. 'in all respects' or nom., 'everything', qualifying the 'we' of *dēbēmur*
paulum for a little
moror 1 dep. delay

33 *sērius* later
citius sooner
34 *sēd-ēs is* 3f. seat, resting-place. *ūnam* here means 'one and the same'
35 *hūmān-us a um**
36 *haec*: 'this [woman]', i.e. Eurydice
mātūr-us a um*
perago 3*
37 *iūris . . . uestrī*: 'of/under your control'
poscō 3 ask for, beg
38 *ueni-a ae* 1f. pardon, mercy
39 *lēt-um ī* 2n. death

25–39: At once he lays the groundwork of his case – he is driven by *amor*, just like the gods. He says he has tried to live without Eurydice, but failed (25), and points out that *Amor* is a god equally well known to the divinities of the upper world and the lower world too (26–9). There is an amusing pause at 27, where one can imagine Orpheus looking around him at the *inamoena rēgna* (15) and wondering whether *amor*, traditionally found in the *locus amoenus* (see Introduction, p. 8), could flourish down here. But he remembers that it can, and quotes the abduction of Persephone, if that was not a false story (28, cf. his question about whether the truth could be told in the underworld, 19–20). The grounds of his case now established, Orpheus goes into the full appeal routine. In the name of the underworld and its terrifying, vast, silences, turn back fate, he begs (29–31). He follows this with sublimely majestic lines arguing that, since death will get us all anyway, sooner or later, Hades is everyone's final destination (32–5). So since Eurydice will eventually come under Hades' control, Hades will not be losing Eurydice, merely lending her (37: note that at 36–7 he argues that she will properly come under Hades' *iūs* only when she has completed her *iūstōs* years on earth). He ends by reaffirming the sincerity of his feelings: I die too if she does not return with me (38–9).

10.40–52: *Eurydice is returned – on one condition*

tālia dīcentem neruōsque ad uerba mouentem   40
exsanguēs flēbant animae; nec Tantalus undam
captāuit refugam, stupuitque Ixīonis orbis,
nec carpsēre iecur uolucrēs, urnīsque uacārunt
Bēlides, inque tuō sēdistī, Sīsyphe, saxō.
tunc prīmum lacrimīs uictārum∧ carmine fāma est   45
∧Eumenidum maduisse genās, nec rēgia coniunx
sustinet ōrantī nec, quī regit īma, negāre,
Eurydicēnque uocant. umbrās erat illa recentēs
inter, et incessit passū dē uulnere tardō.
hanc simul et lēgem Rhodopēius accipit hērōs,   50
nē flectat retrō sua lūmina, dōnec Auernās
exierit uallēs; aut irrita dōna futūra.

41 *exsangu-is e* bloodless. Bloodless souls – *weeping*?
A paradox, but such is the power of Orpheus'
song
Tantal-us ī 2m. Tantalus. He was doomed ever to
stand in water but never to scoop it up to refresh
himself
42 *refug-us a um* flowing away
stupeō 2 be amazed
Ixiōn Ixion-is 3m. Ixion. He was doomed to rotate
for ever on a wheel
43 *iecur -is* 3n. liver (of Tityos, on which birds eternally fed)
*uolucr-is is 3f. bird
urn-a ae 1f. urn
uacō 1 rest from (+ abl.)
44 *Bēlides*: nom. pl. f., descendants of Belus, i.e. the
Danaids, doomed for ever to try to fill buckets
with holes in them
Sīsyph-us ī 2m. Sisyphus, eternally doomed to fail to
push a rock up and over a hill
45 *tunc prīmum . . . genās*: take in order *tunc
prīmum fāma est genās Eumenidum, uictārum*

carmine, maduisse lacrimīs
46 *Eumenidum*: Greek gen. pl. of Eumenides, the
Furies
madeō 2 grow wet
gen-a ae 1f. cheek
rēgi-us a um*
coniunx: i.e. Persephone/Proserpina
47 *sustinet*: controls *ōrantī . . . negāre* 'bear to deny
[to] him begging'
quī: i.e. Pluto
im-us a um deep (here n. pl., used as a noun)
48 *Eurydicēn*: Greek acc. s.
49 *inter*: refers back to *umbrās . . . recentēs*
incēdō 3 *incessī* approach
*pass-us ūs 4m. pace, steps
50 *hanc simul et lēgem*: an amusing syllepsis
hērōs: Greek. nom. s.*
51 *retrō**
Auern-us a um of Avernus, the underworld
52 *uall-is is* 3f. valley
*irrit-us a um (in) vain

40–52: At this the *bloodless* spirits of the dead burst into tears(!) (40–1) and individuals, objects and birds all stop what they are doing to listen to the great singer. Tantalus forgets his thirst, Ixion's wheel stops in amazement, the vultures stop pecking Tityos' liver (song is even tastier), the daughters of Belus abandon their buckets and Sisyphus uses his rock for a seat to enjoy the show (41–4). Even the normally implacable Furies weep (45–6). What chance do Persephone and Pluto stand (46–7)? They summon Eurydice, whose 'physical' condition in Hades is still affected by the way she was killed (48–9, cf. 10), and lay down the terms for her safe return to the upper air (50–2). Note that the gods decree Eurydice's return not as a right but as a gift (*dōna*, 52) – a gift that can be revoked.

10.53–63: *Orpheus looks back, and Eurydice disappears*

carpitur adclīuis per mūta silentia trāmes,
arduus, obscūrus, cālīgine dēnsus opācā,
nec procul āfuerunt tellūris margine summae.   55
hīc, nē dēficeret metuēns, auidusque uidendī,
flexit amāns oculōs, et prōtinus illa relāpsa est,
brācchiaque intendēns, prendīque et prendere certāns,
nīl nisi cēdentēs īnfēlīx arripit aurās.
iamque iterum moriēns nōn est dē coniuge quicquam   60
questa suō (quid enim nisi sē quererētur amātam?)
suprēmumque 'ualē' – quod iam uix auribus ille
acciperet – dīxit, reuolūtaque rūrsus eōdem est . . .

[Orpheus retreats into the Thracian mountains, abjures the love of women but
thoughtfully introduces the Thracians to the love of boys instead. Drawing all
nature after him, he sings a number of songs about love and its effects – including those of Pygmalion (passage 17) and of Venus and Adonis (passage 18) – but
is then spotted by some Maenads who, enraged at his rejection of the female sex,
ferociously attack him.]

53 *adclīu-is e* sloping
*mūt-us a um**
trāmes trāmit-is 3m. path
54 *cālīgō cālīgin-is* 3f. fog, mist
*dēns-us a um**
*opāc-us a um**
55 *tellūris . . . summae*: i.e. the real world above
margō margin-is 3m. edge
56 *dēficiō* 3/4 weaken, falter (Eurydice is the subject)
*auid-us a um**
relābor 3 dep.*
58 *intendō* 3 stretch out. But who is the subject of
these two lines – Orpheus or Eurydice? Without a
change of subject indicated, and the next sentence

certainly having Eurydice as subject, it must still
be Eurydice, desperate to save herself from a
second death (60)
prendō 3 seize, take
certō 1 struggle
arripiō 3/4*
60 *moriēns*: Eurydice is the subject
62 *suprēmum* for the last time
quod . . . acciperet: subj. of characteristic, '[a cry] of
the sort which he could hardly . . .'; almost 'such
that he could hardly . . .'. Characteristic and
result clauses are very similar, **RLQ2(a), W38**
63 *reuoluō* 3*
eōdem to the same place

53–63: The road to the upper world is steep, silent (Orpheus cannot hear Eurydice, 53),
hard-going, dark and shrouded in mist (54). As love drove Orpheus to descend to the
underworld to retrieve his Eurydice, so love now (*amāns*, 57), driven by fear and desire
(56), compels him to look behind him. At once she slips away from him, back into the
underworld. Desperately she tries to seize hold of him, as he her (*prendīque et prendere*),
but clutches only the breezes (58–9). Nor does she make any complaint – as Ovid touchingly points out, her only complaint could be that she was loved (60–1) – and with a final
ualē, which Orpheus could hardly hear, she disappears (62–3).

11.1–19: *Furious Maenads attack Orpheus; their missiles finally get through*

carmine dum tālī siluās animōsque ferārum
Thrēicius uātēs et saxa sequentia dūcit,
ecce nurūs∧ Ciconum, ∧tēctae lymphāta ferīnīs
pectora uelleribus, tumulī dē uertice cernunt
Orphea percussīs sociantem carmina neruīs.   5
ē quibus ūna, leuēs iactātō crīne per aurās,
'en,' ait 'en, hīc est nostrī contemptor!', et hastam∧
uātis Apollineī uōcālia mīsit in ōra,
∧quae, foliīs praesūta, notam sine uulnere fēcit.
alterius tēlum lapis est, quī missus in ipsō   10
āere concentū uictus uōcisque lyraeque est,
ac uelutī supplex prō tam furiālibus ausīs
ante pedēs iacuit. sed enim temerāria crēscunt

Book 11

2 *Thrēici-us a um* Thracian
3 *ecce* look! See!
nur-us ūs 4f. young woman
Ciconum: gen. pl. of Cicones (a Thracian tribe). These women are engaged in a Bacchic (Dionysiac) ritual frenzy. Ironically, the rites of Dionysus were said to have been invented by Orpheus
lymphō 1 make mad
ferin-us a um of wild beasts
4 *uellus ueller-is* 3n. skin
uertex uertic-is 3m. top, summit
5 *Orphea*: Greek acc. s. of Orpheus
sociō 1 join, unite
6 *iactō* 1 toss
7 *en* look!
contemptor -is 3m.*
hast-a ae 1f. spear. This is the thyrsus carried by Bacchic women in honour of their god Bacchus, a wand tipped with a pine-cone (originally concealing a spear-point) and entwined with ivy or vine leaves; hence its inability to hurt Orpheus (9, cf. 27–8)

8 *Apolline-us a um**
uōcāl-is e*
9 *foli-um ī* 2n. leaf, foliage
praesūt-us a um sewn over with
not-a ae 1f. mark
10 *lapis lapid-is* 3m. stone
in ipsō/āere: i.e. as it was travelling through the very air
11 *concent-us ūs* 4m. harmony
*lyr-a ae 1f. lyre
12 *supplex supplic-is* 3m. suppliant (who traditionally fell at another person's knees as (s)he asked forgiveness or sought help)
prō: almost 'to beg forgiveness for'
furiāl-is e frenzied
aus-um ī 2n.*
13 *sed enim* none the less
temerāri-us a um reckless, impetuous
14 *abiit*: for the heavy -*it*, see above on 10.15
insān-us a um*
rēgnō
Erīnŷs: Greek nom. s., Fury, goddess of revenge; here = 'battle frenzy', 'desire for revenge'

1–19: While Orpheus sings his bewitching songs (1–2: observe that the beasts have *animī* but not the woods or rocks, though they still all follow), women from the Cicones tribe (in Thrace) appear, clothed in animal skins, hair tossing in the wind (6) and celebrating their wild Bacchic rites (3–4). Fired with the supernatural power of the god Bacchus/Dionysus inside them, they spot Orpheus and one of them, remembering how he had spurned them, throws an unavailing thyrsus at his mouth (4–9). Why the mouth? Because Orpheus' voice is the source of his appeal and power over all nature (not to mention women); shut his mouth, and he is helpless (one is reminded of Samson and his

bella, modusque abiīt, īnsānaque rēgnat Erīnȳs.
cūnctaque tēla forent cantū mollīta, sed ingēns   15
clāmor, et īnfrāctō Berecyntia tībia cornū,
tympanaque et plausūs et Bacchēī ululātūs
obstrepuēre sonō citharae; tum dēnique saxa
nōn exaudītī rubuērunt sanguine uātis.

11.20–43: *The Maenads attack animals, then Orpheus himself, with everything they can find*

ac prīmum attonitās etiamnum uōce canentis   20
innumerās uolucrēs anguēsque agmenque ferārum
Maenades Orphēī titulum rapuēre theātrī;
inde cruentātīs uertuntur in Orphea dextrīs,

---

15 *forent . . . mollīta*: 'would have been *mollīta . . .*',
  RLE1
cant-us ūs 4m. song
16 *clāmor -is* 3m.*
īnfrāct-us a um bent, curved
Berecynti-us a um from Berecyntia (a region of Caria
  [South-Western Turkey]), i.e. of Cybele (a
  goddess associated with Bacchic worship)
tībi-a ae 1f. pipe
corn-u ūs 4n. horn
17 *tympan-um i* 2n. drum
plaus-us ūs 4m. clapping of hands
Bacchē-us a um Bacchic. Note that *Bacchēī* is in
  hiatus with *ululātūs* (Ovid seems to allow hiatus
  where Greek words are involved: it generates a
  strange rhythmic effect)
ululāt-us ūs 4m. howling
18 *obstrepō* 3 *obstrepuī* drown out (+ dat.)
cithar-a ae 1f. lyre
19 *exaudiō* 4*

rubēscō 2 turn red
20 *attonit-us a um* astonished (*uōce* 'by the voice
  canentis')
etiamnum even now
21 *innumer-us a um**: this line contains the three
  objects of *rapuēre* (22)
*angu-is is 3m. snake
*agmen agmin-is 3n. body, group, column
22 *Maenades*: Greek nom. pl., Maenads (lit. 'mad
  women', i.e. women driven by Bacchic frenzy)
Orphē-us a um of Orpheus, Orpheus'
titul-us i 2m. renown (in apposition to the three
  objects of 22)
*theātr-um i 2n. audience. With *Orphēī titulum* =
  (lit.) 'the renown of Orpheus' audience', i.e.
  'Orpheus' renowned audience', meaning the
  audience of animals Orpheus had attracted to
  listen to him
23 *cruentāt-us a um* bloodied
Orphea: Greek acc. s. of Orpheus

---

hair). The problem the Bacchants will have in doing this becomes clear when one of them throws a stone at him which, charmed by his song (unlike the Bacchants themselves), falls at Orpheus' feet, begging (as it were) for mercy for trying to hurt him (10–13). This in turn creates a problem for Ovid: if nothing the Ciconian women throw at Orpheus is going to get through, how are they going to kill him? But Ovid is up to it. The women redouble their efforts, all hell breaks loose (13–14), and the noise generated by the battle-cries, Bacchic pipes, drums, shouts and howls (15–17) is such that it drowns out the bard. Result? The rocks are now deaf to Orpheus' song, so start to hit home (18–19)!

20–43: The Bacchants turn on Orpheus' followers – birds, snakes and beasts – tearing them apart and, hands bloody from that assault, finally take the attack to Orpheus himself (20–3). Two similes decorate this climactic moment: birds mobbing an owl, and a stag being killed by hounds in the arena (where wild-animal hunts in the morning preceded

et coeunt ut auēs, sī quandō lūce uagantem
noctis auem cernunt, strūctōque utrimque theātrō   25
ceu mātūtīnā ceruus peritūrus harēnā
praeda canum est, uātemque petunt, et fronde uirentēs
cōniciunt thyrsōs, nōn haec in mūnera factōs.
hae glaebās, illae dīreptōs arbore rāmōs,
pars torquent silicēs. neu dēsint tēla furōrī,   30
forte bouēs pressō subigēbant uōmere terram,
nec procul hinc multō frūctum sūdōre parantēs∧
dūra ∧lacertōsī fodiēbant arua ∧colōnī;
agmine quī uīsō fugiunt, operisque relinquunt
arma suī, uacuōsque iacent dispersa per agrōs   35
sarculaquē rāstrīque grauēs longīque ligōnēs.
quae postquam rapuēre ferae, cornūque mināčī
dīuulsēre bouēs, ad uātis fāta recurrunt,

---

24 *ut* like
au-is is 3f. bird (*auis noctis* is probably an owl)
25 *struō* 3 *strūxī strūctus* draw up (begin this clause
    with *ceu* 26)
utrimque on both sides, i.e. the amphitheatre (cf.
    Greek *amphi* 'on both sides')
26 *ceu* or [like]
mātūtīn-us a um in the morning
ceru-us ī 2m. stag
*harēn-a ae 1f. sand (of the amphitheatre/(h)arena;
    animals were slaughtered in the morning,
    humans in the afternoon)
27 *praed-a ae* 1f. prey
*frōns frond-is 3f. leaves, foliage
uireō 2 be green
28 *thyrs-us ī* 2m. thyrsus, Bacchic wand
29 *hae . . . illae . . . pars*: the various groups of
    Bacchants
glaeb-a ae 1f. clod of earth
dīripiō 3/4*
30 *torqueō* 2 throw
*silex silic-is 3m./f. pebble, stone
31 **bōs bou-is* 3m. ox

subigō 3 subdue, plough
uōmer -is 3m. plough
32 *frūct-us ūs* 4m. crop
sudor -is 3m. sweat
33 *lacertōs-us a um* muscular
fodiō 3/4 dig
colōn-us ī 2m. farmer
34 *agmine*: i.e. the column of charging Bacchants
35 *dispers-us a um**
36 *sarcul-um ī* 2n. hoe. Note -*quē* (long), a rare
    scansion
rāstr-um ī 2n. rake
ligō ligōn-is 3m. mattock (for trenching, removing
    weeds, etc.)
37 *ferae*: *sc.* 'women'
cornū: if taken with *mināčēs*, abl. of cause; if taken
    with *dīuulsēre*, abl. of separation, i.e. they tore
    apart the oxen from their horns (to use as
    weapons)
mināx mināc-is threatening
38 *diuellō* 3 *dīuulsī* tear apart
recurrō 3*

---

the gladiatorial contests in the afternoon, 24–7). At first the women throw their thyrsi, but
(as Ovid points out) these are useless for this task (27–8, cf. 9). So they look elsewhere for
weapons. Some come naturally to hand: clods of earth, branches, stones (29–30). But as it
so happens (*forte*), men are working in the fields nearby (31–3). *lacertōsī* they may be (33),
but they know Bacchic women take no prisoners, and they run when they see them. The
women seize their working tools, tear the horns from their oxen (a particularly gruesome
moment) and return to the attack (34–8) on the now defenceless poet. All he can do is
stretch out his arms in supplication (cf. Actaeon, 3.237–41), because his voice will move

tendentemque^ manūs, et in illō tempore prīmum
irrita ^dīcentem, nec quicquam uōce ^mouentem   40
sacrilegae perimunt, perque ōs, prō Iuppiter! illud,
audītum saxīs intellēctumque ferārum
sēnsibus, in uentōs anima exhālāta recessit.

11.44–60: *Nature laments Orpheus; his head still sings as it floats down a river*

tē maestae uolucrēs, Orphēū, tē turba ferārum,
tē rigidī silicēs, tē carmina saepe secūtae   45
flēuērunt siluae, positīs tē frondibus arbor
tōnsa comās lūxit. lacrimīs quoque flūmina dīcunt
incrēuisse suīs, obstrūsaque carbasa pullō
Nāidēs et Dryadēs passōsque habuēre capillōs.
membra iacent dīuersa locīs, caput, Hebre, lyramque   50
excipis; et (mīrum!) mediō dum lābitur amne,
flēbile nescioquid queritur lyra, flēbile lingua
murmurat exanimis, respondent flēbile rīpae.
iamque mare inuectae flūmen populāre relinquunt

39 *tendentem . . . dīcentem . . . mouentem*: acc., referring to Orpheus, object of *sacrilegae perimunt* (41)
41 *sacrīleg-us a um**
perimō 3 kill
43 *sēns-us ūs* 4m.*
exhālō 1*
recēdō 3*
44 *tē . . .*: a long 'funeral' apostrophe, with anaphora
(*tē*), asyndeton and five rising cola.
45 *rigid-us a um**
47 *tondeō* 2 *totondī tōnsum* cut
lūgeō 2 *lūxī* grieve
quoque: take with *flūmina*
48 *incrēscō* 3*
obstrūs-us a um edged
carbas-a ōrum 2n. pl. (linen) garment

pull-um ī 2n. black (material)
49 *Dryadēs*: nom. pl., Dryadēs, nymphs of the woods
pass-us a um loose (*pandō*)
50 *dīuers-us a um* apart, scattered
Hebr-us ī 2m. the river Hebrus in Thrace
51 *excipiō* 3/4*
amn-is is 3m. river
52 **flēbil-is e* lamentable, piteous. Note the (fune-
real? See on passage 13, 8.231) tricolon with
anaphora and asyndeton as lyre and head har-
monise, and the river-banks respond
53 *murmurō* 1*
exanim-is e lifeless
54 *inuehō* 3 *inuexī inuectum* carry into. The understood subjects are Orpheus' head and lyre
populār-is e of his (Orpheus') people

nothing now (39–40). The women kill him, and he breathes his last through that mouth
that once beasts and rocks had understood (41–3). The women's sacrilege (41) lies in the
fact that Orpheus was a priest of Apollo and Bacchus, having (ironically) himself founded
the rites of the latter divinity whom the women themselves worship.

44–60: As is typical in ancient laments, Ovid now uses apostrophe and anaphora to per-
sonalise his mourning for the greatest poet-singer of all time – *tē . . . tē . . . tē . . . tua . . .
tē* – and describes how birds, beasts, rocks, forests, trees, rivers, and nymphs of waters
and woods all joined in grief (44–9; note that the forests shed their leaves like humans
cutting their hair, a traditional sign of mourning). No humans? But Orpheus' genius lay

et Methymnaeae potiuntur lītore Lesbī.   55

hīc ferus expositum∧ peregrīnis anguis harēnis

∧ōs petit et sparsōs stillantī rōre capillōs.

tandem Phoebus adest, morsūsque īnferre parantem

[he holds it back, and into stone the snake's open jaws]

congelat, et patulōs, ut erant, indūrat hiātūs.   60

11.61–6: *Orpheus and Eurydice are reunited in Hades*

umbra subit terrās, et quae loca uīderat ante,

cūncta recognōscit, quaerēnsque per arua piōrum

inuenit Eurydicēn cupidīsque amplectitur ulnīs.

hīc modo coniūnctīs spatiantur passibus ambō,

nunc praecēdentem sequitur, nunc praeuius antēīt,   65

Eurydicēnque suam iam tūtō respicit Orpheus.

---

55 *Methymnae-us a um* where Methymna is (a famous city on Lesbos). The city is eighty miles from the mouth of the Hebrus, over the Aegean sea
Lesbī: gen. s. f. of Lesbos, a Greek island
56 *expōnō* 3*
peregrīn-us a um foreign
57 *stillō* 1 drip
rōs rōr-is 3m. dew
58 *mors-us ūs* 4m. bite
īnferō 3*
parantem: acc., referring to the snake, object of *congelat*, 60
60 *congelō* 1 freeze
patul-us a um gaping
indūrō 1 harden

hiāt-us ūs 4m. mouth
61 *subeō**
62 *recognōscō* 3*
pi-ī ōrum 2 m. pl. the pious (dead), living in the Elysian (blessed) fields
63 *cupid-us a um* desirous
uln-a ae 1f. embrace
64 *coniungō* 3*
spatior 1 dep. stroll
65 *praecēdō* 3 walk ahead (the subject of the sentence is Orpheus, 66)
praeui-us a um in front
anteō*
66 *tūtō*: adverbial
respiciō 3/4 *

---

in the hold he had over all nature, animate and inanimate. Ovid now rounds off the story. He tells how Orpheus' body was torn apart but his head and lyre (said to have been nailed together) were thrown into the river Hebrus by the infuriated Bacchae, but still sang as they floated down it (50–3). Swept into the sea, they reach the town of Methymna on the island of Lesbos (54–5, where they were said to have been buried) – but not before Apollo petrified a snake to prevent it swallowing the head (56–60, a strange detail Ovid lifted from an earlier Greek poet Phanocles, who also says that from then on Lesbos was famous for its lyric poets like Sappho and Alcaeus).

61–6: But what of Orpheus' shade? Ovid saves the best till last. Recognising all the fabled places he had visited before, but continuing to show no interest in them whatsoever, Orpheus seeks out the one person he wants – Eurydice (61–2). Together again, they stroll round the underworld, taking the air, and now, at any rate, Orpheus can look back without any risk of losing her (64–6). He can be grateful, of course, that in the underworld he has a head to look back with; Eurydice's condition in the underworld had been critically affected by what had happened to her in the world above (49).

Learning vocabulary for Passage 16, Orpheus

agmen agmin-is 3n. body, group, column
angu-is is 3m. snake
bōs bou-is 3m. ox
carmen carmin-is 3n. music, song
flēbil-is e lamentable, piteous
frōns frond-is 3f. leaves, foliage
harēn-a ae 1f. sand
irrit-us a um (in) vain
lyr-a ae 1f. lyre

neru-us ī 2m. string (of a lyre)
pass-us ūs 4m. pace, steps
rēgnum ī 2n. kingdom
Rhodopēi-us ī 2m. (man from) Mount
    Rhodope in Thrace, i.e. Thracian
silenti-um ī 2n. silence
silex silic-is 3m./f. pebble, stone
theātr-um ī 2n. audience
uolucr-is is 3f. bird

Study section

1. Compare Ovid's account of Orpheus' descent to the underworld (10.11–16) with Virgil's (*Georgics* 4.464–70, below). Look also for metrical differences (numbers of dactyls and spondees, extent of elision, cf. **Metre**, note 12).

    ipse, cauā sōlāns aegrum testūdine amōrem,
    tē, dulcis coniunx, tē sōlō in lītore sēcum,
    tē ueniente diē, tē dēcēdente canēbat.
    Taenariās etiam faucēs, alta ostia Dītis
    et cālīgantem nigrā formīdine lūcum
    ingressus Mānēsque adiit rēgemque tremendum,
    nesciaque hūmānīs precibus mānsuēscere corda.

    'He himself, consoling his sick love with his hollow tortoise-shell (lyre),
    You, sweet wife, you on the desolate shore alone
    He sang, you at return, you at decline of day.
    Even the jaws of Taenarum, the high gates of Pluto,
    And the grove shrouded in black terror
    And the shades of the dead he approached and entered, and their shuddersome king,
    And hearts that do not know how to soften at human prayers.'

2. Now compare Virgil's account of Orpheus' death (*Georgics* 4.520–7, below) with Ovid's (11.1–53)! What do words like *mirum!* (51), *nescioquid* (52) and *exanimis* (53) suggest about Ovid's 'take' on that scene?

    sprētae Ciconum quō mūnere mātrēs
    inter sacra deum nocturnīque orgia Bacchī
    discerptum lātōs iuuenem sparsēre per agrōs.
    tum quoque marmoreā caput ā ceruīce reuulsum
    gurgite cum mediō portāns Oeagrius Hebrus
    uolueret, 'Eurydicēn!' uōx ipsa et frigida lingua,

'*ā miseram Eurydicēn!' animā fugiente uocābat:*
'*Eurydicēn' tōtō referēbat flūmine rīpae.*

'The mothers of the Cicones, insulted by such devotion [*sc.* to Eurydice*],
amid their rituals for the gods and orgies to Bacchus at night,
tore the young man apart and scattered him across the broad fields.
Then, as for the head ripped from its marble neck,
as Oeagrian Hebrus carrying it rolled it along the middle of the stream,
"Eurydice!" the voice itself and frozen tongue,
"Ah, poor Eurydice", it cried, as the spirit left it:
"Eurydice" echoed back the banks all along the river.'
*It is not at all certain what *mūnere* means here, or whether it is the right
reading.

3. Virgil did not record for us the song he thought Orpheus sang to woo the
spirits of the dead. Ovid does (10.17–39). Is it plain or elaborate? Is it elo-
quent? Ironic? Does it work?

17   Pygmalion, *Metamorphōsēs* 10.243–97

Background

The story of Pygmalion is one of the songs that Orpheus sings to console himself for the loss of his wife Eurydice (see passage 16). Going on to relate tales of transformation on Cyprus, Orpheus sings of the Propoetides, the first women to prostitute themselves in public. Venus turns these hard-hearted women into granite; and that provides Ovid with the transition to the Cypriot Pygmalion who, shocked by this female behaviour, decides never to marry.

10.243–53: *Pygmalion sculpts a beautiful woman, with whom he falls in love*

'quās^ quia Pygmaliōn aeuum per crīmen ^agentēs
uīderat, offēnsus uitiīs, quae plūrima mentī
fēmineae nātūra dedit, sine coniuge caelebs   245

---

243 *quās . . . agentēs*: object of *uīderat. agō* here is used of passing time (with *aeuum*); the women in question (*quās*) are the Propoetides, mentioned in the **Background**
244 *offendō* 3 *offendī offēnsum**

uiti-um i 2n. vice, wickedness
quae plūrima 'which [being] very many' (object of *dedit*)
245 *caelebs caelib-is* unmarried

Unlike their modern equivalents, painters and sculptors in the classical Greek and Roman worlds were seen as technicians whose job was to represent the human body as realistically, and sometimes as idealistically, as possible. They are illusionists. So it is not surprising to find claims in ancient authors that some works of art were so perfect that they could not be distinguished from the real thing (here one must remember that ancient statues were also painted). Indeed, the satirist Lucian (second century AD) tells a story about one young man who was so smitten by a nude statue of Venus in Cnidos that he attempted to copulate with it. From there it was a short step to wonder if such works could ever actually be animate in any sense (a notion with which we are familiar from holy statues that 'bleed' at certain times of the year). In our digital age, the often apparently fine line between reality and illusion is something of which we are all too aware. It is worth noting that *ars* means 'trick, crafty stratagem', as well as 'technical skill'.

244–53: Earlier stories of Pygmalion made him a king on Cyprus who tried the same faintly disgusting trick on a statue of Venus as the young man in Lucian's tale. In an epic of trans

uīuēbat, thalamīque diū cōnsorte carēbat.
intereā niueum∧ mīrā fēlīciter arte
sculpsit ∧ebur fōrmamque dedit, quā fēmina nāscī
nūlla potest, operisque suī concēpit amōrem.
uirginis est uērae faciēs, quam uīuere crēdās,   250
et, sī nōn obstet reuerentia, uelle mouērī:
ars adeō latet arte suā. mīrātur et haurit
pectore Pygmaliōn simulātī corporis ignēs.'

10.254–69: *He touches and kisses the statue, gives it gifts and dresses it up*

'saepe manūs operī temptantēs admouet, an sit
corpus an illud ebur, nec adhūc ebur esse fatētur.   255

246 *cōnsors cōnsort-is* 3f. partner
careō 2 lack (+ abl.)
247 **niue-us a um* snow-white
248 *sculpō* 3 *sculpsī* sculpt
*ebur ebor-is 3n. ivory
quā with which (picking up *fōrmā*); *quā . . . potest*: i.e. impossibly beautiful
249 **concipiō* 3/4 conceive, develop; utter
250 *crēdās*: note the subj., and apostrophe (inviting the reader's agreement)
251 *obstō* 1 stand in the way

reuerenti-a ae 1f. modesty (she was, after all, naked)
uelle mouērī: quam 250, i.e. the statue, is still the subject
252 *ars . . . suā*: a typical Ovidian paradox, the nearest ancient literature comes to expressing the medieval sentiment *ars est celāre artem*, 'the art/skill is hiding the art/skill'
hauriō 4 take in, absorb, experience
253 *ignēs*: i.e. passionate feelings (for)
254 *admoueō* 2*
255 *fateor* 2 dep. admit

formations, however, Ovid sees entirely different possibilities in the tale. He begins by constructing a smooth narrative link with the previous story of the wicked Propoetides, whose dreadful example persuades a shocked Pygmalion not to have anything to do with women, or at least, not *diū*: so we know there is to be a change (243–6). *quae . . . dedit* (244–5) is probably best taken as Pygmalion's thoughts on the matter, though the assumption is common among classical male authors (and Ovid is no exception) that women were not to be trusted where sex and drink were concerned (cf. Cephalus in passage 12, 7.714–19). Observe that Ovid avoids informing us whether Pygmalion was a sculptor by trade (let alone whether he was a king); craftsmen were low-class figures, producing work on commission for clients, unsuitable for major roles in myth (the exception is Daedalus). Likewise, the motivation for Pygmalion's statue remains unclear. *intereā* (247) may suggest that Pygmalion's creation was a form of idealised consolation for his celibacy, but his sudden falling in love (or lust? Cf. *ignēs* 253) with it is quite unexpected (247–9: note ivory, a fantastically expensive material renowned for its warmth of texture). The statue is so lifelike (250) one could even believe it was willing to move; but this would be the last thing any modest girl would do in public, were she by some awful chance to be found naked (hence *reuerentia*, 251; Pygmalion's behaviour here may be intended to contrast with the shocking behaviour of the Pygmalion of the earlier story). There is no doubt that this is a lifeless statue: but Pygmalion is still on fire for it (252–3). One is reminded of Narcissus (passage 8).

254–69: Pygmalion's approach to the statue is carefully delineated. First, there is the physical – from touching to kissing, from kissing to speaking, holding and caressing, abruptly

ōscula dat reddīque putat, loquiturque tenetque,
et crēdit tāctīs digitōs īnsīdere membrīs,
et metuit, pressōs ueniat nē līuor in artūs.
et modo blanditiās adhibet, modo grāta puellīs
mūnera fert illī – conchās teretēsque lapillōs,   260
et paruās uolucrēs et flōrēs mīlle colōrum,
līliaquē pictāsque pilās et ab arbore lāpsās
Hēliadum lacrimās. ōrnat quoque uestibus artūs,
dat digitīs gemmās, dat longa monīlia collō,
aure leuēs bācae, redimīcula pectore pendent.   265
cūncta decent, nec nūda minus fōrmōsa uidetur.
collocat hanc strātīs conchā Sīdōnide tīnctīs,
appellatque torī sociam, acclīnātaque^colla
mollibus in plūmīs, tamquam ^sēnsūra, repōnit.'

256 *reddīque*: i.e. the kisses
257 **īnsīdō* 3 sink into
258 *līuor -is* 3m. bruising
259 *blanditi-a ae* 1f.*
adhibeō 2 offer. There follows a long list of gifts,
    almost compulsively poured out
260 *conch-a ae* 1f. shell
teres teret-is polished
lapill-us ī 2m. pebble
261 *uolucr-is is* 3f. bird
262 *līli-um ī* 2n.*. Note the rare lengthened *-que*
pingō 3 *pīnxī pictum* paint
pil-a ae 1f. ball
263 *Hēliad-es um* 3f. pl. daughters of Helios (the
    sun). They were turned into poplar trees and their
    tears, falling from the tree, were turned by the
    Sun into amber (see **Background** to passage 5)
ōrnō 1 dress, decorate

264 *gemm-a ae* 1f.*
monīl-e is 3n. necklace
265 *bāc-a ae* 1f. pearl
redimīcul-um ī 2n. long ribbons/bands (usually
    attached to a head-dress, and falling down to the
    shoulders)
266 *deceō* 2 be fitting, appropriate
267 *collocō* 1 place
strāt-um ī 2n. bed, bedding, couch
conch-a ae 1f. shell-fish (producing a dye)
Sīdōnis Sīdōnid-is from Sidon (in ancient Phoenicia,
    modern Lebanon, the source of the famous
    purple dye)
tīngō 3 *tīnxī tīnctum* tint, colour
268 *appellat*: sc. 'her'
acclīnō 1 incline, make X lean
269 *plūm-a ae* 1f. feather, down
repōnō 3*

halted (256–8) – and then comes the companionate – sweet nothings, gifts, jewels and
ornaments for fingers, neck, ears, breast (259–66). In all this, Pygmalion is acting as one of
Ovid's elegiac lovers would to a real woman (259 *grāta puellīs*), though the gifts are very
unsophisticated (the sort of simple things a Roman woman in Ovid's elegiac poetry would
scorn). The level of 'intimacy' now rises: Pygmalion prepares the statue for bed and
removes its clothes (*nūda* 266). We might expect the temperature also to rise here, but note
decent and observe that Pygmalion does not see the statue as *more* beautiful when it is
naked: his fixation is not simply sexual. So he lays it on an expensive couch and *calls* it his
bed-fellow (but does not take it to bed with him) and gives it a pillow *as if* it could feel it
(267–9). The statue is now referred to as a woman (*nūda, fōrmōsa* 266, *hanc* 267, and
Pygmalion calls it *sociam* 268), but there is still no doubt that the statue is *ars* (252, cf. *nōn
falsa*, 292); whatever his actions, Pygmalion is living at the moment on belief (*crēdās* 250,
crēdit 257) and thoughts (*pūtat* 256) – as will become even clearer when he approaches
Venus with a prayer. The 'girl' is still a dream, a fantasy, and Pygmalion's thoughts are dom-

10.270–9: *He prays to find a wife like the statue*

'festa diēs Veneris, tōtā celeberrima Cyprō,   270
uēnerat et, pandīs inductae^ cornibus aurum,
conciderant ^ictae niueā ceruīce ^iuuencae,
tūraque fūmābant, cum mūnere fūnctus ad ārās
cōnstitit et timidē "sī, dī, dare cūncta potestis,
sit coniunx^, optō," nōn ausus "eburnea uirgō"   275
dīcere, Pygmaliōn "similis ^mea" dīxit "eburnae."
sēnsit, ut ipsa suīs aderat Venus aurea festīs,
uōta quid illa uelint et, amīcī nūminis ōmen,
flamma ter accēnsa est apicemque per āera dūxit.'

10.280–97: *The statue warms and to his amazement comes to life*

'ut rediit, simulācra suae petit ille puellae,   280
incumbēnsque torō dedit ōscula; uīsa tepēre est.
admouet ōs iterum, manibus quoque pectora temptat;

270 *fest-us a um* festal; *fest-a ōrum* 2n. pl. festival
celeber celebr-is e famous, visited
Cypr-us ī 2f. Cyprus
271 *pand-us a um* curved
indūcō 3 cover with X (acc.) over Y (abl.)
272 *concidō* 3*
īc(i)ō 3 *īcī ictum* strike
ceruīx ceruīc-is 3f. neck
iuuenc-a ae 1f. heifer
273 *tūs tūr-is* 3n. incense

fungor 3 dep. *fūnctus* carry out (+ abl.)
275 *eburn(e)-us a um**
277 *sēnsit*: Venus is the subject
278 *ōmen ōmin-is* 3n.*
ter three times
279 *accendō* 3 *accendī accēnsum* light
apex apic-is 3m. point, tongue (of flame)
281 *incumbō* 3 lean (on)
tepeō 2 be warm

inated by it, living as he is in an over-heated, imagined world of what might be (but is not). It is a brilliant analysis of what, for many people, being in love for the first time can involve.

270–9: Pygmalion's creation has obviously changed his mind about women, and the festival of Venus, goddess of sexual activity, creates an ideal setting in which he can raise the question of a wife. It is a packed occasion on Cyprus (270): oxen with horns covered in gold (a very great honour to the goddess) are being sacrificed, and altars are ablaze with incense (273). But Pygmalion, having made his offering, is not at all sure how to approach the matter (274). He can hardly ask Venus to turn the statue into his wife, he feels, though that is what he really wants (275). So he settles for second best – may he marry a woman *like* her (276). But Venus knows what he really wants (*sēnsit . . . uelint* 277–8) and sends an encouraging sign – the flame flaring up on the altar where he has just placed his offering of incense (278–9).

280–97: Pygmalion returns home and gives the statue a loving kiss (cf. 256). So far, so usual. But – what if . . . ? She (*uīsa*, f.) *seems* to be warm (280–1). This is new. He kisses her again and runs his hands over her breasts (282, cf. 254); this time the ivory is actually

temptātum mollēscit ebur, positōque rigōre
subsīdit digitīs cēditque, ut Hymettia sōle
cēra remollēscit, tractātaque pollice multās   285
flectitur in faciēs, ipsōque fit ūtilis ūsū.
dum stupet et dubiē gaudet fallīque uerētur,
rūrsus amāns rūrsusque manū sua uōta retractat.
corpus erat! saliunt temptātae pollice uēnae.
tum uērō Paphius plēnissima concipit hērōs   290
uerba, quibus Venerī grātēs agat, ōraque tandem
ōre suō nōn falsa premit; dataque ōscula uirgō
sēnsit, et ērubuit, timidumque ad lūmina lūmen
attollēns pariter cum caelō uīdit amantem.
coniugiō, quod fēcit, adest dea, iamque coāctīs   295
cornibus^ in plēnum nouiēns ^lūnāribus orbem,
illa Paphon genuit, dē quā tenet īnsula nōmen.'

<hr>

283 *mollēscō* 3*
rigor -is 3m. hardness
284 *subsīdō* 3 yield to, give way to
Hymetti-us a um from Mount Hymettus (south-east
    of Athens)
285 *remollēscō* 3*
*tractō 1 handle, mould
*pollex pollic-is 3m. thumb
286 *ūtil-is e* useful
287 *stupeō* 2 be amazed
uereor 2 dep. fear
288 *retractō* 1 touch again
289 *saliō* 4 pulse
uēn-a ae 1f. vein
290 *Paphi-us a um* from Paphos (in Cyprus)
hērōs 3m. Greek nom. s., hero

291 *quibus . . . agat*: subj. expressing purpose ('with
    which to offer . . . '); **RL**145(3)
293 *ērubēscō* 3 *ērubuī* blush
294 *attollō* 3*
caelō: it is probably too plodding to ask where is the
    couch so placed that she can see the sky
295 *coniugi-um ī* 2n. marriage
coāgō 3 contract, come together
296 *nouiēns* nine times
lūnār-is e lunar
orbem: i.e. full moon (the whole phrase means 'nine
    months later')
297 *Paphon*: Greek. acc. of Paphos
gignō 3 *genuī* bear
īnsul-a ae 1f. island (but the island is called Cyprus;
    Paphos is one of its towns)

<hr>

softened, her flesh does actually yield to his fingers (282–4, cf. 257–8). A suitably artistic simile accompanies this dramatic moment: her flesh is like wax which softens in the sun and can be worked into many shapes. Pygmalion, joyful and doubtful and afraid that he is being deceived (287 – a cleverly judged combination of feelings at such a time), runs a loving hand over his *uōta* (the object of his prayer) again (288) – to find that the statue is made real flesh, blood pumping through the veins (a close observation, 289). Immediate thanks to Venus are the mark of the truly pious man (290–1), and further kisses follow – not *falsa* any longer (292). But what of Galatea (the name given much later to his wife)? She is so modest (cf. 251) that, although she has had no experience of the real world at all, she blushes to feel Pygmalion's kiss (293, a lovely Ovidian touch); then, looking for the source of the illumination (another fine touch: she does not know what 'light' is), she opens her *timidum* eyes (cf. Pygmalion, 274) to see the man who is in love with her, and the sky, all at once (293–4). Venus attends the marriage, and a child soon follows who will give his name to Paphos on Cyprus: a happy ending, for a change. But not so happy for the descendants, as will become apparent in the next passage . . .

Learning vocabulary for Passage 17, Pygmalion

concipiō 3/4 conceive, develop; utter
ebur ebor-is 3n. ivory
fest-us a um festal; *fest-a ōrum* 2n. pl. festival
īnsīdō 3 sink into

niue-us a um snow-white
pollex pollic-is 3m. thumb
tractō 1 handle, mould

Study section

1. Is Pygmalion (like Narcissus) 'obsessed with a projection of himself rather than with an independent woman'?
2. Is the Pygmalion story a metaphor of the ideal artist, working so close to perfection as to produce the real thing?
3. If the statue is so perfect, why does Venus not enviously destroy it (compare Minerva's destruction of Arachne's work, passage 11)? Or is that not the issue?
4. 'Women readers may feel less enthusiasm for this story of the perfect wife and its implied guarantee that she will never show discontent or independence' (Fantham, 2004, 59). Discuss.
5. Compare Ovid's portrayal of 'being in love' in this story with that of Pyramus and Thisbe (passage 9).

18   Venus and Adonis, *Metamorphōsēs* 10.519–739

Background

Having sung of Pygmalion (passage 17), Orpheus continues his tales on various sexual themes with the story of Myrrha. She was the daughter of Paphos' son Cinyras, and fell in love, and committed incest, with her father. Pregnant, and appalled by what she had done, she prayed for transformation and became a tree. Even so, with the help of Lucina (goddess of child-birth) who split the tree-trunk for her, she gave birth to a son Adonis, a boy of outstanding beauty.

10.519–28: *Time passes, Adonis' beauty increases, and Venus falls for him*

'lābitur occultē fallitque uolātilis aetās,
et nihil est annīs uēlōcius. ille, sorōre   520
nātus auōque suō, quī conditus arbore nūper,
nūper erat genitus, modo fōrmōsissimus īnfāns,
iam iuuenis, iam uir, iam sē fōrmōsior ipsō est.
iam placet et Venerī, mātrisque ulcīscitur ignēs.

519 *occultē* secretly
uolātil-is e fleeting, on wings
520 **uēlōx uēlōc-is* swift
sorōre . . . auōque suō: i.e. Myrrha and Cinyras
521 *au-us ī* 2m. grandfather
arbore: i.e. inside the tree that was his mother
nūper: the repeated *nūper* (in chiasmus), then
  modo and repeated *iam* in tricolon with
  asyndeton (523) push the story quickly
  along
522 *gignō* 3 *genuī genitus* bear

*fōrmōs-us a um handsome. There is amusing polyptoton, *fōrmōsissimus* (superlative) being outdone
  by *fōrmōsior sē ipsō* (523)!
īnfāns infant-is 3m.*
524 *mātrisque*: i.e. Myrrha
ulciscor 3 dep. avenge
ignēs: i.e. the fires of unnatural passion felt by
  Myrrha, which had been stirred by the anger of
  Venus (in some versions of the stories). The
  'revenge' presumably consists in Venus' grief at
  Adonis' death

519–28: Being the offspring of his sister and father, not to mention born from a tree (520–2), Adonis might be expected to have experienced a challenging childhood. Its details, however, Ovid elides by talking about the deceptively fleeting passage of time (519–20) which sees Adonis progress from a beautiful baby through childhood and youth to become an even more handsome adult (522–3); and Ovid then connects Adonis' story to his mother Myrrha's (which he had just told) by claiming that, when Venus falls in love with Adonis, Adonis somehow avenges his mother's unfortunate

[228]

namque pharetrātus dum dat puer ōscula mātrī,   525
īnscius exstantī dēstrinxit harundine pectus.
laesa manū nātum dea reppulit: altius āctum
uulnus erat speciē prīmōque fefellerat ipsam.'

10.529–41: *Venus abandons her usual haunts and practices to be with Adonis*

'capta uirī fōrmā nōn iam Cythereīa∧ cūrat
∧lītora, nōn altō repetit Paphon aequore cīnctam   530
piscōsamque Cnidon grauidamue Amathunta metallīs.
abstinet et caelō; caelō praefertur Adōnis.
hunc tenet, hūic comes est; adsuētaque semper in umbrā
indulgēre sibī fōrmamque augēre colendō,

---

525 *pharetrāt-us a um* with a quiver. The *puer pharetrātus* is Cupid, Venus' playful son, a wound from whose arrows makes the wounded fall in love (see Apollo in passage 2, 1.472–4)
526 *insci-us a um**
exstō 1 protrude
dēstringō 3 *dēstrinxī* graze
harundō harundin-is 3f. shaft
pectus: i.e. Venus' *pectus*
527 *repellō* 3*
altius: comparative adverb
528 *speci-ēs ēī* 5f. appearance (here abl. of comparison)
fefellerat: i.e. at first, Venus had not realised how deeply she had been wounded
529 *Cytherēi-us* of Cythera (an island off the southern tip of Greece associated with Venus' birth)
530 *lītus lītor-is* 3n. shores
Paphon: Greek acc. of Paphos (in Cyprus), where Venus had her main cult centre
531 *piscōs-us a um* full of fish, teeming (the *-que* scans light)
Cnidon: Greek acc. of Cnidos, a promontory at the tip of South-West.Turkey, location of a famous shrine to Venus complete with a notorious nude

female statue of her (see **Comment** on Pygmalion, passage 17)
grauid-us a um prolific, rich in
Amathunta: Greek acc. of Amathus, a town in Cyprus where Venus had another major cult centre
metall-um ī 2n.*
532 *abstineō* 2 shun, stay away from (+ abl.).
abstinet . . . Adōnis makes a neatly antithetical, almost chiastic, line
et: here, 'even'
praeferō 3 prefer X (acc.) to Y (dat.)
533 *umbrā . . . augēre*: the ancients avoided the sun because a tan was low-class (it proved you worked, and in the open air, too); hence the popularity of skin-whitening cosmetics, made of tin oxide for colour, starch for bulk and animal fat for applicability. Likewise, women did not slim, they fattened themselves up (*augēre*) – which Venus certainly will not do chasing over the mountains all day. Such is the effect of Cupid's dart on a goddess
adsuēt-us a um being accustomed (*adsuēscō* 3)
534 *indulgeō* (+ dat.)*
augeō 2 increase, improve

---

passion for her father (524). Not that Venus set out to fall in love with him, Ovid emphasises: it was all down to her being accidentally scratched by her son Cupid's arrow (525–8). Like Apollo before her (see e.g. passage 2, 1.452–74), no divinity is immune to Cupid's darts, even his mother, mistress of sexual passion. Observe how the depth of the wound had deceived even her (528).

529–41: Adonis is a young man, and therefore a hunter. This, then, is what Venus must become if she is to be with her lover all the time (529, 533). So she abandons not only her natural sanctuaries but even Olympus itself (530–2). She puts on unfetching

per iuga, per siluās dūmōsaque saxa uagātur,   535
fine genūs uestem rītū succīncta Diānae.
hortāturque canēs, tūtaeque animālia praedae
aut prōnōs leporēs aut celsum in cornua ceruum
aut agitat dammās; ā fortibus abstinet aprīs,
raptōrēsque lupōs armātōsque unguibus ursōs   540
uītat et armentī saturātōs caede leōnēs.'

10.542–59: *Venus warns Adonis against fierce animals, and relaxes to tell him a story*

'tē quoque, ut hōs timeās, sī quid prōdesse monendō
possit, Adōni, monet, "fortis" que "fugācibus estō"
inquit; "in audācēs nōn est audācia tūta.
parce meō, iuuenis, temerārius esse perīclō,   545

---

535 *iug-um ī* 2n. ridge
dūmōs-us a um full of brambles
536 *fine* up to (+ gen.)
uestem: acc. of respect
rītū in the style of
succingō 3 gird (oneself) up
537 *tūtae . . . praedae*: gen. of description, lit. 'of safe prey', i.e. safe to hunt
animāl-e is 3n.* : *animālia . . . leporēs . . . ceruum . . . dammās* are all objects of *agitat* (539)
538 **prōn-us a um* leaning forward, low to the ground
lepor -is 3m. hare
cels-us a um tall
ceru-us ī 2m. stag
539 *agitō* 1 drive, hunt
damm-a ae 1f. deer
*aper apr-ī 2m. boar

540 *raptor -is* plundering. Note the rising tricolon of animals not to be chased, each described more bloodily than the last
lup-us ī 2m. wolf
armō 1*
ungu-is is 3m. claw
urs-us ī 2m. bear
541 *uītō* 1 avoid
arment-um ī 2n. herd, cattle
saturō 1*
*leō leōn-is 3m. lion
543 **Adōni*: voc. of Adonis
fugācibus: i.e. (*fortis*) against [animals] that flee
estō: imper. of *sum*, RLE1
545 *meō . . . perīclō*: 'with my danger', i.e. at my cost/expense
*temerāri-us a um rash

---

hunter's gear like Diana's and roams the hills (535–6): no more staying out of the sun to avoid a tan, or keeping herself fat, either (533–4). Nevertheless, there are fierce animals out there, and on these she is not keen (539–41; the epithets attached to them suggest her fears about them). So she confines herself to urging on the dogs and hunting the tamer beasts – note the neat contrast in height between hares and stags (537–9).

542–59: With a sympathetic apostrophe towards Adonis (*tē . . . Adōni*, 542–3), Ovid relates Venus' orders to him: he is to be as worried about fierce animals as she is (543–4). Her motives, naturally, are governed by pure self-interest (545–7); she has no idea what *glōria* means to a young male. Her lecture on the implacable ferocity of wild beasts reads pretty richly coming from her (547–52) – as if Adonis did not know anyway – and it is no surprise when he wonders what on earth she is talking about

nēue ferās, quibus arma dedit nātūra, lacesse,
stet mihi nē magnō tua glōria. nōn mouet aetās
nec faciēs nec quae Venerem mōuēre leōnēs
saetigerōsque suēs oculōsque animōsque ferārum.
fulmen habent ācrēs in aduncīs dentibus aprī,   550
impetus est fuluīs et uasta leōnibus īra,
inuīsumque mihī genus est." quae causa rogantī,
"dīcam," ait "et ueteris mōnstrum mīrābere culpae.
sed labor īnsolitus iam mē lassāuit, et, ecce,
opportūna suā blandītur pōpulus umbrā,   555
datque torum caespes; libet hāc requiēscere tēcum"
(et requiēuit) "humō", pressitque et grāmen et ipsum,
inque sinū iuuenis positā ceruīce reclīnis
sic ait, ac mediīs interserit ōscula uerbīs:'

546 *lacessō* 3 wound, harm
547 *stet*: begin the clause with *nē*. *stāre* + abl. means
    lit. 'to stand at the price of', 'cost'; *stāre magnō*
    thus means 'cost X (dat.) dear'. *magnō* is abl. of
    price, **RLL**(f)4(iv)
aetās . . . faciēs . . . quae Venerem mouēre: all subjects
    of *mouet* (547)
549 *saetiger -a um* bristly
*sūs su-is 3m. boar
550 *adunc-us a um* hooked
*dēns dent-is 3m. tusk; tooth
551 *impet-us ūs* 4m. aggression
*fulu-us a um tawny, yellow
uast-us a um*
552 *inuīs-us a um* hateful
quae causa [*esset*] *rogantī*: 'to [him] asking what . . .';
    with *causa*, understand 'of her hatred of lions'

553 *mōnstr-um ī* 2n. monstrous act
554 *insolit-us a um* unaccustomed
lasso 1 exhaust
ecce look!
555 *opportūn-us a um**
blandior 3 dep. entice, beguile
pōpul-us ī 2f. polar tree
556 *caespes caespit-is* 3m. turf, grass
libet 2 (impersonal) it is pleasing
*requiēscō 3 *requiēuī* lie down, rest
557 *grāmen grāmin-is* 3n. grass
558 *sin-us ūs* 4m. lap
ceruix ceruīc-is 3f. neck
reclīn-is e*
559 *interserō* 3 interpose X (acc.) with
    Y (dat.)

(552). So she prepares to tell him a story involving *culpa* (553 – this prompts our curiosity); not before time either, judging by her exhaustion from the chase (554) and her eagerness to take advantage of the convenient *locus amoenus*, complete with *torus* (555–6). She wastes no time in placing herself in prime position on the ground (556–7), dragging him down at the same time (lovely syllepsis at 557 *pressitque . . . ipsum*), placing her head on his breast (558) and taking full advantage (559). We are not told what Adonis made of all this – but then, Adonis is notably speechless throughout, as a young man probably would be with the goddess of sexual passion running the relationship (and telling the story). On the other hand, a young man making his way in the mythic world does not willingly abandon the hunt – one of the main arenas where a man can show he is a man – in favour of lounging on the turf with a woman, even if that woman happens to be Venus. Will Adonis allow himself, like Venus, to be transformed for 'love'?

10.560–74: 'Atalanta decided to marry no one unless they could out-run her'

' "forsitan audieris aliquam certāmine cursūs   560
uēlōcēs superāsse uirōs. nōn fābula rūmor
ille fuit; superābat enim. nec dīcere possēs,
laude pedum fōrmaene bonō praestantior esset.
scītantī deus hūic dē coniuge 'coniuge' dīxit
'nīl opus est, Atalanta, tibī; fuge coniugis ūsum.   565
nec tamen effugiēs, tēque ipsā uīua carēbis.'
territa sorte deī per opācās innuba siluās
uīuit, et īnstantem turbam uiolenta procōrum
condiciōne fugat, 'nec sum potienda, nisi' inquit
'uicta prius cursū. pedibus contendite mecum.   570
praemia uēlōcī coniunx thalamīque dabuntur,
mors pretium tardīs. ea lēx certāminis estō.'
illa quidem immītis, sed (tanta potentia fōrmae est)
uēnit ad hanc lēgem temerāria turba procōrum." '

560 *forsitan* perhaps
aliquam: 'that a certain [woman]'
certāmen certāmin-is 3n. contest
563 *bonō*: here used as a noun
praestāns praestant-is outstanding
564 *scītantī . . . hūic dē . . .* : 'to this [woman]'
    enquiring about . . .' (*scītor* 1 dep.)
deus: the god of oracles, Apollo
565 *opus est* there is a need to X (dat.) of Y (abl.); X
    needs Y
566 *careō* lose (+ abl.). This makes a typical riddling
    answer from the god
567 *opāc-us a um**

innub-us a um unmarried
568 *īnstō* 1 press, urge, insist
**proc-us ī* 2m. suitor
569 *condiciō condiciōn-is* 3f. condition, terms (stated
    in the forthcoming speech)
fugō 1 put to flight, rout
570 *pedibus*: i.e. in a foot-race
contendō 3 compete
571 *praemia*: in apposition to *coniunx*
    thalamīque
572 *preti-um ī* 2n. price
estō: 3rd s. imper. of *sum*
573 *immīt-is e* ruthless

560–74: In seven crisp lines (560–6), Venus sketches the background: the young girl Atalanta, fleet of foot and a great beauty, is given a riddling response by the god to a question about marriage – she should not marry, but she will; and in doing so, she will lose herself. Like all girls in Ovid who decide not to marry, Atalanta at once takes to the woods (567); but not before laying down a challenge to the *īnstantem turbam* of suitors (568–9) – beat me in a race and win me, or die in the attempt (569–72). That she will show no mercy is clear (cf. *uiolenta* 568, *immītis* 573), but it makes no difference to the enthusiasm of her suitors, such is her beauty (573–4, cf. 563). Illogical as this is – if she does not want to marry, why give anyone the chance to marry her? – this is myth, which does not require strict narrative logic; its purpose is to lay the groundwork for Hippomenes' entry into the story.

10.575–99: 'Initially scornful, Hippomenes fell for her when he saw her running'

' "sēderat Hippomenēs, cursūs spectātor inīquī,   575
et 'petitur cūīquam per tanta perīcula coniunx?'
dīxerat, ac nimiōs iuuenum damnārat amōrēs.
ut faciem et positō corpus uēlāmine uīdit,
quāle meum, uel quāle tuum, sī fēmina fīās,
obstipuit, tollēnsque manūs 'ignōscite,' dīxit   580
'quōs modo culpāuī! nōndum mihi praemia nōta,
quae peterētis, erant.' laudandō concipit ignēs
et, nē quis iuuenum currat uēlōcius optat,
inuidiāque timet. 'sed cūr certāminis hūīus
intemptāta mihī fortūna relinquitur?' inquit.   585
'audentēs deus ipse iuuat!' dum tālia sēcum

---

575 *sēderat*: note the plupf. – Hippomenes seems to appear from nowhere. Ovid is imagining a packed stadium (*spectātor*), with seats

*Hippomenēs: Greek nom. s. of Hippomenes

spectātor -is 3m.*

*inīqu-us a um unfair, hostile (to + dat.)

576 *cūīquam*: dat. of interested agent

577 *damnō* 1*

578 *uēlāmen uēlāmin-is* 3n. covering, clothes. Was Atalanta running naked, as Greek male athletes did? It all depends on what is meant by *genuālia* (see on 593 below)

579 *quāle . . . fīās*: a high compliment from the goddess of sexual attraction (who is speaking at the moment) to her mortal lover

580 **obstipescō* 3 *obstipuī* be amazed (strongly placed at the start of the line)

ignōscite: imperative. The (understood) subject is 'You suitors' whom (*quōs*) Hippomenes has recently been blaming

581 *nōt-us a um**

582 *concipiō* 3/4*

584 **inuidi-a ae* 1f. envy, spite, ill-will. It is not clear what Ovid is saying here. The text as printed means 'Hippomenes is afraid because of/in respect of envy', which might be hammered into meaning 'he is filled with envious fear', i.e. that a rival might win; **RLL(f)4**

585 *intemptāt-us a um**

586 *iuuō* 1 help

575–99: Hippomenes appears from nowhere (myth again) as a cynical spectator. *inīquī* (575) suggests his own view of the matter, confirmed by his comment about the *perīcula* involved (576), and *nimiōs* (577) reinforces his point: he is tut-tutting away about the folly of youth as if he is already drawing his pension. At this point, however, he has not actually *seen* a race because he has not seen Atalanta. When he does (578) – and Venus inserts a comment of her own to emphasise Atalanta's desirability (579) – his whole perspective immediately changes (580–2). Observe the device of giving a sense of a person by the reaction (s)he evokes: here Hippomenes' scorn followed by his immediate retraction at the sight of her suggests more about Atalanta's beauty than any detailed description could (compare Homer *Iliad* 3.154–60, where the poet, faced with describing Helen, the most beautiful woman in the world, describes instead the admiring reaction to her of the old men of Troy, all well past it). At once Hippomenes feels passionate about Atalanta and desperately hopes no one will run faster; but then realises there is no reason why *he* should not compete for her too, though he realises that *fortūna* and a god will have to help him (582–6). While turning all this over in his mind, he sees Atalanta up close, flashing past. Her speed enhances her beauty (586–90). His gaze, caught by the flow of her

exigit Hippomenēs, passū uolat ālite uirgō.
quae quamquam Scythicā nōn sētius īre sagittā
Āoniō uīsa est iuuenī, tamen ille decōrem
mīrātur magis; et cursus facit ipse decorum –   590
aura refert ablāta^ citīs ^tālāria plantīs,
tergaque iactantur crīnēs per eburnea, quaeque
poplitibus suberant pictō genuālia limbō;
inque puellārī corpus candōre rubōrem
trāxerat, haud aliter quam cum super ātria^ uēlum   595
^candida purpureum simulātās īnficit umbrās.
dum notat haec hospes, dēcursa nouissima mēta est,
et tegitur festā uictrīx Atalanta corōnā.
dant gemitum uictī, penduntque ex foedere poenās." '

587 *exigō* 3 turn over, reflect on
uolō 1 fly
āles ālit-is winged
588 *Scythic-us a um* Scythian (Scythia was famous
  for its archers)
sētius differently from (+ abl.)
sagitt-a ae 1f. arrow
589 *Āoni-us a um* from Boeotia
591 *cit-us a um* swift
tālār-ia ium 3n. pl. ankle-ribbon
plant-a ae 1f. foot
592 *iactō* 1 toss
eburne-us a um ivory
quaeque: 'and (i.e. 'as were the') the *genuālia* which
  . . .'
593 *poples poplit-is* 3m. knee
subsum be under
pict-us a um colourful (with *limbō*, abl. of description referring to the *genuālia*)
genuāl-ia ium 3n. pl. bands (round the knees, cf.
  genu 'knee'). It might conceivably mean a knee-
  length skirt, but the word appears only here. It
  indeed looks as if Atalanta is running naked,
  except for ankle-ribbons and knee-bands; the
  imagination runs almost as fast as she
limb-us ī 2m. border

594 *puellār-is e**
595 *ātri-a ōrum* 2n. pl. atrium, often the entrance to
  a Roman house. Note the anachronism (Roman
  houses did not exist when Greek myths were
  being told). Above the 'white' (and therefore
  marble) atrium was a rectangular opening
  in the roof, which was covered with awnings
  if the sun was too fierce. Purple awnings
  were very expensive: this is a rich
  man's villa
uēl-um ī 2n. awning
596 *candid-us a um* white (i.e. made of marble)
purpure-us a um*
īnficiō 3/4 *
597 *notō* 1*
*hospes hospit-is 3m. guest, i.e. Hippomenes
dēcurs-us a um run, completed
*mēt-a ae 1f. race, course, lap
598 *fest-us a um* festal, celebratory
uictrīx uictrīc-is*
corōn-a ae 1f.*
599 *pendō* (3) *poenās* pay the penalty. But it is odd
  that there were losers (pl.). What would happen
  were Atalanta to be beaten by two or more of
  them?
foedus foeder-is 3n. terms, conditions

trappings and hair, moves from her ankles (591) to her hair (592) and back down to her
knees (593: observe how erotic Ovid makes the moment by *not* describing what we might
expect him to describe – he leaves that to our imagination). Hippomenes then admires
her whole body, observing its healthy flush (all that running), and a simile decorates the
moment (594–6). Indeed, he is hardly watching the spectacle as a *race* at all, let alone
thinking about the dangers, because while he is eyeing up Atalanta (597), the race suddenly finishes, she is crowned victor – *and the losers pay the penalty* (597–9). But what
does a man suddenly in thrall to a woman care about *that*?

10.600–8: *'Hippomenes declared his ancestry'*

' "nōn tamen ēuentū iuuenis dēterritus hōrum,   600
cōnstitit in mediō, uultūque in uirgine fīxō,
'quid facilem titulum superandō quaeris inertēs?
mēcum cōnfer' ait. 'seū mē fortūna potentem
fēcerit, ā tantō nōn indignābere uincī.
namque mihi genitor Megareus Onchestius, illī   605
est Neptūnus auus, pronepōs ego rēgis aquārum,
nec uirtūs citrā genus est. seū uincar, habēbis
Hippomenē uictō magnum et memorābile nōmen.' " '

10.609–22: *'Atalanta, moved by the young man, wondered whether to race him'*

' " tālia dīcentem mollī Schoenēia uultū
aspicit et dubitat, superārī an uincere mālit,   610
atque ita 'quis deus^ hunc fōrmōsīs' inquit '^inīquus
perdere uult, cāraeque iubet discrīmine uītae

---

600 *ēuent-us ūs* 4m. result
dēterreō 2*
602 *quid* why?
titul-us ī 2m. distinction, claim to glory
iners inert-is slow, laggard (object of *superandō*, RLN, W39)
603 *cōnferō* 3 compete
seu or if
604 *indignor* 1 dep. feel aggrieved (+ inf.)
605 *genitor -is* 3m. father
Megareus: Greek nom. s. of Megareus; cf. *Megarēi-us* 'of Megareus' (659)
Onchesti-us a um from Onchestus (in Boeotia)

606 *au-us ī* 2m. grandfather
pronepōs pronepōt-is great-grandson
607 *citrā* less than (+ acc.)
608 *Hippomenē*: abl. s. of Hippomenes
*memorābil-is e**
609 **Schoenēi-us a um* descended from Schoeneus (Atalanta's father)
610 *aspicit = adspicit*
611 *hunc*: i.e. Hippomenes, object of *perdere*
inīquus: here with dat., 'unfair, hostile to'
612 *cār-us a um* dear, precious
discrīmen discrīmin-is 3n. risk

600–8: Standing up out of the (seated, 575) crowd, gaze firmly fixed on Atalanta (in admiration? confrontation?), Hippomenes casts aspersions on her other suitors and makes his challenge (600–3). His own honour is at stake here, but he knows that hers is too – for if she is beaten, she must marry the victor, and there will be no honour in that unless her opponent has shown he is worthy to defeat and marry her. So Hippomenes reveals that he comes from divine stock, and points out that if she triumphs, she will win a great *nōmen* for herself (603–8): in other words, whatever the result, there will be much for her to take pride in. His effect on Atalanta is immediate. This hard woman (568, 573) looks at him *mollī uultū*; for the first time, as it seems, she does not know what to do (609–10).

609–22: Now, apparently, she speaks (*inquit*, 611, cf. *dīxerat* 636), as if in reply. But this is impossible: for the content of the speech makes it obvious that, far from addressing Hippomenes, she is in fact talking to herself, weighing and assessing her fluctuating

coniugium petere hoc? nōn sum, mē iūdice, tantī.
nec fōrmā tangor (poteram tamen hāc quoque tangī),
sed quod adhūc puer est; nōn mē mouet ipse, sed aetās.   615
quid, quod inest uirtūs et mēns interrita lētī?
quid, quod ab aequoreā numerātur orīgine quārtus?
quid, quod amat, tantīque putat cōnūbia nostra
ut pereat, sī mē fors illī dūra negārit?
dum licet, hospes, abī, thalamōsque relinque cruentōs.   620
coniugium crūdēle meum est, tibi nūbere nūlla
nōlet, et optārī potes ā sapiente puellā. ' " '

10.623–37: *'Regretfully, denying all blame, Atalanta decided to race'*

' " 'cūr tamen est mihi cūra tuī, tot iam ante perēmptīs?
uīderit! intereat, quoniam tot caede procōrum

613 *coniugi-um i* 2n. marriage
tantī: gen. of value, cf. 618, **RLL**(d)5
616 *quid, quod*: 'what [should I make of] the fact
  that . . . ?' , introducing a tremendous rising tricolon with anaphora in the next four lines
interrit-us a um + gen.*
lēt-um i 2n. death
617 *aequore-us a um* from the sea (i.e. from
  Neptune)
numerō 1 count
618 *nostra*: i.e. mine to him

620 *cruent-us a um* bloody. It is hard to see how
  marriage to Atalanta would be 'bloody'. It is
  failure to win her hand that was 'bloody'. Atalanta
  puts it this way to indicate the impossibility of
  Hippomenes' desire
621 *nūbō* 3 marry (+ dat.)
623 *tot iam ante*: i.e. so many previous [suitors] (abl.
  abs. with *perēmptis*)
perimō 3 perēmī perēmptum kill, destroy
624 *uīderit*: 3s. imper.; cf. on 9.519

feelings. Ovid nods? Or is it Venus (who is telling the story) who nods, ignoring the precise
context in order to tell us about Atalanta's thoughts, representing her as talking to herself?
Anyway, *deus . . . inīquus*, *fōrmōsīs*, and *cārae* immediately indicate Atalanta's feelings
about this young man (611–12); she cannot be worth the death of such a one (612–13).
Modest, she is also too nice a girl to admit openly that his looks or person have persuaded
her; she claims it is the fact that he is too young to die (613–15). But immediately she
retracts (*poteram . . . tangī*, 614). She weighs up his *mēns* and his *uirtūs*, of both of which
she can know little, but at least those are 'proper' reasons for a (Roman) girl to admire a
man (616). So too is his ancestry (617). But the last of this tricolon, and most persuasive to
her, is his love for her and readiness (like a good Roman) to die in her cause (618). Note
that the *fors* that may deny her to him will seem to her to be *dūra* (619). So she urges him,
in her mind, not to compete with her, because he will lose: she talks in vivid images of
bloody beds and a cruel marriage (620–1). Her thoughts on what any *sapiēns* girl would do
reflect her own feelings about herself as well as Hippomenes (621–2).

623–37: But now the counter-argument – since many others have died, why should he be
an exception (623–5)? But that is no argument, as she immediately sees: why should
death be the price for someone who feels so passionately about her (626–7)? It is fast

admonitus nōn est agiturque in taedia uītae.—   625
occidet hīc igitur, uoluit quia uīuere mēcum,
indignamque necem pretium patiētur amōris?
nōn erit inuidiae uictōria nostra ferendae.
sed nōn culpa mea est! utinam dēsistere uellēs,
aut, quoniam es dēmēns, utinam uēlōcior essēs!   630
at quam uirgineus puerīlī uultus in ōre est!
a! miser Hippomenē, nōllem tibi uīsa fuissem!
uīuere dignus erās. quodsī fēlīcior essem,
nec mihi coniugium fāta importūna negārent,
ūnus erās, cum quō sociāre cubīlia uellem.'   635
dīxerat, utque rudis prīmōque cupīdine tācta,
quod facit ignōrāns, amat et nōn sentit amōrem. " '

625 *admoneō* 2*
agitur: almost 'he is being (ignorantly and foolishly) pushed into'
taedi-um ī 2n. weariness with (+ gen.)
627 *indign-us a um**
nex nec-is 3f. death
preti-um ī 2n. price (here in apposition to *indignam necem*)
628 *nōn*: take with *ferendae*
inuidiae: gen. describing the nature of the victory of which she is quite confident
629 *dēsistō* 3*

630 *dēmēns dēment-is**
631 *uirgine-us a um**
*pueril-is e**; cf. 615
632 *Hippomenē*: voc. of Hippomenes
nōllem: followed here by the subj.; translate 'I would that [I had] not . . .'; *tibi* is dat. of agent
634 *importūn-us a um* oppressive
635 *sociō* 1 share
636 *utque* 'and like [one]'
rud-is e inexperienced
**cupīdō cupīdin-is* 3m/f. longing, desire

becoming obvious that no other suitor has ever made it clear that he really does love her. But she cannot escape from the logical bind – that she is bound to defeat him (628). As she says, it will not be her fault (629): he does not *have* to race her (630). All she can do is exclaim at his youthful innocence again (631) – which is obviously so appealing to her – and wish he had never seen her (632).

But at this point we may ask – why can she not take the logical step and decide to e.g. trip over and lose? But that is not an option, because at the start of the story, Atalanta was told not to marry (565) or she would lose herself (566). She knows therefore that she *must* defeat Hippomenes or meet an unspecified end. Hence her lament at 633–5: had she only been *fēlīcior* and fate *not* stood in the way, Hippomenes is the only person with whom she would have liked to share a bed. The imperatives of fate, life and desire fight it out in her. Ovid summarises: this is *amor* (which, of course, conquers all), but Atalanta, never having experienced it before, does not know it (636–7). What a master craftsman Ovid shows himself to be in depicting the wavering reflections of a young girl feeling *amor*'s darts for the first time in a situation over which, theoretically, she has complete control, if it were not for *amor*. So – will she or won't she?

10.638–51: '*Hippomenes asked me (Venus) for help; I gave him three golden apples*'

' "iam solitōs poscunt cursūs populusque paterque,
cum mē sollicitā prōlēs Neptūnia uōce
inuocat Hippomenēs 'Cytherēa,' que 'comprecor, ausīs   640
adsit' ait 'nostrīs, et quōs dedit adiuuet ignēs.'
dētulit aura precēs ad mē nōn inuida blandās.
mōtaque sum, fateor, nec opis mora longa dabātur.
est ager (indigenae Tamasēnum nōmine dīcunt),
tellūris Cypriae pars optima, quem mihi prīscī   645
sacrāuēre senēs, templīsque accēdere dōtem
hanc iussēre meīs. mediō nitet arbor in aruō,
fulua comās, fuluō rāmīs crepitantibus aurō.
hinc tria forte meā^ ueniēns dēcerpta ferēbam
aurea pōma ^manū, nūllīque uidenda nisi ipsī   650
Hippomenēn adiī, docuīque quis ūsus in illīs. " '

638 *poscō* 3 demand, call for
paterque: of Atalanta, i.e. Schoeneus
639 *cum*: when
sollicit-us a um uneasy, anxious
*prōlēs prōl-is 3f. offspring
Neptuni-us a um*
640 *inuocō* 1*
*Cytherē-a ae 1f. Cytherean, i.e. Venus (cf. 529);
   nom., not voc., as *adsit*, jussive subj., makes clear
comprecor 1*
641 *quōs*: take in order *ignēs quōs; ignēs* = the flame
   of love Hippomenes feels
adiuuō 1 foster, encourage
642 *dēferō* 3*
inuid-us a um envious, grudging
643 *fateor* 2 dep. admit, confess
644 *indigen-a ae* 1m. inhabitant
Tamasēn-us ī 2m. of Tamasus (in Cyprus)

645 *Cypri-us a um**
quem: picks up *ager*
*prīsc-us a um of old, ancient. *prīscī . . . senēs* are the
   subjects of *sacrāuēre* and *iussēre*
646 *sacrō* 1 make sacred, sanctify
accēdō 3 be added (inf. after *iussēre*)
dōtem/hanc 'this [land] as a gift/dowry' (*dōs dōt-is*
   3f.)
647 *iussēre* = *iussērunt*
niteō 2 shine
648 *crepitō* 1 clatter, tinkle
649 *dēcerpt-us a um* plucked
650 *aure-us a um**
*pōm-um ī 2n. apple
nūllīque . . . ipsī: dat. of agent
651 **Hippomenēn*: Greek acc. of Hippomenes
doceō 2 teach

638–51: The people, not to mention Schoeneus, have a taste for blood (Ovid understands the Roman audience from his experience of gladiatorial games) and demand the next race (638). This is the moment of truth for Hippomenes, and Venus reveals that he now appealed to her for help (639–41). She admits that she was not unsympathetic (that *mōtaque . . . fateor* sounds slightly embarrassed, cradled as she currently is in Adonis' embrace) and she acted at once (642–3). She went to a sanctuary dedicated to her on Cyprus where there grew a tree with golden apples (644–8). Plucking three, she secretly gave them to Hippomenes with instructions how to use them (649–51). She does not describe what the instructions were: Ovid keeps in suspense those who do not know the story.

10.652–80: 'Hippomenes used the apples to delay Atalanta and win the race'

' "signa tubae dederant, cum carcere prōnus uterque
ēmicat, et summam celerī pede lībat harēnam.
posse putēs illōs siccō freta rādere passū
et segetis cānae stantēs percurrere aristās.   655
adiciunt animōs iuuenī clāmorque fauorque
uerbaque dīcentum 'nunc, nunc incumbere tempus!
Hippomenē, properā! nunc uīribus ūtere tōtīs!
pelle moram: uincēs!' dubium, Megarēius hērōs
gaudeat an uirgō magis hīs Schoenēia dictīs.   660
ō quotiēns, cum iam posset trānsīre, morāta est
spectātōsque diū uultūs inuīta relīquit!
āridus ē lassō ueniēbat anhēlitus ōre,
mētaque erat longē. tum dēnique dē tribus ūnum
fētibus arboreīs prōlēs Neptūnia mīsit.   665

652 *tub-a ae* 1f. bugle. Ovid 'romanises' the race
carcer -ris 3m. starting-gate
prōnus: both runners were crouched for the 'off'
653 *ēmicō* 1 flash out
lībō 1 skim
*harēn-a ae 1f. sand
654 *putēs*: Venus draws Adonis into the story
sicc-us a um dry
fret-um ī 2n. sea
rādō 3 graze
655 *seges seget-is* 3f. corn(field)
cān-us a um grey
percurrō 3*
arist-a ae 1f. ear (of corn)
*adiciō 3/4 add

656 *clāmor -is* 3m.*
fauor -is 3m.*
657 *incumbō* 3 forge ahead
658 *Hippomenē*: voc. of Hippomenes
659 *pellō* 3 banish
dubium: understand 'whether', RLS2(e)
*hērōs: nom. s.
661 **trānseō trānsīre* overtake, cross
*moror 1 dep. delay
663 *lass-us a um* exhausted
anhēlit-us ūs 4m. (Hippomenes') panting
665 *fēt-us ūs* 4m. fruit
arbore-us a um*

652–80: Ovid decorates the 'off' with a simile: the pair race across the sand as one might imagine runners skimming over the sea or over a field of standing grain (651–4). The image is Homeric (*Iliad* 20.226–9), used of the racing foals sired by the North Wind: 'These in their frolics could run across a field of corn, brushing the highest ears, and never break one; and when they frolicked on the broad back of the sea, they skimmed the white foam on the crests of the waves' (Rieu–Jones); Virgil uses it of the warrior Camilla at *Aeneid* 7.808–11. The crowd to a man is on Hippomenes' side, urging him on enthusiastically (656–9). Hippomenes is thrilled by the support – but so too is Atalanta (600). So entranced is she by the sight of him that she would rather not overtake, and does so only unwillingly (661–2). He, meanwhile, is in trouble – already breathing hard, and with the finishing post a long way off (663–4: *mēta . . . longē* give us his own view of the matter). Time, then, for the first golden apple – and their purpose, to delay an Atalanta greedy for gold (666), is revealed. *mīsit* does not tell us where Hippomenes threw it; but she *dēclīnat cursūs* (667) so the apple

obstipuit uirgō, nitidīque cupīdine pōmī
dēclīnat cursūs, aurumque uolūbile tollit.
praeterit Hippomenēs; resonant spectācula plausū.
illa moram celerī cessātaque tempora cursū
corrigit, atque iterum iuuenem post terga relinquit;   670
et rūrsus pōmī iactū remorāta secundī
cōnsequitur trānsitque uirum. pars ultima cursūs
restābat; 'nunc' inquit 'adēs, dea mūneris auctor!'
inque latus campī, quō tardius illa redīret,
iēcit ab oblīquō nitidum iuuenāliter aurum.   675
an peteret, uirgō uīsa est dubitāre. coēgī
tollere, et adiēcī sublātō pondera mālō,
impediīque oneris pariter grauitāte morāque.
nēue meus sermō cursū sit tardior ipsō,
praeterita est uirgō, dūxit sua praemia uictor. " '   680

666 *nitid-us a um* shining
667 *dēclīnō* 1 turn away from
uolūbil-is e rolling
668 *resonō* 1 resound
spectācul-um ī 2n. stand
plaus-us ūs 4m. applause
669 *cessō* 1 waste
670 *corrigō* 3 put right
671 *iact-us ūs* 4m. throw
remoror 1 delay, be held up
672 *cōnsequor* 3 dep. catch up with
673 *restō* 1 remain
adēs: imper. of *adsum*

auctor -is 3m/f. provider, source
674 *latus later-is* 3n. side
camp-us ī 2m. plain
quō tardius: + subj. = purpose, RL148
675 *ab oblīquō* off to one side
iuuenāliter with a young man's strength
676 *coēgī*: Venus intervenes to help Hippomenes
677 *māl-um ī* 2n. apple
678 *grauitās grauitāt-is* 3f. weight
679 *meus sermō*: Venus decides to cut the speech
     short
680 *uictor -is* 3m.*

took her off the straight and narrow. The crowd cheers as Hippomenes takes the lead (668), but Atalanta puts on a spurt (*celerī cursū*), makes up the difference and re-takes the lead (669–70). The same thing happens when Hippomenes throws the second apple (671–2). So far, then, the apples have been a complete failure. This is why Hippomenes prays to Venus for help on the final section of the course (672–3). It is the last throw of the apple: if it does not work, he is dead. This time, he throws it right out into the plain, (presumably) at a sharper angle to the 'track' than before (674–5) – so far, indeed, that even Atalanta hesitates to go for it (676). Atalanta, then, was not *that* greedy for gold: so will the third apple be a complete failure as well? No, but little thanks to the apple: Venus reveals that she now took charge, and not only forced Atalanta to chase after it but also added weight to the apples, thus impeding her further (676–8). After such a gross intervention, one rather wonders why Venus bothered with the apples at all; she might just as well have e.g. broken Atalanta's leg. But this is myth. Venus cuts a long story short: Hippomenes passed the girl and won (679–80).

10.681–95: *'Angry that Hippomenes did not thank me, I incited him to sacrilege'*

' "dignane^, cūī grātēs ageret, cūī tūris honōrem

ferret, Adōni, ^fuī? nec grātēs immemor ēgit,

nec mihi tūra dedit. subitam conuertor in īram,

contemptūque dolēns, nē sim spernenda futūrīs,

exemplō caueō, mēque ipsa exhortor in ambōs.   685

templa^, deum Mātrī ^quae quondam clārus Echīōn

fēcerat ex uōtō, nemorōsīs ^abdita siluīs,

trānsībant, et iter longum requiēscere suāsit.

illīc concubitūs intempestīua cupīdō^

occupat Hippomenēn, ā nūmine ^concita nostrō.   690

---

681 *digna cūī*: lit. 'worthy to whom [Hippomenes] should . . . ?', i.e. 'did I deserve that Hippomenes should . . . ?', **RLQ**2(1)

*tūs tūr-is 3n. incense. For offering incense on the altar, see 10.273

683 *conuertor* 3 pass.*

684 *contempt-us ūs* 4m.*

nē: dependent on *caueō*, **RLS**2(d), **W**40

spernō 3 despise, scorn

futūrīs: dat. of agent (presumably 'men' or 'ages')

685 *exempl-um ī* 2n. example ('by [making them both] an example')

in ambōs: i.e. against both of them

686 *deum* (= *deōrum*) *Mātrī*: the goddess in question is Cybele, also called *Magna Mater*, known in Greece by the fifth century BC and brought to Rome from Phrygia (modern Turkey) in 204 BC. She was (among things) a goddess associated with

fertility, wild nature and ecstasy

Echīōn: Greek nom. s., one of the founders of Thebes in Boeotia. Hippomenes is presumably crossing Boeotia with his new bride (*iter longum* 688), taking her home from where her father Schoeneus was king (near Thebes) to Onchestus (605)

687 *ex* (*uōtō*): 'as a result of', 'to fulfil'

nemorōs-us a um wooded

*abdō 3 *abdidī abditum* hide (away), bury

688 *iter longum*: Venus was equally exhausted after hunting (554) and persuaded Adonis to lie down with her – a hint?

689 *concubit-us ūs* 4m. sexual intercourse

intempestiu-us a um untimely

690 *concit-us a um* urged on

nostrō: i.e. Venus's

681–95: Venus' story is at an end. Its subject was, she had claimed at the start (553), an extraordinary *ueteris . . . culpae*, related (apparently) to her hatred of lions, about which Adonis had asked for an explanation (552). No such explanation has emerged so far: but the lion will now begin slowly to creep out of the bag. It emerges that Hippomenes had omitted to thank Venus for her efforts on his behalf (note the enraged questions and sense of personal insult 681–3; contrast Pygmalion, 10.290–1). The result was that Venus' good will towards him was turned to anger, and she decided to make an example of both of them to warn others not to spurn her in the future (683–5: is there a covert warning here to Adonis, on whose breast she is, presumably, still reclining?). All this is typical of the ancient gods, whose love could turn to hatred in a trice, even for those closest to them. For example, when in Homer's *Iliad* Aphrodite ordered Helen (of Troy) to sleep with her abductor Paris, and Helen refused, Aphrodite angrily turned on her (3.414–15): 'Obstinate wretch! Don't get the wrong side of me, or I may desert you in my anger and detest you as vehemently as I have loved you up till now' (Rieu–Jones). Ancient deities are not gods of love. So when, exhausted during their long journey to

lūminis exiguī fuerat prope templa recessus,
spēluncae similis, nātiuō pūmice tēctus,
rēligiōne sacer prīscā, quō multa∧ sacerdōs
∧lignea contulerat ueterum ∧simulācra deōrum;
hunc init et uetitō temerat sacrāria probrō." '   695

10.696–707: 'Shocked, Cybele turned them both into lions – you, too, Adonis, watch out for wild animals'

' "sacra retorsērunt oculōs, turrītaque Māter
an Stygiā sontēs dubitāuit mergeret undā.
poena leuis uīsa est; ergō modo lēuia fuluae

691 *recess-us ūs* 4m. secluded spot
692 *spēlunc-a ae* 1f. cave
nātiu-us a um natural. This gives the place an
    ancient air, as if priests had been using it long
    before human ingenuity enabled temples to be
    built
pūmex pūmic-is 3m. pumice stone
693 *rēligiō rēligiōn-is* 3f. ritual, worship
quō to where
sacerdōs sacerdōt-is 3m. priest
694 *ligne-us a um* wooden (such statues were
    thought to be of great antiquity)
cōnferō 3*
695 *temerō* 1 profane, violate
sacrāri-um ī 2n. shrine
probr-um ī 2n. offence. Sexual intercourse was felt by
    Greeks to be incompatible with the sacred
    (perhaps because gods, being immortal, required
    insulation from processes to do with life and

death). So intercourse in a sacred place, let alone
    in the presence of the gods' statues, was felt to be
    a great sacrilege
696 *sacra*: i.e. the sacred statues there
retorqueō 2 *retorsī* avert
turrīt-us a um towered (Cybele is often depicted
    wearing a crown like a tower; one of her functions
    was to protect her people in war)
697 *an*: take in order *turrītaque Māter dubitāuit an*
    . . .
Stygiā: the dead usually cross the river Styx to reach
    the far bank. Here the lovers are (dramatically) to
    be plunged into it, such is the goddess' fury at
    what they have done
sōns sont-is (the) guilty
698 *lēu-is e* smooth (note the long *ē* and compare
    leuis)

Hippomenes' home, the couple were crossing a temple tucked away in the woods and dedicated to the goddess Cybele (686–8), Venus prompted in Hippomenes a desire to have sexual intercourse with Atalanta (689–90). In a nearby, dimly lit cave, sacred of old to the gods and filled with their (ancient) wooden images (691–4), he took her and did the sacrilegious deed (695). The fact that Venus had planted the desire in him does not remove his guilt. Nor would it have made any difference if he had not *known* it was an area dedicated to the gods (it was, after all, dimly lit, 691). Intentions count for nothing with these deities; only what you *do* counts. Compare Homer's *Iliad* 9.533–8, where king Oeneus makes a sacrifice to all the other gods, but not to Artemis: 'perhaps he forgot her, perhaps he did not intend to do it – but in either case, it was a seriously deluded act. In her rage, Artemis . . .' (Rieu–Jones).

696–707: The result is dramatic – even the statues look away in horror (696) – and Cybele, deciding that sending the couple to Hades there and then is too lenient a penalty

colla iubae uēlant, digitī curuantur in unguēs,
ex umerīs armī fiunt, in pectora tōtum   700
pondus abit, summae caudā uerruntur harēnae.
īram uultus habet, prō uerbīs murmura reddunt,
prō thalamīs celebrant siluās, aliīsque timendī
dente premunt domitō Cybelēia frēna – leōnēs!
hōs tū, cāre mihī, cumque hīs genus omne ferārum,   705
quod nōn terga fugae, sed pugnae pectora praebet,
effuge, nē uirtūs tua sit damnōsa duōbus! " '

---

699 *iub-a ae* 1f. mane
curuō 1*
ungu-is is 3m. claw
700 *arm-us ī* 2m. forequarter
701 *uerrō* 3 sweep
702 *murmur -is* 3n. growl. 702–3 make a tremendous
  tricolon with asyndeton
703 *prō thalamīs*: Ovid's point is that these animals
  copulate in woods (as Hippomenes and Atalanta
  had just done), not bedrooms
celebrō 1 throng, crowd
704 *domit-us a um* tamed
Cybelēi-us a um of Cybele
frēn-um ī 2n. bit. Cybele, as goddess of wild nature,
  can tame wild animals to serve her

leōnēs: in apposition, 'as lions'. Cybele reckoned
  death was too light a penalty (*poena leuis*, 698).
  Would eternal life as a domesticated lion pulling a
  chariot have appealed to ancient mythic heroes
  and heroines?
705 *hōs*: 'these [animals]' – object of *tū . . . effuge*
  (707); Venus now turns to Adonis to remind him
  of the lesson of her story – steer clear of wild
  beasts (543 ff.)
cār-us a um dear, precious
706 *terga . . . pectora*: neat chiasmus
707 *damnōs-us a um* ruinous

(696–8), decides to – what? Ovid presents us with an unannounced transformation
which offers a predominantly front-on image: he picks out a tawny mane that clothes
their 'smooth' necks, the claws that their fingers become (698–9: note the 'curve' of the
claws, like the curve of the fingers); the broadening and deepening of their shoulders
and chests (and only then does his imagination travel down the body to the tail, sweep-
ing the sand, 700–1); their angry faces (cf. 551); the growls they now emit; the woods
which they use for intercourse – though now, tamed, they pull Cybele's chariot (702–4).
What are they? The last word reveals it – *leōnēs* (704). And so Atalanta's oracle (564–6)
is fulfilled. Venus ends by drawing the lesson for Adonis – steer clear of lions and every
kind of wild animal that does not flee but stands and fights, because your courage may
be disastrous for both of us (705–7). Nevertheless, it is not at all clear precisely *how* this
story explains Venus' fear and hatred of wild animals, the reason for which Adonis
specifically asked at 552. If the logic is 'I hated Hippomenes and Atalanta: they became
wild animals: therefore I hate wild animals', it is a pretty thin train of reasoning, especially since the wild animals (lions) in question are now tame ones. Not too thin,
however, for Ovid, who has used it to insert another (wonderful) story into his
Metamorphōsēs; and a useful excuse too for Venus to spend some time on the ground in
Adonis' arms.

10.708–16: *Venus leaves, and at the hunt Adonis is killed by a wild boar*

'illa quidem monuit, iūnctīsque per āera cycnīs
carpit iter; sed stat monitīs contrāria uirtūs.
forte suem∧ latebrīs uestīgia certa secūtī   710
excīuēre canēs, siluīsque exīre ∧parantem
fixerat oblīquō iuuenis Cinyrēius ictū.
prōtinus excussit pandō uēnābula rōstrō
sanguine tīncta suō, trepidumque et tūta petentem
trux aper īnsequitur, tōtōsque sub inguine dentēs   715
abdidit, et fuluā moribundum strāuit harēnā.'

10.717–39: *Venus returns, grieves and establishes a festival in Adonis' name; his blood turns into a flower*

'uecta leuī currū mediās Cytherēa per aurās
Cypron olōrīnīs nōndum peruēnerat ālīs;

---

708 *cycn-us ī* 2m. swan. Venus is typically trans-
ported by birds: swans and sparrows (said to have
aphrodisiac qualities) are especially popular.
When the Greek poetess Sappho (c. 600 BC) in a
famous poem remembers calling on Aphrodite to
help her, Aphrodite arrives 'in a golden chariot,
with pretty sparrows bringing you swiftly from
heaven through the air across the black earth,
wings whirring madly' – as they would have to if
you were sparrows pulling a goddess in a chariot
709 *contrāri-us a um**
710 *latebr-a ae* 1f. hiding place, cover
cert-us a um unmistakable
711 *exciō* 4 rouse, start
parantem: refers to the boar, object of *fixerat*
712 *oblīqu-us a um* from the side

*Cinyrēi-us a um of Cinyras (father of Adonis)
ict-us ūs 4m. blow, thrust
713 *excutiō 3/4 *excussī* shake/knock X (acc.) out/off
pand-us a um wide
uēnābul-um ī 2n. spear
rōstr-um ī 2n. snout. The boar uses his snout to
knock the spears out
714 *trepidum** . . . *petentem*: refers to Adonis
715 *trux truc-is* savage
inguen inguin-is 3n. groin
716 *moribund-us a um**
sternō 3 *strāuī* lay low
717 *uehor* 3 pass. *uectus* be carried, borne; travel
718 *Cypron*: Greek acc. of Cyprus
olōrīn-us a um of a swan

708–16: Venus gives her advice and swans off (708–9), but she has a limited understanding
of a young man's priorities. To someone like Adonis, *uirtūs* is not some airy ideal to which
he must occasionally nod. It has to be demonstrated, here and now, if he wants to be
counted in the ranks of heroes. In other words, all his training stands in denial of Venus'
injunctions (709, cf. 547). Ovid cuts at once to the chase, with brilliant concision portray-
ing the unfolding scene (710–12): boar – hiding place – definite tracks – follow them – dogs
– roused it out – the woods the boar is preparing to leave – he hit him! – from the side –
Adonis did – with a blow. With its economy and precision, and with a master such as Ovid
wielding it, Latin does all this quite brilliantly. The boar knocks out the spears with his
snout and goes for Adonis, buries his tusks in his (ah!) groin and flattens him (713–16). In
seven lines and forty-one words, a complete hunt has unfolded vividly before our eyes.

717–39: So immediate has been Adonis' return to the hunt that Venus has not even
reached home in Cyprus before she hears his scream of agony, turns back and sees from

agnōuit longē gemitum morientis, et albās
flexit auēs illūc, utque aethere uīdit ab altō   720
exanimem inque suō iactantem sanguine corpus,
dēsiluit, pariterque sinum pariterque capillōs
rūpit, et indignīs percussit pectora palmīs;
questaque cum fātīs "at nōn tamen omnia uestrī
iūris erunt" dīxit. "luctūs^ monimenta manēbunt   725
semper, Adōni, ^meī, repetītaque mortis imāgō
annua^ plangōris peraget ^simulāmina nostrī.
at cruor in flōrem mūtābitur. an tibi quondam
fēmineōs artūs in olentēs uertere mentās,
Persephonē, licuit – nōbīs Cinyrēius hērōs   730
inuidiae mūtātus erit?" sīc fāta, cruōrem
nectare odōrātō sparsit, quī tāctus ab illō
intumuit sīc, ut fuluō perlūcida caenō

719 *agnōscō* 3 *agnōuī* recognise
alb-us a um white
721 *exanim-is e* dead
iactō 1 shake, make X (acc.) writhe
722 *dēsiliō* 4 *dēsiluī* jump down
sin-us ūs 4m. breast
723 *rumpō* 3 *rūpī* tear at
indign-us a um guiltless
palm-a ae 1f.*
724 *uestrī iūris*: 'under your control'
725 *moniment-um ī* 2n.*
726 *mortis*: i.e. of Adonis' death
727 *annu-us a um**: this is a golden line
plangor -is 3m.*
peragō 3 bring about (i.e. there will be an annual,
    ritual enactment of your death). The Adonia was
    a cult, celebrated by women, that originated in
    Cyprus and Byblos (in modern Lebanon) and was
    well established in Greece by the seventh century
    BC. Evidence for it is known from only three cities
    – Athens, Alexandria (Egypt) and Byblos itself.
    The ritual combined both mourning and
    rejoicing on behalf of Aphrodite and Adonis

simulāmen simulāmin-is 3n. imitation
728 *an*: the force here is 'or is it the case that it was
    possible for you, Persephone, to . . . but it will not
    be for us?'
729 *olēns olent-is* fragrant
ment-a ae 1f. mint
730 *Persephonē*: the story was that the nymph
    Minthe, a concubine of Persephone's husband
    Hades, was turned by Persephone into garden
    mint (*menta*)
inuidiae: predicative dative: '[A changed Adonis]
    will be for [an object of] envy [to us]', i.e. will be
    refused us, **RL**88.6, **WSuppl**.syntax
731 *fāta*: participle from *for fārī fātus* 1 dep. speak
732 *nectar -is* 3n. nectar, the drink of the gods
*odōrāt-us a um**
spargō 3 *sparsī* scatter
quī: picks up *cruōrem*
733 *intumēscō* 2 *intumuī* swell up
ut: introduces a simile
perlūcid-us a um clear, translucent
caen-um ī 2n. mud (see **Study section**)

the skies his bloodied corpse (717–21). Leaping down, she goes into full lamentation
routine (722–3: note the alliteration with 'p'), swears to establish an annual festival in his
name to commemorate her grief (724–7) and, drawing on Persephone's example,
demands that Adonis too be allowed to be transformed (728–31). Adonis' blood,
drenched in nectar, swells like a bubble, and an hour later a flower rises from it, rather
like that of a pomegranate, but short-lived and easily flattened by the winds – the
anemone. This is Ovid's aetiology; its purpose is to compare the fall of the youthful
Adonis with the fall of the short-lived flower. Pliny the Elder offers a different account:
the anemone is so called because it opens only when the wind blows.

surgere bulla solet, nec plēnā longior hōrā
facta mora est, cum flōs dē sanguine concolor ortus,   735
quālem, quae lentō cēlant sub cortice grānum,
pūnica ferre solent. breuis est tamen ūsus in illō;
namque male haerentem et nimiā leuitāte cadūcum
excutiunt īdem, quī praestant nōmina, uentī.'

---

734 *bull-a ae* 1f. bubble
735 *concolor -is* of the same colour
736 *quālem*: object of *pūnica ferre solent; quae* picks
    up *pūnica*
lent-us a um tough
cēlō 1 hide
cortex cortic-is 3m. rind
grān-um ī 2n. seed

737 *pūnic-um* (*pōmum*) bright-red (apple), i.e
    pomegranate
illō: i.e. the flower emerging from Adonis' blood
738 *leuitās leuitāt-is* 3f. lightness
cadūc-us a um fragile, likely to fall
739 *īdem*: refers forward to *uentī*; the flower is the
    anemone, 'wind-flower' (Greek *anemos*, 'wind')
praestō 1 provide, produce

Learning vocabulary for Passage 18, Venus and Adonis

abdō 3 *abdidī abditum* hide (away), bury
abstineō 2 shun, stay away from (+ abl.)
adiciō 3/4 add
Adōnī: voc. of Adonis
aper apr-ī 2m. boar
certāmen certāmin-is 3n. contest
Cinyrēi-us a um of Cinyras (father of Adonis)
Cytherē-a ae 1f. Cytherean, i.e. Venus
coniugi-um ī 2n. marriage
cupīdō cupīdin-is 3m./f. longing, desire
dēns dent-is 3m. tusk; tooth
excutiō 3/4 *excussī* shake/knock X (acc.)
    out/off
fōrmōs-us a um handsome
fulu-us a um tawny, yellow
harēn-a ae 1f. sand
hērōs: nom. s.
Hippomenēn: Greek acc. s. of Hippomenes
Hippomenēs: Greek nom. s. of Hippomenes
hospes hospit-is 3m. guest
inīqu-us a um unfair, hostile (to + dat.)
inuidi-a ae 1f. envy, spite, ill-will

leō leōn-is 3m. lion
Megareus: Greek nom. s. of Megareus; cf.
    Megarēi-us 'of Megareus'
mēt-a ae 1f. race, course, lap
moror 1 dep. delay
nitid-us a um shining
obstipescō 3 *obstipuī* be amazed
pōm-um ī 2n. apple
prīsc-us a um of old, ancient
proc-us ī 2m. suitor
prōlēs prōl-is 3f. offspring
prōn-us a um leaning forward, low to the
    ground
requiēscō 3 *requiēuī* lie down, rest
Schoenēi-us a um descendant of Atalanta's
    father Schoeneus
seu or if
sūs su-is 3m. boar
temerāri-us a um rash
trānseō trānsīre overtake, cross
tūs tūr-is 3n. incense
uēlōx uēlōc-is swift

Study section

1. 'Orpheus describes Adonis . . . as a man, but Venus's relationship with him is
   more like that of a mother' (Fantham, 2004, 81). Do you agree? How would
   you characterise their relationship?

2. What is the function of the oracle (10.564–6)?

3. Are there comparisons to be drawn between Hippomenes and Apollo in passage 2? How is Atalanta different from Daphne?

4. At 733, most manuscripts print *caelō*, yielding '[as a clear bubble swells up] in the yellow sky', which does not make a lot of sense; but '[as a clear bubble swells up] in yellow mud' is not a great improvement. Since the colour *fuluō* 'yellow' is irrelevant to the simile (the anemone is red), replace it with *pluuiō*: *pluuiō* with *caelō* ('rainy sky') looks hopeful, as if the text hides the idea of bubbles formed by rain dropping on water. But that leaves us with 'as a clear bubble swells up from a rainy sky' – not a lot of sense either. Can you do any better?

5. Here are the opening lines of Shakespeare's *Venus and Adonis*.

a. What is the difference between Shakespeare and Ovid in the *mise-en-scène* and relationship between Venus and Adonis?

b. How 'Ovidian' is Shakespeare? Look for word-plays, balance, antithesis, tricola, chiasmus, paradox, imagery, and so on.

> Even as the sun with purple-coloured face
> Had ta'en his last leave of the weeping morn,
> Rose-cheeked Adonis hied him to the chase.
> Hunting he loved, but love he laughed to scorn.
>   Sick-thoughted Venus makes amain unto him,   5
>   And like a bold-faced suitor 'gins to woo him.
>
> 'Thrice fairer than myself,' thus she began,
> 'The fields' chief flower, sweet above compare,
> Stain to all nymphs, more lovely than a man,
> More white and red than doves or roses are –   10
>   Nature that made thee with herself at strife
>   Saith that the world hath ending with thy life.
>
> 'Vouchsafe, thou wonder, to alight thy steed
> And rein his proud head to the saddle-bow;
> If thou wilt deign this favour, for thy meed   15
> A thousand honey secrets shalt thou know.
>   Here come and sit where never serpent hisses;
>   And, being sat, I'll smother thee with kisses,
>
> 'And yet not cloy thy lips with loathed satiety,
> But rather famish them amid their plenty,   20
> Making them red, and pale, with fresh variety;

Ten kisses short as one, one long as twenty.
  A summer's day will seem an hour but short,
  Being wasted in such time-beguiling sport.'

With this, she seizeth on his sweating palm,   25
The precedent of pith and livelihood,
And, trembling in her passion, calls it balm -
Earth's sovereign salve to do a goddess good.
  Being so enraged, desire doth lend her force
  Courageously to pluck him from his horse.   30

Over one arm, the lusty courser's rein;
Under her other was the tender boy,
Who blushed and pouted in a dull disdain
With leaden appetite, unapt to toy.
  She red and hot as coals of glowing fire;   35
  He red for shame, but frosty in desire.

5. Study the two pictures of Venus and Adonis (Titian and Rubens) How would
   you compare and contrast them (position of the couple, dress, hunting
   implements, Cupids, dogs, etc.)? Are they more Ovidian or Shakespearean in
   the 'story' they tell?

Figure 4   Titian, *Venus and Adonis*.

Figure 5   Rubens, *Venus and Adonis*.

19 Midas, *Metamorphōsēs* 11.100–45

Background

Bacchus, enraged at the death of Orpheus, the singer of his mysteries (see passage 16), punished his killers the Maenads by turning them into oak trees. He also abandoned Thrace, and took himself off with his followers to Lydia (southern Turkey). But Bacchus' foster-father Silenus was not among them; he had been captured by Phrygians (central Turkey) and presented to their king Midas. Midas, who had been initiated into Bacchic rites, was delighted when he recognised Silenus and celebrated his arrival with a ten-day festival. Next day, Midas left Phrygia for Lydia to return Silenus to a grateful Bacchus – who gives Midas a wish.

11.100–5: *Midas asks for everything he touches to become gold*

hūic deus∧ optandī grātum, sed inūtile, fēcit	100
mūneris arbitrium, ∧gaudēns altōre receptō.	
ille, male ūsūrus dōnīs, ait 'effice, quicquid	
corpore contigerō, fuluum uertātur in aurum.'	
adnuit optātīs nocitūraque mūnera soluit	
Līber, et indoluit quod nōn meliōra petisset.	105

100 *hūic*: i.e. to Midas
deus: i.e. Bacchus
optandī . . . mūneris: this is the *arbitrium* Midas was offered by Bacchus, 'of a gift to be wished for', 'of wishing for a[ny] gift [he cared for]'
*inūtil-is e**
101 *arbitri-um ī* 2n. choice
altor -is 3m. foster-father (i.e. Silenus)
102 *ille*: denoting change of subject, = Midas

ūsūrus: the fut. denotes 'fated to . . .'
effice: + subj., see **RL**135
103 *fulu-us a um* yellow
104 *adnuō* 3 agree to (+ dat.)
105 *Līber -ī* 2m. Bacchus
indoleō 2*
petisset: subj. as part of Bacchus' thoughts on the matter, **RL**R4, **W**Suppl.syntax

100–5: Since the ancients placed a very high value indeed upon the advantages to be derived from wealth, tending to associate it with all sorts of other desirable qualities (good looks, good fortune, happiness, etc.), Bacchus' agreement to grant Midas' wish does indeed seem like a dream come true (*grātum*, 100). But Midas had not thought through the consequences. That he is a dim-wit is hinted at by *inūtile* (100) and clinched by *male ūsūrus* (102), *nocitūra* (104) and Bacchus' regrets at Midas' choice (105). Note in particular *corpore* (103): if Midas had said 'with my hands', his wish would not have had quite such disastrous consequences.

11.106–26: *Thrilled at first, Midas comes to realise the drawbacks*

laetus abit gaudetque malō Berecyntius hērōs,
pollicitīque fidem tangendō singula temptat,
uixque sibī crēdēns, nōn altā fronde uirentem
īlice dētrāxit uirgam: uirga aurea facta est.
tollit humō saxum: saxum quoque palluit aurō.   110
contigit et glaebam: contāctū glaeba potentī
massa fit. ārentēs Cereris dēcerpsit aristās:
aurea messis erat. dēmptum tenet arbore pōmum:
Hesperidas dōnāsse putēs. sī postibus altīs
admōuit digitōs, postēs radiāre uidentur.   115
ille etiam liquidīs palmās ubi lāuerat undīs,
unda fluēns palmīs Danaēn ēlūdere posset.
uix spēs ipse suās animō capit, aurea∧ fingēns

106 *Berecynti-us a um*: Phrygian (Mount Berecyntus was in Phrygia)
hērōs: Greek nom. s., 'hero'
107 *pollicit-um ī* 2n. promise
singula: object of *tangendō*
108 *uireō* 2 be green
109 *īlex īlic-is* 3f. holm-oak (which sprouts low to the ground)
dētrahō 3*
110 *palleō* 2 *palluī* grow pale (Romans frequently described gold as 'pale')
111 *glaeb-a ae* 1f. clod of earth
contāct-us ūs 4m.*
112 *mass-a ae* 1f. solid lump (of gold)
ārēns ārent-is dry
Cer-es Cerer-is 3f. grain
dēcerpō 3*
arist-a ae 1f. ear
113 *mess-is is* 3f. harvest

dēmō 3 *dēmpsī dēmptum* pluck
pōm-um ī 2n. apple
114 *Hesperidas*: Greek acc. of Hesperides, the daughters of Hesperus who guarded Atlas' orchard in which golden apples grew
115 *post-is is* 3m. post, gate
radiō 1 shine, gleam
116 *palm-a ae* 1f. palm of the hand
lauō 3 *lāuī* wash
117 *fluō* 3*
Danaēn: Greek acc. of Danaē, seduced by Jupiter who came to her disguised as a shower of gold
ēlūdō 3 trick, deceive
posset: conditional subj.; cf. *uidērēs* 126
118 *capiō* 3/4 contain, grasp (i.e. Midas is overwhelmed by the possibilities his wish appears to open up to him)
fingō 3 imagine

106–26: the paradoxical *gaudet malō* puts the situation in a nutshell (106, *malō* being Ovid's comment). Hardly able to believe his luck (108), Midas tests his new powers (107: perhaps we are to imagine him doing so on his joyful way back from Lydia to Phrygia). He touches the branch of a holm-oak, which turns at once to gold (109). Ovid now produces a delightful list of objects that Midas touches, dividing the act of touching from the golden result either by caesura or line-end. Continuing on his journey, Midas tests different types of substance, vegetable and mineral, though not animal (110–14). Perhaps *postibus altīs* indicates he has reached home, where he tries out his gift on his man-made palace, then on water, the first liquid (114–17). It all 'works'. Thrilled at the prospect (118–19), he orders from his slaves a superb celebratory meal, delicious food piled high (119–20). *tum uērō* (121) – dream becomes nightmare. Whatever he touches hardens into gold (121–2). So, forgoing use of his hands, he tears at the food with his teeth (note *auidō* 123: he's getting hungry), with the same result (123–4 – cf. *corpore*, 103). Drinking

^omnia. gaudentī mēnsās posuēre ministrī
exstrūctās dapibus nec tostae frūgis egentēs.   120
tum uērō, sīue ille suā Cereālia dextrā
mūnera contigerat, Cereālia dōna rigēbant.
sīue dapēs auidō conuellere dente parābat,
lammina fulua dapēs, admōtō dente, premēbat.
miscuerat pūrīs auctōrem mūneris undīs;   125
fūsile per rictūs aurum fluitāre uidērēs.

11.127–45: *Bacchus agrees when Midas asks for his wish to be reversed*

attonitus nouitāte malī dīuesque miserque
effugere optat opēs, et quae modo uōuerat, ōdit.
cōpia nūlla famem releuat; sitis ārida guttur
ūrit, et inuīsō meritus torquētur ab aurō;   130

119 *mēns-a ae* 1f. table (*exstrūctās* and *egentēs* agree with *mēnsās*)
minister ministr-ī 2m. slave
120 *exstruō* 3 *exstrūxī exstrūctum* pile high
*daps dap-is 3f. food
tost-us a um baked
frūx frūg-is 3f. produce (of the earth)
121 *sīue . . . sīue* whether . . . or
*Cereāl-is e of Ceres, grain (i.e. bread)
122 **rigeō* 2 grow hard
123 *auid-us a um**
conuellō 3 tear
dēns dent-is 3m. tooth
124 *lammin-a ae* 1f. sheet (metal)
125 *misceō* 2 *miscuī* mix
pūr-us a um*
auctōrem mūneris: lit. 'the source of the gift'. This is

Bacchus, god of wine; and therefore the gift, wine, itself
126 *fūsil-is e* molten, fluid
rict-us ūs 4m. jaw
fluitō 1 flow
127 *nouitās nouitāt-is* 3f.*
dīues dīuit-is rich
128 *uoueō* 2 *uōuī* pray for
ōdī (perf.) hate, RLF1(a)
129 *fam-ēs is* 3f. hunger
releuō 1*
sit-is is 3f. thirst
arid-us a um*
guttur -is 3n. throat
130 *inuīs-us a um* hated
merit-us a um deserving, deservedly
torqueō 2 torture

wine mixed with (ironically useless) 'pure' water also makes no difference (125–6, the last line producing a brilliantly horrible image).

127–45: At last the *attonitus* Midas, realising the truth (127 *malī*, cf. 105–6) – the fine antithesis *dīuesque miserque* sums up him and his situation perfectly – desperately longs to be rid of the powers he so keenly desired. Having all he wants but incapable of being satisfied – and deserving all he gets (129–30: note the brilliant paradox *cōpia nūlla famem releuat*, cf. Narcissus at 3.466) – he lifts his *splendida brācchia* (nice touch) to the heavens, admits he has made a serious mistake and asks to be relieved of the gift that seemed to promise so much (*speciōsō*, another fine oxymoron, 131–3). Bacchus kindly (134) agrees, emphasising the vanity of human wishes (*male optātō* 136, cf. 102, 106, 127–8), and instructs Midas to purify himself of his powers by washing in the river Pactolus in Sardis (136–41). The river absorbs the power Midas has been given and from then on cakes the surrounding fields with gold (142–5). This is another aetiology: the Pactolus was one of

ad caelumque manūs et splendida brācchia tollēns
'dā ueniam, Lēnaee pater! peccāuimus' inquit,
'sed miserēre, precor, speciōsōque ēripe damnō!'
mīte deum nūmen; Bacchus peccāsse fatentem
restituit, pactīque fidē data mūnera soluit   135
'nē' ue 'male optātō maneās circumlitus aurō,
uāde' ait 'ad magnīs uīcīnum Sardibus amnem,
perque iugum rīpae lābentibus obuius undīs
carpe uiam, dōnec ueniās ad flūminis ortūs,
spūmigerōque tuum^ fontī, quā plūrimus exit,   140
subde ^caput corpusque simul, simul ēlue crīmen.'
rēx iussae succēdit aquae: uīs aurea tīnxit
flūmen et hūmānō dē corpore cessit in amnem.
nunc quoque iam, ueteris perceptō sēmine uēnae,
arua rigent aurō madidīs pallentia glaebīs.   145

131 *splendid-us a um* shining
132 *ueni-a ae* 1f. pardon
Lēnae-us ī 2m. Bacchus
*peccō 1 go wrong, make a mistake
133 *misereor* 2 dep. have mercy
speciōs-us a um seductive
ēripiō 3/4*
damn-um ī 2n. curse
134 *mīt-is e* kindly
deum = *deōrum*
fateor 2 dep. admit ([*sē*] *peccāuisse*)
135 *restituō* 3 restore
pact-um ī 2n. agreement (referring to Bacchus' original promise)
fidē: abl. after *data*
136 *circumlit-us a um* smeared, coated
137 *uādō* 3 go
Sard-es ium 3f. Sardis, a town in Lydia
*amn-is is 3m. river (the Pactolus, which flowed
  through Sardis)

138 *iug-um ī* 2n. ridge (i.e. the ridged bank of the
  river, which was presumably running very low in
  the summer)
obui-us a um confronting (+ dat.), i.e. going
  upstream
139 *ort-us ūs* 4m. source
140 *spūmiger -a um* foaming
141 *subdō* 3 submerge
ēluō 3 wash away
142 *succēdō* 3 approach (+ dat.)
uīs aurea: 'golden power', i.e. power to turn things to
  gold
tingō 3 *tīnxī* tinge
143 *hūmān-us a um**
144 *percipiō* 3/4 receive
sēmen sēmin-is 3n. seed
uēn-a ae 1f. vein (of gold)
145 *madid-us a um* wet, dripping

five 'gold-bearing' rivers, according to Pliny the Elder (*Natural History* 33.66), the others
being the Tagus (Spain), the Po (Italy), the Hebrus (Thrace) and the Ganges (India).
Ovid is again in literary heaven as he brilliantly exploits the paradoxes and ironies of the
cretinous Midas' decision, especially 100–5 and 127–33.

Learning vocabulary for Passage 19, Midas, 11.100–45

amn-is is 3m. river
Cereāl-is e of Ceres, grain (i.e. bread)
daps dap-is 3f. food
fulu-us a um yellow
glaeb-a ae 1f. clod of earth

palleō 2 *palluī* grow pale
palm-a ae 1f. palm of the hand
peccō 1 go wrong, make a mistake
post-is is 3m. post, gate
rigeō 2 grow hard

Study section

1. Do you see any similarities between the stories of Midas, Phaethon (passage 4), Semele (passage 6) and Daedalus (passage 13)?
2. You are a leading member of a religious community. Preach a sermon based on Ovid's story of Midas.
3. See 'Some assessments' (pp. 13–15). Do you now share any of those views?

Total learning vocabulary

This list contains all the words that are shared between the learning vocabularies of *Reading Latin* and *Wheelock* (i.e. no word is here which occurs in just *one* of the lists); plus all the vocabulary set to be learned in passages 1–8 of this selection.

A

ā/ab (+ abl.) from, away from
abeō abīre abiī abitum go/come away, depart
ablāt-: see *auferō*
absēns absent-is absent, away
abstul-: see *auferō*
absum abesse āfuī be away from, be absent; be distant
ac (or *atque*) and
accēdō 3 *accessī accessum* approach, come near, reach; be added
access-: see *accēdō*
accipiō 3/4 *accēpī acceptum* receive, accept, take, welcome; learn; obtain, get; sustain; meet with
accūsō 1 accuse (X acc. of Y gen.)
ācer ācr-is e keen, sharp, eager, severe; red-hot
acerb-us a um bitter, harsh, grievous
ācerrim-us a um sup. of *ācer*
aci-ēs ēī 5f. battle-line; sharp edge, point; keenness (of sight); eyes
āct-: see *agō*
ad (+ acc.) towards; at, up to, near; for the purpose of; *usque ad* right up to
addō 3 *addidī additum* add
adeō adīre adiī aditum go/come to, approach
adeō to such an extent, so
adferō adferre attulī allātum bring to
adhūc so far
adiuuō 1 *adiūuī adiūtum* help, aid
admīror 1 dep. be surprised, wonder at
admoueō 2 *admōuī admōtum* move, bring near
adspiciō 3/4 *adspexī adspectum* observe, catch sight of, see

adsum adesse adfuī be present (with), be at hand, be near, assist (+ dat.)
aduers-us a um hostile; facing, opposite; unfavourable, adverse
adulēscēns adulēscent-is 3m. youth, young man
aegrē with difficulty, hardly, scarcely
aequor -is 3n. sea
aequ-us a um fair, balanced, even, equal, level, favourable, just
āēr āer-is 3n. air, atmosphere, sky
aest-us ūs 4m. heat
aetās aetāt-is 3f. age; lifetime, life; generation, time
aethēr -is 3m. upper air, heaven
aeu-um ī 2n. age
ager agr-ī 2m. land, field, farm, territory
agō 3 *ēgī āctum* do, act; drive, lead, direct; develop; spend, pass; (*dē* + abl.) discuss; *gratiās agō* thank
aiō irr. say, assent; *ait* (s)he says, *aiunt* they say
āl-a ae 1f. wing
aliēn-us a um someone else's, foreign, strange, alien
aliī . . . aliī some . . . others
aliquis aliqua aliquid someone, something (pron.)
aliquis aliqua aliquod some (adj.)
aliter ac/quam otherwise than
ali-us a ud other (two different cases in same clause = 'different . . . different')
ali-us ac different from; other than
alō 3 *aluī altum* feed, nourish, rear; support, sustain, cherish; strengthen
alter alter-a um one (or other) of two; *alter . . . alter* (any)one . . . (any) other
alt-us a um high; deep

ambō (nom.) both
ambulō 1 walk
amīciti-a ae 1f friendship
amīc-us ī 2m. friend, ally (adj. friendly)
āmittō 3 *āmīsī āmissum* lose, let go
amō 1 love, like
amor amōr-is 3m. love; pl. girl-friend, sexual
    intercourse
amplector 3 dep. *amplexus* embrace
an = ne = ? (in direct questions); whether, if,
    or (in indirect questions: + subj. = *num);*
    (on its own) or, it can be that
anim-a ae 1f. soul, spirit, breath
anim-us ī 2m. mind, spirit, heart, soul; pl.
    anim-ī high spirits, pride, courage
ann-us ī 2m. year
ante (+ acc.) before, in front of; (adv.) earlier,
    before
anteā (adv.) before, formerly
antr-um ī 2n. cave
appellō 1 address; name, call
appropinquō 1 (+ dat.) approach, draw near to
apud (+ acc.) at the house of, in the hands of,
    in the works of
aqu-a ae 1f. water
ār-a ae 1f. altar
arbitror 1 dep. think, consider; give judgement
arbor arbor-is 3f. tree
arbore-us a um of/from trees
arc-us ūs 4m. arch; bow
ardeō 2 *arsī arsum* burst into flames
ardu-us a um looking upwards; steep, difficult;
    tall, high
argent-um ī 2n. silver; silver-plate; money
arid-us a um dry, parched
arm-a ōrum 2n. pl. arms; tools; armed men
ars art-is 3f. skill, art, accomplishment
art-us ūs 4m. limb
aru-um ī 2n. field
arx arc-is 3f. citadel, stronghold
Asi-a ae 1f. Asia Minor
asper asper-a um rough, harsh
at but; mind you; you say
atque (or *ac*) and, and also, and even
attul-: see adferō
auctor -is 3m. originator
auctōritās auctōritāt-is 3f. weight, authority
audāci-a ae 1f. boldness, cockiness, daring
audāx audāc-is brave, bold, daring, resolute
audeō 2 semi-dep. *ausus* dare

audiō 4 hear, listen to
auferō auferre abstulī ablātum take away, carry
    off (X acc. from Y dat.)
aur-a ae 1f. breeze, wind
aure-us a um golden
aurīg-a ae 1m. charioteer
aur-is is 3f. ear
Aurōr-a ae 1f. Dawn
aur-um ī 2n. gold
aus-: see audeō
aut or
aut . . . aut either . . . or
autem but, however, moreover (2nd word)
auxili-um ī 2n. help, aid

B

Bacch-us ī 2m. the god Dionysus/Bacchus
bell-um ī 2n. war
bellum gerō wage war
bell-us a um pretty, beautiful, handsome,
    charming
bene well, thoroughly, rightly; good! fine!
    (comp. *melius*; sup. *optimē*)
bibō 3 *bibī* drink
bland-us a um coaxing, flattering, charming
bon-us a um good, brave, fit, honest (comp.
    melior; sup. *optimus*)
brācchi-um ī 2n. arm, fore-arm
breu-is e short, brief, small

C

cadō 3 *cecidī cāsum* fall; die
caed-ēs is 3f. slaughter, blood
caelest-is e in the heavens; (as a noun) gods
cael-um ī 2n. sky, heavens
calamitās calamitāt-is 3f. disaster, calamity,
    misfortune
calēscō 3 *caluī* become hot, excited (with
    desire)
candid-us a um white; bright, shining,
    beautiful
candor -is 3m. radiance, whiteness
capill-us ī 2m. hair
capiō 3/4 *cēpī captum* take, capture, seize, get
captō 1 try to get hold of, snatch at
caput capit-is 3n. head; source, fount
carpō 3 *carpsī carptum* pick, harvest; take;
    plunder; weaken, consume

cās-us ūs 4m. outcome; event, occurrence; accident, chance; disaster, death

caud-a ae 1f. tail

caueō 2 *cāuī cautum* be wary, beware, avoid; take precautions lest (*nē*)

caus-a ae 1f. case, situation; reason; cause (often for complaint); *causā* (+ gen. – which precedes it) for the sake of

cecid-: see *cadō*

cēdō 3 *cess-ī cess-um* yield (to), step aside; withdraw; come to an end; go

celer celer-is celer-e swift, quick, rapid

celeritās celeritāt-is 3f. speed, swiftness

celeriter quickly

cēn-a ae 1f. dinner

centum 100

cēp-: see *capiō*

cēr-a ae 1f. wax

cernō 3 *crēuī crētum* discern, perceive

certē without doubt, certainly

cert-us a um sure, certain, definite, reliable

ceru-us ī 2m. stag

cēter-ī ae a the rest, the others

cingō 3 *cīnxī cinctum* surround, encircle, gird up; pass. be situated, lie round

cinis ciner-is 3m./f. ashes

circumdō 1 surround, put X (acc.) round Y (dat.)

cīuis cīu-is 3m. and f. citizen

cīuitās cīuitāt-is 3f. state, citizenship

clāmō 1 shout, cry out to/for

clār-us a um famous, well-known, renowned, illustrious; clear, bright

claudō 3 *clausī clausum* close, enclose, trap

coeō coīre gather, come together; be united (often sexually)

coepī (perf. form: past part. act./pass. *coeptus*) began

cognit-: see *cognōscō*

cognōscō 3 *cognōuī cognitum* get to know, examine, become acquainted with; learn; recognise (perf. tense = know, plup. = knew, fut. perf. = shall know)

cōgō 3 *coēgī coāctum* force, compel; gather

colligō 3 *collēgī collēctum* collect, gather; gain, acquire

coll-um ī 2n. neck

colō 3 *coluī cultum* worship; cherish; cultivate, till; inhabit; care for (one's looks)

color -is 3m. colour, tinge, hue

com-a ae 1f. hair

comes comit-is 3m. comrade, companion

committō 3 *commīsī commissum* commit, entrust

commūn-is e shared in, common, general, universal

comparō 1 prepare, provide, get ready, get

condō 3 *condidī conditum* hide, bury; build, found; compose; preserve

cōnfiteor 2 dep. *cōnfessus* confess, acknowledge, reveal

cōniciō 3/4 *coniēcī coniectum* throw, hurl; put together, conjecture

coniunx coniug-is 3f. wife, spouse

cōnor 1 dep. try, attempt

cōnseruō 1 keep safe, preserve, maintain

cōnsili-um ī 2n. plan, purpose; advice; judgement

cōnsistō 3 *cōnstitī* stop, stand one's ground, take one's place; freeze; depend on

cōnspiciō 3/4 *cōnspexī cōnspectum* catch sight of, see, observe

cōnstit-: see *cōnsistō*

cōnsul cōnsul-is 3m. consul

contingō 3 *contigī* happen (to + dat.), come in touch/contact with

contrā (+ acc.) against

cōnūbi-um ī 2n. marriage, right to marry

conuocō 1 summon, call together

cōpi-a ae 1f. control over, use of (X gen.) for sexual purposes; plenty

cōpi-ae ārum 1f. pl. troops

corn-ū ūs 4n. wing (of army); horn

corpus corpor-is 3n. body

cotīdiē daily

crēber crēbr-a um frequent, numerous; thick, close

crēdō 3 *crēdidī crēditum* believe in (+ dat.); entrust (X acc. to Y dat.); accept as true (+ acc.)

crēscō 3 *crēuī crētum* grow, be born, increase, swell, advance

crīmen crīmin-is 3n. charge; scandal, offence

crīnis crīn-is 3m. hair

croce-us a um yellow

crūdēl-is e cruel

cruor -is 3m. gore, blood, bloodshed

cui dat. s. of *quī/quis*

cuidam dat. s. of *quīdam*

cuiquam dat. of *quisquam*

cuius gen. s. of *qui/quis*

cuiusdam gen. s. of *quidam*

culp-a ae 1f. fault; blame; scandal

culpō 1 blame, find fault

cum (+ abl.) with; (+ subj.) when; since; although; (+ ind.) whenever

cūnctor 1 dep. delay; hesitate (+ inf.)

cūnct-us a um all

cupiditās cupiditāt-is 3f. lust, greed, avarice, passion, desire, longing

cupiō 3/4 *cupiuī cupītum* desire, wish, long for, yearn for; want desperately

cūr why?

cūr-a ae 1f. care; attention, thought of; worry, concern, anxiety, caution

cūrō 1 look after, care for, attend to; heal; see to it that

currō 3 *cucurrī cursum* run

curr-us ūs 4m. chariot

curs-us ūs 4m. running, race; course; direction; voyage

curu-us a um curved, bending, winding

custōs custōd-is 3m. and f. guard, guardian

D

dat-: see *dō*

dē (+ abl.) about, concerning; from, down from; made from, of

de-a ae 1f. goddess

dēbeō 2 ought, must (+ inf.); owe

decim-us a um tenth

dēcipiō 3/4 *dēcēpī dēceptum* deceive, trick

decor decōr-is 3m. beauty, grace, charm; skill

ded-: see *dō*

dēfendō 3 *dēfendī dēfēnsum* defend, ward off, protect

deinde then, next

dēleō 2 *dēlēuī dēlētum* destroy, wipe out, erase

dēnique finally; in a word

dēprendō 3 *dēprēndī dēprēnsum* catch out, catch red-handed (often *dēprehendō*)

dēscendō 3 *dēscendī dēscensum* descend, go down

dēsum dēesse to be unforthcoming; offer no (more) access to; lack, fail (+ dat.)

dēui-us a um remote, out of the way

de-us ī 2m. god (nom. pl. *deī* or *dī*) god

dexter dextr-a um right; favourable; *dext(e)r-a ae* 1f. right hand

dī nom. pl. of *deus*

Diān-a ae 1f. Diana (Artemis), goddess of chastity and the hunt

dīc imper. s. of *dīcō*

dīcō 3 *dīxī dictum* speak, say, tell, name

dict-um ī 2n. word, saying

diēs diē-ī 5m. and f. day

difficil-is e difficult, hard, troublesome

diffīdō 3 mistrust, distrust

digit-us ī 2m. finger

dignitās dignitāt-is 3f. distinction, position; honour; rank, high office

dign-us a um worthy; worthy of (+ abl.); worthy to (+ inf.)

dīligēns dīligent-is careful, diligent

dīligenti-a ae 1f. care, diligence

dīligō 3 *dīlēxī dīlēctum* love, esteem

dīmittō 3 *dīmīsī dīmissum* send away, release, direct

discēdō 3 *discessī discessum* depart, go away

distō 1 be distant from (+ abl.)

diū for a long time; comp. *diūtius*; sup. *diūtissimē*

dīuiti-ae ārum 1f. pl. riches, wealth

dīu-us a um divine; as noun, god(dess)

dō 1 *dedī datum* give, grant, permit ('grant X to' + inf.)

doct-us a um skilled (in X: abl.); learned, taught, skilled

doleō 2 suffer pain, grieve; be stung

dolor dolōr-is 3m. pain, anguish, grief

domī at home

domin-us ī 2m. master, lord

domō from home

domum to home, homewards

dom-us ūs 4f. (irr.) house, home

dōnec until

dōn-um ī 2n. gift

dormiō 4 sleep

dubitō 1 doubt; hesitate (+ inf.)

dūc imper. s. of *dūcō*

dūcō 3 *dūxī ductum* lead; shape; draw out, continue; descend from; extend, prolong; think, consider; acquire, take on

dulc-is e sweet, pleasant agreeable

dum (+ indic.) while; (+ indic./subj.) until; (+ subj.) provided that (also *dummodo, modo*)

duo duae duo two

dūr-us a um hard, tough, robust, harsh, severe, strict

dux duc-is 3m. leader, guide, general
dūx-: see *dūcō*

E

ē (+ abl.) out of, from (also *ex*)
eā abl. s. f. of *is*
ea nom. s. f. or nom./acc. pl. n. of *is*
eādem abl. s. f. of *īdem*
eadem nom. s. f. or nom./acc. pl. n. of *īdem*
eae nom. pl. f. of *is*
eam acc. s. f. of *is*
eandem acc. s. f. of *īdem*
eārum gen. pl. f. of *īdem*
eās acc. pl. f. of *is*
eāsdem acc. pl. f. of *īdem*
ecce behold! look!
ecquis: '[Is] anyone?'
ēdūcō 3 *ēdūxī ēductum* lead out, bring out
efficiō 3/4 *effēcī effectum* bring about (that, *ut* + subj.); cause, make; complete
effugiō 3/4 *effūgī* escape, feel from, away
ēg-: see *agō*
egeō 2 lack, need, be in want of (+ abl. or gen.)
ego I
ēgredior 3/4 dep. *ēgressus* go/come out, depart
ēgress-: see *ēgredior*
ēheu (cf. *heu*) a cry of anguish
eī dat. s. or nom. pl. m. of *is*
eīs dat./abl. pl. of *is*
eius gen. s. of *is*
enim for, in fact, truly (2nd word)
eō īre iī itum go/come
eōdem abl. s. m. or n. of *īdem*
eōrum gen. pl. of *is*
eōs acc. pl. m. of *is*
eōsdem acc. pl. m. of *īdem*
eques equit-is 3m. horseman; pl. cavalry; 'knight' (member of the Roman business class)
equitāt-us ūs 4m. cavalry
equus ī 2m. horse
ergō therefore; well then, so then
ēripiō 3/4 *ēripuī ēreptum* snatch (from, + dat.), wrench away, rescue
errō 1 be wrong; wander
error -is 3m. mistake, deviation; delusion; dead end
et and; also, too; even; *et . . .et* both . . . and
etiam still, even, as well; yes indeed

etsī although, even though, even if
ex (or *ē*) (+ abl.) out of, from
excipiō 3/4 *excēpī exceptum* sustain; take, receive; welcome; catch; make an exception of
exeō exīre exiī set out, leave; go beyond, exceed
exercit-us ūs 4m. army
exigu-us a um narrow, small, light, dim
exiti-um ī 2n. death, destruction
exsili-um ī 2n. exile
exspectō 1 await, wait for
extrēm-us a um furthest, outermost, last, extreme

F

fābul-a ae 1f. story; play
fac imper. s. of *faciō*
faci-ēs -ēī 5f. looks, appearance, sight, beauty, face
facil-is e easy, agreeable, affable; superl. *facillimus*
faciō 3/4 *fēcī factum* make, do, accomplish
fact-: see *fīō*
fact-um ī 2n. deed, act, achievement
fallō 3 *fefellī falsum* cheat, deceive; disappoint; fail, beguile (of time); go unnoticed by
fals-us a um fake, counterfeit, deceptive
fām-a ae 1f. rumour, report; reputation
famili-a ae 1f. household
fās, indecl., n., right, sacred duty; fitting, lawful
fāt-um ī 2n. fate, destiny, death
fēc-: see *faciō*
fēmin-a ae 1f. woman
fēmine-us a um woman's, feminine, female
fer imper. s. of *ferō*
fer-a ae 1f. wild animal
ferē almost, nearly, generally
ferō ferre tulī lātum bear, suffer, endure; bring, carry away/off; lead; *ferunt* can mean 'they say'; *fertur* can mean 'he/she/it is said'
ferr-um ī 2n. sword; iron
fer-us a um savage, wild
fess-us a um tired
festīnō 1 hurry
fidēs fid-ēī 5f. loyalty, honour; trust, faith; promise, pledge; protection; fulfilment (of a promise)
figō 3 *fīxī fīxum* pierce, transfix; attach, plant
figūr-a ae 2f. beauty, shape, appearance

fīli-a ae 1f. daughter
fīli-us ī 2m. son
finiō 4 end, finish
fin-is is 3f. end
fīō fierī factum become; be done, be made (passive of *faciō*)
firmō 1 reinforce, strengthen, confirm
flamm-a ae 1f. flame (often of passion)
flāu-us a um yellow, blonde (-haired)
flectō 3 *flexī flexum* bend, curve, avert, steer
fleō 2 *flēuī flētum* weep
flōs flōr-is 3m. flower
flūmen flūmin-is 3n. river
fōns font-is 3m. spring, fountain, flowing water; source
fore = futūrum esse to be about to be; *fore ut* (+ subj.) that it will/would turn out that
fōrm-a ae 1f. shape, looks; beauty
fōrmō 1 shape, form, mould
fors fort-is 3f. chance, luck, destiny (usually only in nom. or abl. *forte*, 'by chance')
fortasse perhaps
fort-is e brave, courageous, strong
fortūn-a ae 1f. good or bad fortune, luck, chance; pl. wealth
fortunāt-us a um fortunate, lucky, happy
for-um ī 2n. forum (main business centre)
frāter frātr-is 3m. brother
frēnum ī 2n. rein, control
frōns front-is 3f. forehead
frūstrā in vain
fu-: see *sum*
fug-a ae 1f. flight
fugāx fugāc-is fleeting
fugiō 3/4 *fūgī fugitūrus* escape, run off, flee, avoid, shun; fall away
fugō 1 put to flight, rout
fulgeō 2 *fulsī* shine, flash
fulmen fulmin-is 3n. thunderbolt
fūmō 1 smoke
fundō 3 *fūdī fūsum* pour
furor furōr-is 3m. rage, fury; madness; mad passion (often pl.)
fūrtim secretly

G

gaudeō 2 semi-dep. *gāuisum* find pleasure, rejoice, be happy in (+ gen./abl.)
gaudi-um ī 2n. joy, delight, pleasure

gelid-us a um cold
gemin-us a um twin, double
gemit-us ūs 4m. groan
gemm-a ae 1f. gem
gēns gent-is 3f. tribe, clan; race; family; people, nation
genu gen-ūs 4n. knee
genus gener-is 3n. family; stock; tribe; type, kind
gerō 3 *gessī gestum* do, conduct, carry on; manage; accomplish, perform; reveal, show; wear
gladi-us ī 2m. sword
glōri-a ae 1f. glory, renown, fame
Graec-us a um Greek
grāti-a ae 1f. thanks, favour, recompense
grātiās/grātēs agō (+ dat.) thank
grāt-us a um pleasing (to X, dat.), welcome
grau-is e serious, important, weighty; heavy; severe
grauitās grauitāt-is 3f. weight; seriousness; solemnity; importance, authority

H

habēn-a ae 1f. rein
habeō 2 have; hold, regard
haereō 2 *haesī haesum* cling (on/to), be fixed to; stay put; persist; doubt, hesitate
haud not, not at all (strong negative)
herb-a ae 1f. herb, plant, grass
hēu alas!
hīc haec hoc this; this person, thing; pl. these; he/she/it, they; the latter
hīc here
hinc from here
hodiē today
homo homin-is 3m. man, human being, fellow
honor honōr-is 3m. respect, esteem; (mark of) honour; public office
hōr-a ae 1f. hour
hortor 1 dep. urge, encourage
hospes hospit-is 3m. host; friend; guest; connection
hostis host-is 3m. enemy (of the state)
hūc (to) here
humī on the ground
humō on, from the ground
hum-us ī 2f. earth, soil, ground

I

ī imper. s. of *eō*

i-: see *eō*

iaceō 2 lie, lie prostrate/dead

iaciō 3/4 *iēcī iactum* throw (away), hurl; pile up

iam now, by now, already; presently

iānu-a ae 1f. door

ibi there

īdem eadem idem the same

igitur therefore

ignār-us a um ignorant, unaware

ignis ign-is 3m. fire

ignōrō 1 be ignorant, not know

ignōscō 3 *ignōuī ignōtum* forgive, pardon, overlook (+ dat.)

ille ill-a illud that; that person, thing; pl. those; the former; the famous; he/she/it, they

illīc there

illinc from there; from that/one point of view

imāgō imāgin-is 3f. image, guise; reflection; portrayal

imitor 1 dep. imitate

immēns-us a um immeasurable

impedīment-um ī 2n. hindrance

impediō 4 prevent, impede, hinder

imperātor imperātōr-is 3m. leader, general, commander

imperi-um ī 2n. order, command; power (to command), authority; control; dominion

imperō 1 give orders (to), command (+ dat.: often followed by *ut/nē* + subj. 'to/not to')

impleō 2 *implēuī implētum* fill

imprīmīs see *in prīmīs*

in (+ acc.) into, onto; (+ abl.) in, on; (+ acc.) against

in dubiō = in doubt; *dubi-us a um* uncertain, doubtful, ambiguous

in prīmīs especially

incalēscō 3 *incaluī* become hot, excited (with desire)

incendi-um ī 2n. fire, conflagration

incert-us a um uncertain, doubtful, unpredictable

inde from there, as a result, from then on

indūcō 3 *indūxī indūctum* draw X (acc.) over Y (dat.)

ineō inīre iniī initum enter

infect-us a um stained, tinged

infēlix infēlic-is unhappy, unfortunate

ingeminō 1 repeat, reiterate, intensify

ingeni-um ī 2n. talent, ability

ingēns ingent-is huge, large, lavish

inimīc-us a um hostile, personal enemy

inquam say (*inquis, inquit; inquiunt*)

īnsequor 3 dep. *īnsecūtus* follow, pursue

īnstituō 3 *īnstituī īnstitūtum* begin, establish; construct; resolve

integer integr-a um whole, untouched

intellegō 3 *intellēxī intellēctum* perceive, understand, comprehend, grasp

inter (+ acc.) among; between

intereā meanwhile

interficiō 3/4 *interfēcī interfectum* kill

intrō 1 enter

inueniō 4 *inuēnī inuentum* find

inuideō 2 *inuīdī inuīsum* envy, begrudge (+ dat.)

inuīt-us a um unwilling(ly)

ioc-us ī 2m. joke, joking, fun

Iou-: see *Iuppiter*

ipse ips-a ips-um very, actual, self

īr-a ae 1f. anger, rage, wrath

īrāscor 3 dep. *īrātus* grow angry (with X: dat.)

īrāt-us a um angry

irrit-us a um undone, vain

is ea id that; he/she/it

iste ist-a istud that of yours

it-: see *eō*

ita so, thus; yes

Ītali-a ae 1f. Italy

itaque and so, therefore

iter itiner-is 3n. journey, route

iterum again

iubeō 2 *iussī iussum* order, command, tell

iūcund-us a um pleasant, agreeable, gratifying

iūdex iūdic-is 3m. judge, juror

iūdicō 1 judge

iug-um ī 2n. yoke

iungō 3 *iūnxī iūnctum* join (often 'in marriage' or 'sexually')

Iūnō -nis 3f. Juno (Greek Hera), wife of Jupiter

Iuppiter Iou-is 3m. Jupiter, Jove

iūrgi-um ī 2n. abuse, insult

iūs iūrand-um iūr-is iūrand-ī 3n. oath

iūs iūr-is 3n. law, justice, right, bond, obligation

iuss-: see *iubeō*

iussū by the order (of X: gen.)

iuss-um ī 2n. injunction, order, command

iūst-us a um just, righteous, proper, lawful, fair
iuuat it pleases
iuuenc-a ae 1f. cow, heifer; *iuuenc-us ī* 2m. bull
iuuen-is iuuen-is 3m. young man
iuuō 1 *iūuī iūtum* please; help, assist

L

lābor 3 dep. *lāpsus* slip, glide, fall down; make a mistake
labor labōr-is 3m. toil, effort, hard work; trouble, hardship, suffering
lacert-us ī 2m. (upper) arm, embrace
lacrim-a ae 2f. tear
laedō 3 *laesī laesum* wound, hurt, injure, annoy
laet-us a um joyful, happy
lateō 2 lie hidden, be covered, hide
Latin-us a um Latin
lāt-us a um wide, broad; *lātē* (adv.) broadly, widely
laudō 1 praise
laus laud-is 3f. reputation, praise, merit, renown
lect-us ī 2m. couch; bed
lēgāt-us ī 2m. commander, ambassador, deputy
legiō legiōn-is 3f. legion
legō 3 *lēgī lēctum* read; select, choose; traverse
leu-is e light, trivial, capricious, inconstant
leuō 1 relieve, lighten, raise, lift, undo
lēx lēg-is 3f. law, statute, control; terms, conditions
liber liber-a um free
liber-ī ōrum 2m. pl. children
liberō 1 free, release
lībertās libertāt-is 3f. freedom, liberty
licet 2 it is permitted (to X dat. to Y inf.); that X should (subj.)
lingu-a ae 1f. tongue; language
līn-um ī 2n. net, thread, cord
liquid-us a um clear, fluid
litter-ae ārum 1f. pl. letter(s); literature
loc-us ī 2m. place; birthplace; passage in literature; pl. *loc-a ōrum* 2n.
locūt-: see *loquor*
longē far
long-us a um long
loquor 3 dep. *locūtus* be speaking, say
lōr-um ī 2n. rein

luct-us ūs 4m. cause of grief, mourning, lamentation
lūdō 3 *lūsī lūsum* play; tantalise; trick, deceive, make a fool of
lūmen lūmin-is 3n. eye, light
lūn-a ae 1f. moon
lūx lūc-is 3f. light

M

maest-us a um anguished, unhappy
magis more, rather
magnopere greatly (comp. *magis*; sup. *maximē*)
magn-us a um great, large, important (comp. *māior*; sup. *maximus*)
māior māiōr-is greater, bigger
mālō mālle māluī prefer (X *quam* Y)
mal-um ī 2n. trouble, evil
mal-us a um bad, evil, wicked (comp. *pēior*; sup. *pessimus*); *male* badly
maneō 2 *mānsī mānsum* remain, wait, continue, stay
man-us ūs 4f. hand; touch; band
mare mar-is 3n. sea (abl. *marī*)
margō margin-is 3m. edge, border
marīt-us a um married; husband; *marīta* wife
mātern-us a um maternal, mother's
maximus see *magnus*
mē acc. or abl. of *ego*
meditor 1 dep. think, ponder on, devise; practise (*meditātus* is often used in a passive sense)
medi-us a um middle (of)
melior meliōr-is better (see *bonus*)
membr-um ī 2n. limb
meminī (perfect form) remember (usually + gen.)
memor memor-is remembering (X: gen.); mindful of (X: gen.)
memori-a ae 1f. remembering, memory, recollection; record
mēns ment-is 3f. mind, thought, intention; sanity, resolve
mergō 3 *mersī mersum* plunge, bury, overwhelm
mēt-a ae 1f. turning-point, a metaphor from racing chariots round a track; in the case of the sun, its two *mētae* are East and West
metuō 3 *metuī metutum* fear

met-us ūs 4m. fear, terror

me-us a um my, mine (voc. s. m. *mī*)

mī = *mihi* (dat. s. of *ego*)

mī voc. s. m. of *meus*

mihi dat. s. of *ego*

mīles mīlit-is 3m. soldier

mīlitār-is e military

mīlle 1,000 (pl. *mīlia*)

minim-us a um smallest, fewest, least (see *paruus*)

minor minōr-is smaller, fewer, less (see *paruus*)

minus less (adv.); less of (+ gen.)

mīrābil-is e admirable, wonderful, amazing

mīror 1 dep. wonder, be amazed at

mīr-us a um amazing, wonderful

mīs-: see *mittō*

miser miser-a um miserable, unhappy, wretched

miserābil-is e pitiful

miss-: see *mittō*

mittō 3 *mīsī missum* send; throw

mixt-us a um mixed (*misceō*)

modo now, just now; only, after all

mod-us ī 2m. way, fashion, manner; measure, bound, limit

molliō 4 soften, calm, weaken, appease, allay, tame

moll-is e soft, tender, gentle; pleasant; weak

moneō 2 advise, warn

monit-a ōrum 2n. pl. advice, warning, precepts

mōns mont-is 3m. mountain

mor-a ae 1f. delay

morior 3/4 dep. *mortuus* die, be dying

mortāl-is e mortal, human

mōs mōr-is 3m. way, habit, custom; pl. character

mōt-: see *moueō*

moueō 2 *mōuī mōtum* remove (from: abl.); move; cause, begin

mox soon

mulier mulier-is 3f. woman, wife

multum (adv.) much

mult-us a um much, many

mūnus mūner-is 3n. gift; duty, function, office; purpose

mūtō 1 change, alter, exchange

N

Nāis Nāid-is 3f. water nymph

nam for

nam moreover, again (indicating a transition)

nārrō 1 tell, relate

nāscor 3 dep. *nātus* be born, arise, come into being, be suited; *nāt-us a um* can = (X years) old; son/daughter of (+ abl.), e.g. *Ioue nātus* son of/born from Jupiter; *nāta* daughter, etc.

nātūr-a ae 1f. nature

nāuigō 1 sail

nāuis nāu-is 3f. ship

naut-a ae 1m. sailor

nē (+ subj.) 'not to', 'that x should not . . .'; 'lest', 'in order that not', 'in order not to. . .'; 'that', 'lest'; (+ perf. subj.) 'don't'

-ne (added to the first word of a sentence) = ?

nē . . . quidem not even (emphasising the enclosed word)

nē . . . quidem not even (emphasising the word in between)

nē quis 'that no one'; 'in order that no one . . .'

nec and . . . not; neither; nor

necesse est it is necessary, inevitable (for X dat. to Y inf.)

necō 1 kill

nefās n. wrong, crime, sacrilege, horror

neglegō 3 *neglēxī neglēctum* ignore, overlook, neglect

negō 1 deny, say that X is not the case (acc. + inf.)

nēmō nēmin-is 3m. no one, nobody

nemus nemor-is 3n. wood, forest, grove

nepōs nepōt-is 3m./f. grandchild

neque and . . . not; neither; nor (also *nec*)

nesciō 4 do not know

nesci-us a um ignorant (of)

neu = *nēue*

nēue (+ subj.) 'and not to', 'and that X should not . . .', 'and in case'

niger nigr-a um black, dark

nihil (indecl. n.) nothing

nīl nothing

nimis too much (of X: gen.)

nimium too (much); too much (of X: gen.)

nimi-us a um excessive

nisi unless, if . . . not: except

noceō 2 harm, injure (+ dat.)

nōlī (+ inf.) do not

nōlō nōlle nōluī refuse, be unwilling (+ inf.)

nōmen nōmin-is 3n. name

nōn not

nōndum not yet

nōnne surely?

nōnnūll-us -a um some, several

nōn-us a um ninth

nōs we

nōscō 3 *nōuī nōtum* get to know (perfect tenses = know)

nōsse(t)=nōuisse(t)

noster nostr-a um our(s)

nōt-us a um usual, well-known, familiar

nōu-: see *nōscō*

nou-us a um new, recent, last

nox noct-is 3f. night

nūbil-um ī 2n. cloud, mist

nūd-us a um naked

nūll-us a um no, none, not any; of no value (gen. s. *nūllīus;* dat. s. *nūllī*)

num surely . . . not?; (+ subj.) whether (indirect question)

nūmen nūmin-is 3n. power, divinity

numer-us ī 2m. number

numquam never

nunc now

nūntiō 1 announce, proclaim

nūnti-us ī 2m. messenger

nūper recently

nymph-a ae 1f. (and *nymph-ē*) young woman; semi-divine female spirit

O

obdūrō 1 be firm, hold out, persist

obscūr-us a um obscured, dark, unrecognised

occāsiō occāsiōn-is 3f. opportunity

occidō 3 *occidī occāsum* fall, die, set (of the sun)

occīdō 3 *occīdī occīsum* kill, cut down, slay

occupō 1 seize, take

ocul-us ī 2m. eye

offici-um ī 2n. duty, service, job

omittō 3 *omīsī omissum* give up; let fall; omit, leave aside

omnīnō altogether, completely, wholly, altogether

omn-is e all, every; *omnia* everything

onus oner-is 3n. load, burden

oper-a ae 1f. attention; service, work, help

opēs, op-um 3f. pl. power, resources, wealth

oportet 2 it is right/fitting for X (acc.) to Y (inf.), X (acc.) ought to Y (inf.)

opportūn-us a um strategic, suitable, favourable, advantageous

oppress-: see *opprimō*

opprimō 3 *oppressī oppressum* surprise; catch; crush, overpower

oppugnō 1 attack, assault

ops op-is 3f. help, aid

optim-us a um best (see *bonus*)

optō 1 wish

opus oper-is 3n. job, work, task, deed; effect; fortification; matter, stuff

ōrācul-um ī 2n. oracle

ōrātiō ōrātiōn-is 3f. speech

orb-is is 3m physical world; orb; course (of the sun); ball (of wool); wheel

ōrdō ōrdin-is 3m. rank, class (i.e. section of society or line of soldiers); order

orīgō orīgin-is 3f. birth, origin, line of descent

orior 4 dep. *ortus* rise, proceed; begin, spring from, originate

ōrō 1 beg, pray, entreat

ōs ōr-is 3n. face; mouth; often used in pl. *ōra*

os oss-is 3n. bone

ōscul-um ī 2n. little mouth, i.e. (usually) kiss

ostendō 3 *ostendī ostēnsum* (or *ostentum*) show, reveal, exhibit, display

ōti-um ī 2n. cessation of conflict; leisure, inactivity

ouis ou-is 3f. sheep

P

paelex paelic-is 3f. mistress

palam openly, plainly

par par-is equal, like

parcō 3 *pepercī parsūrus* spare, be lenient to (+ dat.); take care not (to)

parēns parent-is 3m. father, parent; f. mother

pāreō 2 obey (+ dat.)

pariō 3/4 *peperī partum* bring forth, bear, produce; obtain, acquire

pariter equally

parō 1 prepare (for), get ready; provide, obtain

pars part-is 3f. part; side

paru-us a um small (comp. *minor;* sup. *minimus*)

pass-us ūs 4m. step, stride, pace

pastōr -is 3m. shepherd

patefaciō 3/4 *patefēcī patefactum* reveal, expose, disclose, throw open *pater patr-is* 3m. father

patern-us a um father's, paternal

patior 3/4 *passum* endure, suffer; allow, permit

patri-a ae 1f. fatherland

patri-us a um paternal, of one's father

pauc-ī ae a a few

paueō 2 be frightened, fear; tremble

pauid-us a um terror-struck, fearful

pauper pauper-is 3m. poor man; (adj.) poor, cheap, meagre

pāx pāc-is 3f. peace; *pāce* with the permission of

pectus pector-is 3n. breast, chest, heart

pecūni-a ae 1f. money

pēior pēiōr-is worse (see *malus*)

pendeō 2 *pependī* hang (down); hang on, be uncertain; depend on

penn-a ae 1f. feather, wing

peper-: see *pariō*

per (+ acc.) through; in the name of

percutiō 3/4 *percussī percussum* beat, strike

perdō 3 *perdidī perditum* lose; destroy, ruin

pereō perīre periī peritum perish, die

perferō perferre pertulī perlātum endure (to the end); complete; carry to; announce

perficiō 3/4 *perfēcī perfectum* finish, complete, carry out; *perficiō ut* (+ subj.) bring it about that

perfundō 3 bathe

peri-: see *pereō*

perīcul-um ī 2n. danger

perit-: see *pereō*

perscrībō 3 *perscrīpsī perscrīptum* write in detail, put on record

persequor 3 dep. *persecūtus* pursue, follow after, take vengeance on

persuādeō 2 *persuāsī persuāsum* persuade (+ dat.) (to/not to *ut/nē* + subj.)

pertimēscō 3 *pertimuī* be afraid of

perueniō 4 *peruēnī peruentum* reach, arrive at, come to (*ad* + acc.)

pēs ped-is 3m. foot

pessim-us a um worst (see *malus*)

petō 3 *petīuī petītum* beg; seek; proposition, court; attack, make for; stand for (public office)

pharetr-a ae 1f. quiver

Phoeb-us ī 2m. Phoebus ('bright, shining'), i.e. Apollo; also used of the sun

pi-us a um holy, dutiful, faithful, just

placeō 2 *placuī placitum* I please (+ dat.)

placet 2 it is pleasing (to X dat. to Y inf.); X (dat.) votes/agrees/resolves (to Y inf.);

plānē clearly

plangō 3 *planxī* mourn; beat

plēn-us a um full (of) (+ gen. or abl.)

plūrim-us a um most, very much (see *multus*)

plūs plūr-is 3n. more; more

poen-a ae 1f. penalty, punishment

pondus ponder-is 3n. weight

pōnō 3 *posuī positus* place, position, set up; lay/put aside (= *dēpōnō*)

pōns pont-is 3m. bridge

pont-us ī 2m. sea

popul-us ī 2m. people, a people, nation

porrigō 3 *porrēxī porrēctum* offer, stretch

posit-: see *pōnō*

possideō 2 *possēd-ī possess-um* hold, possess

possum posse potuī be able, can; be powerful, have power (+ adv.)

post (adv.) afterwards, later; (+ acc.) behind, after

posteā afterwards

postquam (conjunction) after

posu-: see *pōnō*

pot-: see *possum*

potēns potent-is powerful

potenti-a ae 1f. power

potior 4 dep. control; gain control of (+ gen., abl.)

potius quam rather than

potu-: see *possum*

praebeō 2 supply, provide, lend

praeceps praecipit-is headlong

praeclār-us a um very famous, outstanding, brilliant

praeficiō 3/4 *praefēcī praefectum* put (X acc.) in charge of (Y dat.)

praemi-um ī 2n. reward, prize

praesum praeesse praefuī be in charge of (+ dat.)

praetereō praeterīre praeteriī praeteritum pass by, over; overtake; neglect, omit

prec-ēs -um 3f. pl. prayers

precor 1 dep. pray to/for, entreat

premō 3 *pressī pressum* press (on), overlay; press after; oppress; bite on

prīmō at first

prīmum (adv.) first

prīm-us a um first

princeps princip-is 3m. leader, chieftain; (adj.) first

prior -is former, earlier (of two), having prior place, elder

prius (adv.) before, earlier; first

prō (+ abl.) for, in return for; on behalf of; in front of; instead of; in accordance with

probō 1 approve of, prove

procul at a distance

proeli-um ī 2n. battle

proficīscor 3 dep. *profectus* set out

prohibeō 2 prevent, restrain, inhibit, hinder, keep X (acc.) from Y (abl./ā(*ab*) + abl.)

prōiciō 3/4 *prōiēcī prōiectum* throw down, forward

properō 1 hurry, perform/do X in haste

prōpōnō 3 *prōposuī prōpositum* set before; imagine; offer

propter (+ acc.) on account of

prōsum prōdesse prōfuī prōfutūrum be an advantage

prōtinus at once; straight on

prōuideō 2 *prōuidī prōuisum* take care of (that), foresee

proxim-us a um nearest, next

pudor pudōr-is 3m. modesty, sense of shame; cause for shame

puell-a ae 1f. girl

puer puer-ī 2m. boy

pugn-a ae 1f. battle, fight

pugnō 1 fight

pulcher pulchr-a um beautiful; (sup.) *pulcherrimus a um*; (comp.) *pulchrior*

pūniō 4 punish

putō 1 reckon, suppose, judge, think, imagine

Q

quā where, by which route; in what way, how

quadrāgintā 40

quaerō 3 *quaesiuī quaesītum* seek, look for; ask

quam how! (+ adj. or adv.); (after comp.) than

quam prīmum as soon as possible

quamquam although

quamuīs (often + subj.) although; (+ adj.) however

quandō since, when

quant-us a um how much, how great

quārē why?; therefore

quārt-us a um fourth

quasi as if, like

quattuor four

-que (added to the end of the word) and

quemadmodum how

queror 3 dep. *questus* complain (about)

quī- quae- quod- cumque who/which/what-ever

quī quae quod which? what?; who, which; (+ subj.) since (also with *quippe*); (+ subj.) in order that/to

quid what?; why? (see *quis*)

quīdam quaedam quid-/quod-dam a, a certain, some

quidem indeed, certainly, at least, even (places emphasis on the preceding word)

quiēs quiēt-is 3f. sleep, rest

quippe quī (quae quod) inasmuch as he (she, it)

quis qua quid (after *sī*, *nisi*, *nē*, *num*) anyone, anything

quis quid who, what?

quisquam quicquam (after negatives) anyone

quisque quaeque quodque (quidque) each

quisquis quidquid (or *quicquid*) whoever, whatever

quō to where?; whither, to where

quod sī but if

quondam once (upon a time)

quoque also, too

quot how many, as (many as)

quotiēns how often

R

rām-us ī 2m. branch

rapiō 3/4 *rapuī raptum* snatch, seize, rape, carry away, plunder

ratiō ratiōn-is 3f. plan, method; reason; count, list; calculation, judgement, consideration

recēns recent-is fresh, new

recēp-: see *recipiō*

recipiō 3/4 *recēpī receptum* welcome, receive, take in, regain, get back, admit; *mē recipiō* retreat

reddō 3 *reddidī redditum* return, give back, repeat; restore; render (of an artist)

redeō redīre rediī reditum return, go back (intrans.)

redūcō 3 *redūxī reductum* lead/bring back, retract

referō referre rettulī relātum bring/carry/put back (again); tell, answer; record, pay

refugiō 3/4 *refūgī* recoil from

relict-: see *relinquō*

relinquō 3 *relīquī relictum* leave behind, leave, abandon

remaneō 2 *remānsī remānsum* remain, stay behind, continue

remittō 3 *remīsī remissum* let go of, let down; send back, return

remoueō 2 *remōuī remōtum* remove, disperse

reperiō 4 *repperī repertum* find, discover, learn, get

repetō 3 *repetīuī repetītum* return/go back to, recall, repeat, take up again, seek again, attack again

repugn-ō 1 fight against, militate against

requīrō 3 *requīsiuī requīsitum* seek out; ask for; miss, need

rēs pūblic-a rē-ī pūblic-ae state, republic

rēs rē-ī 5f. thing, matter, business, affair; property; affair

resistō 3 *restitī* resist (+ dat.); stand back; halt, pause

respondeō 2 *respondī respōnsum* reply answer

retineō 2 *retinuī retentum* hold back, keep, keep hold of

reuocō 1 call back, ask, ask for

rīm-a ae 1f. crack

rīp-a ae 1f. bank

rogō 1 ask (*ut* + subj.)

Rōm-a ae 1f. Rome (*Rōmae*, locative, at Rome)

Rōmān-us a um Roman

rot-a ae 1f. wheel, i.e. chariot (cf. 'wheels')

rubor rubōr-is 3m. blush, redness, modesty

rūmor rūmōr-is 3m. rumour, (piece of) gossip, unfavourable report

ruō 3 *ruī rutum* run wild(ly), rush headlong; collapse, lay flat

S

sacer sacr-a um holy, sacred

saepe often

saeu-us a um savage, cruel

salūs salūt-is 3f. safety, health; greeting

salu-us a um safe, sound

sanct-us a um sacrosanct, sacred, holy, blessed, upright, pure

sanguis sanguin-is 3m. blood

sapienti-a ae 1f. wisdom

satiō 1 satisfy, fill with

satis enough (of) (+ gen.)

Sāturni-a ae 1f. daughter of Saturn, i.e. Juno

Sāturni-us ī 2m. son of Saturn, i.e. Jupiter

saxum ī 2n. stone, rock

scelus sceler-is 3n. crime, villainy; criminal, villain

sciō 4 know

scrībō 3 *scrīpsī scrīptum* write

sē himself, herself, itself/themselves

sēcum with/to himself/herself

secund-us a um second, favourable

secūt-: see *sequor*

sed but

sedeō 2 *sēdī sessum* seat

semel once

semper always

senāt-us ūs 4m. senate

senex sen-is 3m. old man

sēns-: see *sentiō*

sententi-a ae 1f. opinion; judgement; sentence, vote; maxim

sentiō 4 *sēnsī sēnsum* feel; understand; perceive, realise

septem seven

sepulc(h)r-um ī 2n. tomb, grave

sequor 3 dep. *secūtus* follow

sermō sermōn-is 3m. conversation, discussion

serpēns serpent-is 3m./f. snake (*serpō* crawl)

seruō 1 keep safe, preserve, guard

seru-us ī 2m. slave

sī + impf. subj., impf. subj. 'if X were happening (now), Y would be happening' (sometimes: 'if X had happened, Y would have happened')

sī + plupf. subj., plupf. subj. 'if X had happened, Y would have happened'

sī + pres. subj., pres. subj. 'if X were to happen, Y would happen'

sī if

sīc thus, in this way, so

sīdus sīder-is 3n. star

sign-um ī 2n. seal, signal, sign; statue; standard; trumpet-call

silu-a ae 1f. wood, forest

sim pres. subj. of *sum*

simil-is e alike, similar, like (+ gen.)

simul as soon as, once; together, at the same time

simulācr-um ī 2n. image, likeness

simulō 1 imitate, simulate, disguise oneself as

sine (+ abl.) without

singul-ī ae a individual, one by one

sit-is is 3f. thirst

soci-us ī 2m. ally, friend

sōl sōl-is 3m. sun

soleō 2 semi-dep. *solitum* be accustomed, be used (+ inf.)

solit-: see *soleō*

sollicitō 1 bother, worry; stir up, incite; tempt

sōlum (adv.) only; *nōn sōlum . . . sed etiam* not only . . . but also

soluō 3 *soluī solūtum* unleash, release, let go; cancel; weaken; (of vows) fulfil

sōl-us a um (gen. s. *sōlīus*: dat. s. *sōlī*) alone; lonely

somn-us ī 2m. sleep

son-us ī 2m. sound

soror -is 3f. sister

sors sort-is 3f. oracle, lot, fortune; group chosen by lot, allocation

spars-us a um loose, streaming; scattered (*spargō* 3 *sparsī sparsum* sprinkle, scatter)

spectō 1 look at, observe, see

spērō 1 hope (for); expect

spēs spē-ī 5f. hope(s); expectation

statim at once

stell-a ae 1f. star

stet-: see *stō*

stil-us ī 2m. stylus (for writing in wax)

stō 1 *stetī statum* stand

studi-um ī 2n. enthusiasm, zeal

stult-us a um stupid, foolish, a fool

Stygi-us a um Stygian, of the River Styx; underworld, hellish

suādeō 2 *suāsī suāsum* recommend, urge, advocate

sub (+ abl.) beneath, under, up under, close to; (+ acc.) right up till/into, under cover of

subitō suddenly

sublāt-: see *tollō*

succurrō 3 *succurrī succursum* run to help, assist (+ dat.)

sum esse fuī futūrus be

summ-us a um highest, final; top of

sūmō 3 *sūmpsī sūmptum* take; put on; choose; assume, catch; eat *supplicium sūmō* (*dē* + abl.) exact the penalty (from)

sūmpt-: see *sūmō*

sūmpt-us ūs 4m. expense(s)

super up, i.e. high, tall; *super* + acc., above

super-ī ōrum 2m. powers above, gods; as adj., *super-us a um* upper

superō 1 conquer, overcome; get the upper hand; remain, have yet to run

supersum superesse superfuī remain, be left over, survive (from + dat.)

supplici-um ī 2n. punishment *summum supplicium* the death penalty

supplicium sūmō (*dē* + abl.) exact the penalty (from)

surgō 3 *surrēxī surrēctum* rise, arise, get up

sustineo 2 *sustinuī sustentum* withstand, endure, bear to; stand up to (+ dat.); support; hang up

sustul-: see *tollō*

su-us a um his, hers/theirs

Syrācūs-ae ārum 1f. pl. Syracuse (*Syrācūsīs* at Syracuse)

T

tabell-ae ārum 1f. pl. writing-tablets

taceō 2 be silent, leave unmentioned

tāct-: see *tangō*

tāl-is e of such a kind

tam so, to such a degree

tamen however, but (second word)

tamquam as though

tandem at length

tangō 3 *tetigī tāctum* touch, lay hands on; move, touch the heart of

tantum only

tant-us a um so great, so much, so important

tard-us a um slow, late

tēcum with you/yourself

tegō 3 *tēxī tēctum* cover, hide, protect

tellūs tellūr-is 3f. earth

tēl-um ī 2n weapon

templ-um ī 2n. temple

temptō 1 try out, test, investigate, examine, try

tempus tempor-is 3n. time

tendō 3 *tetendī tēnsum* (*tentum*) stretch out, draw; proceed, reach, aim (at)

teneō 2 *tenuī tentum* hold, hold back; possess, keep; restrain, control; catch (out)

tener -a um delicate

tenu-is e thin, slim, fine, clear

terg-um ī 2n. back, rear, far side

terr-a ae 1f. land

terreō 2 frighten

terti-us a um third

tetig-: see *tangō*

thalam-us ī 2m. marriage (-bed)

timeō 2 fear, be afraid of; (*nē* + subj.) be afraid that/lest

timid-us a um fearful, timid

timor timōr-is 3m. fear

tollō 3 *sustulī sublātum* lift, remove, take away, destroy

tor-us ī 2m. bed, marriage-bed; bolster, mattress

tot so many

totidem the same number of

tōt-us a um (gen. s. *tōtīus*; dat. s. *tōtī*) whole, complete, entire

trādō 3 *trādidī trāditum* hand over, transmit

trahō 3 *trāxī tractum* attract, acquire, bring in one's wake; drag, draw after, carry off; extend

trāns (+ acc.) across

trēdecim thirteen

trēs tri-a three

trīgintā thirty

trīst-is e sad, gloomy, unhappy

tū you (s.)

tul-: see *ferō*

tum then

tumul-us ī 2m. tomb, mound, hill

turb-a ae 1f. crowd, mob, pack; uproar, disturbance

turbō 1 disturb, confuse

turp-is e disgusting, filthy, outrageous, ugly

tūt-us a um safe, protected, secure

tu-us a um your(s) (s.)

U

uacc-a ae 1f. cow

uacu-us a um empty; free (from: + abl. or *ā/ab* + abl.); not busy, unoccupied

uagor 1 dep. wander, roam

ualē(te) goodbye!

ualeō 2 be strong; be well, be powerful; be able; prevail, succeed (cf. *ualē* = 'Farewell!' 'Goodbye!')

uari-us a um diverse, various

uāt-ēs is 3m. prophet, seer; poet, bard

ubi where?; when?

uehemēns uehement-is impetuous, violent, emphatic

uel . . . uel either . . . or;

uel even

uelim pres. subj. of *uolō*

uellem impf. subj. of *uolō*

uēlō 1 veil, cover, conceal

uēlōx uēlōc-is fast, speedy

uelut(ī) like, as if, as

ueniō 4 *uēnī uentum* come, arrive

uent-: see *ueniō*

uent-us ī 2m. wind

Venus Vener-is 3f. the goddess Venus; sex; desire, passion

uerber uerber-is 3n. blow; whip

uerb-um ī 2n. word

uērō indeed, in truth, to be sure

uers-us ūs 4m. verse, line; pl. poetry

uertō 3 *uertī uersum* turn (trans.)

uēr-us a um true

uester uestr-a um your(s) (pl.)

uestīgi-um ī 2n. footstep, footprint, track, walk, trace

uest-is is 3f. clothes, dress; cloth

uetō 1 *uetuī uetitum* forbid

uetus ueter-is old; long-established

ui-a ae 1f. way, road

uīc-: see *uincō*

uīcīn-us ī 2m. neighbour; as adj., nearby, neighbouring

uict-: see *uincō*

uictōri-a ae 1f. victory

uideō 2 *uīdī uīsum* see, observe, understand

uideor 2 passive *uīsum* be seen; seem; (sometimes) seem best

uincō 3 *uīcī uictum* conquer

uīn-um ī 2n. wine

uiolent-us a um savage, excessive

uir uir-ī 2m. man, husband, hero

uirg-a ae 1f. rod, wand, branch

uirgine-us a um virgin

uirgō uirgin-is 3f. young girl, virgin

uirid-is e green

uirtūs uirtūt-is 3f. manliness, courage; goodness

uīs 2nd s. of *uolō*

uīs irr. force, violence (acc. *uim*; abl. *uī*); pl. *uīrēs uīr-ium* 3f. strength; military forces

uīs-: see *uideō/uideor*

uīt-a ae 1f. life

uīuō 3 *uīxī uictum* be alive, live

uix scarcely, hardly

ūll-us a um (gen. s. *ūllīus*; dat. s. *ūllī*) any
  (cf. *nūllus*)
ultim-us a um final, last
umbr-a ae 1f. shadow, darkness; shade, ghost
umer-us ī 2m. shoulder
umquam ever
und-a ae 1f. wave, water
unde from where, whence
ūn-us a um (gen. s. *ūnīus*; dat. s. *ūnī*) one,
  single, alone; *ūnā* alongside, in company
uōbīscum with you (pl.)
uocō 1 call, summon
uolō uelle uoluī wish, want, be willing
uoluntās uoluntāt-is 3f. will, wish
uōs you (pl.)
uōt-um ī 2n. prayer, desire, vow
uōx uōc-is 3f. voice; word
ūrō 3 *ussī ustum* burn up, set on fire, inflame
ūs-: see *ūtor*
usque ad (+ acc.) right up to
usque continually, without a break; as far as
ūs-us ūs 4m. use, employment; experience;
  function, utility, life; need; loan
ut (+ indic.) how!; (+ indic.) as, when;
  (+ subj.) to, that . . . should; (+ subj.) that

(after *accidit, perficiō* etc.); (+ subj.) that
  (result); (+ subj.) in order to/that
  (purpose); (+ subj.) that . . . not (after verbs
  of fearing)
uterque utriusque both, each (cf. *uter utr-a um*)
utī = *ut*
utinam would that, O that (+ subj.)
ūtor 3 dep. *ūsus* use, make use of; adopt
  (+abl.)
utrum . . . an (+ subj.) whether . . . or
  (indirect question: negative *necne*)
utrum . . . an (double question) A or B?
  (negative *annōn* = or not?); (+ subj.)
  whether . . . or (indirect question) (negative
  necne = or not)
utrum . . . an = double question, i.e. A or B?
  (negative *annōn*)
uulnus uulner-is 3n. wound
uult 3rd s. of *uolō*
uultis 2nd pl. of *uolō*
uult-us ūs 4m. face; feature(s), distinctive look,
  aspect; expression (often used in pl.)
uxor uxōr-is 3f. wife

Grammar index

This index lists the grammatical features referred to in the notes running with the texts, with references.

RL = Peter Jones and Keith Sidwell, *Reading Latin: Grammar, Vocabulary and Exercises* (Cambridge: Cambridge University Press, 1986). A plain number, e.g. **RL**88, refers to sections of the Running Grammar; letter + number, e.g. **RL**A4, refers to the Reference Grammar at the back.

W = F. M. Wheelock, *Wheelock's Latin* (sixth edition, rev. R. A. LaFleur, New York: HarperCollins, 2000). The number, e.g. **W**38, refers to the grammatical chapters; Suppl.syntax = Supplementary Syntax.